Security and
Loss Prevention

Security and Loss Prevention

An Introduction
Fourth Edition

Philip P. Purpura, CPP

BUTTERWORTH
HEINEMANN

An Imprint of Elsevier

Amsterdam   Boston   Heidelberg   London   New York   Oxford   Paris   San Diego
San Francisco   Singapore   Sydney   Tokyo

Butterworth–Heinemann is an imprint of Elsevier

Library of Congress Cataloging-in-Publication Data
Purpura, Philip P.
   Security and loss prevention : an introduction / Philip P.
Purpura.—4th ed.
      p. cm.
   Includes bibliographical references and index.
   ISBN-13: 978-0-7506-7437-9   ISBN-10: 0-7506-7437-7 (alk. paper)
   1. Private security services.   2. Burglary protection.
3. Employee theft—Prevention.   4. Fire prevention.   5. Shoplifting—
Prevention.   6. Security systems.   I. Title.
HV8290.P87   2002
658.4'73—dc21   2001058969

British Library Cataloguing-in-Publication Data
A catalogue record for this book is available from the British Library
ISBN-13: 978-0-7506-7437-9
ISBN-10: 0-7506-7437-7 (alk. paper)
The publisher offers special discounts on bulk orders of this book.
For information, please contact:

Manager of Special Sales
Elsevier
225 Wildwood Avenue
Woburn, MA 01801-2041
Tel: 781-904-2500
Fax: 781-904-2620

For information on all Butterworth–Heinemann books available,
contact our World Wide Web home page at: http://www.bh.com

10 9 8 7 6 5

This edition is dedicated to the United States
and its allies, to the victims of terrorism,
and to the millions of military, public safety,
and security professionals who strive
to create a safe and secure world.

Contents

About the Author

Philip P. Purpura, Certified Protection Professional, is a college educator, consultant, expert witness, and writer. He began his security career in New York City and held management and proprietary and contract investigative positions. He also worked with a public police agency. Mr. Purpura is the author of three other security textbooks: *The Security Handbook* (Delmar, 1991; Butterworth–Heinemann, 2002), *Retail Security and Shrinkage Protection* (Butterworth–Heinemann, 1993), and *Modern Security and Loss Prevention Management* (Butterworth–Heinemann, 1989). He also wrote *Police and Community: Concepts and Cases* (Allyn & Bacon, 2001), *Criminal Justice: An Introduction* (Butterworth–Heinemann, 1997), and numerous articles in journals, magazines, and newsletters. He served as a contributing editor to three security periodicals. Mr. Purpura holds bachelor's and master's degrees in criminal justice from the University of Dayton and Eastern Kentucky University, respectively. He also studied in several foreign countries. He serves on the American Society for Industrial Security Council on Academic Programs. Presently, he is Director of the Security Training Institute and Resource Center and coordinator of the Security for Houses of Worship Project in South Carolina.

Preface

When a new edition of a textbook is published, the reader often wants to know how it has been updated, what features were retained, and how it is different from the previous edition. This preface seeks to answer these questions.

A new era of security emerged on September 11, 2001, when terrorists launched the devastating attack on the World Trade Center and Pentagon. Not only did tighter security and increased vigilance prevail, but the issues of homeland defense, security, and safety became etched in the minds of people throughout the world. Two major questions surfaced from this attack: How can security and safety be improved? What can be expected in the future from criminals? The first question is complex and it can lead to a variety of answers, several of which are suggested in this book. To assist the reader in formulating conclusions and making decisions about security, Chapter 1 begins with critical thinking skills. In Chapter 3, critical thinking is applied to security planning by suggesting that each security strategy be placed under one the following three models: it protects people and assets; it accomplishes nothing; or it helps offenders. Practitioners will benefit by thinking critically as they plan, select vendors, and implement and manage improved security strategies. Chapter 19 offers insights into the future, although this is a complex and risky venture. Anticipating the future is safer than attempting to predict it.

The fourth edition of *Security and Loss Prevention: An Introduction* continues to focus on loss problems and those countermeasures that protect against crimes, fires, and accidents. Because many fields of study hold answers to protection problems, the foundation of this text is interdisciplinary and draws on such disciplines as law, criminal justice, business, accounting, risk management, fire protection, safety, sociology, and psychology. The traditional focus of security—security officers, fences, and alarms—is too narrow to deal with an increasingly complex world. Practitioners are being asked to do more with less resources and prove that the money spent on protection has a return on investment (ROI). In a world of rapid change, management expects protection personnel to produce answers quickly. The true professional maintains a positive attitude and sees problems as challenges that have solutions. An interdisciplinary approach can be an immense aid to the practitioner.

This fourth edition has been updated to reflect new laws, technology, security strategies, and statistics. Many new references from the years 2000 and 2001 provide support for the contentions made in each chapter. This new edition also serves as a helpful directory; professional organizations that enhance protection programs are included with Web addresses, street addresses, and telephone numbers.

A major intent of the author while writing this new edition was to help the reader develop an improved understanding of the security and loss prevention *profession* while providing information and tools to enhance the success of practitioners. Since we are in the "information age" and the protection of information technology (IT) and proprietary information is so important today, a major theme of this fourth edition is to *connect the traditional security manager and physical security specialist to IT security.* This is not a claim to make the reader an IT security expert. Rather, the reader will learn about similarities and differences of physical and IT security, internal and external IT risks and countermeasures, and the mind-set of the IT security specialist.

Our "information age" has brought with it an explosion of data, information, and "hype" that challenge us to probe and shape knowledge for our personal and professional life. The critical thinking skills presented offer an extra edge or tool for the security professional seeking to plan security in a complex, rapidly changing world.

Other differences from earlier editions include career boxes that explain various specializations in security, Web exercises at the end of each chapter to link the reader to a wealth of professional information, more boxes on international perspectives, and more end-of-chapter case problems on a variety of topics ranging from IT threats to racist e-mail.

The first five chapters provide an introduction and foundation for protection strategies. Chapter 1 defines security and loss prevention and presents a critical perspective of the history of security and loss prevention. The second chapter concentrates on the growth of the security industry and its problems. The next three chapters provide a foundation from which protection programs can become more efficient and effective: Chapter 3 focuses on security as a profession, risk analysis, planning, evaluation, research, performance measures, and security standards; Chapter 4 provides an overview of civil and criminal law and includes discussions of premise protection and negligence and arrest law; and Chapter 5, "Internal and External Relations," explains the why and how of recruiting people and organizations to assist with loss prevention efforts. Chapters 6, 7, and 8 emphasize strategies for curbing internal and external crime threats. These include job applicant screening, policies, procedures, and physical security. Chapter 9, on purchasing security services and systems, is vital because not all security specialists are wise consumers, and the best plans are useless when followed by poor purchasing decisions. Chapter 10 provides practical information on investigations. The strategies of accountability, accounting, and auditing described in Chapter 11 provide an understanding as to why these areas are essential for survival. Chapters 12, 13, and 14 cover fire and other disasters, safety, and risk management. Specialized security programs are explained in the next three chapters. These include retail, IT, nuclear, Department of Defense, education, healthcare, finance, and government. Chapter 18 concentrates on protection of sensitive information, communications security, terrorism, executive protection, substance abuse, and workplace violence. The final chapter covers the future, research directions, and employment opportunities. Topics that have been expanded and added in the fourth edition are listed here:

Topics Expanded	Topics Added
Theoretical foundations	Critical thinking skills
Ethics	September 11, 2001, attack on the United States
Diversity	Cyberlaw
Cybercrime	Marketing security through intranet and e-mail
IT security	Open architecture
System integration	Identity theft and countermeasures
Standards	E-business risks and countermeasures
Outsourcing	Enterprise risk management
Contraband detection	Racial profiling in security
Terrorism	Performance-based fire protection
Information sources for investigators	Dangers of safety incentive programs
	Lockout/tagout
Business fraud	Ergonomics
	Internet insurance

The student or practitioner will find this book to be user-friendly and interactive. Several features will assist the reader in understanding not only the basics but also the "reality" of the field. Within each chapter the loss problems are described and are followed by a discussion of the nuts-and-bolts countermeasures. Sidebars in each chapter emphasize significant points and facilitate critical thinking about security issues. Cases titled "You Be the Judge" appear in the text. These are fictional accounts of actual cases that deal with security-related legal problems. The reader is asked for a verdict based on the material at hand and then is directed to the end of the chapter for the court's ruling. Additional boxed cases appear in chapters and offer bits of interesting information or analyze a loss problem relevant to the subject matter of the chapter. Boxes on international perspectives provide a global view of protection. The case problems at the end of most chapters bridge theory to practice and ask the reader to apply the general concepts of the chapter to real-world situations. This activity enables the reader to consider alternative strategies, helps to stimulate controversy in group discussions, and allows the reader to make mistakes and receive feedback, thereby acquiring the skills for problem solving.

This book also helps applicants prepare for the Certified Protection Professional examination, which is sponsored by the American Society for Industrial Security. Numerous topics included in the examination are covered in this textbook.

The tremendous growth of the security and loss prevention field provides fertile ground to advance in a rewarding career. In such a competitive world, the survival and protection of businesses, technological innovations, and even the national interest will depend greatly on security and loss prevention programs. This book should inspire and motivate students and practitioners to fulfill these vital protection needs.

Acknowledgments

I thank the many people who contributed to this fourth edition. Gratitude goes to my wife, Amyie, for her superb typing and editorial assistance, and to my family for their patience. I am thankful to the many security practitioners and librarians who helped to provide a wealth of information to support the contents of this book. The hardworking editorial team at Butterworth–Heinemann—Assistant Editor Jennifer Packard, Associate Acquisitions Editor Mark Listewnik, and Production Manager Maura Kelly—are to be recognized for their talents and skills in publishing this book. I am grateful for the team effort, among so many people, for without it this book could not be published.

INTRODUCTION TO SECURITY AND LOSS PREVENTION

1

The History of Security and Loss Prevention: A Critical Perspective

OBJECTIVES

After studying this chapter the reader will be able to:

1. Explain the purpose of critical thinking and how to think critically.
2. Define security and loss prevention.
3. List the benefits of studying the history of security and loss prevention.
4. Trace the early development of security and policing.
5. Describe the growth of security companies in the United States.
6. Explain how information technology and terrorism have impacted security.

WHY CRITICAL THINKING?

September 11, 2001, marked a turning point in the history of security. In a devastating terrorist onslaught, knife-wielding hijackers crashed two airliners into the World Trade Center in New York City, creating an inferno that caused the 110-story twin skyscrapers to collapse. About 3,000 people were killed, including responding firefighters and police. During the same morning another hijacked airliner crashed into the Pentagon, causing additional deaths and destruction. A fourth hijacked airliner failed to reach its target and crashed when heroic passengers learned of the other attacks and struggled with hijackers to control the airliner.

Because of these devastating attacks, not only have homeland defense, security, safety, and military strategies changed, but also our way of thinking has changed. We cannot afford to have failures in our planning and imagination of what criminals can do. To improve security, we must seek new tools to assist us in our thinking processes.

Here we begin with critical thinking skills to counter "business as usual." Critical thinking helps us to become active learners: to not only absorb information, but to probe and shape knowledge. The critical thinker cuts through "hype" and emotion and goes beyond collecting "facts" and memorizing information in an effort to understand causes, motives, and changes. Critical thinking skills provide a foundation for creative planning while helping us to anticipate future events.

The critical thinker asks many questions, and the questions are often easier to formulate than the answers. Critical thinking requires us to "jump out of our own skin" to see the world from the perspective of others. Although this is not an easy process, we are much better informed before we make our conclusions and decisions.

Critical thinking is not to be used as a tool to open up the floodgates of criticism in the workplace. It is to be applied discreetly to understand the world and to meet challenges.

A professional's success depends on his or her thinking process applied to everyday duties and long-range planning. Critical thinking adds an extra edge to the repertoire of tools available to security and loss prevention practitioners.

Security challenges have become increasingly complex because as we plan for protection and face a multitude of threats in a rapidly changing environment, we must expect the unexpected, while staying within our budgets. The security practitioner should be creative, have an excellent imagination, apply critical thinking skills, and carefully prioritize security strategies to produce the best possible security program.

Although critical thinking skills are applied to a critical perspective of history in this chapter, students and practitioners are urged to continue this thinking process throughout this book. It is hoped that your conclusions and decisions will be enhanced to improve security and loss prevention.

> To prime the reader's mind for the explanation of critical thinking, Chapter 3 applies critical thinking to security planning by suggesting that each security strategy be placed under one of the following three models: it protects people and assets; it accomplishes nothing; or it helps offenders.

HOW CAN WE THINK CRITICALLY?

Our world is filled with many efforts to influence our thinking. Examples are the media, advertisers, politicians, educators, and writers. This author is biased just like other writers, and within these pages is a North American interpretation of security. Although an effort has been made to write an objective book here, it is impossible for any writer, and biases surface. Objectivity is fostered in this book through an introduction to critical thinking skills, an interdisciplinary approach, international perspectives, boxed topics and questions, a variety of references, Web exercises, and case problems at the end of chapters that bridge theory to practice and ask the reader to make decisions as a practitioner.

With so much competition seeking to influence us, choices become difficult and confusing. And, as we think through complex challenges, we need a method of sorting conflicting claims, differentiating between fact and opinion, weighing "evidence" or "proof," being perceptive to our biases and those of others, and drawing logical conclusions. David Ellis suggests a four-step strategy for critical thinking:

> *Step1: Understanding the point of view.*
> - Listen/read without early judgment
> - Seek to understand the source's background (e.g., culture, education, experience, and values)
> - Try to "live in their shoes"
> - Summarize their viewpoint
>
> *Step 2: Seek other views.*
> - Seek viewpoints, questions, answers, ideas, and solutions from others
>
> *Step 3: Evaluate the various viewpoints.*
> - Look for assumptions (i.e., an opinion that something is true, without evidence), exceptions, gaps in logic, oversimplification, selective perception, either/or thinking, and personal attacks
>
> *Step 4: Construct a reasonable view.*
> - Study multiple viewpoints, combine perspectives, and produce an original viewpoint which is a creative act and the essence of critical thinking[1]

WHY THINK CRITICALLY ABOUT THE HISTORY OF SECURITY AND LOSS PREVENTION?

The intent here is to stimulate the reader to go beyond memorizing historical events, people, and dates. If you have read several books in this field, the history chapters sound very similar. Did the writers, including this one, become complacent and repeat what has been written over and over again about the history of this field? How do you know that the history of security and loss prevention as presented in this book and in others is objective?

Recorded history is filled with bias. Historians and scholars decide what subjects, events, innovations, countries, ethnic groups, religions, men, and women should be included or excluded from recorded history. In reference to the history of security and loss prevention, what have we missed? What subjects have been overemphasized? (A case problem at the end of this chapter asks the reader to critically think about the history of security and loss prevention.) In the policing field, for example, history and research reflect a bias toward urban police, at the expense of rural police.[2] Also, do security writers overemphasize proprietary security programs and security services of large corporations? What about the thousands of proprietary security programs at small companies and the thousands of small security service firms? Another question is, what role did women and minorities play in the history of this field?

What country do you think has had the most impact on police and security in the United States? Our language, government, public and private protection, law, and many other aspects of our lives have deep roots in England. But what about the role of other countries in the development of police and private security methods? Stead writes of the French as innovators in crime prevention as early as the 1600s under King Louis XIV.[3] During that time, crime prevention was emphasized through preventive patrol and street lighting. Germann and colleagues write of early Asian investigative methods that used psychology to elicit confessions.[4]

A critical thinking approach "opens our eyes" to a more objective perspective of historical events. The author is not seeking to rewrite history, nor to change the basic strategies of security and loss prevention. Rather, the aim is to expand the reader's perception and knowledge as a foundation for smarter protection in a complex world.

SECURITY AND *LOSS PREVENTION* DEFINED

Within our organized society, security is provided primarily by our armed forces, public safety agencies (e.g., police and fire departments), and private security. This text focuses on the private sector.

The methods of private security have become more specialized and diverse. Methods not previously associated with security have emerged and become important components of the total security effort. Security officers, fences, and alarms have been the hallmark of traditional security functions. Today, with society becoming increasingly complex, additional specialization—accounting, auditing, safety, fire protection, safeguarding hazardous materials, insurance, and environmental design, to name a few—continuously are being added to the security function. Because of the increase in diverse specialization within the security function, many practitioners favor a broader term for all of these functions, known as *loss prevention*.

Another reason for the growing shift in terminology from *security* to *loss prevention* involves the negative connotations of security. Saul Astor points out:

> In the minds of many, the very word "security" is its own impediment.
> . . . Security carries a stigma; the very word suggests police, badges, alarms, thieves, burglars, and some generally negative and even repellent mental images. . . . Simply using the term "loss prevention" instead of the word "security" can be a giant step toward improving the security image, broadening the scope of the security function, and attracting able people.[5]

Because of additional specialization included in the security function and the frequently negative connotations associated with the term *security*, the all-encompassing term for describing the contents of this text is *loss prevention*. The security function and other specialized fields (safety, auditing, insurance, etc.) are subsumed in loss prevention.

Security is narrowly defined as traditional methods (security officers, fences, alarms) used to increase the likelihood of a crime-controlled, tranquil, and uninterrupted environment for an individual or organization in pursuit of objectives.

Loss prevention is broadly defined as any method (e.g., security officers, safety, auditing, insurance) used by an individual or organization to increase the likelihood of preventing and controlling loss (e.g., people, money, productivity, materials) resulting from a host of adverse occurrences (e.g., crime, fire, accident, error, poor supervision or management, bad investment). This broad definition provides a foundation for the loss prevention practitioner whose innovations are limited only by his or her imagination. It is hoped that these concepts not only will guide the reader through this text but also reinforce a trend in the use of these definitions.

Security is narrowly defined; *loss prevention* is broadly defined.

HISTORY

Why Study the History of Security and Loss Prevention?

We should study the history of security and loss prevention because:

- We learn of the origins of the profession and how it developed.

- We can see how voids in security and safety within society were filled by the private sector.
- We learn of noted practitioners and their challenges, failures, and successes.
- We can compare security in the past to security in the present to note areas of improvement and areas requiring improvement.
- We learn how security services and systems have been controlled and regulated.
- We learn of the interaction of private and public police over time.
- History repeats itself. We should strive to avoid the mistakes of the past and continue with successes.
- We can learn how social, economic, political, and technological forces have affected security over time.
- The past assists us in understanding the present and it offers us a foundation to anticipate future events.

EARLY CIVILIZATIONS

Prehistoric human beings depended on nature for protection, because they had not learned how to build strong houses and fortifications. In cold climates, caves provided protection and shelter, whereas in the tropics, trees and thickets were used. Caves were particularly secure because rocky walls guarded tribes on all sides except at the cave mouth. To protect the entrance, redundant (i.e., duplicating to prevent failure) security was employed: large rocks acted as barriers when they were rolled in front of entrances; dogs, with their keen sense of smell, served to alarm and attack; and fires added additional defense. By living on the side of a mountain with access via a narrow, rocky ledge, cave dwellers were relatively safe from enemies and beasts. Early Pueblo Indians, living in what is now New Mexico and Arizona, ensured greater protection for themselves in their dwellings by constructing ladders that could be pulled in, and this defense proved useful until enemies attacked with their own ladders. *In fact, in early civilizations, as today, security measures have never been foolproof, and adversaries typically strive to circumvent (i.e., to go around) defenses.*

> Throughout history, redundant security has been used to block adversaries attempting to circumvent defenses.

The Great Wall of China is the longest structure ever built. It was constructed over hundreds of years beginning in the 400s B.C. Hundreds of thousands of workers lived their lives near the wall and participated in this huge project that stretched 4000 miles and reached heights of 25 feet. Unfortunately, the wall provided protection only from minor attacks; when a major invasion force struck, the defense could not withstand the onslaught. The army of Mongol leader Genghis Khan swept across the wall during the 1200s A.D. and conquered much of China. (Since 1949, the Chinese government has restored some sections of the mostly collapsed wall, which is a major tourist attraction.)[6]

It is interesting to note the changing character of security through history. In earlier years, huge fortifications could be built with cheap labor. Today, physical barriers such as fences and walls are expensive, as is the posting of security forces at physical barriers; a king could secure a perimeter with many inexpensive guards. Today, one 24-hour post costs tens of thousands of dollars a year.

As societies became more complex, the concepts of leadership, authority, and organization began to evolve. Mutual association created social and economic advantages but also inequities, so people and assets required increased protection. Intergroup and intragroup conflicts created problems whose "solutions" often took the form of gruesome punishments, including stoning, flaying, burning, and crucifying. A person's criminal record was carried right on his or her body, through branding and mutilation. By 1750 B.C. the laws of *Hammurabi, king of Babylon*, not only codified the responsibilities of the individual to the group and the rules for private dealings between individuals but also discussed retributive penalties.[7]

Ancient Greece

Between the ninth and the third centuries B.C. ancient Greece blossomed as an advanced commercial and culturally rich civilization. The Greeks protected their advancing civilization through the use of the *polis*, or city-state, which consisted of a city and the surrounding land protected by a centrally built fortress overlooking the countryside. A stratified society brought the ruling classes constant fear of revolution from below. Spartans, for example, kept their secret agents planted among the lower classes and subversives. *During the time of the Greek city-states, the first police force evolved to protect local communities, although citizens were responsible for this function.* The Greek rulers did not view local policing as a state responsibility, and when internal conflicts arose, they used the army. During this era, the Greek philosopher Plato introduced an advanced concept of justice, in which an offender not only would be forced to pay a sort of retribution but also would be forced into a method of reform or rehabilitation.

Ancient Egyptians sealed the master locksmith in the tomb to prevent security leaks.

Ancient Rome

The civilization of ancient Rome also developed both commercially and culturally before the birth of Christ. Rome was located only 15 miles from the sea and could easily share in the trade of the Mediterranean. This city sat on seven hills overlooking the Tiber River, which permitted ease in fortification and defense. A primitive but effective alarm system was used by placing geese at strategic locations so their very sensitive hearing would trigger squawking at the sound of an approaching army.

The Roman regime was well designed to carry on the chief business of the Roman state, which was war. A phalanx of 8000 foot soldiers became the basic unit of a Roman army equipped with helmets, shields, lances, and swords. Later, a more maneuverable legion of 3600 men armed in addition with iron-tipped javelins was used. These legions also were employed to maintain law and order. The first emperor of Rome, Augustus (27 B.C.–14 A.D.), created the *Praetorian Guard* to provide security for his life and property. These urban cohorts of 500 to 600 men were deployed to keep the peace in the city. Some believe that after about 6 A.D. this was the most effective police force until recent developments in law enforcement. Modern-day coordinated patrolling and preventive security began with the subsequent nonmilitary *vigiles*, night watchmen who were active in both policing and firefighting.[8]

The Romans have an interesting history in fire protection. During the 300s B.C., slaves were assigned firefighting duties. Later, improved organization established divisions encompassing hundreds of people, who carried water in jars to fires or brought large pillows so victims trapped in taller structures could jump with improved chances for survival. The completion of the aqueducts to Rome aided firefighting by making water easier to obtain. Hand pumps and leather hoses were other innovations.

The Middle Ages in Europe

During the Dark Ages, the period in history after the destruction of the ancient Greek and Roman empires, *feudalism* gradually developed in Europe. Overlords supplied food and security to those who farmed and provided protection around castles fortified by walls, towers, and a drawbridge that could be raised from its position across a moat. Even then, security required registration, licensing, and a fee—Henry II of England (reigned 1154–1189 A.D.) destroyed more than 1100 unlicensed castles that had been constructed during a civil war![9]

Another mutual arrangement was the war band of the early Germans, the *comitatus*, by which a leader commanded the loyalty of followers, who banded together to fight and win booty. (Today, the term *posse comitatus* denotes a body of citizens that authority can call on for assistance against offenders.) To defend against these bands of German barbarians, many landowners throughout Europe built their own private armies.

Much of the United States' customs, language, laws, and police and security methods can be traced to its English heritage. For this reason, England's history of protection is examined here.

Between the seventh and tenth centuries, the frankpledge system and the concept of tithing fostered increased protection. The *frankpledge system*, which originated in France and spread to England, emphasized communal responsibility for justice and protection. The *tithing*, or group of ten families, shared the duties of maintaining the peace and protecting the community.

In 1066, William, Duke of Normandy (in present-day France), crossed the English Channel and defeated the Anglo-Saxons at Hastings. A highly repressive police system developed under martial law as the state appropriated responsibility for peace and protection. Community authority and the tithing system were weakened. William divided England into 55 districts, or *shires*. A *reeve*, drawn from the military, was assigned to each district. (Today, we use the word *sheriff*, derived from *shire-reeve*.) William is credited with changing the law to make a crime an offense against the state rather than against the individual and was instrumental in separating police from judicial functions. A traveling judge tried the cases of those arrested by the shire-reeves.

In 1215 King John signed the *Magna Carta*, which guaranteed civil and political liberties. Local government power increased at the expense of the national government, and community protection increased at the local level.

Another security milestone was the *Statute of Westminster* (1285), issued by King Edward I to organize a police and justice system. A *watch and ward* was established to keep the peace. Every town was required to deploy men all night, to close the gates of walled towns at night, and to enforce a curfew.

> What similarities can you draw between security strategies of earlier civilizations and those of today?

MORE CONTEMPORARY TIMES

England

For the next 500 years, repeated attempts were made to improve protection and justice in England. Each king was confronted with increasingly serious crime problems and cries from the citizenry for solutions. As England colonized many parts of the world and as trade and commercial pursuits brought many people into the cities, urban problems and high crime rates persisted. Merchants, dissatisfied with the protection afforded by the government, hired private security forces to protect their businesses.

By the eighteenth century, the Industrial Revolution compounded urban problems. Many citizens were forced to carry arms for their own protection, because a strong government policing system was absent. Various police and private security organizations did strive to reduce crime; *Henry Fielding*, in 1748, was appointed magistrate, and he devised the strategy of preventing crime through police action by helping to form the famous *Bow Street Runners*, the first detective unit. The merchant police were formed to protect businesses, and the Thames River police provided protection at the docks. During this period, more than 160 crimes, including stealing food, were punishable by death. As pickpockets were being hanged, others moved among the spectators, picking pockets.

> Do you think policing and justice were impotent during the early Industrial Revolution in England? Do you think we have a similar problem today in the United States?

Peel's Reforms

In 1829, *Sir Robert Peel's* efforts produced the *Metropolitan Police Act*, a revolution in law enforcement. Modern policing was born. Peel's innovative ideas were accepted by Parliament, and he was selected to implement an act that established a full-time, unarmed police force with the major purpose of patrolling London. Peel is credited also with reforming the criminal law by limiting its scope and abolishing the death penalty for more than 100 offenses. It was hoped that such a strategy would gain public support and respect for the police. Peel was very selective in hiring his personnel, and training was an essential part of developing a professional police force. Peel's reforms are applicable today and include crime prevention, the strategic deployment of police according to time and location, a command of temper rather than violent action, record keeping, and crime news distribution.

> Although Sir Robert Peel produced a revolution in law enforcement in 1829, crime and the private security industry continued to grow.

Early America

The Europeans who colonized North America had brought with them the heritage of their mother countries, including various customs of protection. The watchman system and collective responses remained popular. A central fortification in populated areas provided increased security from hostile threats. As communities expanded in size, the office of sheriff took hold in the South, whereas the functions of constable and watchman were the norm in the Northeast. The sheriff's duties involved apprehending offenders, serving subpoenas, and collecting taxes. Because a sheriff was paid a higher fee for collecting taxes, policing became a lower priority. Constables performed a variety of tasks such as keeping the peace, bringing suspects and witnesses to court, and eliminating health hazards. As in England, the watch system had its share of inefficiency, and to make matters worse, those convicted of minor crimes were sentenced to serve time on the watch.

The watch also warned citizens of fire. In colonial towns, each home had to have two fire buckets, and homeowners were subject to a fine if they did not respond to a fire, buckets in hand. A large fire in Boston in 1679 prompted the establishment of the first paid fire department in North America.[10]

The Growth of Policing

The period of the middle 1800s was a turning point for both law enforcement and private security in America, as it had been in England. Several major cities (e.g., New York, Philadelphia, San Francisco) organized police forces, often modeled after the London Metropolitan Police. However, corruption was widespread. Numerous urban police agencies in the Northeast received large boosts in personnel and resources to combat the growing militancy of the labor unions in the late 1800s and early 1900s. According to Richard Holden, to a large extent, many of the large urban police departments originally were formed as strikebreakers.[11] Federal policing also experienced growth during this period. The U.S. Treasury had already established an investigative unit in 1864. As in England, an increase in public police did not quell the need for private security.

The History of Loss Prevention in a Nutshell

Loss prevention has its origin in the insurance industry. Before the Civil War, insurers gave minimal attention to the benefits of loss prevention. For instance, in the fire insurance business, executives generally viewed fires as good for business. Insurance rates were based on past loss experience, premiums were paid by customers, losses were paid to unfortunate customers, and a profit was expected by the insurer. When excessive fire losses resulted in spiraling premiums, the changing nature of the fire insurance business created a hardship for both the insurer and the insured. Insurance executives were forced to raise premiums to cover losses and customers complained about high rates. The predominance of wooden construction (even wooden chimneys) in dense urban areas made fire insurance unaffordable for many. A serious fire peril persisted.

After the Civil War, loss prevention began to gain momentum as a way to reduce losses and premiums. Fire insurance companies formed the National Board of Fire Underwriters, which, through the use of engineers, investigation, research, and education, was credited with preventing losses. In 1965, the board was merged into the American Insurance Association (AIA). AIA activities have brought about the development of the National Building Code, a model code adopted by many municipalities to reduce fire losses.

Today, executives throughout the insurance industry view loss prevention as essential. Many insurers have loss prevention departments to aid themselves and customers. Furthermore, customers (i.e., the insured), to reduce premiums, have become increasingly concerned about preventing losses. Management in many businesses instituted loss prevention strategies (e.g., fire protection). These strategies repeatedly are handled by the security departments within businesses, which results in an expanded role for security. Expansion of the security function to such fields as fire protection and safety has led to the use of the broader term *loss prevention* rather than *security*.

The Growth of Security Companies

In 1850, *Allan Pinkerton*, a cooper, opened a detective agency in the United States after becoming the Chicago Police Department's first detective. Because public police were limited by geographic jurisdiction, they were handicapped when investigating and apprehending fleeing offenders. This limitation facilitated the growth of private security. Pinkerton (see Figure 1-1) and others became famous as they pursued criminals across state boundaries throughout the country. Today, Pinkerton Service Corporation, is a subsidiary of Securitas, based in Stockholm, Sweden.

During the 1800s, because public police were limited by geographic jurisdiction and restrained from chasing fleeing offenders, private security filled this need and became a growth industry.

To accompany Americans' expansion westward during the nineteenth century and to ensure the safe transportation of valuables, *Henry Wells* and

Figure 1–1   Major Allan Pinkerton, President Lincoln, and General John A. McClellan, Antietam, MD, October 1862. Courtesy: National Archives.

William Fargo supplied a wide-open market by forming Wells, Fargo & Company in 1852, opening the era of bandits accosting stagecoaches and their shotgun riders. Today, Wells Fargo is a division of Burns International Services Corporation, which is a subsidiary of Securitas.

Another security entrepreneur, *William Burns*, first was a Secret Service agent who directed the Bureau of Investigation that preceded the FBI. In 1909, this experienced investigator opened the William J. Burns Detective Agency (see Figure 1-2), which became the investigative arm of the American Bankers Association. Today, Burns International Services Corporation is a subsidiary of Securitas.

Figure 1–2 In 1910, William J. Burns, the foremost American investigator of his day and the first director of the government agency that became the FBI, formed the William J. Burns Detective Agency.

Washington Perry Brink, in 1859, also took advantage of the need for the safe transportation of valuables. From freight and package delivery to the transportation of payrolls, his service required increased protection through the years as cargo became more valuable and more vulnerable. Following the killing of two Brink's guards during a robbery, the armored truck was initiated in 1917. Today, Brink's, Inc., a subsidiary of the Pittston Co., is the world's largest provider of secure transportation services. It also maintains a large business monitoring home security systems.

Edwin Holmes is another historical figure in the development of private security in the United States. He pioneered the electronic security alarm business. During 1858, Holmes had a difficult time convincing people that an alarm would sound on the second floor of a home when a door or window was opened on the first floor. His sales strategy was to carry door-to-door a small model of a home containing his electric alarm system. Soon sales soared, and the first central office burglar alarm monitoring operation began. Holmes Protection Group, Inc., was acquired by ADT Security Services, Inc., at the end of the twentieth century.

Since 1874, *ADT Security Services, Inc.,* has been a leader in electronic security services. Originally known as American District Telegraph, ADT has acquired numerous security companies since its inception. Today, it is a unit of Tyco Fire and Security Services. ADT is the largest single provider of electronic security services (i.e., intrusion, fire protection, CCTV, access control) to nearly three million commercial, federal, and residential customers throughout North America and the United Kingdom.

The *Wackenhut Corporation* is another leader in the security industry and it provides correctional and human resources services. Founded in 1954 by George Wackenhut, a former FBI agent, the corporation extended its services to government agencies, which resulted in numerous contracts since its inception. The corporation has operations throughout the United States and in more than fifty countries.

Railroads and Labor Unions

The history of private security businesses in the United States must include two important events of the nineteenth century: the growth of railroads and labor unions.

Although railroads were valuable in providing the vital East–West link that enabled the settling of the American frontier, these powerful businesses used their domination of transportation to control several industries, such as coal and kerosene. Farmers were especially hurt in economic terms, because they had no alternative but to pay high fees to transport their products via the railroads. The monopolistic practices of railroads created considerable hostility; when Jesse James and other criminals robbed trains, citizens applauded. Railroads could not rely on public police protection because of jurisdictional boundaries. Consequently, numerous states passed laws enabling railroads to organize proprietary security forces with full arrest powers and the authority to apprehend criminals transcending multiple jurisdictions. Railroad police numbered 14,000 by 1914. During World War I, they were deputized by the federal government to ensure protection of this vital transportation network.

The growth of labor unions at the end of the nineteenth century resulted in increased business for security firms who acted as strikebreakers for large corporations. However, this venture proved costly. A bloody confrontation between Pinkerton men and workers at the Carnegie steel plant in Homestead, Pennsylvania, resulted in eight deaths (three security men and five workers). Pinkerton's security force surrendered. The plant then was occupied by federal troops. Senate hearings followed the Homestead disaster and "anti-Pinkertonism" laws were enacted to restrict private security. However, local and state police forces began to emerge quickly to deal with strikers.[12] Later, the Ford Motor Company and other businesses were involved in bloody confrontations. Henry Ford had a force of about 3500 security personnel, spies, and "sluggers" (i.e., private detectives), who were augmented by various community groups such as the Knights of Dearborn and the Legionnaires. The negative image brought to the public eye by newspaper coverage tarnished many businesses and security firms. Prior to World War II, pressure from Congress, the Roosevelt Administration, labor unions, and the ACLU caused corporate management to shift its philosophy to a softer "public relations" approach.[13]

The Great Wars

World Wars I and II brought about an increased need for protection in the United States. Sabotage and espionage were serious threats. Key industries and transportation systems required expanded and improved security. The social and political climate in the early twentieth century reflected urban problems, labor unrest, and worldwide nationalism. World War I compounded these turbulent times and people's fears. Security became a primary concern. A combination of the "war to end all wars," Prohibition, intense labor unrest, and the Great Depression all overtaxed public police. Private security companies helped fill the void.

By the late 1930s, Europe was at war again, and the Japanese were expanding in the Far East. A surprise Japanese bombing of the Pacific Fleet at Pearl Harbor in 1941 jolted the United States into World War II, and security concerns appeared again. The United States went into full production, and protection of vital industries became crucial, leading the federal government to bring plant security personnel into the army as an auxiliary to military police. By the end of the war, more than 200,000 of these security workers had been sworn in.

The Third Wave

In the decades following World War II private security expanded even more; during the 1950s, the Korean war and the unrelenting "cold war" created worldwide tension and competition between the democracies and communist regimes. The Department of Defense, in 1952, strengthened the security requirements of defense industries to protect classified information and materials. When the Soviets successfully launched the first earth satellite (Sputnik, in 1957) and first reached the moon with an unmanned rocket (1959), Americans were stunned. The technological race became more intense and information protection became more important.

The turbulent 1960s created massive social and political upheaval in the United States, and public police forces were overwhelmed by responses to the unpopular Vietnam war; protests over the denial of civil rights to minority groups; the assassinations of President John F. Kennedy, Senator Robert Kennedy, and the Reverend Martin Luther King, Jr.; and rising crime and drug problems. Private security boomed.

Protests, crime, terrorism, and limited public police resources marked the 1970s, 1980s, and 1990s. By this time the advanced nations of the world had developed into what Alvin Toffler's *The Third Wave*[14] and John Naisbitt's *Megatrends*[15] call *third wave* societies: societies based on information and technology. ("First wave" societies had agriculture as a foundation, and these dominated the world for thousands of years, deriving energy from human and animal power. Offenders stole cattle, gold, and other valuables. The "second wave" occurred during the Industrial Revolution when production was powered by irreplaceable energy sources such as coal and oil. Criminals focused on money and booming economic conditions.) With the depletion of world resources, the world is becoming more dependent on technology and information; and "third wave" criminals exploit technology to commit their crimes, the extent of which is limited only by technological innovation and the offenders' imaginations.

IT and Physical Security

Today, the third wave is continuing with three notable occurrences affecting security. First, terminology is changing. Examples are "cybercrime," "denial of service," and "e-security." Second, two distinct security camps have emerged: the information technology (IT) security specialists and the physical security specialists. Generally, the former possess a background geared to protect against computer-related crime and unauthorized intrusions into computer systems, whereas the latter focus on traditional security duties (e.g., perimeter security and contract security forces). Third, both camps often use similar terminology and perform similar duties. Terms common to both groups include "denial of access" and "intrusion detection." Similar duties can be far reaching and include investigations, information protection, loss prevention, and risk management. A survey by *Security Management* magazine found that in 35 percent of companies, IT and security remain separate functions, but in 20 percent of companies, security assists IT with investigations, while 11 percent said security coordinates with IT on policy and projects as requested.[16] Jim Spencer, writing in *iSecurity*, adds that these two groups have their own suppliers, consultants, publications, associations, and trade shows.[17]

For several years "cross-training" has been a buzzword for various vocations, such as for investigators and auditors. History repeats itself and we now have a need for cross-training with IT and physical security specialists. Each specialist can assist the other with data, technologies, access controls, biometrics, investigations, and disaster planning and recovery, among other areas. Cooperative planning is essential. Suppose an employee is fired at a company. Security officers and access control systems customarily deny the former employee entrance to the company facility. However, today, protection requires broader applications because of remote access to computer systems. *An offender no longer has to physically trespass to steal and do harm to an organization.* We can only guess at the number of times the traditional security manager has done an excellent job of ensuring that security officers are patrolling, that intrusion detection systems and lighting are operational, and the facility is protected through the night, except that during the night a hacker has stolen proprietary information or caused other harm to the business. Physical security specialists and IT specialists must work together for comprehensive protection.

Another player in corporate management change is the facility manager. This individual, often an engineer, ensures that the company's infrastructure, which houses people and operations, functions at optimum efficiency to support business goals. The traditional security department is likely to feel a "pull" toward IT or the facility manager because its boundaries are dissolving as a result of information and communications technology. The process of management is increasingly dependent on information, who controls it, what is done with it, and its dissemination. The power of IT especially is growing.[18]

Finally, there are those who may claim the demise of the traditional security manager, who will be replaced by the IT manager or facility manager. The argument is that if an offender enters a facility and steals a computer, this crime is minor in comparison to, say, a hacker accessing a company's computer system and stealing proprietary information or altering the payroll. Such reasoning misses the broad, essential functions performed by the traditional security manager and staff. Examples are preventing crimes against people, responding to crimes, rendering first aid, conducting investigations, working with public police to arrest offenders, life safety, and fire protection. At the same time, traditional security practitioners must be put on notice to become involved in lifelong learning of computers and computer systems which touch all aspects of their traditional duties.

Many companies have two security directors, one for IT and the other for physical security. Do you agree with this approach? Why or why not?

Twenty-First Century Security Challenges

The last decade of the twentieth century offered warnings of what was to come in the next century. The 1990s brought the first bombing of the World Trade Center, the bombing of the Murrah Federal Building in Oklahoma City, the war with Iraq, crimes resulting from the Internet, the increased value of proprietary information, and the attention to violence in the workplace.

As we know, not long into the twenty-first century, on September 11, 2001, terrorists attacked the World Trade Center and the Pentagon, killing about 3,000 people. These bold, surprise attacks, subsequent bio-terrorism, and the war in Afghanistan show the difficult challenges facing our world in this new century. A rethinking of defense and security strategies will meet these threats. Security professionals are on the front lines, facing not only terrorism, but also a variety of crimes, fire, accidents, and disasters. Through improved education and training, increased professionalism, creativity, astute planning, and support from our community and leaders, security professionals will provide a safe environment.

Search the Web

Access the Web and seek an international perspective by visiting the New Scotland Yard, which includes links to history: http://www.met.police.uk
 Use your favorite search engines to check the sites of major security companies. For example: http://www.pinkertons.com/
 What did you learn from these sites?

CASE PROBLEMS

1A.   As a security manager you are asked to speak to a local college class on the history and development of the security and loss prevention field. What five significant points in the history of this field do you emphasize?

1B.   As a part-time security officer and a full-time college student, you are now working on an assignment, which is to think critically about the history of security and loss prevention and prepare a typed report. The assignment requires you to focus on some aspect of the history of security and loss prevention that you believe is biased or inaccurate, and to explain your interpretation of historical events.

NOTES

1. David Ellis, *Becoming a Master Student,* 6th ed. (Rapid City, SD: College Survival, Inc., 1991), pp. 184–185.
2. R. Weisheit, L. Baker, and D. Falcone, *Crime and Policing in Rural and Small Town America: An Overview of the Issues* (Washington, D.C.: National Institute of Justice, 1995), p. 1.

3. P. Stead, *The Police of France* (New York: Macmillan, 1983), pp. 14–15.

4. A. C. Germann, Frank Day, and Robert Gallati, *Introduction to Law Enforcement and Criminal Justice* (Springfield, IL: Thomas Pub., 1974), pp. 45–46.

5. Saul D. Astor, *Loss Prevention: Controls and Concepts* (Stoneham, MA: Butterworths, 1978), p. 27.

6. *World Book Encyclopedia* (Chicago: World Book, 1986), p. 348.

7. A. C. Germann, et al., *Introduction to Law Enforcement and Criminal Justice*, p. 43.

8. See Richard S. Post and Arthur A. Kingsbury, *Security Administration: An Introduction*, 3rd ed. (Springfield, IL: Charles C. Thomas, 1977); and Henry S. Ursic and Leroy E. Pagano, *Security Management Systems* (Springfield, IL: Charles C. Thomas, 1974).

9. Crane Brinton, et al., *Civilization in the West* (Englewood Cliffs, NJ: Prentice-Hall, 1973), p. 167.

10. Percy Bugbee, *Principles of Fire Protection* (Boston: National Fire Protection Assoc., 1978), p. 5.

11. Richard N. Holden, *Modern Police Management* (Englewood Cliffs, NJ: Prentice-Hall, 1986), p. 23.

12. Randall Shelden, *Controlling the Dangerous Classes* (Boston, MA: Allyn & Bacon, 2001), p. 84.

13. Ibid., p. 92.

14. Alvin Toffler, *The Third Wave* (New York: Morrow, 1980).

15. John Naisbitt, *Megatrends* (New York: Warren Books, 1982).

16. "Polling Corporate Practices," *Security Management* (June 2000), p. 39.

17. Jim Spencer, "Of a Single Mind," *iSecurity* (November 2000), p. 1–13.

18. Joseph P. Freeman, "Security Director as Politician," *Security Technology & Design* (August 2000), p. 10.

2

The Business
and Careers of Security
and Loss Prevention

OBJECTIVES

After studying this chapter the reader will be able to:

1. Describe the variety and extent of losses facing our society.
2. Discuss the security industry and the types of employment available in this field.
3. Explain the limitations of the criminal justice system.
4. List and discuss the challenges of the security industry.

> The millions of employees in the security and loss prevention field protect people and assets.

WHAT IS THE EXTENT OF LOSSES?

Risk is exposure to possible loss. A variety of risks face businesses, institutions, and organizations. Table 2-1 depicts several risks that can cause losses. The frequency and cost of each loss varies.

Three major risks are crimes, fires, and accidents. Here is a summary of losses from these categories.

Crimes. According to the FBI *Uniform Crime Reports* (UCR) and the Bureau of Justice Statistics *National Crime Victimization Survey* (NCVS), crime has been consistently declining for several years. However, the volume of crime is still staggering. The NCVS reported 7.4

23

Table 2–1   Risks

Criminal Acts	Natural Disasters	Miscellaneous
Larceny/theft	Floods/excessive rain	Poor supervision
Burglary	Excessive snow/ice	Error
Robbery	Lightning	Waste
Embezzlement	Pestilence	Bad investment
Fraud	Earthquake	Poor safety
Shoplifting	Landslide	Equipment failure
Murder	Tornado	Fire
Terrorism	Hurricane	Explosion
Computer crime	Volcanic eruption	Pollution
Product tampering	Tidal wave	Power outage
Counterfeiting		Strike
Arson		Mine disaster
Vandalism		Oil spill
Riot		Sonic boom
Extortion		Nuclear accident
Kidnapping		War
Espionage		
Sabotage		

million crimes of violence and 21.2 million property crimes in 1999 in the United States.[1] The National Institute of Justice calculated that direct and indirect costs of crime, which includes property and productivity losses and medical expenses, is about $105 billion annually. When the value of pain, long-term emotional trauma, disability, and risk of death are put in dollar terms, the costs climb to $450 billion annually.[2]

Fires. The National Fire Protection Association reports that the United States has one of the highest fire death rates in the industrialized world. Data from the Web in 2001, from the National Fire Data Center, showed that in 1999, 3,570 Americans lost their lives and another 21,875 were injured as a result of fire, more Americans were killed by fire than all natural disasters combined, and about 1.8 million fires were reported, causing direct property loss of $10 billion.[3]

Accidents. The American Red Cross reports that in the workplace each year: 10,000 people die, almost 6 million injuries occur, 50,000 people are permanently impaired, 30 million workdays are lost, and $60 billion is spent on lost wages, health care, lawsuits, and worker's compensation claims.[4]

Each type of risk has its own specialist to work toward solutions. For instance, a rash of robberies in a liquor store may require additional public law enforcement assistance and the installation of a more sophisticated alarm system from the private sector. Numerous injuries at a manufacturing plant may require assistance from a safety specialist. The loss prevention manager—a specialist in his or her own right or with the assistance of a specialist—must plan, implement, and monitor programs to anticipate, prevent, and reduce loss.

Why Emphasize Both Direct and Indirect Losses?

Businesses, institutions, and organizations can suffer extensive direct losses from risks. Additionally, indirect losses can be devastating and often surpass direct losses. *Direct losses* are immediate, obvious losses, whereas *indirect losses* are prolonged and often hidden. A burglary at a business, for example, may show the loss of, say, $300 from a safe. However, on close inspection of indirect losses, total losses may include the following: damage to the door or window where the break-in occurred, replacement of the destroyed safe, insurance policy deductible, loss of sales from a delay in opening the business, and employee time required to speak with police, insurance representatives, and repair people. *Security practitioners can help justify their position and their value to the business community by demonstrating total losses resulting from each incident.*

THE SECURITY INDUSTRY

The security industry is a multibillion-dollar business. Every decade seems to bring an increased need for security services. Street crime, terrorism, computer crime, and so on bring greater demands for the protection of people and assets.

Research of the private security industry, in the early 1990s, sponsored by the National Institute of Justice, U.S. Department of Justice, showed the following:

- Private security is clearly the nation's primary protective resource, outspending public law enforcement by 73 percent and employing 2 1/2 times the workforce (see Figure 2-1).
- Annual spending for private security is $52 billion, and private agencies employ 1.5 million persons. Public law enforcement spends $30 billion a year and has a workforce of about 600,000 (see Figure 2-1).
- The average annual rate of growth in private security is 8 percent, double that of public law enforcement.[5]

What Is the Picture Today?

More recently the Bureau of Justice Statistics listed 531,496 full-time employees of local police departments, of which 420,000 were sworn

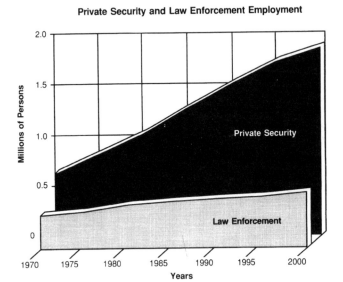

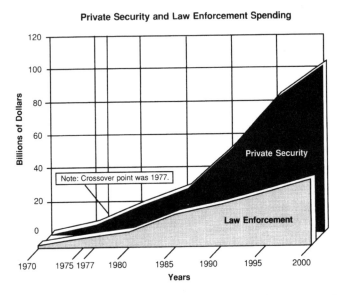

Figure 2–1 Private security and law enforcement employment and spending. Source: William C. Cunningham et al., *Private Security: Patterns and Trends* (Washington, D.C.: National Institute of Justice, August 1991), p. 3.

personnel. Sheriffs' departments had 263,427 full-time employees, including 175,000 sworn personnel. State and federal police consist of 59,000 and 70,000 sworn officers, respectively. Annual spending for police is about $58 billion. Private security employs between 1.2 and 1.4 million people.[6]

The Security Industry Association, the trade group that represents security businesses, reported that revenues of security-related manufacturers and service providers for the United States and Canada during 2000 would be about $103 billion. Major categories, with revenues in billions of dollars, were manufacturers of electronic security systems ($37.2), contract security officer services ($21.5), proprietary security ($16), alarm companies ($14), private investigators ($4.6), and armored car services ($1.3).[7]

The Freedonia Group, a Cleveland-based market research firm, published *World Security Services* to report that the world market for private security services grew 8.3 percent annually from 1989 to 1999 and will grow 8.4 percent annually through 2004, approaching $100 billion. By 2009 revenues are expected to be $150 billion. In the United States such revenues are projected at $40 billion in 2004 and $59 billion in 2009. (The Freedonia study emphasizes revenues from "security services," whereas the Security Industry Association study is broader and includes manufacturers of electronic security systems.) The Freedonia study noted that contractual security officer services will remain the largest segment of the market and benefit from the outsourcing of public and proprietary protection; however, growth will be hindered by more affordable electronic security systems. The report stated that six large companies account for 18 percent of global revenues: Securitas, Secom, Brinks, Tyco, Group 4 Falck, and Wackenhut.[8] The larger companies have been acquiring the smaller firms at a record pace since the 1980s when in the United States there were 10,000 contract security officer firms, 26,000 investigative firms, and 10,000 alarm installation firms.[9]

Do you think the gap between public police and private security is narrowing? Will more affordable electronic security systems reduce the need for security officers? How do you think federal funds to hire 100,000 more police in the late 1990s affected this gap? Will privatization (see subsequent page) widen the gap?

Contract versus Proprietary Security Officers

Contract security officers work for a company that seeks a profit by providing the services of security officers to businesses and institutions. Depending on its unique needs and weighing several factors, an organization needing security may prefer to establish a proprietary (in-house) security force, of which there are thousands. Also, an organization may use both contract and proprietary security (see Figure 2-2).

Figure 2–2   Businesses often employ both proprietary and contract security personnel

The *Report of the Task Force on Private Security* lists several factors to consider concerning contract versus proprietary security.[10] Contract security generally is less expensive, although there are exceptions. The service company typically handles recruitment, selection, training, and supervision. Hiring unqualified security officers and rapid turnover are two primary disadvantages of a contract service. Many contract officers are "moonlighting" and subject to fatigue. Questions concerning insurance and liability between the security company and the client often are hazy.

A major advantage of a proprietary force is that greater control is maintained over personnel, including selection, training, and supervision, and of course, such a force is more familiar with the unique needs of the company. Salaries and benefits, however, often make establishment of a proprietary force more expensive.

CAREERS: LOSS PREVENTION SERVICES AND SPECIALISTS

Many services and specialists from the private sector can help the loss prevention practitioner develop an effective loss prevention program. These services and specialists can be in-house or attainable through outside sources. Tables 2-2, 2-3, and 2-4 point out various facilities requiring loss

Table 2-2   Locations Requiring Loss Prevention Programs

Industrial	Hospital
Retail	Campus
Wholesale/warehouse	School
Railroad	Government
Airport/airline	Museum
Financial institution	Library
Office building	Park and recreation
Nuclear plant	Hotel/motel/restaurant
Computer	Sports/entertainment
Housing/residential	Others

Table 2-3   Security Services and Equipment from the Private Sector

Services	Equipment
Security officer protection	Access control systems
Investigation	Locks and keys
Undercover investigation	Intrusion detection systems
Central alarm station	Closed-circuit television
Armored truck (see Figure 2-3)	Fire alarm systems
Security survey	Barriers
Guard dog (canine)	Glazing
Deception detection	Doors
Honesty shopping service	Lighting
Terrorism countermeasures	Safes and vaults
Bodyguard/executive protection	Security vehicles
Information protection	Weapons
Sweeps for bugging devices	Others
Others	

prevention programs, security services and equipment from the private sector, and specialists and consultants who can aid in loss prevention efforts. These tables are not conclusive, because loss prevention programs are becoming increasingly specialized and diversified. Therefore, additional specialization will evolve to aid these programs.

Most loss prevention managers are generalists, which means that they have a broad knowledge of the field plus a specialized knowledge of their particular loss prevention problems. When feasible, a loss prevention manager should develop an interdisciplinary staff to assist in loss prevention objectives. The staff should represent various specializations as appropriate, such as security, safety, and fire protection.

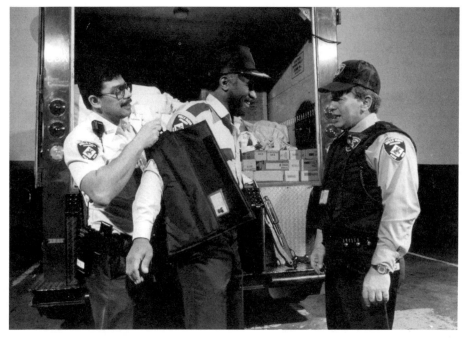

Figure 2–3   Employees wear bullet-resistant vests and personal hold-up alarms to help protect them as they pick up and deliver valuable shipments.

Table 2-4   Specialists and Consultants Who Can Aid Loss Prevention Efforts

Manufacturing loss prevention specialist	General loss prevention specialist
Institutional loss prevention specialist	Security design and engineering
Contingency planning/crisis management	Architect
Locksmith	Computer scientist
Electronic surveillance specialist (CCTV, photog-raphy)	Criminologist
	Forensic scientist
Lighting specialist	Industrial engineer
Audio surveillance countermeasures specialist (debugging)	Electrical engineer
	Civil engineer
Fire and safety specialist	Nuclear engineer
Education/training specialist	Nuclear safety specialist
Legal specialist/attorney	Others
Insurance/bonding specialist	
Accountant	
Auditor	

Career: Manufacturing Security

Manufacturers make products that are sold to wholesalers, distributors, or directly to consumers.

Duties: Protect people, sales transactions, transportation, raw materials, and finished goods; interview; investigate; allocate resources; supervise; conduct meetings; deal with public affairs; and contribute to the growth of the company.

Prerequisites: Undergraduate or advanced degree; 3–5 years of experience for entry management; 10+ years for upper management.

Demographics of typical practitioner: Undergraduate degree; 10–15 years in security; 10–15 years in specialty; salary of $50,000–150,000 yr.; titles: Security Officer, Manager of Plant Protection, Director, Vice President of Security.

Source: American Society for Industrial Security, *Career Opportunities in Security* (Alexandria, VA: ASIS, 1998), p. 13.

The Basic Differences Between Public Police and Private Security

The primary differences pertain to the *employer*, the *interests served, basic strategies*, and *legal authority*. Public police are employed by governments and serve the general public. Tax dollars support public police activities. On the other hand, private police are employed by and serve private concerns (e.g., businesses) that provide the funds for this type of protection. There are exceptions to these general statements. For instance, government agencies sometimes contract protection needs to private security agencies to cut costs. Also, public police often are involved in efforts to assist business owners in preventing crimes through security surveys and public education.

Another difference involves basic strategies. Public police devote considerable resources to *reacting* to crimes. This entails detection, investigation, and apprehension of offenders. Law enforcement is a key objective. In contrast, private police stress the *prevention* of crimes; arrests are often de-emphasized.

The degree of police powers among public and private police is another distinguishing characteristic. Public police derive their authority from statutes and ordinances, whereas private police function commonly as private citizens. Public police have greater arrest, search, and interrogation powers. Depending on jurisdiction and state laws, private police may be deputized or given special commissions that increase powers.

THE LIMITATIONS OF THE CRIMINAL JUSTICE SYSTEM: IMPLICATIONS FOR LOSS PREVENTION PRACTITIONERS

Federal, state, and local governments spent nearly $130 billion for criminal and civil justice in 1997.[11] Despite this huge sum, many theories underpinning crime prevention and law enforcement measures have come under increased scrutiny. For example, the strategy of deterrence has been questioned. This criminal justice system strategy seeks to prevent crime through state-imposed punishment. This model points out that offenders rationally consider the risks and rewards of crime prior to acting. Numerous offenders simply find that "crime pays," because the certainty of punishment is a myth and the odds are in the offender's favor. John E. Conklin, a criminologist, writes: "People have imperfect knowledge of the maximum penalties for various crimes, but their perceptions of the severity of sanctions, the certainty with which they will be administered, and the promptness of punishment influence their choice of behavior."[12] Since the impact of deterrence is questionable, crime prevention is a key strategy to reduce losses.

Another limitation of the criminal justice system is that tight budgets and limited resources and personnel are the main reasons why public safety agencies play a very minor role in private loss prevention programs. Public police agencies cannot afford to assign personnel to patrol inside business establishments or watch for employee theft. An occasional (public) police patrol and a response to a crime are the primary forms of assistance that public police can provide to businesses. Prosecutors are unwilling to prosecute certain crimes against businesses because of heavy caseloads. Consequently, public protection is being supplemented or replaced by private security and volunteer efforts in many locales.

The U.S. law enforcement community employs an average of 2.3 full-time officers for every 1,000 inhabitants.[13]

In your opinion, what are the most serious problems of the criminal justice system, and what are your solutions?

CHALLENGES OF THE SECURITY INDUSTRY

Business and government leaders have realized that the growing private security industry is a great ally of the criminal justice system. Both crime-fighting sectors have mutual and overlapping functions in controlling crime. With this thinking in mind, the U.S. Department of Justice provided financial support for the production of important research reports. *The Rand Report* (1972) focused national attention on the problems and needs of the private security industry. This report stated that "the typical private guard is an aging white male, poorly educated, usually untrained, and very poorly paid."[14] This conclusion has met with criticism because the research sample was small and thus did not represent the entire security industry. However, with the assistance of this report and its recommendations, the professionalism of private security improved.

The Rand Report was a great aid (because of limited literature in the field) to the *Report of the Task Force on Private Security* (1976). This report of the National Advisory Committee on Criminal Justice Standards and Goals represented the first national effort to set realistic and viable standards and goals designed to maximize the ability, competency, and effectiveness of the private security industry for its role in the prevention and reduction of crime.[15] A major emphasis of the report was that all businesses that sell security services should be licensed and all personnel in private security work should be registered.

The task force's urging of stricter standards for the security industry reflected a need to reduce ineptitude and industry abuses, while striving toward professionalism. For example, in the private security industry, minimal hiring, training, and salary standards are pervasive. These minimal standards enable companies to reduce costs and provide potential clients with low bids for contract service. Thus, professionalism is sacrificed to keep up with competition. The task force recommended improved hiring criteria, higher salaries (especially to reduce turnover), and better training, among other improvements. Both studies recommended state-level regulation of the security industry in general as a means of creating more uniformity.

Another major study of the security industry funded by the U.S. Department of Justice was published in 1985. *Private Security and Police in America: The Hallcrest Report*, prepared by Hallcrest Systems, Inc., focused research on three major areas: (1) the contributions of both public police and private security to crime control, (2) the interaction of these two forces and their level of cooperation, and (3) the characteristics of the private security industry.[16] Several industry problems and preferred solutions were discussed in this report, as covered in subsequent pages.

The U.S. Department of Justice funded a second Hallcrest Report, entitled *Private Security Trends: 1970–2000, The Hallcrest Report II*. This report provided a study of security trends to the twenty-first century. Some of its findings follow:

- Crime against business in the United States will cost $200 billion by the year 2000.
- Since the middle 1980s, companies have been less inclined to hire security managers with police and military backgrounds and more inclined to hire those with a business background.

- During the 1990s, in-house security staffs will diminish with an increase reliance on contract services and equipment.
- The negative stereotypical security personnel are being replaced with younger, better-educated officers with greater numbers of women and minority group members. However, the problems of quality, training, and compensation remain.
- The false-alarm problem is continuing. There is a massive waste of public funds when police and fire agencies must respond to current levels of false alarms. Between 97 and 99 percent of all alarms are false.[17]

Cooperation Between Public Police and Private Security

A persistent problem noted by several research reports involves disrespect and even conflict between public and private police.

Some law enforcement officers believe that being a "public servant" is of a higher moral order than serving private interests. . . . They then relegate private security to an inferior status. . . . This perceived status differential by law enforcement personnel manifests itself in lack of respect and communication, which precludes effective cooperation.[18]

To reduce conflict, the Task Force Report and the Hallcrest Reports recommended liaison be implemented between public and private police. During the 1980s, the International Association of Chiefs of Police, the National Sheriffs' Association, and the American Society for Industrial Security (ASIS) began joint meetings to foster better cooperation between the public and private sectors.[19] This effort continued into the 1990s. In 1996, ASIS members testified before Congress in support of legislation to increase cooperation between private security and public law enforcement.[20] Avenues of increased cooperation include appointing high-ranking practitioners from both sectors to increase communication and instituting short training lessons in established training programs.

As we begin the twenty-first century, cooperative efforts must continue in an effort to enhance the resources and capabilities of each sector. Suggested areas of cooperation are sharing data, information and technology; and sharing expertise in combating fraud, cybercrime, and terrorism.

Regulation of the Industry

The security field has its share of charlatans, who tarnish the industry, and as with many types of services offered the public, government intervention has taken the form of licensing and registration. State agencies screen applications of those interested in security work (e.g., check criminal records).

The Task Force Report and Hallcrest Reports recommend regulation of the security industry by all states. The majority of states have such legislation, but it is varied. Although government regulation does not guarantee that all security practitioners will perform in a satisfactory manner, it does prevent people who have criminal records from entering the profession.

Attempts have been made through Congress to pass a national law to regulate the security industry. H.R. 2092, *The Private Security Officers Quality Assurance Act of 1995*, was introduced by Rep. Bob Bar (R-GA). It languished in Congress in various forms when Rep. Matthew Martinez (D-CA) introduced a similar bill. Known as the Barr-Martinez Bill, if passed, it would have provided state regulators with expedited FBI criminal background checks of prospective and newly hired security officers. The minimal training standards of the bill were stricken, which would have required 8 hours of training and 4 hours of on-the-job training for unarmed officers and an additional 15 hours for armed officers. Critics argue that states are against such a national law and state regulations are sufficient.[21]

Which government agency in your state regulates the private security industry? What are the requirements?

The Issue of Privatization

Privatization is the contracting out of government programs, either wholly or in part, to for-profit and not-for-profit organizations. There is a growing interdependence of the public and private sectors. A broad array of services are provided to government agencies by the private sector today, from consulting services to janitorial services. Hospitals, schools, and other institutions formerly dominated by the government are being operated by both the public and private sectors. For crime control efforts, we see private security patrols in residential areas, private security officers in courts, and private prisons. Business people make themselves attractive to governments when they claim that they can perform services more efficiently and at a lower cost than the public sector.

Privatization is not a new concept. In the late 1600s, much security and incarceration for early urban areas was supplied by the private sector. By the 1700s, government dominated these services. Today, privatization can be viewed as a movement to demonopolize and decentralize services dominated by government. This movement to privatize criminal justice services encourages shared responsibility for public safety.[22]

Another factor fueling the privatization movement is victim and citizen dissatisfaction with the way in which government is handling crime. Increasing numbers of citizens are confronting crime through neighborhood watches, citizen patrols, crime stoppers, hiring private attorneys to assist prosecutors, and dispute resolution.

Critics of privatization argue that crime control by government is rooted in constitutional safeguards and crime control should not be contracted to the private sector. Use of force and searches by the private sector, punishment in private prisons, and liabilities of governments and contractors are examples of the thorny issues that face privatization.

What are your views on privatization? Do you view it as a wise choice to improve crime control strategies?

The Need for Training

Numerous research reports and other publications have pointed to the need for more training of personnel in the security industry. Training of all security officers should be required by law prior to assignment. The harsh realities of the contract security business make this objective difficult to reach. Low pay and the enormous turnover of officers lead many security executives to consider costly training difficult to justify. With liability a constant threat and with insurance often unaffordable, many security firms are simply gambling by not adequately preparing their officers for the job. The Task Force Report and the Hallcrest Reports stress the need for improved recruitment, selection, pay, and training within the security industry.

The Hallcrest Report II noted that the typical uniformed security officer receives an estimated 4 to 6 hours of training before assignment. Seventeen states require minimum training for unarmed officers, 32 states mandate some firearms training for armed officers, and amazingly, 14 states require not even a minimal background check for armed officers. The Task Force on Private Security recommended 24 hours of training for armed security officers. Because of potential liability and the rise in insurance premiums, it was estimated that by the year 2000, only 5 percent of officers will be armed.[23] Today, these trends continue: security training is inconsistent and, at times, nonexistent; a small percentage of security officers are armed.

In essence, what we have seen following these national reports and recommendations is an industry that needs to do more to help professionalize the industry and security personnel. It is easy to forget about these reports and rec-

ommendations as a businessperson under pressure to reduce expenses and turn a profit while facing employee turnover, the pressure to ensure security officers are on client posts, and competition from low bidders. Furthermore, the security industry plays a strong role in influencing government laws and regulations that can result in added expenses for businesses. Unfortunately, we have seen changes resulting from many lawsuits claiming negligent security. Fear of such litigation motivates the industry to change. On the bright side, there are many security service companies that are professional, set high standards for themselves, and have improved the industry. It is hoped that these companies continue to set an example to be followed by others.

Ethics

A code of ethics is a partial solution to strengthen the professionalism of security practitioners. Such a code helps to guide behavior by establishing standards of ethical conduct. Twomey, Jennings, and Fox describe *ethics* as a branch of philosophy dealing with values that relate to the nature of human conduct. They write that "conduct and values within the context of business operations become more complex because individuals are working together to maximize profit. Balancing the goal of profits with the values of individuals and society is the focus of *business ethics*." Twomey and colleagues note that capitalism succeeds because of trust; investors provide capital for a business because they believe the business will earn a profit.[24]

Customers rely on business promises of quality and the commitment to stand behind a product or service. Having a code makes good business sense because consumers make purchasing decisions based on past experience or the experiences of others. Reliance on promises, not litigation, nurtures good business relationships.

Twomey and colleagues write of studies that show that those businesses with the strongest value systems survive and do so successfully. Citing several companies, they argue that "bankruptcy and/or free falls in the worth of shares are the fates that await firms that make poor ethical choices."[25] Multiple DePaul University studies found that companies with a defined corporate commitment to ethical standards outperformed companies that do not have such standards.[26]

A host of problems can develop for a business and its employees when unethical decisions are made. Besides a loss of customers, unethical decisions can result in criminal and civil liabilities. Quality ethics must be initiated and supported by top management, who must set an example without hypocrisy. All employees must be a part of the ethical environment through a code of ethics and see it spelled out in policies, procedures, and training.

International business presents special challenges when promoting ethical decision making because cultures differ on codes of ethics. Business management must take the lead and research and define guidelines for employees.

Another challenge develops when a security practitioner's employer or supervisor violates ethical standards or law. What you do not want to do is to become part of the problem and subject yourself to a tarnished reputation or criminal and civil liabilities. When faced with such difficult dilemmas, refer to your professional background and its code of ethics.

The Web is a rich source of information on ethics. The Corporate Social Responsibility Resource Center for Business Ethics (http://www.bsr.org/resourcecenter) focuses on many topics such as ethics training, competitive intelligence, corruption and bribery, "cyberethics" challenges, defense industry initiative on ethics, and what a variety of corporations are doing. The Markkula Center for Applied Ethics (http://www.scu.edu/Ethics/) provides training and educational tools to heighten ethical awareness and improve ethical decisions.

The Task Force Report and the American Society for Industrial Security are sources for codes of ethics for the security profession. The former has one code for security management (as does ASIS) and a code for security employees in general. A sample of the wording, similar in both codes, includes: "to protect life and property," and "to be guided by a sense of integrity, honor, justice and morality. . . ."[27] Management, supervision, policies, procedures, and training help to define what these words mean.

Here are guidelines for ethical decisions:

- Does the decision violate law, a code of ethics, or company policy?
- What are the short-term and long-term consequences of your decision for your employer and yourself?
- Is there an alternative course of action that is less harmful?
- Are you making a level-headed decision, rather than a decision based on emotions?
- Would your family support your decision?
- Would your supervisor and management support your decision?

The False Alarm Problem

Another persistent problem that causes friction between public police and the private sector is false alarms. It is generally agreed that more than 95 percent of all alarm response calls received by public police are false alarms. However, the definition of *false alarm* is subject to debate. It often is assumed that, if a burglar is not caught on the premises, the alarm was false. Police do not always consider that the alarm or the approaching police could have frightened away a burglar.

The Task Force and Hallcrest Reports from the last quarter of the twentieth century discussed the problem of false alarms. Many police agencies nationwide continue to spend millions of dollars each year in personnel and equipment to respond to these calls. For decades municipalities and the alarm industry have tried various solutions. Police agencies have selectively responded or not responded to alarms. City and county governments have enacted false alarm control ordinances that require a permit for an alarm system and impose fines for excessive false alarms. The industry claims that 80 percent of the problems are caused by the end users. It continues its education campaign while trying a multitude of strategies, such as offering a class for repeat offenders instead of a fine, setting standards of exit delay at no fewer than 45 seconds and entry times of at least 30 seconds, and audio and video verification of alarms. Since the industry is installing 15 percent more systems each year, these efforts must continue.[28]

What do you think are the most serious problems of the private security industry, and what are your solutions?

Search the Web

Several security associations exist to promote professionalism and improve the security field. Go to the Web site of the American Society for Industrial Security (http://www.asisonline.org/). With a membership over 30,000, the ASIS is the leading general organization of protection executives and specialists. Its monthly magazine, *Security Management,* is an excellent source of information. Courses, seminars, and a certification program for the Certified Protection Professional (CPP) also are available.

Another major association in this field is the International Foundation for Protection Officers (http://www.ifpo.org/). The IFPO publishes *The Protection Officer* magazine and offers the Certified Protection Officer (CPO) and Certified Security Supervisor (CSS) programs.

CASE PROBLEMS

2A.   As a city police detective specializing in white-collar crime, you enjoy the challenges of your work and look forward to retirement in five years to become an insurance fraud investigator. You often work with the private sector and you are frequently in contact with corporate security investigators. As an active member of a local police-security council, you are assigned the task of developing a plan to improve police-security cooperation at all levels in the city. What are your specific plans that you will present to the council?

2B.   As a uniformed security officer, how would you handle the following situations?

- Another security officer says that you can leave two hours early during second shift and she will "punch you out."
- You are assigned to a stationary post at a shipping and receiving dock and a truck driver asks you to "look the other way" for $500 cash.
- A security officer that you work with shows you how to make the required physical inspections around the plant without leaving your seat.
- During the holidays a group of coworkers planning a party on the premises ask you if you want to contribute to a fund to hire a stripper/prostitute.
- You are testifying in criminal court in a shoplifting case and the defense attorney asks you to state whether you ever lost sight of the defendant when the incident occurred. The case depends on you stating that you never lost sight of the defendant. You actually lost sight of the defendant once. How do you respond?
- Your best friend wants you to provide a positive recommendation for him when he applies for a job where you work, even though he has an arrest record.
- You see your supervisor take company items and put them in the trunk of her vehicle.

2C.   As a corporate security manager, how would you handle the following situations?

- Two contract security officers fail to show up for first shift. The contract manager says that screened and trained replacements are unavailable, but two new applicants are available. You are required to make an immediate decision. Do you accept the two applicants, who lack a background investigation and state-mandated training?
- A vendor offers you a condo at the beach for a week if you support his firm's bid for an access control system. You know that the system is not the best and that it will cost your company slightly more than the best system. The condo will save you about $1,500 on your summer vacation. What is your decision?
- Your employer is violating environmental laws. You know that if the government learns of the violations, your company will be unable to survive financially criminal and civil action and pollution controls and you will certainly lose your job. What do you do?

- While reviewing CCTV video footage, you see your boss inappropriately touching a coworker who recently filed a sexual harassment suit against the boss, who vehemently denied the allegations. You placed the pinhole-lens camera in the office supply closet to catch a thief, not expecting to see your boss touching the coworker. No one knows of the placement of the camera and the video footage, except you. Your boss, who is the vice-president of finance, has been especially helpful to your career, your excellent raises and bonuses, and the corporate security budget. What do you do?

- You are testifying in a case of negligent security concerning a retail store in your region. The plaintiff's attorney asks you if any security surveys have ever been conducted at the store where the murder occurred. You know that a survey conducted prior to the murder showed the need for increased security at the store. Such information would secure a victory for the plaintiff. What is your response to the question?

NOTES

1. FBI (1999), *Uniform Crime Reports*. http://www.fbi.gov/ (February 19, 2001). And, Bureau of Justice Statistics (1999), *National Crime Victimization Survey*. http://www.ojp.usdoj.gov/bjs (February 19, 2001).

2. Ted Miller, et al., *Victim Costs and Consequences: A New Look* (Washington, D.C.: National Institute of Justice, 1996).

3. National Fire Data Center (2000), *The Overall Fire Picture-1999*. http://www.usfa.fema.gov/ (February 16, 2001).

4. American Red Cross (2001), *The Annual Cost of Workplace Injuries Nationwide*. http://www.redcross.org/atlanta (February 16, 2001).

5. William C. Cunningham, et al., *Private Security: Patterns and Trends* (Washington, D.C.: National Institute of Justice, August 1991).

6. Bureau of Justice Statistics (1999). http://www.ojp.usdoj.gov/bjs (February 20, 2001). And, "Law Enforcement Count Dwarfed by Private Security," *Security* 37 (January 2000), p. 7.

7. Susan Whitehurst, "1980-2000: What a Ride!" *Security* 37 (February 2000), p. 14. And, telephone call to Security Industry Association, 703-683-2075 (February 22, 2001).

8. "Global Security Market Growth Continues, Finds Researchers," *Security Letter* XXXI (February 2001).

9. Sources: U.S. Department of Justice, National Institute of Justice, *Crime and Protection in America: Executive Summary of the Hallcrest Report* (Washington, D.C.: U.S. Government Printing Office, 1985), pp. 19–21; "Exploring Security Trends," *Security* [Cahners Publishing Co.] (1989); and *Security Letter* 19 (September 1, 1989).

10. U.S. Department of Justice, *Report of the Task Force on Private Security* (Washington, D.C.: U.S. Government Printing Office, 1976), pp. 146–147 and 249–257.

11. Bureau of Justice Statistics (1997), *Expenditure and Employment Statistics.* http://www.ojp.usdoj.gov/bjs (February 20, 2001).
12. John E. Conklin, *Criminology,* 7th ed. (Boston: Allyn & Bacon, 2001), p. 466.
13. Brian Reaves and Andrew Goldberg, *Law Enforcement Management and Administrative Statistics, 1997* (Washington, D.C.: Bureau of Justice Statistics, 1999).
14. U.S. Department of Justice, *Private Police in the United States: Findings and Recommendations* 1 (Washington, D.C.: U.S. Government Printing Office, 1972), p. 30.
15. U.S. Department of Justice, National Criminal Justice Reference Service, Abstract for the *Report of the Task Force on Private Security* (1976).
16. William C. Cunningham and Todd H. Taylor, *Private Security and Police in America: The Hallcrest Report* (Portland, OR: Chancellor Press, 1985).
17. William C. Cunningham, et al., *Private Security Trends: 1970-2000, The Hallcrest Report II* (Boston: Butterworth–Heinemann, 1990).
18. U.S. Department of Justice, *Law Enforcement and Private Security: Sources and Areas of Conflict* (Washington, D.C.: U.S. Government Printing Office, 1976), p. 6.
19. William C. Cunningham, et al., *Private Security: Patterns and Trends,* p. 2.
20. Kate Doherty, "Public/Private Cooperation Needed, ASIS Tells Congress," *Access Control* (October 1996), p. 6.
21. Robert King, "Security Guard Bill Referred out of Committee," *Security Concepts* (October 1996), p. 1.
22. Gary Bowman, et al., *Privatizing the United States Justice System* (Jefferson, NC: McFarland Pub., 1992), pp. 15–57.
23. King, "Security Guard Bill," p. 16; Cunningham et al., *Private Security,* p. 4.
24. David Twomey, Marianne Jennings, and Ivan Fox, *Anderson's Business Law and the Regulatory Environment,* 14th ed. (Cincinnati, OH: West Legal Studies, 2001), pp. 28–31.
25. Ibid., p. 32.
26. The Corporate Social Responsibility Resource Center for Business Ethics. *Business Ethics.* http://www.bsr.org/resourcecenter (February 24, 2001).
27. U.S. Department of Justice, *Report of the Task Force on Private Security,* p. 24.
28. Randy Southerland, "Dispatch to Nowhere," *Access Control & Security Systems Integration* (February 2000), p. 1.

II

REDUCING THE
PROBLEM OF LOSS

3

Foundations of Security and Loss Prevention

OBJECTIVES

After studying this chapter the reader will be able to:

1. Explain precisely how the security and loss prevention field has reached the status of a profession.
2. List and explain the three-step risk analysis process.
3. Discuss planning and its importance.
4. Explain and illustrate how to evaluate security and loss prevention programs.
5. Discuss standards for protection.
6. Describe the characteristics of proprietary security programs.

THE SECURITY AND LOSS PREVENTION PROFESSION

The security and loss prevention field has reached the status of a profession. If we look to other professions as models to emulate, we see the following in each, just as we see in the security and loss prevention profession: a history and body of knowledge recorded in books and periodicals; associations that promote advancement of knowledge, training, certification, and a code of ethics; and programs of higher education that prepare students for the profession.

Theoretical Foundations

The challenges of security and loss prevention in a complex world have created an intense search among practitioners to seek answers to protection problems. Many fields of study offer answers for the practitioner, and thus, an interdisciplinary approach to the problem of loss is best. Here we present a summary of theories and concepts to illustrate the interdisciplinary nature of security and loss prevention and its theoretical foundation.

The work of Oscar Newman is the bedrock of many security designs worldwide. He argued that informal control of criminal behavior can be enhanced through architectural design that creates "defensible space" and changes residents' use of public places while reducing fear.[1]

From the field of criminology, routine activities theory stresses that some people engage in regular or routine activities that increase their risk of victimization. Three factors must occur for victimization under this theory: (1) an attractive target; (2) a motivated offender; and (3) the absence of "guardianship" (e.g., nearby people who can protect an intended victim).[2] Corporate security and executive protection programs can benefit from this theory and related research.

Employee theft and embezzlement are huge problems for businesses. Criminologist Donald Cressey's formula offers insight into causation and preventive measures. The formula is: motivation + opportunity + rationalization = theft. Cressey, in his classic study, observed that embezzlers' financial problems are "nonshareable" because of embarrassment or shame, and they rationalize their illegal behavior.[3] More recent research on embezzlement sees a new form of it called "collective embezzlement," which involves groups of two or more people. Financial industries, such as banks, stock brokerage, and insurance, have been victimized by collective embezzlement.[4]

Psychologist Abraham Maslow is noted for his "hierarchy of human needs." He claimed that people have a variety of needs such as basic physiological needs, safety and security needs, and societal needs. These needs can be met in the workplace through, for instance, clean lavatories, a safe working environment, and praise and rewards.[5] The implications are that as employers do more to meet human needs, losses (e.g., internal theft) may drop. Research should focus on the relationship among types of needs met by employers and types of losses reduced.

The snapshot of theory presented here is a beginning point from which to build. The social sciences are by no means the only disciplines helpful to security and loss prevention. In subsequent chapters, theory and concepts are drawn from law, marketing, accounting, fire science, safety, and risk management.

Security Periodicals and the Web

There are many security periodicals published by a variety of associations and organizations. Periodicals serve as a platform not only for the theoretical foundation of the security and loss prevention field but also to introduce readers to new developments, security strategies and technology, law, and a host of other topics. What follows are noted periodicals in this field.

Security Journal is published by Perpetuity Press United Kingdom and supported by the American Society for Industrial Security Foundation. The editorial staff is from the United States and the United Kingdom. The journal publishes articles on a variety of topics on the latest developments and techniques of security management. Articles include findings and recommendations of independent research. Two other journals from this publisher are *Risk Management: An International Journal* and *Crime Prevention and Community Safety: An International Journal.* Web site: http://www.perpetuitypress.co.uk/

Journal of Security Administration is a scholarly semi-annual journal that presents excellent articles on a variety of security topics. It is affiliated with the Security and Crime Prevention Section of the Academy of Criminal Justice Sciences. Web site: http://www.wiu.edu/users/mfkac/jsa/

Security Management is a monthly magazine published by the American Society for Industrial Security. Each issue contains a wealth of informative articles on a broad range of topics written by experienced security professionals. It is the best general security periodical. Web site: http://www.asis.com/

Protection News, published by the International Foundation of Protection Officers, is a newsletter containing current trends of the security industry and covering topics on life safety and the protection of property. Its Web site has an excellent "security surfer" with links to numerous security associations and organizations and related periodicals. Web site: http://www.ifpo.org/

An alternative to the above "security surfer" is a good search engine. By typing "school security," "healthcare security," "bank security," "computer security," or whatever type of security, you will be introduced to the many specializations in this profession. And, each specialization is likely to have an association, an agenda of objectives to advance the profession, training, certification, and a periodical. In this book, as specialized topics are covered, the reader will be introduced to related associations.

Security Associations

Several security associations exist to promote professionalism and improve the security field. The American Society for Industrial Security (ASIS) and the International Foundation for Protection Officers (IFPO) were covered in the "Search the Web" exercise at the end of the previous chapter. Other associations and the certification provided include the Academy of Security Educators and Trainers, offering the Certified Security Trainer (CST) and the Association of Certified Fraud Examiners (CFE).

The National Association of Security and Investigative Regulators contains members who are state employees involved in the licensing and regulation of the private security industry. This group promotes effective regulation and enforcement, assists in training and education, and influences legislation. Most states are represented in the membership. The group's Web site lists state licensing information for security officers, armored car officers, private investigators, and electronic security companies (www.nasir.org).

The National Association of Security Companies represents the private security industry and its membership includes large contract security companies. Its goals are to monitor proposed state and federal legislation that might affect the quality or effectiveness of private security services, upgrade standards within the industry, and foster uniformity of regulation throughout the United States.

METHODS FOR PROTECTION PROGRAMS

Before a program of security and loss prevention can be implemented, careful planning is necessary. Such planning should begin by identifying the threats that face the organization. A retailer, for example, typically incurs losses from internal theft and shoplifting, and fire and accidents also are serious threats. The expansion of E-commerce presents retailers with additional security concerns. Once the security planner has pinpointed the organization's vulnerabilities, the next step is to use this information to plan and implement countermeasures.

Risk Analysis

The term *risk analysis* is used interchangeably with *risk assessment* and *risk evaluation*. This chapter uses *risk analysis*, defining it as a method to estimate the expected loss from specific risks using the following three-step process: (1) the loss prevention survey, (2) identifying vulnerabilities, and (3) determining probability, frequency, and cost.

The Loss Prevention Survey

The purpose of a loss prevention survey is to pinpoint risks and vulnerabilities (e.g., inadequate access controls, unsafe conditions) and develop a foundation for improved protection. The survey should tailor its questions to the unique needs of the premises to be surveyed. *The merging of information technology (IT) specialists into the risk analysis process is vital for comprehensive protection.* Essentially, the survey involves a day-and-night physical examination of the location requiring a loss prevention program. The list that follows is a beginning point for topics for the survey, which can take several days.

1. Geography and climate (possible natural disaster)
2. Social and political climate surrounding the facility (possible high crime rate and unrest)

3.   Past incidents causing loss
4.   Condition of physical security, fire protection, and safety measures
5.   Hazardous substances and protection measures
6.   Policies and procedures and their enforcement
7.   Quality of security personnel (e.g., applicant screening, training, and supervision; properly registered and licensed)
8.   Protection of people and assets
9.   Protection of information systems and information
10. Protection of communications systems (e.g., telephones and fax machines)
11. Protection of utilities
12. Protection of parking lots[6]

The survey document usually consists of a checklist in the form of questions that remind the loss prevention practitioner or committee of what to examine. A list attached to the survey can contain the targets—for example, people, money, equipment, IT systems—that must be protected and the present strategies, if any, used to protect them. Blueprints of the facility and a map of the surrounding area also are helpful to the survey.

Identifying Vulnerabilities

Once the survey is completed, vulnerabilities can be isolated. For example, merchandise stacked high in a retail store provides "cover" and aids shoplifters. Poor record keeping and accountability can benefit employee thieves. A lax atmosphere concerning changing passwords aids hackers. These vulnerabilities can be minimized through loss prevention measures: an improved store plan, better accountability, and periodic changing of passwords. Vulnerabilities may also show that security, fire, and life-safety strategies are outdated and must be brought up to current codes and standards.

Determining Probability, Frequency, and Cost

The third step requires an analysis of the probability, frequency, and cost of each loss. Shoplifting and employee theft are common in retail stores, and numerous incidents can add up to serious losses. Fire and explosion are potential risks at a petrochemical facility: Even one incident can be financially devastating. The frequency of shoplifting and employee theft incidents at a retail store will likely be greater than the frequency of fires and explosions at a petrochemical facility. However, it is impossible to pinpoint accurately when, where, and how many times losses will occur. When the questions of probability, frequency, and cost of losses arise, practitioners must rely on their own experience, records and statistics, communication with fellow practitioners, and information provided by trade publications. Also helpful is risk analysis software such as PPM 2000 (http://www.ppm2000.com/), CAP Index (http://www.capindex.com/), and Risk Watch (http://www.riskwatch.com/).

It is argued that security directors of large, complex organizations should use quantitative risk analysis when exposures cannot be evaluated intuitively, especially for the protection of IT and e-business.[7] The process begins with a mathematical model that can be simple or complex. A simple formula is ALE = I × F, where "ALE" is annual loss exposure, "I" is impact (i.e., dollar loss if the event occurs), and "F" is frequency (i.e., the number of times the event will occur each year). Software tools are available to organize and automate complex risk analyses. Debate continues over when to use quantitative risk analysis, its cost and value, how much guesswork goes into the process, and which formula and software is best. Two points are clear: (1) there are many opinions and styles of risk analysis, and (2) what works for one organization may not work for another.

In the previous chapter the importance of totaling direct and indirect losses was covered. Here we apply this financial strategy to potential losses to IT systems, as an illustration. Trusecure conducted research on 300 organizations following the Melissa virus catastrophe in 1999. The average victimized company had 1120 employees and 196 infected PCs, and 8.7 infected servers (including e-mail and e-commerce) that were down for two days. Respondents claimed an average of $1700 in losses. Total costs were probably more than sevenfold higher when consideration is given to such losses as staff time spent repairing damage, lost productivity, public relations damage, and lost business.[8] Thus, when determining potential losses, include total potential losses.

Planning

Planning results in a design used to reach objectives. It is better to know where one is going and how to get there than to adhere to a philosophy of "we'll cross that bridge when we get to it." One serious consequence of that philosophy is the panic atmosphere that develops when serious losses occur; emotional decisions are made when quickly acquiring needed loss prevention systems and services. This sets up the organization for unscrupulous salespeople who prey on the panic.

An integral purpose of the planning process is to fulfill organizational goals and objectives. Those who plan protection should have a clear understanding of the organization and its needs. Because of global competitiveness, downsizing, and restructuring, today's corporations are in a state of constant change and reengineering. To survive, a support function such as security must be a team player, adapt quickly to change, meet challenges in a positive and creative manner, and contribute to the corporate mission.[9]

Budgeting is closely related to planning because it pertains to the money required to fulfill plans. Modern practitioners state their protection plans in financial terms that justify the expenditures, save the organization money, and if possible, bring in a return on the investment. The concept of *value added* means that all corporate departments must demonstrate their value to the organization by translating expenditures into bottom-line impact. Corporate financial officers ask, "Is security contributing to our business and profit success, and if it is, how?" Illustrations of financial leverage for security include calculating total direct and indirect losses for each loss incident, conducting an undercover investigation to pinpoint not only theft but also substance abuse and safety problems, hiring a bad check specialist who recovers several times his or her salary, purchasing an access control system that performs multiple roles such as producing time and attendance data, and installing a CCTV system that not only assists investigations but helps to locate production problems to improve efficiency and cut costs.

> Modern security and loss prevention practitioners state their protection plans in financial terms that justify expenditures, save the organization money, and if possible, bring in a return on investment.

A risk analysis provides input for planning protection. Security strategies generally take the form of personnel, hardware, and policies and procedures, as discussed throughout this book. Some of the many factors that go into the planning process follow:

1. Has the problem been carefully and accurately identified?
2. How much will it cost to correct the problem, and what percent of the budget will be allocated to the particular strategy?
3. Is the strategy practical?
4. Is the strategy cost effective? For example, a loss prevention manager debates an increase in the staff of loss prevention officers or the purchase of a closed-circuit television system. The staff increase will cost $20,000 per officer (three officers × $20,000 per year = $60,000 per year). CCTV will cost $75,000. After considering the costs and benefits of each, the manager decides on the CCTV system because by the second year the expense will be much lower than hiring three extra officers.
5. Does the cost of the strategy exceed the potential loss? For example, it would not be cost effective to spend $5000 to prevent the burglary of a $50 petty cash fund.
6. Does the strategy relate to unique needs? Often, strategies good for one location may not be appropriate for another location.

7.   How will the strategy relate to the entire loss prevention program? A systems approach is wise. The interrelatedness of each strategy should be considered. For example, CCTV can be used in a retail store to prevent both shoplifting and employee theft. Also, personnel are needed to respond to incidents. Furthermore, a high-quality CCTV system can act as a cost savings by reducing personnel at certain locations.

8.   Does the strategy conform to the goals and objectives of the organization or business and the loss prevention program?

9.   How does the strategy compare to contract loss prevention programs? Will the strategy interfere with any contract services?

10. How will the insurance carriers react?

11. If a government contract is involved, what Department of Defense regulations must be considered?

12. Does the strategy create the potential for losses greater than what is being prevented? For example, applying a chain and lock to the inside handles of a double door makes it more difficult for a burglar to enter; however, what if a fire takes place and employees must escape quickly?

13. Does the strategy reduce the effectiveness of other loss prevention strategies? For example, a chain-link fence with colorful plastic woven through the links and high hedges will prevent people from seeing into the property and hinder an offender's penetration, but this strategy also will cause observation problems for patrolling police.

14. To what extent will the loss prevention strategy interfere with productivity? For example, in a high-risk environment, how much time will be necessary to search employees who leave and return at lunchtime? What if 1000 employees leave for lunch? As another example, if the loss prevention manager requires merchandise loaded into trucks to be counted by three separate individuals, will this strategy slow the shipping process significantly?

15. Will the strategy receive support from management, employees, customers, clients, and visitors? Can any type of adverse reaction be predicted?

16. Does the strategy have to conform to local codes, ordinances, or laws? For example, in certain jurisdictions, perimeter fences must be under a specific height and use of barbed wire is restricted.

17. Will the strategy lower employee morale or lead to a distrust of management?

18. Are there any possible problems with civil liberties violations?

19. How will the union react to the strategy?

20. Was participatory management used to aid in planning the strategy?

21. Can the strategy be effectively implemented with the present number of loss prevention personnel?

22. Will the strategy cause a strain on personnel time?

23. What are the characteristics of the area surrounding the location that will receive the loss prevention strategy? These characteristics must be considered to improve the quality of strategies. For example, if loss prevention strategies are planned for a manufacturing plant, what factors outside the plant must be considered? (Factors of consideration include crime, fire, and accident rates.) Also, certain nearby sites may be subject to disaster: nuclear plants, airports, railroads (transportation of hazardous materials), educational institutions (student unrest), forests (fire), hazardous industries (chemicals), and military installations, among others. Weather conditions are important to consider as well. Storms can activate alarms. Excessive rainfall can cause losses due to flooding. Heavy snow can result in a variety of losses. Earthquake and volcanic actions are additional factors to consider.

24. When considering loss prevention strategies such as burglar or fire alarms, what is the response time of public services such as police, fire, and emergency medical service? Where is the nearest facility housing each service?

25. Will loss prevention strategies be able to repel activity from local criminals, a gang, or organized crime?

26. Will the strategy shift crime to another target?

27. Does the strategy attempt to "loss-proof" or eliminate all losses? This often is an impossible objective to reach. Loss prevention practitioners sometimes are surprised by the failure of a strategy that was publicized as a panacea.

28. If the strategy is not implemented, what is the risk of loss?

29. Will a better, less expensive strategy accomplish the same objective? For example, "According to a survey by the U.S. General Services Administration, one 24-hour guard post can cost as much as $100,000 per year, including salaries, maintenance, uniforms, equipment, benefits, and insurance. By injecting an electronic backup such as a CCTV or alarm into the security force, guard manpower can be reduced."[10]

30. Can any other present strategy be eliminated when the new strategy is implemented? Can security be consolidated?

31. What other strategies are more important? Are priorities established?

32. Should a pilot program be implemented (say, at one manufacturing plant instead of all plants) to study the strategy for problems and corrective action?

33. How will the strategy be evaluated?

Incomplete Protection Plans[11]

Andrew Smith, security manager at Tecsonics, Inc., a fast-growing electronics firm, was assigned the task of preparing a plan and one-year budget for the protection of proprietary information. Two months later, Andrew was in front of senior executives who were eager to learn how proprietary information would be protected in such a fiercely competitive industry. At the beginning of the presentation, Andrew emphasized that the survival and growth of Tecsonics depended on its information protection program. The four major strategies for protection for the first year included electronic soundproofing, also referred to as shielding, which would involve the use of a copper barrier throughout one conference room to cut off radio waves from a spy's bugging equipment. Cost: $250,000. The second strategy was to spend $85,000 for countermeasure "sweeps" to detect bugs in select locations on the premises. The third strategy was to install a card access control system at a cost of $200,000. The fourth strategy was to hire an IT security specialist for $80,000 annually.

Before Andrew was five minutes into his presentation, the rapid-fire questions began: "What is the return on investment?" "Are the plans cost effective?" "Did you perform a risk analysis?"

"What are other similar businesses doing?" "Why should we spend so much money on shielding and sweeps when we can use cheaper methods, such as holding meetings in unexpected locations, preparing good policies and procedures, promoting employee education, and keeping certain sensitive information out of the computer and locked up in a safe?" One sarcastic, hard-nosed executive quipped: "You would probably spend millions on shielding and sweeps and not realize that one of our male scientists could go out of town to a seminar, get cornered by a foxy broad, and get drunk as she pumps him for information!" Unfortunately for Andrew, everybody was laughing while he wished he had known about these questions beforehand.

Planning from a Systems Perspective

The *systems perspective* looks at interactions among subsystems. When actions take place in one subsystem, other subsystems are affected. For example, the criminal justice system is composed of three major subsystems: police, courts, and corrections. If, during one day, 100 public drunk arrests are made by the police, then the court and corrections subsystems must react by accommodating these arrestees. There are many other examples of systems: a loss prevention department, business, government, school, an automobile, the human body, and so on. All these systems have subsystems that interact and affect the whole system. In each system, subsystems are established to attain overall system objectives and goals.

In a loss prevention system, for instance, the investigation subsystem is dependent on the patrol subsystem for information and assistance. Likewise, the patrol subsystem depends on the investigation subsystem for indepth follow-up.

Similar to other systems, a loss prevention department can be analyzed in terms of inputs, processes, outputs, and feedback. As an example, look at a loss prevention department's immediate reaction and short-term planning concerning an employee theft incident (see Figure 3-1). The loss prevention department receives a call from a supervisor who has caught an employee stealing: the input. The process is the analysis of the call; planning; and the action taken, dispatching of loss prevention personnel. The output (activity at the scene) is the arrival of the personnel, questioning, and note taking. Feedback involves communications from the on-site loss prevention personnel to the loss prevention department. This helps to determine if the output was proper or if corrections are necessary. For instance, suppose that an on-the-spot arrest was required. Then additional outputs might be necessary, possibly including assistance from a local public police department.

The systems perspective described in Figure 3-1 is for planning a short-term immediate action. Figure 3-2 illustrates long-term loss prevention planning from a systems perspective.

In Figure 3-2, the inputs of goals and objectives relate to upper management's expectations of the loss prevention function. The resources basically are money, material, and personnel. Information, research, reports, risk analyses, and statistics all aid in decision making within the planning process. The output is the loss prevention programs and strategies evolving from the planning process that will prevent and reduce losses while increasing profits. Feedback, an often overlooked activity, is essential for effective planning; and evaluation is an integral part of feedback. Ineffective programs and strategies must be eliminated. Other programs and strategies may need modification. Evaluation helps to justify programs and strategies.

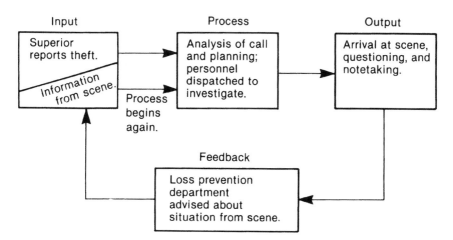

Figure 3-1 A systems perspective of a loss prevention department's immediate reaction and short-term planning relevant to an employee theft incident.

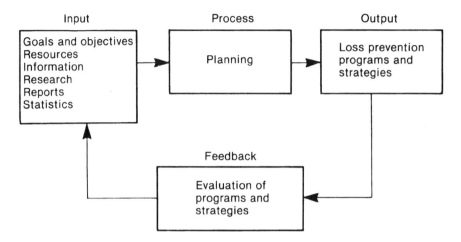

Figure 3–2   Long-term loss prevention planning from a systems perspective.

Loss prevention practitioners must be prepared when asked by upper management, "How do you know the loss prevention plans and strategies are working?"

Critical Thinking for Security Planning

Maxims of Security

1. Security is never foolproof. The term *foolproof* is a misnomer. Instead of *burglarproof, fireproof,* or *bulletproof,* replace *proof* with *resistant.*
2. State-of-the-art security has its vulnerabilities. History is filled with grand security strategies that failed.
3. Security often is as good as the time it takes to get through it. The longer the time delay facing the offender, the greater the protection and chances that he or she will abort the offense, be apprehended, or seek another victim.
4. Security must focus on not only what is leaving a facility (e.g., company assets) but also what is entering (e.g., weapons, explosives, illegal drugs, and anger).

Three Models of Security

All security strategies fall under one of the following models:
1. It protects people and/or assets.
2. It accomplishes nothing.
3. It helps offenders.

Illustrations of security protecting people or assets are seen when a hospital security officer escorts nurses to their vehicles at night or when a safe proves too formidable for a burglar, who leaves the scene. Security accomplishes nothing when security officers sleep on the job or fail to make their rounds or when alarm systems remain inoperable. Sometimes unknown to security practitioners and those they serve are the security strategies that actually help offenders. This can occur when security officers are poorly screened and they commit crimes. The ordinary padlock is an example of how physical security can assist offenders. An unlocked padlock hanging on an opened gate can invite *padlock substitution*, in which the offender replaces it with his or her padlock, returns at night to gain access, and then secures the gate with the original padlock. Such cases are difficult to investigate because signs of forced entry may be absent. Fences, another example, often are built with a top rail and supports for barbed wire that are strong enough to assist and support people, rather than the fence and barbed wire. Also, attractive-looking picket fences have been knocked down by offenders and used as ladders.

Security practitioners should identify and classify all security strategies under these models to expose useful, wasteful, and harmful methods. This endeavor should be a perpetual process within risk analysis, careful planning, critical thinking, testing, and research to facilitate cost-effective, results-oriented security. Although these challenging goals require time and effort, the net result is a superior security and loss prevention program.

EVALUATION OF LOSS PREVENTION PROGRAMS

How can a loss prevention program be evaluated? First, a research design can assist in the evaluation. A look at a few simplified research designs demonstrates how loss prevention programs are determined to be successful or unsuccessful.

One design is the *pretest-posttest design*. A robbery prevention program can serve as an example. First, the robbery rate is measured (by compiling statistics) before the robbery prevention program is implemented. The program then is implemented and the rate measured again. Robbery rates before and after program implementation are compared. If the robbery rate has declined, then the robbery prevention program may be the causative factor.

A loss prevention training program can serve as another example. Loss prevention personnel are tested prior to the training program, and their test scores are saved. The training program is implemented. After the program is completed, another similar test is given the personnel. The pretest scores are compared to the posttest scores. Higher posttest scores indicate that the training program probably was effective.

Another evaluation design or research method is called the *experimental control group design*. As an example, a crime prevention program within a corporation is subject to evaluation. Within the corporation, two plants that are characteristically similar are selected. One plant (the experimental plant) receives the crime prevention program, while the other plant (the control plant) does not. Before the program is implemented, the rate of crime at each plant is measured. After the program has been in effect for a predetermined period of time, the rate of crime is again measured at each plant. If the crime rate has declined at the "experimental" plant while remaining the same at the "control" plant, then the crime prevention program may be successful.

A good researcher should be cautious when formulating conclusions. In the crime prevention program at the plant, crime may have declined for reasons unknown to the researcher. For instance, offenders at the experimental plant may have refrained from crime because of the publicity surrounding the crime prevention program. However, after the initial impact of the program and the novelty expired, offenders continued to commit crimes without being detected by the program. In other words, the program may have been successful in the beginning but soon became ineffective. Thus, continued evaluations are vital to strengthen research results.

Research

To assist planning and research, the *scientific method* can be used. *Four steps are involved: statement of the problem, hypothesis, testing, and conclusion.* As an example, employee theft will serve as the problem. The hypothesis is a statement whereby the problem and a possible solution (i.e., loss prevention strategy) are noted. Testing involves an attempt to learn whether the strategy reduces the problem. Several research designs are possible. Here is an example of the presentation of the problem according to the style of scientific methodology:

- *Problem*: Employee theft
- *Hypothesis*: Employee theft can be reduced by using CCTV.
- *Testing*: Control group (plant A—no CCTV); experimental group (plant B—CCTV)
- *Conclusion*: After several months of testing, plant A maintained previous levels of employee theft, whereas plant B showed a drop in employee theft. Therefore, CCTV appears to be an effective loss prevention strategy in reducing employee theft.

To strengthen research results, continued testing is necessary. In the example, CCTV can be tested at other, similar locations. Further, other strategies can be combined with CCTV to see if the problem can be reduced to a greater extent.

Sources of Research Assistance

Obviously, a need exists for more loss prevention research; at this time it is limited. A unified national effort is needed. Four potential sources of research assistance are in-house, university, private consulting, and insurance companies.

In-house research may be the best because proprietary personnel are familiar with the unique problems at hand. Salary costs could be a problem, but a loss prevention practitioner with a graduate degree can be an asset to loss prevention planning and programming. In-house research, however, can result in increased bias by the researcher because superiors may expect results that conform to their points of view.

University researchers usually have excellent credentials. Many educators are required to serve the community and are eager to do research that can lead to publication. The cost is minimal.

Private consulting firms often have qualified personnel. This source can be the most expensive because these firms are in business for profit. Careful consideration and a scrutiny of the consulting staff are wise. The buyer should beware.

Insurance companies are active in making inspections of risks and recommending strategies (i.e., risk management) to reduce possible losses. They also participate in varying degrees in research projects relevant to crime, fire, and safety. Other sources of research assistance and information are described in the standards section of this chapter.

Performance Measures

Traditionally, public police performance has been measured by reported crime rates, overall arrests, crimes cleared by arrest, and response time to incidents. These measures have become institutionalized, and substantial investments have been made to develop information systems to capture such data. However, this data may tell little about police effectiveness in reducing crime and the fear of crime.[12] Furthermore, do these measures reflect outmoded policing and do they fail to account for many important contributions police make to the quality of life, such as efforts at community cohesion and crime prevention?

Here is an example of performance measures for police which have implications for security:

- *Goal:* promoting secure communities.
- *Methods and activities:* promoting crime prevention and problem-solving initiatives.
- *Performance indicators:* programs and resources allocated to crime prevention, public trust and confidence in police, and reduced public fear of crime.[13]

> What lessons can security practitioners learn from research on performance measures in the public sector? Do security programs contain traditional systems of measuring performance that reflect outmoded security efforts, while failing to account for important contributions to protection? Performance measures are surfacing in security programs.[14] (For performance measures in health-care security, see Chapter 17.) To improve security programs, research should be directed at enhancing traditional performance measures and introducing new measures that more accurately reflect customer satisfaction, security expenditures, and return on investments.

STANDARDS

Standards are written and tested guidelines that promote uniformity and quality. Manufacturers can adhere to standards in the production of protection products, businesses in the same industry can follow standards to ensure an adequate level of protection for people and assets on the premises, and in general, standards prevent people from installing unsafe systems.

Manufacturers have been producing their products in accordance with safety standards for many years. During the 1920s, for example, *Underwriters Laboratory* (UL), an independent testing organization, worked with insurers to establish a rating system for alarm products and installations. This system assists insurance agents in setting premiums for customers. An alarm company may show customers that its service is of a higher standard than a competitor's. UL has various listings, and it requires that an alarm company advertise its listing specifically. What a company has to do to obtain a listing as a central station burglar alarm company differs widely from what it has to do to be listed as a residential monitoring station; providing fire-resistant construction, backup power, access controls, and optimal response time following an alarm are a few examples (UL, http://www.ul.com/; 1285 Walt Whitman Rd., Melville, NY 11747-3081; Tel.: 631-271-6200).

Consumers, in general, are more familiar with UL as an organization promoting the electrical safety of thousands of retail products. Companies pay a fee to have UL test their products for safety according to UL standards. The famous UL label often is seen attached to the product.

Another organization producing standards is the *National Fire Protection Association* (NFPA). This group has established standards for fire protection equipment and construction that have been adopted by government agencies, in addition to companies in the private sector. Beginning in 1898, in cooperation with the insurance industry, the NFPA has produced standards covering sprinklers, fire hoses, and fire doors, among other forms of fire protection (NFPA, http://www.nfpa.com/; 1 Batterymarch Park, Quincy, MA 02269-9101; Tel.: 617-770-3000).

The *American Society for Testing and Materials* (ASTM), organized in 1898, has grown into one of the largest voluntary standards development systems in the world. ASTM is a nonprofit organization providing a forum for producers, consumers, government, and academia to meet to write standards for materials, products, systems, and services. Among its 132 standards-writing committees are committees that focus on security, safety, and fire protection (ASTM, http://www.astm.org/; 100 Barr Harbor Dr., West Conshohocken, PA 19428; Tel.: 610-832-9500).

The *American National Standards Institute* (ANSI), organized in 1918, is a nonprofit organization that coordinates U.S. voluntary national standards and represents the United States in international standards bodies such as the International Organization for Standardization. ANSI serves both private and public sectors in an effort to develop standards that exist in all industries, such as safety and health, information processing, banking, and petroleum (ANSI, http://www.ansi.org/; 11 West 42nd St., New York, NY 10036; Tel.: 212-642-4900).

The *International Organization for Standardization* (with the initials ISO) is a worldwide federation of national standards bodies from about 130 countries, one from each country. It is a nongovernmental group based in Geneva, Switzerland, established in 1947 with the purpose of promoting standardization globally to facilitate the international exchange of goods and services. Its agreements are published as International Standards (ISO http://www.iso.ch/).

Loss prevention practitioners are also guided by law through city, state, and federal code requirements that are often based on standards. Legislation also provides legal guidelines (e.g., Occupational Safety and Health Act; Americans with Disabilities Act).

> Standards promote uniformity and quality.

For the security industry as a whole, we should also remember the *Report of the Task Force on Private Security* (1976). As discussed in the previous chapter, this report was prepared by the National Advisory Committee on Criminal Justice Standards and Goals, which endeavored to set standards that would make the security industry more professional.

Some security standards focus on uniform standards of protection for specific industries, as seen at banks, through the Bank Protection Act; at airports, through the Federal Aviation Administration (FAA); and at companies with a U.S. Department of Defense (DOD) contract. Specific types of security characterize these different industries. Unfortunately, many types of businesses and institutions have no uniform standards of protection (for

example, retail businesses, hotels, restaurants, office buildings, and manufacturing plants).

Security magazine states the following:

> Facility security standards, in some form and coverage, do exist at U.S.
> colleges, some health care facilities, some convenience stores and at
> some federal government facilities—all where specific federal, state or
> local laws or industry regulations come into play.
>
> Most existing United States premises security standards exist as
> ever-changing *de facto* guidelines determined by common application,
> case law, insurance or arising from liability concerns.[15]

To make matters worse, in settling lawsuits involving negligent security, courts have ruled inconsistently. Acceptable security in one jurisdiction may be unacceptable in another. Security standards would curb this
problem and enable the private sector and the courts to foster uniform security. Those against standards cite costs and argue that it is impossible to
standardize security because each location and business is unique.

> Why is it so difficult to develop security standards for all propri-
> etary security programs?

PROPRIETARY SECURITY

A trend in proprietary (in-house) security programs is *security reengineering*. It
involves critical thinking about security to improve performance and quality of
service to customers at a lower cost. This entails justifying personnel financially and helping them to work more efficiently to enhance their value to the
business. Security reengineering includes using fewer people by outsourcing
their duties or using technology, whichever is more cost-effective. Although
people resist change and fear it, reengineering makes good business sense.

Proprietary security programs, and organizations in general, are characterized by the organization terms and practical management tools in the
following two lists.

Basics of Organization: The Vocabulary

- *Division of work.* Work is divided among employees according to such
  factors as function, clientele, time, and location.
- *Authority.* The right to act.

- *Responsibility.* An obligation to do an assigned job.
- *Power.* The ability to act.
- *Delegation of authority.* A superior delegates authority to subordinates to spread the workload. A superior can delegate authority, but a person must accept responsibility. Responsibility cannot be delegated. For example, the sergeant delegated to loss prevention officers the authority to check employee lunch boxes when employees left the plant.
- *Chain of command.* Communications go upward and downward within an organized hierarchy for the purpose of efficiency and order.
- *Span of control.* The number of subordinates that one superior can adequately supervise. An example of a broad span of control would be one senior investigator supervising twenty investigators. An example of a narrow span of control would be one senior investigator supervising five investigators. An adequate span of control will depend on factors such as the amount of close supervision necessary and the difficulty of the task.
- *Unity of command.* To prevent confusion during an organized effort, no subordinate should report to more than one superior.
- *Line personnel.* Those in the organized hierarchy who have authority and function within the chain of command. Line personnel can include uniformed loss prevention officers, sergeants, lieutenants, captains, and other superiors.
- *Staff personnel.* Specialists with limited authority who advise line personnel. For example, the loss prevention specialist advised the captain about a more efficient method of reducing losses.
- *Formal organization.* An official organization designed by upper management whereby the "basics of organization" are applied to produce the most efficient organization possible.
- *Informal organization.* An unofficial organization produced by employees with specific interests. For example, several employees spend time together (during "breaks" and lunch) because they are active as community volunteers.
- *Organization chart.* A pictorial chart that visually represents the formal organization. Many of the "basics of organization" actually can be seen on organization charts (see Figure 3-3).

Basics of Organization: The Practical Management Tools

- *Directive system.* A formal directive system is a management tool used to communicate information within an organized group. The communications can be both verbal and written. A verbal directive can be as simple as a superior telling a subordinate what work needs to be done. The formal verbal directive system also can include meetings in which verbal communications are exchanged.
- *Policies.* Policies are management tools that control employee decision making. Policies reflect the goals and objectives of management.

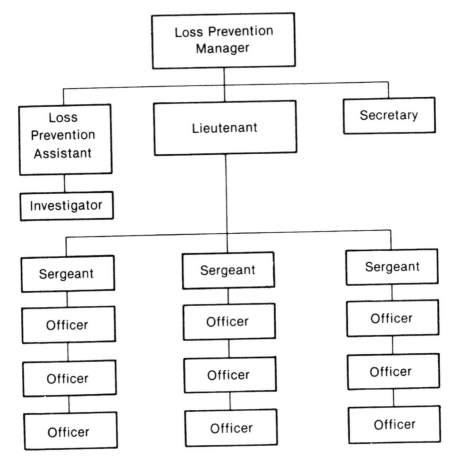

Figure 3–3   Small loss prevention department.

- *Procedures.* Procedures are management tools that point out a particular way of doing something: they guide action. Many procedures actually are plans that fulfill the requirements of policies. The loss prevention manager must maintain an open mind when feedback evolves from policies and procedures. For instance, suppose only two security officers are assigned to search the belongings carried by 1,000 employees as they end their shift. Long lines of irritated employees may develop. Consequently, changes must be made.
- *The manual.* A manual is like a "rule book" for an organized group; it contains policies and procedures.

It is important to note that if an organization's structure is too rigid, employees may be hindered from fulfilling business objectives. Participation by subordinates in decision making and a team atmosphere of cooperation have been shown to increase morale and motivation. Leadership style will also influence success. The *autocratic style* sees managers making all decisions, whereas the *democratic style* seeks opinions from employees as input for decisions. Following decades of research, psychologists have concluded that no one style is best. Effective managers use both. For example, a manager may be autocratic with a trainee and democratic with a seasoned employee.[16]

What Are the Duties of a Security Manager?

The duties of security managers vary widely. Here, a generalization is presented.

Security managers plan, prioritize tasks, concentrate on pressing problems, and strive to stay within their budget. They delegate tasks and supervise subordinates and contractors who perform security services. Another duty is to ensure that security systems are functioning properly. Security managers may spend all day at their desks and computers sending and responding to e-mails, preparing reports, conducting research on the Web, reading, or talking on the telephone. On other days they may split their time in the office with visits to various locations on the premises for inspections or investigations. They may attend meetings, conduct or receive training, or go off-site on business or for training or a college course. Since they are interacting with people so much, they must have excellent human relations skills.

Physical security and access controls are often part of the job; only authorized people should be on the premises. Security managers also realize that offenders can cause harm from remote locations by using a computer; consequently, security managers and IT specialists are increasingly working together. If an alleged crime occurs or an incident requires investigation, the manager may conduct the investigation, delegate the task, or contract the work to an outside firm. Workplace safety is another important issue, and this includes fire safety and the prevention of accidents. All security personnel and volunteers from the workforce may receive special training to prevent and suppress fires and render first aid. As risks surface, security managers prepare policies and procedures, in cooperation with other employees, in an effort to prevent losses.

A company may require the manager to spend a great deal of time providing training programs to employees on a host of topics, from employee protection to protecting proprietary information. Security managers may be responsible for a certain geographic area and visit corporate locations over several weeks to conduct a variety of duties as described above. To reduce costs, businesses may add additional duties—outside of traditional security duties—to the security manager's position. Examples include supervision of: landscaping, parking, a fleet of vehicles, a mail system, and a cafeteria. Security managers must be flexible and available for emergencies at any hour since the employer and employees depend on them for protection.

What is your opinion of the duties of a security manager?

Search the Web

The Web contains a wealth of information on the security and loss prevention profession. Using at least two Web addresses from this chapter, explore this profession.

CASE PROBLEMS

3A. As a loss prevention manager you have been asked to prepare a speech to a group of security practitioners. The topic is Prerequisites to Planning Security and Loss Prevention Programs and Strategies. Outline the speech or prepare note cards for your presentation.

3B. Refer to the box in this chapter entitled "Incomplete Protection Plans." If you were an outside security consultant hired by Andrew Smith, what would you suggest to help him prior to his meeting with top executives?

3C. As a security manager, you believe that the 3 P.M. meeting today with the Vice President of Finance will not bring good news. Each business quarter seems to show poor profits and the need for cutbacks in all departments. When you enter her office for the meeting, the VP, Alaine Nell, gets right to the point: "Your security budget to protect the four openings at the plant must be cut by 50 percent." She draws a sketch of the huge square plant and notes that each of the four openings on the sides of the facility is costing $100,000 annually for 24-hour-a-day security officer protection. She states that each post requires four officers (three on and one off during each 24-hour period) at $20,000 apiece. She requests a financial plan for the next five years. Prepare such a plan, providing hypothetical information if needed.

3D. Design an organization chart for a loss prevention department of 35 people at an industrial plant. Write a one-page justification of your design to satisfy management. Provide hypothetical information about the plant if needed.

NOTES

1. Oscar Newman, *Defensible Space* (New York: Macmillan, 1972).
2. Marcus Felson, *Crime and Everyday Life: Insights and Implications for Society* (Thousand Oaks, CA: Pine Forge Press, 1998).

3. Donald Cressey, *Other People's Money: A Study in the Social Psychology of Embezzlement* (Belmont, CA: Wadsworth, 1971).

4. Henry Pontell and Kitty Calavita, "The Savings and Loan Industry." In *Beyond the Law: Crime in Complex Organizations*, edited by Michael Tonry and Albert Reiss (Chicago: University of Chicago Press, 1993).

5. Abraham H. Maslow, *Motivation and Personality* (New York: Harper & Row, 1954).

6. Jay B. Crawford, "Security, Heal Thyself," *Security Management* (May 1995), pp. 85–90.

7. Robert Jacobson, "What Is a Rational Goal for Security?" *Security Management* 44 (December 2000), pp. 142–144.

8. Peter Tippett, "Calculating Risk," *Information Security* 4 (March 2001), pp. 36–38.

9. Richard D. Roberts, "Changing of the Guard: Corporate Downsizing's Effect on Security," *Security Technology and Design* (October 1996), pp. 8–12.

10. Wayne Siatt, "Doubled Systems Promise Documented Savings," *Security World* 17 (January 1980), p. 30.

11. Philip P. Purpura, *Modern Security and Loss Prevention Management* (Boston: Butterworth–Heinemann, 1989), pp. 43–44.

12. U.S. Department of Justice, *A Police Guide to Surveying Citizens and Their Environment* (Washington, D.C.: U.S. Government Printing Office, October 1993), p. ix.

13. John J. DiIulio, Jr., et al., *Performance Measures for the Criminal Justice System* (Washington, D.C.: Bureau of Justice Statistics, October 1993), pp. 113–135.

14. Steven Placek, "Smithsonian Displays New Security Model," *Security Management* (August 1996), pp. 62–68.

15. "NFPA Shuts Door, Again, to Security Standards," *Security* (March 1996), p. 108.

16. Michael Levy and Barton Weitz, *Retailing Management* (New York: McGraw-Hill, 2001), p. 534.

4

Law

OBJECTIVES

After studying this chapter the reader will be able to:

1. Explain the origins of law.
2. List and define at least five torts.
3. Discuss premises protection and negligence.
4. Explain contract law.
5. Explain the relationship among administrative law, compliance auditing, and the Federal Sentencing Guidelines.
6. Summarize criminal justice procedure.
7. Explain arrest law, use of force, searches, and questioning.

A good foundation in law is an essential prerequisite to loss prevention programming. Many crucial decisions by practitioners are circumscribed by legal parameters, and the consequences of these decisions can be serious. An arrest without the proper legal authority and evidence can result in civil and criminal action against security personnel. Negligence is a serious concern that results from the failure to exercise due care in the use of force, for example. This is why training is so important; it becomes a major issue in a lawsuit against security. Numerous lawsuits also have been directed at those responsible for security, who are claimed to be negligent for not providing a safe environment, which caused a person to become a crime victim. Consequently, security and loss prevention decisions must take into consideration the legal environment.

ORIGINS OF LAW

Three major sources of law are common law, case law, and legislative law. English common law is the major source of law in the United States. *Common law* generally refers to law founded on principles of justice determined by reasoning according to custom and universal consent handed down from one generation to another. The development of civilization is reflected in

Legal Quiz

Prime your mind with the following questions that are answered in this chapter.

1. Do most employers monitor Internet access by employees?
2. Do employers customarily place covert CCTV cameras in restrooms?
3. Which of the following is subject to the most lawsuits alleging inadequate security: Office buildings, restaurants, apartment and condominium complexes, retail stores, or hotels?
4. Comparing the early 1990s with the late 1990s, which period saw federal prosecutors charging more people with environmental crimes?
5. Are private security personnel required by the U.S. Supreme Court to read suspects "Miranda warnings"?

common law. Specific acts were, and still are, deemed criminal. These acts, even today, are referred to as common law crimes: treason, murder, robbery, battery, larceny, arson, kidnapping, and rape, among others. Common law is reinforced by decisions of courts of law. After our nation gained independence from England, the common law influence remained. Nineteen states have perpetuated common law through case law (i.e., judicial precedent). Eighteen states have abolished common law and written it into statutes. The remaining states have either adopted common law via ratification or are unclear about exactly how it is reflected in the state system.

Case law, sometimes referred to as *judge-made law*, involves the interpretation of statutes or constitutional concepts by federal and state appellate courts. Previous case decisions or "precedent cases" have a strong influence on court decisions. Precedents clarify both statutes and court views to limit ambiguity. When a new case comes into existence, earlier case decisions are used as a reference for decision making. Because the justice system is adversary in nature, opposing attorneys refer to past cases (i.e., precedents) that support their individual contentions. The court makes a decision between the opposing parties. Societal changes often are reflected in decisions. Because the meaning of legal issues evolves from case law, these court decisions are the law. Of course, later court review of previous decisions can alter legal precedent.

Legislative law from the federal government is passed by Congress under the authority of the U.S. Constitution. Likewise, individual state constitutions empower state legislatures to pass laws. Legislative laws permit both the establishment of criminal laws and a justice system to preside over criminal and civil matters. A court later may decide that a legislative law is unconstitutional; this illustrates the system of "checks and balances" that enables one government body to check on another.

Criminal law deals with crimes against society. Each state and the federal government maintains a criminal code that classifies and defines offenses. *Felonies* are considered more serious crimes, such as burglary and robbery. *Misdemeanors* are less serious crimes such as trespassing and disorderly conduct.

Civil law adjusts conflicts and differences between individuals. Examples of civil law cases are accidental injuries, marital disputes, breach of contract, sales that dissatisfy customers, and disputes with a government agency. When a *plaintiff* (i.e., a person who initiates a lawsuit) wins a case against another party, monetary compensation commonly results.

Cyberlaw

The rapid change brought on by computers and the Internet has been characterized as a "Wild West" legal environment.[1] Security specialists, whether involved in IT, physical security, or other areas, should be knowledgeable of legal trends and issues pertaining to cyberlaw. What follows here is a list of helpful Web sites that the reader may want to consult and bookmark in their computer.

U.S. Department of Justice Cybercrime. (www.usdoj.gov/criminal/cybercrime) This site contains a broad array of topics. The list includes federal codes related to cybercrime, how to report Internet-related crime, search and seizure of computers and electronic evidence, computer intrusion cases, intellectual property crime, economic espionage, privacy issues, and manuals, reports, and documents.

David Loundy's E-Law. (http://www.loundy.com/) This is a personal site of an attorney and cyberlaw professor who is a leader in electronic law. The site contains a long list of links to other legal Web sites and sites helpful to security in general.

Stein Schjolberg, Moss City Court. (http://www.mossbyrett.of.no/info/legal.html) Laws governing electronic information vary among states, the federal government, and countries. Legislators and judges are having difficulty facing the destruction of traditional geographic boundaries in cyberspace. Stein Schjolberg, city court of Moss, Norway, is an expert on cybercrime legislation. He has constructed a Web site on the cyberlaws of more than thirty countries.

Lawyers and the Law. (http://lawyers.com/) Sponsored by legal publisher Martindale-Hubbell, this Web site contains a wealth of general information on lawyers and the law. It offers a search engine that can locate members of the bar of any state. A broad variety of legal subjects are presented, as well as "Ask a Lawyer," plus a glossary containing 10,000 legal terms, pronunciations, and definitions.

TORT LAW

Public police officers have greater police powers than private sector officers, who typically possess citizen's arrest powers. In conjunction with greater police powers, public officers are limited in their action by the Bill of Rights of the U.S. Constitution. On the other hand, private officers, possessing fewer powers, for the most part, are not as heavily restricted by constitutional limitations. Authority and limitations on private officers result from *tort law*, the body of state legislative statutes and court decisions that governs citizens' actions toward each other and allows lawsuits to recover damages for injury. Tort law is the foundation for civil actions in which an injured party may litigate to prevent an activity or recover damages from someone who has violated his or her person or property. Most civil actions are based not on a claim of intended harm but on a claim that the defendant was negligent. This is especially so in cases involving private security officers. Tort law requires actions that have regard for the safety and rights of others; otherwise negligence results. *The essence of the tort law limitations on private sector officers is fear of a lawsuit and the payment of damages.*

The primary torts relevant to private security are as follows:

1. *False imprisonment.* The intentional and forceful confinement or restriction of the freedom of movement of another person, also called *false arrest.* The elements necessary to create liability are detention and its unlawfulness.
2. *Malicious prosecution.* Groundless initiation of criminal proceedings against another.
3. *Battery.* Intentionally harmful or offensive touching of another.
4. *Assault.* Intentional causing of fear of harmful or offensive touching.
5. *Trespass to land.* Unauthorized entering upon another person's property.
6. *Trespass to personal property.* Taking or damaging another person's possessions.
7. *Infliction of emotional distress.* Intentionally causing emotional or mental distress in another.
8. *Defamation (libel and slander).* Injury to the reputation of another by publicly making untrue statements. *Libel* refers to the written word; *slander*, to the spoken word.
9. *Invasion of privacy.* Intruding on another's physical solitude, the disclosure of private information about another, public misrepresentation of another's actions.
10. *Negligence.* Causing injury to persons or property by failing to use reasonable care or by taking unreasonable risk.

Civil action is not the only factor that hinders abuses by the private sector. Local and state ordinances, rules, regulations, and laws establish guidelines for the private security industry. This usually pertains to licens-

---

Match the Tort

Suppose you are a security manger: identify the tort(s) related to each scenario.

- A retail customer was frightened by one of your security officers who, in front of other customers, loudly accused the customer of shoplifting and hurt the customer's arm.
- You learn that an employee of a company department that is missing cash has been locked in an office by the department manager and ordered not to leave.
- An administrative assistant in the human resources department told people in the community that a specific employee is to be fired for sexual harassment, although you are only investigating allegations of such behavior.

---

ing and registration requirements. Improper or illegal action is likely to result in suspension or revocation of a license. Criminal law presents a further deterrent against criminal action by private sector personnel. Examples are laws prohibiting impersonation of a public official, electronic surveillance, breaking and entering, and assault.

Some court cases have applied select constitutional limitations to private sector action. Union contracts also can limit private security. These contracts might stipulate, for instance, that employee lockers cannot be searched and that certain investigative guidelines must be followed.

PREMISES PROTECTION AND NEGLIGENCE

Negligence results when a failure to exercise a reasonable amount of care in a situation causes harm to another (see Figure 4-1). For instance, management should take steps to ensure the safety of individuals on the premises. Numerous premises security claims have been directed at management for failing to provide adequate protection for employees, customers, residents, or students who were injured by a third-party criminal act (e.g., robbery).

The legal theory of premises security claims follows. States allow monetary damages to the plaintiff who is injured as a proximate cause of the defendant's (e.g., management's) breach of a legal duty to provide protection. The definitions of "legal duty," "proximate cause," and the related concept of "foreseeability" distinguish the law among the states. Legal duty refers to management's duty to maintain the premises in a reasonably safe condition for invitees (e.g., customers on the property of a retail store). Proximate cause means that the breach of the legal duty is the actual cause of the harm. Foreseeability refers to whether the harm was likely to occur based on the safety history of the premises and nearby property. If harm was likely, there is a duty to protect invitees.

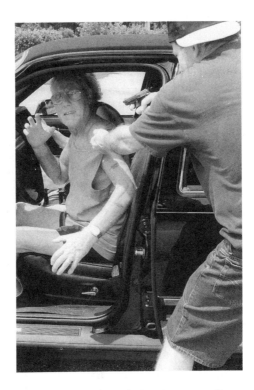

Figure 4–1   Assaults in parking lots have led to lawsuits alleging negligent security. Source: Philip P. Purpura, *Criminal Justice: An Introduction* (Boston: Butterworth–Heinemann, 1997), p. 4.

This theory has evolved over the years. The *prior similar incidents rule*, for instance, means that a plaintiff must demonstrate that there had been a prior similar incident on the premises. However, courts became critical of this rule in the 1990s because it had the effect of being a "one free rape rule." At that time, the majority of jurisdictions shifted to a *totality of the circumstances* test: prior similar incidents and other factors, such as the nature of the business, its surrounding locale, security training, and whether customary security measures for the particular industry were applied.[2] A third test courts place on security-related cases is *conscious disregard*: whether management or the security program knew of a problem or vulnerability, but did nothing.

What is your opinion of privacy issues such as employer monitoring in the workplace?

Employee Privacy

Technical advances have the potential to invade privacy, and there is the potential for abuse. The issues include employer monitoring of computer, Internet, e-mail, and telephone use by employees, and CCTV surveillance.

The American Management Association reported that 73 percent of major U.S. companies conduct some form of employee monitoring at work. Fifty-four percent of employers surveyed monitor Internet access and 38 percent monitor e-mail.[3] Courts attempt to balance business justifications against employees' expectation of privacy.

When an employer electronically measures the productivity of an employee on a computer, stress can result and privacy issues can surface. Employers should communicate with employees about the monitoring and why it is being used (e.g., as a supervisory tool). For use of the Internet by employees, written policies should clearly state guidelines and the consequences of violations. Employers may choose to state that employees should assume there is no privacy, that they should reserve personal Internet access and e-mail for their home computers, and that the employer reserves the right to access employee e-mail.

Telephone monitoring is another thorny issue. Businesses are capable of generating reports on the number of calls made by telemarketers, and to improve quality, supervisors may listen to telephone conversations. Legal risks may surface under the Wiretap Act of 1968, as modified by the Electronic Communications Privacy Act of 1986. Essentially, an employer may listen to a telephone conversation when one party consents. As an employer, it is best to notify employees of telephone monitoring and obtain their consent in writing. If a conversation becomes personal during monitoring, the listening must stop. Since many states require "two-party" consent to monitor, provide customers with the following message: "This call may be monitored for quality purposes."[4]

Closed-circuit television (CCTV) presents additional concerns. It is a widely used method of preventing crime and conducting investigations. Cameras may be placed overtly or covertly to observe people in public areas. Employers must avoid placing cameras in rest rooms, dressing rooms, locker rooms, and areas containing an expectation of privacy.

Employers will strengthen their position when they inform employees of the types of monitoring conducted in the workplace, post signs, and ask employees to sign a consent form containing policies. The enforcement of policies must be done in a uniform manner to avoid charges of unfair employment practices.

Research by Liability Consultants, Inc. (http://www.liabilityconsultants.com/) provides a picture of trends of premises liability cases from 1993 to 1997 and draws comparisons to the company's first report covering 1983 to 1992.

- Defendants are winning more and paying less when they lose.
- Crimes in parking lots are more likely to lead to litigation against the property owner than crimes occurring elsewhere on the premises.
- Apartment and condominium complexes are sued most often. This was true in the first study. Office building and restaurants placed second and third in the newer study, while hotels and retail stores were second and third earlier. This change could be due to lawsuits leading to increased security at hotels and retail stores and a shift in crime to less secure locations.
- Both studies show the most litigious states as New York, Texas, Florida, and California.
- The new study found that the largest percentage of case verdicts and settlements was for under $250,000. In the earlier study, the figures were between $250,000 and $500,000.
- The reasons why most verdicts favored the defense are as follows: property owners are increasing crime prevention efforts; defense attorneys and insurers are learning how to improve their defense strategies; and the standards of foreseeability are changing in certain jurisdictions (i.e., establish a connection between the crime and the alleged security deficiency).[5]

You Be the Judge[*]

On August 1, Ken Yates and his family arrived at their motel about 6:30 P.M. While he was unloading the car, Yates was approached, threatened at gunpoint, and told to hand over his money. He resisted and was shot in the ensuing scuffle. Even though there had been a security officer on duty, no one intervened to help Yates.

Yates sued the motel, claiming that his injuries were caused by management's failure to provide an adequate number of trained security officers. Yates' expert witness supported this claim. However, he conceded that even if the motel had two officers on duty, the incident might have occurred outside of the officers' direct observation. In addition, under cross-examination, the expert witness conceded that he had never developed or studied a security plan for a hotel or motel whose security needs required two security officers, so his expertise in the manner was limited.

The trial court dismissed the case, saying there was no evidence that having two officers on duty would have prevented the assault. Yates appealed, insisting that the Inn could have done more to ensure his safety.

How did the appeals court rule?

Make your decision; then turn to the end of the chapter for the court's decision.

---

*Reprinted with permission from *Security Watch* (January 15, 2000), Aspen Pub. (http://www.aspenpublishers.com/).

A lawsuit means that security faces a very big test. Management either pays for adequate protection initially to prevent a serious incident or possibly pays later, following a lawsuit. In addition to providing basic protection for people and assets, a good security and loss prevention program becomes an investment in litigation prevention.

Negligence involves many types of situations pertaining to protection programs. Security personnel have been held liable for negligent use of force and firearms. Managers and supervisors have been found negligent in the areas of applicant screening and the training and supervision of employees. And such negligence is not only restricted to the security industry. Any organization and employee can be subject to negligence. A hospital, for example, may find itself in a lawsuit after a patient is sexually assaulted by an orderly because the human resources department did not check on the orderly's background.

> Do businesses and institutions in your locale provide reasonable protection for people on the premises? Should premises security lawsuits be permitted? Why or why not?

CONTRACT LAW

A *contract* is an agreement between parties to do or to abstain from doing some act. The law may enforce the agreement by requiring that a party perform its obligation or pay money equivalent to the performance. These court requirements are known as *remedies for breach of contract*. Specific circumstances may create defenses for failure to perform contract stipulations. Contracts may be express or implied. In an express contract, written or oral, the terms are stated in words. An implied contract is presumed by law to have been made from the circumstances and relations of the parties involved.

Several areas in the security and loss prevention field are relevant to the law of contracts. The company that provides a service or device to a client company may be liable for breach of contract following a dispute. A contract usually states liabilities for each party. For instance, if a third party is harmed (e.g., a person illegally arrested on the premises by a private officer from a contract service hired by a client company), the contract will commonly establish who is responsible and who is to have insurance for each risk. However, in third-party suits, courts have held a specific party liable even though the contract stipulated that another party was to be responsible in the matter. This principle is known as *nondelegable duty*.

In the common law principle of *respondeat superior* (i.e., let the master respond), an employer (master) is liable for injuries caused by an employee (servant). This is also called *vicarious liability*. Typically, the injured party will look beyond the employee, to the employer, for compensation for damages. Proper supervision and training can prevent litigation.

Another form of contract is the union contract. If a proprietary force is employed on the premises, it may be under a union contract. For regular employees, their union contract may stipulate guidelines for locker searches and investigations.

ADMINISTRATIVE LAW

Administrative law is designed to ensure that as businesses seek profit, fairness and safety are maintained. Many U.S. federal and state agencies and executive departments influence loss prevention policies and programs. On the federal level, these include the Occupational Safety and Health Administration (OSHA), the National Labor Relations Board (NLRB), and the Equal Employment Opportunity Commission (EEOC), among others. (All three are discussed in various sections of this book.) Likewise, on the state level, similar bodies exist to regulate various activities such as the security industry. These agencies were formed because legislative and executive branches of government typically lack the expertise to regulate specialized areas. Therefore, independent agencies are formed that are less susceptible to direct political influence. *Administrative agencies* are government bodies that regulate various activities, make rules, conduct investigations, perform law-enforcement functions, issue penalties, and initiate criminal and civil litigation. Federal agencies document rules in the *Federal Register*, published by the General Services Administration. State agency manuals perform a similar function. Local governments follow generally accepted fire and building codes.

Compliance Auditing

Compliance auditing involves a survey of whether an organization is conforming to government regulations. A business, for example, can prepare its own checklist, based on the requirements of regulatory laws, such as the posting of laws, licenses, certificates, and policies and plans. OSHA is one of many agencies that requires such compliance, subject to penalties amounting to a $10,000 fine, six months imprisonment, or both.[6]

Environmental compliance is an especially important area of growing concern. During the 1970s and 1980s, federal, state, and local governments in the United States passed hundreds of environmental statutes and regulations focusing on discharges to the air, land, and water; the manufacture, transport, storage, and disposal of goods and their by-products; and the location of facilities. The 1990s became the era of enforcement of these laws on the federal, state, and local levels. Consequently, U.S. industry spends tens of billions of dollars to comply with these laws and prevent severe criminal and civil penalties, imprisonment, and liability for personal injuries and property damage. The American Society for Testing and Materials standard practices E1527 and E1528 on environmental site assessment often are referred to as the foundation for designing an environmental compliance audit. This type of audit often is used as part of a due diligence investigation when, for example, a company buys a plant and land. Also, it will help in the "innocent landowner defense" under federal environmental law.[7] *Due diligence* is the attention and care legally expected in checking on the accuracy of information and omissions. Businesses that audit themselves and put forth efforts to reach compliance may receive a lighter sanction under the Federal Sentencing Guidelines and in certain states.[8]

Federal Sentencing Guidelines

Today, the federal government views incarceration of corporate executives as a strong deterrent to corporate crime. The *Federal Sentencing Guidelines*, which apply to all federal crimes, contain stiff sentencing provisions and strong economic penalties for corporate crimes such as environmental violations, fraud, and safety and health violations. Compared to the early 1990s, the late 1990s saw federal prosecutors charging more than three times as many people with environmental crimes, and the sentences were longer. For example, the former chairman of a Georgia chemical company was sentenced to nine years in prison for exposing workers to dangerous chemicals in the workplace. In another case, a Florida man received 13 years for dumping toxic waste into Tampa's sewer system. The states show a similar trend and judges are taking environmental crimes more seriously.[9]

The sentencing guidelines are a judicial strategy to encourage corporations to enforce compliance with legal requirements and avert ignorance of the law throughout a corporation. Communications and training are essential to corporate compliance programs. The guidelines themselves state the importance of corporate programs exercising due diligence (i.e., attention and care) in preventing, detecting, and reporting criminal conduct of employees and other agents—customary duties of security programs. Research reveals that many companies had compliance programs in place when their problems occurred, but the programs failed to penetrate the culture. Consequently, an effective ethics program must embrace the entire corporation.[10]

It is argued that corporate crime overshadows street crime. A list of the Top 100 Corporate Criminals can be found at http://www.corporatepredators.org/top100.html.[11]

Do you believe our government is too tough on businesses? Why or why not?

A Comprehensive Environmental Compliance Program[12]

Because environmental compliance is such a serious issue, seven recommendations are presented here that can assist a corporation in proving it has taken steps to comply with environmental laws. These recommendations can apply to other compliance programs as well.

1. Ensure that line management is attentive to regulatory compliance.
2. Communicate relevant policies, procedures, and standards to all employees.
3. Audit and monitor all relevant activities.
4. Establish a training program for all employees.
5. Establish an incentive program.
6. Discipline wrongdoers.
7. Evaluate the whole effort through an outside expert.

CRIMINAL JUSTICE PROCEDURE

The following list briefly describes *procedural law*, which covers the formal rules for enforcing substantive law and the steps required to process a criminal case. (*Substantive law* defines criminal offenses and specifies corresponding fines and punishment.) Because jurisdictional procedures vary, a generalization is presented here.

1. The purpose of an arrest is to bring the person into the criminal justice system so that he or she may be held to answer the criminal charges.
2. A citation frequently is used by public police instead of a formal arrest for less serious crimes (e.g., traffic violations). If the conditions set forth in the citation are not followed, a magistrate of the appropriate court will issue a misdemeanor warrant.
3. All arrests must be based on probable cause, which is stated in arrest warrants. *Probable cause* is reasonable grounds to justify legal action, more than mere suspicion. Police officers, security officers, and reli-

able witnesses and victims typically provide the foundation of probably cause through their observations of offenders.

4. Booking takes place when an arrestee is taken to a police department or jail so that a record can be made of the person's name, the date, time, location of offense, charge, and arresting officer's name. Fingerprinting and a photograph are part of the booking process.

5. Because our system of justice has a high regard for civil liberties as expressed in the Bill of Rights, the accused is informed of his or her *Miranda* rights, by the public police, prior to questioning.

6. After booking, and without unnecessary delay, the accused is taken before a magistrate for the "initial appearance." At this appearance, the magistrate has the responsibility of informing the accused of constitutional rights, stating the charge, and fixing bail (if necessary).

7. Also after booking, the arresting officer will meet with the prosecutor, or a representative, to review evidence. A decision is made whether to continue legal action or to drop the case. A case may be dropped by the prosecutor for insufficient evidence or because the defendant is suffering from a problem better handled by a social agency.

8. The prosecutor prepares an "information" when prosecution is initiated. It cites the defendant's name and the charge and is signed by the complainant (e.g., the person who witnessed the crime). Then an arrest warrant is prepared by the proper judicial officer. The defendant already may be in custody at this point.

9. At the initial appearance, the magistrate will inform the defendant about the right to have a preliminary hearing. The defendant and the defense attorney make this decision. This hearing is used to determine if probable cause exists for a trial. The courtroom participants in a preliminary hearing are a judge, defendant, defense attorney, and prosecutor. The prosecutor has the "burden of proof." Witnesses may be called by the prosecutor to testify.

10. Federal law and the laws of more than half the states require that probable cause to hold a person for trial must result from grand jury action. The Fifth Amendment of the Bill of Rights states such a requirement. When probable cause is established in an action ordered by a judge or prosecutor, the grand jury will return an "indictment" or "true bill" against the accused. A "presentment" results from an investigation initiated by a grand jury establishing probable cause. Based on the indictment or presentment, an arrest warrant is issued.

11. At an "arraignment," the accused enters a plea to the charges. The four plea options are guilty, not guilty, nolo contendere (no contest), and not guilty by reason of insanity.

12. Few defendants reach the trial stage. Plea bargaining is an indispensable method to clear crowded court dockets. Essentially, it means that the prosecutor and defense attorney have worked out an agreement whereby the prosecutor reduces the charge in exchange for a guilty plea. Charges also may be dropped if the accused becomes a witness in another case.

13. "Pretrial motions" can be entered by the defense attorney prior to entering a plea at arraignment. Some examples would be a "motion to quash" an indictment or information because the grand jury was improperly selected, a "continuance" requested by the defense attorney because more time is needed to prepare the case, or a "change of venue" requested when pretrial publicity is harmful to the defendant's case and the defense hopes to locate the trial in another jurisdiction so that an impartial jury is more likely to be selected.

14. The accused is tried by the court or a jury. The system of justice is basically adversarial, involving opponents. This is apparent in a trial, where the prosecutor and defense attorney make brief opening statements to the jury. The prosecutor then presents evidence. Witnesses are called to the stand to testify; they go through direct examination by the prosecutor, followed by defense cross-examination. The prosecutor attempts to show the defendant's guilt "beyond a reasonable doubt." The defense attorney strives to discredit the evidence. Redirect examination rebuilds evidence discredited by cross-examination. Recross-examination may follow. After the prosecutor presents all the evidence, the defense attorney may move for acquittal. This motion commonly is overruled by the judge. Then, the defense attorney presents evidence. Defense evidence undergoes direct and redirect examination by the defense and cross- and recross-examination by the prosecutor.

15. Next, the judge will "charge the jury," which means that the jury is briefed by the judge on the charge and how a verdict is to be reached based on the evidence. In certain states, juries have a responsibility for recommending a sentence after a guilty verdict; the judge will brief the jury on this issue. Closing arguments are then presented by opposing attorneys.

16. The jury retires to the deliberation room; a verdict follows. A not guilty verdict signifies release for the defendant. A guilty verdict leads to sentencing. Motions and appeals may be initiated after the sentence.

How Much Power Is in the Hands of Private Security Officers?

Can they:

- Make an arrest without probable cause?
- Arrest for a felony?
- Arrest for a misdemeanor?
- Use force to complete an arrest?
- Search an arrestee following an arrest?
- Question a suspect or arrestee without public police being present?
- Be barred from using seized evidence as the police are under the exclusionary rule?

These questions are answered in the nearby paragraphs.

ARREST LAW

Because our justice system places a high value on the rights of the individual citizen, private and public personnel cannot simply arrest, search, question, and confine a person by whim. A consideration of individual rights is an important factor. The Bill of Rights of the U.S. Constitution affords citizens numerous protections against government. The Fourth and Fifth Amendments of the Bill of Rights demonstrate how individual rights are safeguarded during criminal investigations.

> Amendment IV—The right of the people to be secure in their persons, houses, papers, and effects, against unreasonable searches and seizures, shall not be violated, and no Warrants shall issue, but upon probable cause, supported by Oath or affirmation; and particularly describing the place to be searched, and the person or things to be seized.

> Amendment V—. . . nor shall [any person] be compelled in any criminal case to be a witness against himself, nor be deprived of life, liberty, or property, without due process of law.

The Sixth, Eighth, and Fourteenth Amendments are other important amendments frequently associated with our criminal justice process. Briefly, the Sixth Amendment pertains to the right to trial by jury and assistance of counsel. The Eighth Amendment states that "excessive bail shall not be required, nor excessive fines imposed, nor cruel and unusual punishments inflicted." The Fourteenth Amendment bars states from depriving any person of due process of law or equal protection of the laws.

The Fourth Amendment stipulates guidelines for the issuance of warrants. Public police obtain arrest and search warrants from an impartial judicial officer. Sometimes immediate action (e.g., chasing a bank robber) does not permit time to obtain warrants before arrest and search. In such a case, an arrest warrant is obtained as soon as possible. Private police should contact public police for assistance in securing warrants and in apprehending suspects.

A knowledge of arrest powers is essential for those likely to exercise this authority. These powers differ from state to state and depend on the statutory authority of the type of individual involved. Generally, public police officers have the greatest arrest powers. They also are protected from civil liability for false arrest, as long as they had probable cause that the crime was committed. Those in the private sector usually have arrest powers equal to citizen's arrest powers, which means that they are liable for false arrest if a crime was not, in fact, committed—regardless of the reasonableness of their belief. An exception is apparent if state statutes point out that these personnel have arrest powers equal to public police only on the protected property. If private sector personnel are deputized or given a special constabulary commission, their arrest powers are likely to equal those of public police.

Whoever makes an arrest must have the legal authority to do so. Furthermore, the distinction between felonies and misdemeanors, for those making arrests, is of tremendous importance. *Felonies*, more serious crimes, include burglary, armed robbery, murder, and arson. *Misdemeanors*, less serious crimes, include trespassing, disorderly conduct, and being drunk in public. Generally, public police can arrest someone for a felony or a misdemeanor committed in his or her view; the viewing amounts to probable cause. Arrest for a felony not seen by the public police is lawful with probable cause. Arrest for a misdemeanor not seen by the public police generally is unlawful; a warrant is needed based on probable cause. There are exceptions to this misdemeanor rule; for example, public police can arrest in domestic violence cases or cases of driving under the influence, when the offense is fresh although not observed by the police. On the other hand, private police have fewer powers of arrest (equal to citizen's arrest powers). Basically, citizen's arrest powers permit felony arrests based on probable cause, but prohibit misdemeanor arrests.

A serious situation exists when, for example, a private officer arrests and charges a person for a felony when in fact the offense was a misdemeanor and the jurisdiction does not grant security officers such misdemeanor arrest power. Many employers in the private sector are so afraid of an illegal arrest and subsequent legal action that they prohibit their officers from making arrests without supervisory approval. It is imperative that private sector personnel know state arrest law; proper training is a necessity.

Force

During the exercise of arrest powers, force may be necessary. The key criterion is *reasonableness*: force should be no more than what is reasonably necessary to carry out legitimate authority. If an arrestee struggles to escape, but is subdued to the ground and stops resisting, it would be unreasonable for the arrestor to step on the arrestee's face. *Deadly force* is reserved for life-threatening situations, never to defend property. Unreasonable force can lead to difficulties in prosecuting a case, as well as civil and criminal litigation.

Searches

Ordinarily, public police conduct a search of an arrestee right after an arrest. This has been consistently upheld by courts for the protection of the officer who may be harmed by a concealed weapon. However, *evidence obtained through an unreasonable search and seizure is not admissible in court*; this is known as the *exclusionary rule*.

The Fourth Amendment prohibition against unreasonable searches and seizures applies only to government action. Searches by private citizens, including security officers, even if "unreasonable," are therefore not "unconstitutional" and the exclusionary rule does not apply (*Burdeau v. McDowell*, 256 U.S. 465, 1921).[13] At the same time, the law of searches by private security officers is not clear and varies widely. Even though private security may not be restrained by the Fourth Amendment, a lawsuit may result following a search. A search is valid when consent is given and where, in a retail environment, a shoplifting statute permits the retrieval of merchandise. A search for weapons following an arrest may be justified through common law, which states that citizens have the right of self-defense. The recovery of stolen goods as the basis for a search is typically forbidden, except in some state shoplifting statutes. Whenever possible, private sector personnel should let public police conduct searches in order to transfer potential liability.

Call It "Inspection," Not "Search and Seizure"[14]

Norman M. Spain, an authority on legal issues in security, states that private security officers generally are not bound by constitutional constraints of search and seizure as public police, unless they are "tainted by the color of law"—that is, jointly working with public police. Spain favors the term *inspection* instead of *search* for private security, because the Fourth Amendment does not apply in most private settings. He cites various targets for inspections in private settings: a locker, a vehicle entering or leaving a facility, or the belongings of an employee.

Spain recommends a formal inspection policy that would be backed by common law—employers have the right to take reasonable measures to protect their property against theft. All parties (e.g., employees, contractors, visitors) should be given notice through, for example, signs and publications. The policy should have four components:

1. A formal statement that the company reserves the right to inspect
2. Illustrations of types of inspections
3. A list of items that employees should not have in their possession (e.g., illegal drugs, weapons, company property removed without authorization)
4. A statement of penalties, including those for not cooperating

Spain cautions that a "pat-down" of a person's body or inspections of pockets may result in a civil action alleging invasion of privacy, unless the site requires intense security.

Questioning

An important clause of the Fifth Amendment states that a person cannot be compelled in any criminal case to be a witness against himself or herself. Therefore, what constitutional protections does a suspect have on being approached by an investigator for questioning? Here again, the law differs with respect to public and private sector investigations.

A person about to be questioned about a crime by public police must be advised of:

1. The right to remain silent
2. The fact that statements can be used against the person in a court of law
3. The right to an attorney, even if the person has no money
4. The right to stop answering questions

These rights, known as the *Miranda warnings*, evolved out of the famous 1966 U.S. Supreme Court case known as *Miranda v. Arizona*. If these rights are not read to a person (by public police) before questioning, statements or a confession will not be admissible as evidence in court.

Are private security personnel required to read a subject the "*Miranda warnings*" prior to questioning? The U.S. Supreme Court has not yet required the reading. However, any type of coercion or trick during questioning is prohibited for private as well as public police. A voluntary confession by the suspect is in the best interests of public and private investigators. Many private sector investigators read suspects the "*Miranda warnings*" anyway, to strengthen their case. If security personnel are working jointly with public police (as in a cooperative protection effort), or if a police officer is working part-time in security, then the warnings should be read.

Another topic concerning questioning of subjects pertains to disciplinary hearings. The National Labor Relations Board (NLRB) regulates management–labor issues, and it extended another right to nonunion employees—the right to have a witness at a disciplinary meeting (Epilepsy Foundation of Northeast Ohio, 331 NLRB No. 92, 2000). Union members have had this right since the U.S. Supreme Court decision, *NLRB v. Weingarten* (1975).[15]

Career: Gaming/Wagering Security

Gaming is big entertainment. With advancing technology in this industry comes new opportunities for security practitioners.

Duties: Protect people, assets, and gamblers' interests; exercise good human relations skills; safely transfer funds; operate security systems; surveillance; prevent and detect scams and thefts; render first aid; and supervising, planning, and budgeting.

Prerequisites: For management, associate degree, but undergraduate degree preferred; 4–8 years of experience; depending on organization, special clearance and certification.

Demographics of typical practitioner. Undergraduate degree; 10–15 years in security; 6–8 years in specialty; Gaming Commission license; CPP; salary of $30,000–60,000 yr.; titles: Security Officer, Manager, and Loss Prevention Director.

Source: American Society for Industrial Security, *Career Opportunities in Security* (Alexandria, VA: ASIS, 1998), p. 8.

Search the Web

Suppose you are a security manager for a corporation. Refer to the beginning of this chapter to the box on cyberlaw, check out the Web sites offered, and explain how you would use any of the information in the Web sites to help you in your job.

CASE PROBLEMS

4A. You are a loss prevention officer with three years of experience and a newly acquired college degree. The plant manager of loss prevention has selected you for a special assignment: design and conduct an eight-hour training program on law for company loss prevention officers. The grapevine indicates that success on this project could lead to a promotion to training officer, a position vacant at this time. You are required to (1) formulate an outline of topics to be covered and the hours for each topic, (2) justify in one to three sentences why each topic is important, and (3) prepare an examination of 10 (or 20) questions.

4B. Research and prepare a report on the laws of arrest and search and seizure in your state for citizens, private security officers, private detectives, and public police.

4C. Create, in writing, situations where each of the previous types of individuals in problem 4B can make a legal arrest. In each of the situations you create, describe appropriate search and seizure guidelines.

4D. You are a member of a jury on a civil case involving the question of negligent security. In this case, a young man was killed by a stray bullet at a restaurant parking lot at night during the weekend as he approached a group of rowdy people about to fight. The restaurant had a history of three gun incidents prior to the murder: one month earlier a shot was fired into the restaurant, without injury; three months earlier police arrested a subject for assault in the parking lot and confiscated a pistol; and five months earlier police found a revolver in the bushes in the parking lot following an arrest for public intoxication. Each incident occurred at night during the weekend.

Following these three incidents the restaurant maintained the same level of security on the premises, which was good lighting and training for employees to call police when a crime occurred. Does the business owe a duty to provide a safe environment to those who enter the premises? Is the restaurant negligent? Why or why not?

THE DECISION FOR "YOU BE THE JUDGE"

The appeals court said the trial court acted properly. Yates had failed to show that another security officer would have prevented the assault. [*Walsh v. Ramada Franchise Systems, Inc. et al.*, No. 98-5040, U.S. Ct. of App. for the 6th Circ., 1999 U.S. App. Lexis 11281.]

    Comment: What methods do you use to arrive at staffing levels for your officers? How would you defend those methods in court?

    The motel was lucky; Yates' expert failed to show that more security officers would have been more effective. If the expert had testified that similarly sized and located motels used more security officers, the motel would have been in the difficult position of defending its use of only one officer.

    Benchmarking your practices against industry norms and against companies in your neighborhood is an excellent way to assess whether your company is doing enough to secure your grounds.

NOTES

1. Jay Heiser, "You'll Hear From My Lawyer," *Information Security* 3 (October 2000), p. 24.
2. Corey L. Gordon and William Brill, *The Expanded Role of Crime Prevention Through Environmental Design in Premises Liability* (Washington, D.C.: National Institute of Justice, April 1996), pp. 2–3.
3. Michael Blotzer, "Privacy in the Digital Age," *Occupational Hazards* 62 (July 2000), pp. 29–31.
4. "Limits on Electronic Surveillance," *Security Watch* 2916 (August 15, 2000), pp. 6–7.
5. Norman Bates and Jon Groussman, "More Wins for Defendants in Premises Liability Cases," *Security Management* 44 (February 2000), p. 94.
6. John D. McCann, "Preparing a Case for Compliance," *Security Management* (February 1994), pp. 72–73.
7. American Society for Testing and Materials, *Practice E1527-00 Standard Practice for Environmental Site Assessments* (http://www.astm.org/) (March 10, 2001).
8. Dan M. Chilcutt, "Making Sense of Environmental Compliance," *Risk Management* (November 1995), pp. 41–43.
9. Tom Kenworthy, "It's a New World: Polluters Go to Prison," *USA Today* (April 21, 2000), p. 3A.

10. Gary Edwards and Rebecca Goodell, "Three Years Later: A Look at the Effectiveness of Sentencing Guidelines," *Ethics Journal* (Fall-Winter 1994), pp. 1 and 4.
11. Robert Trigaux, "As Street Crime Declines, Corporate Crime Climbs," *Florence Morning News* (October 10, 1999), p. 8-D.
12. Janet S. Kole and Hope Lefeber, "The New Environmental Hazard: Prison," *Risk Management* (June 1994), pp. 37–40.
13. Fred Inbau, Bernard Farber, and David Arnold, *Protective Security Law*, 2nd ed. (Boston: Butterworth–Heinemann, 1996), p. 54.
14. "Call It 'Inspection' (Not 'Search and Seizure')," *Security Management Bulletin* (May 10, 1996), pp. 4–7.
15. "NLRB Ruling Gives Nonunion Workers Right to Request Witness at Disciplinary Meetings," *Safety Compliance Letter* 2362 (September 15, 2000), pp. 1–2.

5

Internal and External Relations

OBJECTIVES

After studying this chapter the reader will be able to:

1. Define internal and external relations.
2. Explain the value of marketing security.
3. Discuss internal relations.
4. Explain how an intranet and e-mail can assist security.
5. Discuss external relations.
6. Debate the issues of prosecution.
7. Debate the issues of loss prevention attire.

INTERNAL AND EXTERNAL RELATIONS

This chapter explains why it is so important to recruit people and organizations to assist with security and loss prevention efforts. With practitioners being asked to handle increasingly complex problems, often with limited resources, it is vital that all possible sources of assistance be solicited. Strategies are delineated here for improving relations between the loss prevention department and those groups that loss prevention serves and works with in reducing losses. *Internal relations* refers to cooperative efforts with individuals and groups within an organization that a loss prevention department serves. *External relations* refers to cooperative efforts with external individuals and groups that assist in loss prevention objectives.

To elaborate on the internal and external relations charts (Figures 5-1 and 5-2), lines of communications are important for an improved loss prevention program. For instance (clockwise, Figure 5-1, internal relations chart), upper management dictates loss prevention goals. Both the human resources and loss prevention departments should coordinate activities relevant to applicant screening and workplace violence. When labor problems (e.g., unrest, strike) are anticipated, losses can be minimized. In addition, labor

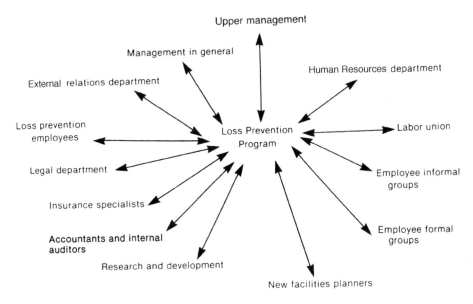

Figure 5–1   Internal relations.

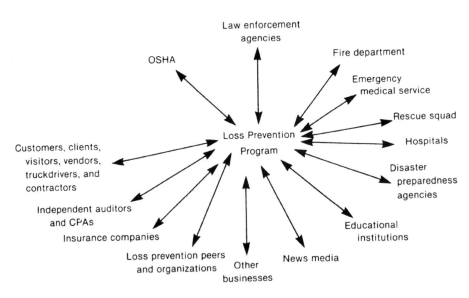

Figure 5–2   External relations.

union contracts may stipulate limitations on loss prevention activities (e.g., the questioning of suspect employees). Loss prevention practitioners are wise to tune in on feedback and criticism from formal and informal employee groups. By listening to and satisfying employee needs (e.g., clean restrooms, a well-run cafeteria, and recreational programs), losses can be reduced. When new facilities are being planned, architects, engineers, and loss prevention practitioners can jointly design prevention strategies into the plan and thereby save money by not having to install equipment after construction is completed. Trade secrets and other proprietary information must be under strict security, especially in research and development. Accountants and auditors can help create cooperative strategies against losses. Furthermore, the loss prevention manager should be given an opportunity to review their findings. Insurance specialists often assist in planning prevention strategies and reducing premiums. At various times, legal assistance may be required by a loss prevention department. Because loss prevention personnel are the backbone of the program, the manager should do everything possible (e.g., give praise and pay raises, and institute participatory management) to satisfy their needs. Good rapport with the external relations department ensures that appropriate loss prevention information is released to outsiders and that this information is in the best interest of the organization. Communicating with management in general is vital for many reasons. For instance, the objectives of the loss prevention program can be transmitted to all employees via meetings with management. Feedback from management also assists in planning loss prevention strategies that do not hinder productivity or profit.

In reference to the external relations chart (clockwise, Figure 5-2, beginning with law enforcement), public service agencies are an essential ingredient of private sector loss prevention programs. Good communications and cooperation are important in case crimes occur or a disaster strikes. Educational institutions also can provide research assistance as well as potential employees. The loss prevention manager may want to serve on an advisory committee or speak to classes to spread the word about loss prevention. When possible, the news media should be recruited to aid in loss prevention objectives. Other businesses and loss prevention peers with similar problems can be a good source of ideas. Insurance companies, like internal insurance specialists, can provide information to improve prevention strategies while reducing premiums. Independent auditors and certified public accountants can point out weaknesses in the loss prevention program. When people (e.g., customers) visit the organization, they should not be seriously inconvenienced by loss prevention devices (e.g., access control), but at the same time, losses must be prevented. Friendly dialogue and cooperative efforts should be emphasized when OSHA and other government agencies are involved in a loss prevention program. *To enhance all of the above relations, the security and loss prevention practitioner is wise to emphasize two-way communication and understanding, and partnering for mutual benefits.*

Benefits of Good Relations

The following are reasons why good internal and external relations are important to a loss prevention program. Good relations:

1. Build respect for the loss prevention department, its objectives, and its personnel
2. Reinforce compliance with policies and procedures to prevent losses
3. Foster assistance with loss prevention activities such as programs and investigations
4. Provide a united front against vulnerabilities, which creates lower losses, extends the impact of strategies, and saves money
5. Educate employees, community residents, and others
6. Improve understanding of complex security problems
7. Reduce rumors and false information
8. Improve understanding of the loss prevention program
9. Stimulate consciousness-raising relevant to loss prevention
10. Make the loss prevention job easier

> Good internal and external relations enhance the effectiveness of security and loss prevention programs.

Marketing

Marketing consists of researching a target market and the needs of customers and developing products and services to be sold at a profit. Marketing also is considered the study of consumer problems as opportunities.

The concepts of marketing are universally applicable. *Market segmentation* divides a market into distinct groups of consumers. When one or more of the market segments is chosen for a specific product or service, this is known as *target marketing*. To illustrate, for security programs, market segmentation within a corporation can yield the following groups: executives, women, salespeople, production workers, and truck drivers. Once the market is segmented, a protection program can be designed for each target market. Research and risk analyses will produce a foundation from which to satisfy the protection needs of each type of customer. For those security programs that are so general in nature that few customers find them appealing, marketing strategies may be the solution to generate interest. Loss prevention influence over a target group or groups is better than no influence at all.[1]

These seven strategies contain a heavy emphasis on marketing and are designed to produce a high-quality security program:

1. Identify all internal and external customers of security services and determine what the customers want and how security can tell whether they are satisfied with the quality of the services rendered.

2. Focus on the customer and his or her perspective. Security should avoid an "us versus them" viewpoint.

3. Facilitate teamwork by meeting with representatives of all internal departments to discuss security issues and to seek solutions.

4. Listen and be receptive to customer concerns. In one hospital, employees complained about the need to enter their departments outside of regular business hours. In response, the security department used its technology to customize access control for each department.

5. Develop definitions. Ensure that customers and security share each group's definitions of security and loss prevention.

6. Set priorities among customers. One hospital ranked its customers as follows: patients or outside customers, employees, and employees' families.

7. Take action and be prepared to constantly adapt to new circumstances.[2]

Do you think marketing concepts can really assist a security manager, or does marketing consist of theories that have no practical value in the real world?

International Perspective: Market Research to Improve Crime Prevention[3]

Crime prevention by residents in the community is not a unitary construct; it is composed of various types of preventive activities. Research from a British crime survey revealed that citizens take part in five clear groupings of preventive activities. An understanding of the groupings, and the characteristics of citizens who choose the groupings, can assist those in the public and private sectors who market crime prevention programs. Here are the groupings:

- *Evening Precautions*: Actions taken at night to protect against attack, such as special transportation arrangements.
- *Self-Defense*: Taking self-defense classes and carrying weapons and personal alarms.
- *Neighborhood Watch*: Membership in a watch group and marking property.
- *Technological Security*: Burglar alarms and timed lights.
- *Fortress Security*: Door and window locks and grills.

This British research showed that people's use of various preventive methods represents their different perceptions of crime, their "routine activities," their aims and needs, and to a lesser extent, demographic variables. Only particular types of people will adopt certain crime prevention methods, and more extensive research is needed on this topic.

Corporate security practitioners should consider surveying employees to ascertain what is on their minds (i.e., understanding customers) as input for selecting the best possible security methods. Survey questions can focus on perceptions of security and safety on and off the premises, their "routine activities," and their needs. Such information provides a foundation for market segmentation and target marketing.

INTERNAL RELATIONS

Human Relations on the Job

Getting along with others is a major part of almost everyone's job. Many say it is half of the job. The result of such effort is increased cooperation and a smoother working environment.

These suggestions can help a person develop good human relations:

1. Make getting along with all employees as well as possible a conscious goal. Cooperation increases productivity.
2. Say hello to as many employees as possible, even if you do not know them.
3. Smile.
4. Think before you speak.
5. Be aware that nonverbal communication such as body language, facial expression, and tone of voice may reveal messages not included in your oral statements.
6. Listen carefully.
7. Maintain a sense of humor.
8. Try to look at each person as an individual. Avoid stereotyping (applying an image of a group to an individual member of a group).
9. Personalities vary form one person to another.
10. People who are quiet may be shy, and these people should not be interpreted as being aloof.
11. Carefully consider rumors and those who gossip. Such information often is inaccurate.
12. Remember that when you speak about another person your comments often are repeated.

13. If possible, avoid people with negative attitudes. A positive attitude increases the quality of human relations and has an impact on many other activities (e.g., opportunity for advancement).
14. Do not flaunt your background.
15. Everybody makes mistakes. Maintain a positive attitude and learn from mistakes.

Management Support

Management support is indispensable for an effective loss prevention program, and management support can be enhanced through good human relations. Frequent dialogue between loss prevention practitioners and management should be a high priority. One method of gaining the interest of management is to emphasize loss prevention as an investment for increasing profits. A good knowledge of business principles and practices can aid the practitioner who must speak "business management language" for effective communications. A loss prevention practitioner who does not speak "business management language" would be wise to enroll in management and accounting courses at a local college.

In one large corporation, the strategy of the security department to gain management support is to quantify its worth and prove it can provide services more efficiently than an outside contractor. This is the reality of proprietary security today as it struggles to survive and escape the outsourcing and downsizing trends. This corporation's security department tracks everything from the number of investigations conducted to the turnover rate of security officers. Such information helps the security function evaluate and improve its services to its in-house customers. Internal customer satisfaction is further measured via surveys. Additionally, the department measures losses avoided because of security action. For example, the department takes credit for the annual savings from an investigation that reveals that a workers' compensation claim that the corporation has been paying for several years is fraudulent. Another avenue to gain management support is to show that a $50,000-a-year investigator can recover an average of $500,000 in lost inventory each year.[4]

Orientation and Training Programs

Beginning with a new employee's initial contact with a business, an emphasis should be placed on loss prevention. Through the employment interview, orientation, and training, an atmosphere of loss prevention impressed on the new people sets the stage for consciousness-raising about the importance of reduced losses through prevention strategies.

Specifically, orientation and training sessions should include a description of the loss prevention plan pertaining to crime, fire, and accident. Program objectives, benefits to employees, and how employees can help reduce losses also are topics of concern. Other possible topics include prosecution policies, photo ID cards, emergency exits, and various loss prevention services, devices, policies, and procedures.

Loss Prevention Meetings

Meetings with superiors, with employees on the same level as the prevention manager, and with subordinates all strengthen internal relations because communication is fostered. When the loss prevention manager meets with superiors, goals and objectives often are transmitted to the manager. Essentially, the manager does a lot of listening. However, after listening, the manager usually has an opportunity to explain the needs of the loss prevention program while conforming to upper management's expectations. This two-way communication facilitates mutual understanding.

Meetings with other managers vary, depending on the type of organization. For instance, a meeting between the human resources manager and the loss prevention manager helps to resolve problem areas. One typical conflict pertains to disciplinary decisions. Another problem area between both departments evolves from applicant screening. Both departments should meet, work together, and formulate a cooperative plan.

When a loss prevention manager meets with subordinates, internal relations are enhanced further. Morale and productivity often are heightened when subordinates are given an opportunity to express opinions and ideas. A manager who is willing to listen to subordinates fosters improved internal relations.

Intranet and E-Mail

The communications technology of today offers a security and loss prevention program superb opportunities to market its services.[5] This involves informing customers of available services, providing helpful information, requesting assistance from customers, seeking input on the needs of customers to improve protection, and illustrating the value of security and loss prevention to the organization.

Intranets are in-house, proprietary electronic networks that are similar to the Internet. To prepare an internal Web page for security, a committee can be formed composed of management, security personnel, a Web master to take a leadership role, and an employee from the internal relations department. Next, ascertain through a survey what the customers of security would like to see on the Web page. Consideration must be given to what not to post and possible external access by nonemployees. Moderation should be used with visual images so the site does not require excessive time to load to a customer's computer. Visuals of police badges and handcuffs should be avoided to favor a partnering, loss prevention approach. To help market the site, it can be placed on the home page of the organization's intranet.

An organization's security and loss prevention internal Web site can contain the following:

- Goals, objectives, polices, and procedures
- Services offered
- Educational material on a host of topics such as personal protection, property protection, Internet and computer security, and protecting information
- Answers to frequently asked questions
- Links to resources and information
- Information on how to obtain parking privileges and access cards
- Information on how to handle various emergencies
- An incident form for reporting, and avenues to report off-line anonymously
- A bomb threat form
- A survey form for feedback to improve security
- A quarterly report on incidents and accomplishments to show the value of security and security personnel
- An e-mail feature for ease of interaction and to request information
- A counter to record the number of "hits" at the Web site

E-mail is a convenient way to communicate. Management can be sent a quarterly report on vulnerabilities, incidents, direct and indirect losses, prevention strategies, and achievements. "Tooting one's own horn" should not be perceived as bragging, but a method to inform others that the past budget allocation was worthwhile. For example, achievements may include lowering of shrinkage and increasing profits, a low accident rate, foiling a criminal conspiracy, and quickly extinguishing a fire. Such a report for superiors will better prepare them for meetings, budgets, and decisions associated with loss prevention.

> As a security manager, what types of information would you avoid placing on the Internet and a company intranet?

Involvement Programs

The essence of involvement programs is to motivate employees who are not directly associated with the loss prevention department to participate in loss prevention objectives. How can this be accomplished? Here are some suggestions: The employee responsible for the lowest shrinkage among several competing departments within a business wins $200 and a day off. The employee with the best loss prevention idea of the month wins $50. Those people who become involved should be mentioned in loss prevention reports to show others the benefits of participating in loss prevention activities.

EXTERNAL RELATIONS

Law Enforcement

Without the assistance of public law enforcement agencies, criminal charges initiated by the private sector would not be possible. Public police and prosecutors are the main components of public law enforcement. Police frequently are guided by a prosecutor, who is often referred to as the "chief law enforcement officer." The prosecuting attorney has broad discretion to initiate criminal cases. Community sentiment and powerful groups almost always have an influence on a prosecutor's discretion. Various alternatives are open to a prosecutor. If there is sufficient evidence, the prosecutor can charge an individual. Charges frequently are reduced after a defendant has agreed to plead guilty to a lesser offense. This is called *plea bargaining.* It avoids an expensive trial and the prosecutor obtains a conviction.

Unless private security officers adhere to the basic requirements within local jurisdictions, cases cannot be prosecuted successfully. An example can be seen in shoplifting cases. Depending on state law and local prosecutor requirements, a jurisdiction may require apprehension of a shoplifter after the offender leaves the store with the item, rather than apprehending within the store. Many prosecutors feel that this strengthens the case.

External relations with law enforcement agencies are vital for loss prevention programs. Sharing information is a major factor in enhancing this working relationship. Law enforcement agencies often provide information that aids the private sector. Intelligence information pertaining to the presence in an area of professional criminals, bad-check violators, counterfeiters, and con artists assists the private sector in preventing losses. Because of cybercrime, police agencies—especially federal police agencies—are increasingly working with the private sector to investigate and prosecute hackers and other cyberoffenders.

Public Service Agencies

In addition to law enforcement, other public service agencies such as fire departments, emergency medical services, and rescue squads are helpful to loss prevention programs. An analysis of these services is particularly important when a new facility is being planned. Factors relevant to emergency response time, equipment, and efficiency assist in planning the extent and expense of a loss prevention program.

Very little is accomplished by overtly criticizing local public service agencies for their deficiencies. This action results in negative attitudes and strained relations. Moreover, in the future, the severity of losses very well may depend on action taken by these public service agencies.

Several strategies help create good relations with public service agencies:

1. Do not become too aggressive when striving toward good external relations.
2. Speak on the same vocabulary level as the person with whom you are communicating.
3. Do not brag about your education and experience.
4. Do not criticize public service practitioners, because these comments often are repeated.
5. Try to have a third party, such as a friend, introduce you to public service personnel.
6. Join organizations to which public service personnel belong.
7. Join volunteer public service organizations (e.g., the local public police reserve or volunteer fire department), if possible.
8. Speak to civic groups.
9. Ask to sit in on special training programs and offer to assist in training.
10. Try to join local or regional criminal intelligence meetings, where information is shared and crimes are solved.
11. Create a softball league with private and public sector participation. Have a picnic at the end of the season. Try to obtain company funds for these activities.
12. Obtain a position on an advisory committee at a college that has a criminal justice, security and loss prevention, or fire science program.
13. Form an external loss prevention advisory board and ask local public service heads to volunteer a limited amount of time. Secure company money to sponsor these as dinner meetings.
14. Accept official inspections and surveys by public service practitioners.
15. Begin an organization, such as a local private sector–public sector cooperative association, that has common goals.

The Community

When a new industry moves to a community, external relations become especially important. Residents should be informed about safety plans. Safety is a moral obligation, as well as a necessity, to ensure limited losses and business survival. As shown in the media, over and over again, community resistance to certain industries is strong. Consequently, an industry with a history of adverse environmental impacts must cultivate relations that assure residents that safety has improved to the point of causing minimal problems and an extremely low probability of accidents. Engineers, scientists, upper management, and other support personnel are needed to provide community residents, politicians, and resistance groups with a variety of information and answers. Another consideration involves reassuring the community that a proposed industry will not adversely drain public service resources while creating additional community problems.

To promote strong ties to the community, companies often become involved in community service projects. Employees volunteer time to worthy causes such as helping the needy and mentoring youth. The American Society for Industrial Security promotes a Security for Houses of Worship Project that offers security practitioners an opportunity to partner with college security and criminal justice academic programs to protect houses of worship.[6]

The Media

The media can help or hinder a loss prevention program. Efforts must be made to recruit the media. Difficulties often arise because members of the media usually are interested in information beyond that offered by interviewees. It is worthwhile to maintain positive relations; negative relations may create a vicious cycle leading to mutual harm.

In almost all large organizations, educated and experienced media relations personnel handle the media. Loss prevention practitioners should take advantage of such an organizational structure. This, in effect, insulates the loss prevention department from the media. Policy statements should point out that comments to the media are released through a *designated spokesperson*. When all loss prevention personnel clearly understand the media policy, mistakes and embarrassing situations are minimized. An example of a mistake is the story about a young police officer who was confronted by an aggressive news reporter about a homicide investigation. Investigators had one lead: clear shoe prints under the window of entry to the crime scene. It was hoped that the suspect would be discovered with the shoes that matched the prints. Unfortunately, the news reporter obtained this information from the young officer. The local newspaper printed the story and mentioned the shoes. After reading the newspaper, the offender destroyed the shoes, and the case became more difficult to solve. There had never been a clear policy statement concerning the media within this organization. Another blunder may take place if the amount of valuables (e.g., cash) stolen in a burglary or robbery is revealed to the media, or the fact that the offenders overlooked high-priced valuables during the crime. Both types of information, broadcast by the media, have been known to cause future crimes at the same location.

An article in *Security Management*, "Stress from the Press—and How to Meet It,"[7] states many useful ideas concerning relations with the media. The article stresses the importance of preparation, knowing what you want to say, being prepared for tricky questions, and carefully phrasing answers. Numerous firms are training executives in effective communication techniques. These courses vary, but most participants learn how to deal with hostile questioning and receive feedback and coaching with the assistance of videotaping. The courses generally run for one to three days and can cost thousands of dollars per participant.

The article recommends several "don'ts" for interviews with the media:

1. Don't return any hostility from the interviewer.
2. Don't lose the audience. Remember the type of audience you are communicating with at home.
3. Don't say "no comment." If you can't answer the questions, at least tell the audience why.
4. Don't make up answers. If you do not know an answer, say so.
5. Don't say "off the record." If you don't want it repeated, don't say it.
6. Don't offer personal opinions. You are on the air to represent your company, and everything you say will appear to be company policy.

External Loss Prevention Peers

The practitioner who exists in a vacuum is like a student who doesn't pay attention. No knowledge is obtained. Through formal and informal associations with peers, the practitioner inevitably becomes involved in a learning experience. One of the results of relations with peers is information that can improve loss prevention programming.

No individual is an expert about everything. If a group of experts comes together, a broad spectrum of ideas results. When a loss prevention practitioner does not know the answer to a particular question, a call to a peer can produce an answer. Peers are helpful in the selection of services and devices, budget preparation, and even presentations to management.

Many formal organizations are open to practitioners. The one organization known by almost all practitioners is the American Society for Industrial Security. This organization is at the forefront in upgrading the security and loss prevention field by educating members and increasing professionalism. Local chapters, national meetings, seminars, and specialized committees and councils bring peers together for mutually beneficial relations.

SPECIAL PROBLEMS

Certain select areas of concern overshadow both internal and external relations. Two important areas are prosecution decisions and loss prevention attire.

Prosecution Decisions

Prosecution decisions concerning employee–offenders, usually for theft, often are difficult for management. The difficulty arises because a wise manager considers numerous variables. No matter what decision is made, the company may suffer in some way. The situation is tantamount to "damned if we do and damned if we don't." The following are benefits of prosecuting:

1. Prosecuting deters future offenders by setting an example. This reduces the potential for future losses.
2. The company will rid itself of an employee–offender who may have committed previous offenses.
3. The company will appear strong, and this will generate greater respect from employees.
4. Morale is boosted when "rotten apple" employees are purged from the workforce.
5. If a company policy states that all offenders will be prosecuted, then after each prosecution, employees will know that the company lives up to its word and will not tolerate criminal offenses.
6. The company aids the criminal justice system and the community against crime.
7. Local law enforcement will feel that the company is part of the war against crime. This will reinforce cooperation.
8. A strong prosecution policy will become known inside and outside the company. Those seeking employment who also are thinking of committing crimes against the company will be deterred from applying for work.

The following are benefits of not prosecuting:

1. The company shows sympathy for the employee–offender. Therefore, employees say the company has a heart. Morale is boosted.
2. Not prosecuting saves the company time, money, and wages for those employees such as witnesses and the investigator, who must aid in the prosecution.
3. If the employee–offender agrees to pay back the losses to the company and he or she is not fired, the company will not lose an experienced and trained employee in whom it has invested.
4. The criminal justice system will not be burdened by another case.
5. Sometimes companies initiate prosecution, an arrest is made, and then management changes its mind. This creates friction with law enforcement agencies.
6. Possible labor trouble is avoided.
7. Possible litigation is avoided.
8. Prosecution sometimes creates friction among human resources, internal and external relations, and loss prevention departments.

9. Giving bad news to financial supporters, stockholders, customers, and
    the community is avoided.

To complicate the prosecution decision even more, the policy statement concerning prosecution must be carefully worded by management.
There is no perfect statement that can apply to all incidents. A look at a
strict policy statement illustrates this problem. Suppose a company policy
states that all employees committing crimes against the business will be
impartially and vigorously prosecuted. Thereafter, what if a 15-year
employee, with an excellent work record, and accumulated company-paid
training, is caught stealing a box of envelopes? Obviously, such a strong policy statement can be detrimental.

Employees Smoking Marijuana

An undercover investigation at the Southern Manufacturing Plant by public
and private investigators revealed that seven experienced and well-trained
employees smoke marijuana before work.

The company loss prevention and human resources managers met with
upper management to decide what to do. One solution was to fire all the
employees; however, these offending employees had good work records and
considerable work experience, and the company had invested heavily in their
training. The loss prevention and human resources managers suggested that
the employees be confronted and threatened with firing unless they participated in an Employee Assistance Program through a local alcohol and drug
abuse program and submitted to drug testing. The managers stated that
another local business had a similar problem and a contract was formulated
between the business and the government agency dealing with alcohol and
drug abuse problems. Upper management at Southern favored this idea.

Later, the employees were confronted and surprised. They all admitted
that they liked their jobs and were willing to participate in a drug abuse program on their own time to avoid being fired. By this time, the local alcohol
and drug abuse commission had agreed to conduct a program for these
employees. The local police chief and prosecutor favored the program as an
innovative diversion from the criminal justice system.

Upper management was satisfied. Internal and external relations were
improved. The company provided a second chance for the employees and did
not lose experienced workers or the money invested in their training.

The *Report of the Task Force on Private Security* adds interesting perspectives to the prosecution issue:

[I]t would appear that a large percentage of criminal violators known to
private security personnel are not referred to the criminal justice system.
A logical conclusion would be that there is a "private" criminal justice

system wherein employer reprimands, restrictions, suspensions, demotions, job transfers, or employment terminations take the place of censure by the public system. . . . [I]n many instances private action is more expedient, less expensive, and less embarrassing to the company. Fear of lawsuits or protecting the offender from a criminal record may be important. However, violations of due process, right to counsel, and other individual rights are more likely to occur under such a system. The criminal justice system is established for the purpose of resolving criminal offenses and can be a viable resource for the private security sector in this regard.[8]

Another factor affecting a company's prosecution decision is the *prosecution threshold*, which is the monetary level of the alleged crime that must be met before prosecution. Trends indicate a rise in dollar amounts of individual instances of theft that are partly tied to employee perception of changes in company and prosecutor policies concerning prosecution thresholds. "In the 1970s, an employee who stole $10,000 would have been prosecuted. Today, in many places, that amount won't even produce a criminal referral."[9]

> Should management in companies seek to prosecute or not prosecute employee offenders?

Loss Prevention Attire

The appearance of loss prevention personnel has a definite impact on how people perceive a loss prevention program. A vital part of appearance is attire (i.e., uniforms). Wrinkled, messy uniforms send a message to observers that loss prevention objectives are not very important. A variety of people observe loss prevention personnel: employees, customers, visitors, salespeople, truck drivers, law enforcement personnel, and the community in general. What type of message to these people is desired from an effective loss prevention program? Obviously, neat, good-looking attire is an asset.

Attire can project two primary images: subtlety or visibility. Subtle attire consists of blazers or sports jackets (see Figure 5-3). It is generally believed that blazers project a warmer, less threatening, and less authoritarian image. Increased visibility and a stricter image are projected through traditional uniforms. However, it is vital that traditional uniforms do not look similar to those worn by public police; this can cause mistakes by citizens needing aid, and the public police resent private sector officers wearing such uniforms.

Figure 5–3   Security officers at a museum. Courtesy of Wackenhut Corporation. Photo by Ed Burns.

"All security and loss prevention personnel must realize that they have only one opportunity to create a first, favorable impression."[10]

Research on the psychological influence of the public police uniform should be considered by those who plan uniforms for the private sector. It has been shown in psychological tests that individuals associate the color blue with feelings of security and comfort, and the color black with power and strength. Other research shows black and brown being perceived as strong and passive, but also bad, and eliciting emotions of anger, hostility, and aggression. Darker police uniforms may send negative subconscious signals to citizens. One experiment showed that lighter colored sheriff's uniforms were rated higher for warmth and friendliness than darker uniforms. Furthermore, a half-dark uniform (i.e., light shirt, dark pants) sends a better message than an all-dark uniform. Research on the traditional uniform versus the blazer shows mixed results. The Menlo Park, California, police tried the blazer for eight years, but found that assaults on police increased and that it did not command respect. After 18 months of wearing blazers, the police of this department displayed fewer authoritarian characteristics when compared to police from other nearby agencies.[11] For the private sector, research questions are: Do light colored uniforms or blazers send more positive signals than dark colored apparel? Do blazers really create a less authoritarian atmosphere than uniforms? What impact do blazers have on assaults and respect for private sector security officers?

Do you favor traditional uniforms or blazers for security officers? Why?

Career: Transportation Security

Security in the transportation industry—airports, trucking, rail, ports and sea operations—is a multifaceted and challenging endeavor.

Duties: Protect people, assets, and cargo; prevent theft, terrorism, and other vulnerabilities; establish security for transportation facilities, modes of transportation, parking lots, restaurants, and retail stores; and process and screen passengers, identify unusual behavior, conduct investigations, perform risk analyses, and adhere to regulatory laws and security standards.

Prerequisites: For management, graduate degree, five years of experience, possible security clearance, CPP preferred.

Demographic of typical practitioner: Undergraduate degree, some master's degree; 15–20 years in security; 12–15 years in specialty; salary of $40,000–100,000+ yr.; titles: Security Director, Security Manager, and Security Supervisor.

Source: American Society for Industrial Security, *Career Opportunities in Security* (Alexandria, VA: ASIS, 1998), p. 16.

Search the Web

Check out the following sites to see the broad range of helpful resources on the Web:

Public Relations (http://publicrelations.about.com/mbody.htm) offers information on marketing, media relations, case studies, and many other topics.

Police Officer's Internet Directory (http://www.Officer.com/) offers a variety of links to law enforcement sites.

CASE PROBLEMS

5A. As a security supervisor you have received reports that a security officer assigned to the employee parking lot is having repeated verbal confrontations with employees. One report described the officer's use of profane language and threats. Specifically, what do you say to this officer, and what actions do you take? How do you repair internal relations?

5B. You are a loss prevention supervisor, and two company employees report to you that a loss prevention officer is intoxicated while on duty. You approach the officer, engage in conversation, and smell alcohol on his breath. What do you do? An added complication is that this particular officer has a brother in the local police department who has provided valuable aid during past loss prevention investigations. Furthermore, the officer has had a good work record while employed by the company for five years. After carefully studying the advantages and disadvantages of various internal and external ramifications to proposed actions, what do you do?

5C. While a loss prevention officer was routinely patrolling the inner storage rooms of a manufacturing facility, he accidentally stumbled on two employees engaged in sexual intercourse. All three were shocked and surprised. The man and woman should have been selecting orders for shipment. The woman cried and begged the loss prevention officer to remain silent about this revelation. The man also pleaded for mercy, especially because both were married to other people. When the officer decided that he should report the matter, the man became violent. A fight developed between the officer and the man and woman. The officer was able to radio his location and within 10 minutes other officers arrived. The pair has been brought to the loss prevention office. What do you do as the loss prevention supervisor?

5D. You are a newly hired security manager for an electronics company of 2000 employees. You were told by your supervisor, the vice-president of human resources, "You are here to bring our security program into the twenty-first century." Apparently, the previous security manager did not meet management's expectations. As you speak with employees and public safety practitioners in the community, you get the impression that you need to "build many bridges." What are your ideas for improving internal and external relations?

5E. An unfortunate explosion and injuries took place at Smith Industries and a company vice president designates you, a loss prevention supervisor, to speak to the media. It has been only one hour since the explosion, the investigation is far from complete, and you have no time to prepare for the media representatives who have arrived. As you walk to the front gate, several news people are anxiously waiting. The rapid-fire questions begin: "What is the extent of injuries and damage?" "Is it true that both high production quotas and poor safety have caused the explosion?" "What dangers will the community face due to this explosion and future ones?" "What are your comments about reports that safety inspectors have been bribed by Smith Industries executives?" As a loss prevention supervisor with the authority and responsibility to respond to media questions, what are your answers to each question?

5F. Because of your experience and college education you are appointed manager of loss prevention at a large manufacturing facility in a small city. It is your understanding that the local police chief is introverted and uncooperative with strangers. The chief has an eighth-grade education and is extremely sensitive about this deficiency. He refuses to hire college graduates. Despite these faults, he is respected and does a good job as a police administrator.

The local fire chief is the police chief's brother. Both have similar backgrounds and character traits. Furthermore, the local prosecutor is a cousin of both chiefs. A "clannish" situation is apparent.

As the loss prevention manager you know that you will have to rely on as much cooperation as possible from these public officials. What do you do to develop good relations with them?

5G. Allen Dart has worked for the Music Manufacturing Company for 14 years. He has always done above-average work and was recently promoted to production supervisor. One afternoon when Allen was leaving the facility, he dropped company tools from under his coat in front of a loss prevention officer. Allen was immediately approached by the officer, who asked Allen to step inside to the loss prevention office. At this time, Allen broke down and began crying. Before anybody could say a word, Allen stated that he was very sorry and that he would not do it again. Later, the loss prevention and human resources managers met to discuss the incident. An argument developed because the loss prevention manager wanted to seek prosecution, whereas the human resources manager did not. As a vice-president in this company, how do you resolve the situation?

NOTES

1. Philip Purpura, *Modern Security and Loss Prevention Management* (Boston: Butterworth–Heinemann, 1989), pp. 141–148.
2. Dennis Wozniak, "Seven Steps to Quality Security." *Security Management* (March 1996), pp. 25–28.
3. Tim Hope and Steven Lab, "Variation in Crime Prevention Participation: Evidence from the British Crime Survey," *Crime Prevention and Community Safety: An International Journal* 3 (2001), pp. 7–22.
4. Brian R. Hollstein, "Internal Security and the Corporate Customer," *Security Management* (June 1995), pp. 61–63.
5. Nigel Richardson, "A Blueprint for Value," *Security Management* 44 (March 2000), pp. 24–26. And, Johnnie Huneycutt, "Nothing But Net," *Security Management* 44 (December 2000), pp. 103–107.

6. Philip Purpura, *Security for Houses of Worship: A Community Service Manual for ASIS Chapters* (Alexandria, VA: American Society for Industrial Security, 1999).
7. "Stress from the Press—and How to Meet It," *Security Management* 24 (February 1980), pp. 8–11.
8. U.S. Department of Justice, *Report of the Task Force on Private Security* (Washington, D.C.: U.S. Government Printing Office, 1976), p. 128. Research in 1980 and 1990 confirmed that much economic crime is disposed of privately. See William C. Cunningham, et al., *Private Security: Patterns and Trends* (Washington, D.C.: National Institute of Justice, August 1991), p. 4.
9. "Finding Where the (Financial) Bodies Are Buried," *Security Management Bulletin* (August 25, 1993), pp. 4–5.
10. Philip Purpura, *Security Handbook* (Albany, NY: Delmar, 1991), p. 41.
11. Richard R. Johnson, "The Psychological Influence of the Police Uniform," *FBI Law Enforcement Bulletin* 70 (March 2001), pp. 27–32.

6

Applicant Screening and Employee Socialization

OBJECTIVES

After studying this chapter the reader will be able to:

1. Define applicant screening and employee socialization.
2. Summarize the legal guidelines for applicant screening.
3. Explain each of the following and how it relates to the employment environment: equal employment opportunity, affirmative action, quotas, diversity, and sexual harassment.
4. List and explain at least four applicant screening methods.
5. Describe how to enhance employee socialization.

One of the most important assets of an organization is its personnel. The purpose of *applicant screening* is to find the most appropriate person for a particular job. Several methods are available for screening applicants, such as interviewing and testing.

The culmination of the applicant screening process results in hiring an applicant. At this stage, an organization already has invested considerable personnel, money, and time in making the best possible choice. The next step is to develop a productive employee. This can be accomplished through adequate *socialization*, which is a learning process that, it is hoped, produces an employee who will benefit the organization. Two primary methods of socialization are employee training and example setting by superiors.

Both applicant screening and employee socialization are primary loss prevention strategies. If an organization can select honest, stable, and productive people, less has to be done to protect the organization from employees and protect employees from employees. If employees can be socialized to act safely and protect company assets, security and loss prevention strategies are enhanced further.

> Applicant screening and employee socialization are primary loss prevention strategies.

EMPLOYMENT LAW

Government regulation affects the balance and working relationship between employers and employees in three major areas: (1) the prohibition of employment discrimination; (2) the promotion of a safe and healthy workplace; and (3) fair negotiation between management and labor concerning terms of employment.[1] Here we begin with major federal laws prohibiting employment discrimination, followed by applicant screening methods. The laws on workplace safety and labor are covered in later chapters.

Federal Legislation

* *The Equal Pay Act of 1963.* This legislation requires that men and women be paid equally if they work at the same location at similar jobs. Exceptions include a seniority or merit system and earnings through quantity or quality of production. The act is enforced by the Equal Employment Opportunity Commission (EEOC).
* *The Civil Rights Act of 1964, Title VII.* This law prohibits employment discrimination based on race, color, religion, gender, or national origin. Title VII prohibits discrimination with regard to any employment condition, including recruiting, screening, hiring, training, compensating, evaluating, promoting, disciplining, and firing. Congress established the Equal Employment Opportunity Commission to enforce Title VII.
* *The Age Discrimination in Employment Act of 1967.* This law prohibits employment discrimination on the basis of age in areas such as hiring, firing, and compensating. It applies to private employers with twenty or more employees and all government units. Mandatory retirement is also prohibited, absent a suitable defense. The act is enforced by the EEOC.
* *The Equal Employment Opportunity Act of 1972.* The purpose of this federal law (EEO) is to strengthen Title VII by providing the EEOC with additional enforcement powers to file suits and issue cease-and-desist orders. Further, EEO expands coverage to employees of state and local governments, educational institutions, and private employers of more than fifteen persons. EEO programs are implemented by employers to

prevent discrimination in the workplace and to offset past employment discrimination.

- *The Rehabilitation Act of 1973.* This act requires government agencies and contractors with the federal government to take affirmative action to hire those with physical or mental handicaps. The act is enforced by the Office of Federal Contract Compliance Procedures.

- *The American with Disabilities Act of 1990.* This legislation prohibits discrimination against individuals with disabilities and increases their access to services and jobs. The law requires employers to make reasonable accommodations for employees with a disability if doing so would not create an undue hardship for the employer. Reasonable accommodations include making existing facilities accessible and modifying a workstation. The ADA has had a significant impact on the security and safety designs of buildings. Access controls, doorways, elevators, and emergency alarm systems are among the many physical features of a building that must accommodate disabled people. The act is enforced by the EEOC.

- *The Civil Rights Act of 1991.* This legislation provides additional remedies to deter employment discrimination by codifying disparate impact concepts and allowing plaintiffs to demand a jury trial and seek damages. "Disparate impact or unintentional discrimination occurs when a facially neutral employment practice has the effect of disproportionately excluding a group based upon a protected category."[2] (The U.S. Supreme Court expanded the definition of illegal discrimination to include disparate impact as illustrated in the *Griggs* case.) It requires businesses to prove that the business practice that led to the charge of discrimination was not discriminatory but job related for the position and consistent with business necessity. The act is enforced by the EEOC.

- *The Family and Medical Leave Act of 1993.* This legislation requires employers to provide twelve weeks of unpaid leave for family and medical emergencies without employees suffering job loss. The act is enforced by the Department of Labor.

U.S. Supreme Court Decisions

When laws are passed, the courts play a role in helping to define what the legislation means. Such court cases evolve, for example, when the EEOC develops and enforces guidelines based upon their interpretation of legislation. Confusion over how to interpret the legislation has led to many lawsuits and some conflicting court decisions. What follows here are two famous U.S. Supreme Court cases from an historical context to illustrate the development of the issues and laws.

Griggs v. Duke Power (1971). In 1968, several employees of the Duke Power Company in North Carolina were given a pencil-and-paper aptitude test for manual labor. Willie Griggs and twelve other black workers sued their employer with the charge of job discrimination under the Civil Rights Act of 1964. Their contention was that the pencil-and-paper aptitude test had little to do with their ability to perform manual labor. The Supreme Court decided that a test is inherently discriminatory if it is not job related and differentiates on the basis of race, sex, or religion. Furthermore, employers are required to prove that their screening methods are job related.

Bakke v. University of California (1978). Reverse discrimination was the main issue of this case. Allan Bakke, a white man, sued the Davis Medical School under the "equal protection" clause of the Fourteenth Amendment because it set aside 16 of 100 openings for minorities, who were evaluated according to different standards. The Court concluded that the racial quota system was unacceptable because it disregarded Bakke's right to equal protection of the law, and that affirmative action programs are permissible as long as applicants are considered on an individual basis and a rigid number of places has not been set aside. Race can be a key factor in the selection process; however, multiple factors must be considered.

In addition to federal legislation and court cases, executive orders have been issued by presidents of the United States to deal with problems of discrimination. Furthermore, every state has equal employment laws of one form or another, and state court decisions have interpreted these state laws.

What do all these laws and cases mean for those involved in applicant screening? Basically, all screening methods must be job related, valid, and nondiscriminatory. Included in this mandate are interviews, background investigations, and tests. Simply put, the EEOC regards all screening tools as capable of discriminating against applicants.

The EEOC does not have the power to order employers to stop a discriminatory practice or to provide back pay to a victim. However, the EEOC has the power to sue an employer in federal court. The EEOC requires employers to report employment statistics annually. It investigates claims, collects facts from all parties, seeks an out-of-court settlement, and promotes mediation.

According to the EEOC, 79,900 cases were filed during FY 2000. This figure was about 2,500 higher than in 1999, but lower than the 1994 figure of 91,200. During FY 2000 327 suits were filed by EEOC, with monetary benefits of $47 million. A year earlier the figures were 465 and $97 million, respectively.[3]

EEO, AA, and Quotas[4]

Equal employment opportunity, affirmative action, and quotas are important terms relevant to staffing organizations. *Equal employment opportunity*

You Be the Judge*

Facts of the Case

When security officer Bronislav Zaleszny was passed over for promotion to supervisor, he decided that his Eastern European origin was at least one of the reasons (his English was rather thickly accented). So he went to the Equal Employment Opportunity Commission and filed a charge against his employer, Hi-Mark Home Products, alleging discrimination on the basis of national origin.

During the month after the EEOC notified the company of the charge, Zaleszny's troubles multiplied. First, Hi-Mark informed the police that products had been disappearing for months, that the disappearances evidently had occurred during Zaleszny's shift, and that Zaleszny was a reasonable suspect. Second, the company terminated him on suspicion of theft. Police arrested Zaleszny, but a preliminary hearing resulted in dismissal of the charges against him.

Zaleszny fumed with anger at his former employer. He sued, alleging that Hi-Mark had prosecuted him maliciously and had fired him in retaliation for his EEOC complaint.

Exactly Who Prosecuted, and Exactly Who Knew about the EEOC Complaint?

In court, the company argued that Zaleszny's allegations really couldn't stand up to logical analysis. *We didn't prosecute him, maliciously or otherwise,* Hi-Mark noted. *We truthfully told the police everything we knew about the disappearance of our products, and we said that on the basis of the facts, Mr. Zaleszny seemed to us to be logical suspect. Then, completely on their own discretion, the police and the district attorney initiated charges against him. We disagree that the prosecution was malicious, but whether it was or not, we're not the ones who prosecuted.*

In answer to Zaleszny's retaliatory-firing allegation, Hi-Mark's director of corporate security took the stand. "I'm the company official who recommended Mr. Zaleszny's termination," she testified, "and when I made the recommendation, I *didn't know* about his EEOC complaint. Yes, the Commission had notified our company, and yes, our HR department knew, but I didn't! And if I didn't know about the complaint when I fired him, then the firing obviously wasn't a retaliation."

Did Zaleszny win his suit against Hi-Mark Home Products?

Make your decision; then turn to the end of the chapter for the court decision.

*Reprinted with permission from *Security Management Bulletin*, a publication of the Bureau of Business Practice, Inc., 24 Rope Ferry Road, Waterford, CT 06386.

(EEO) refers to practices that are designed so that all applicants and employees are treated similarly without regard to protected characteristics such as race and sex. For example, suppose a vacant position requires applicants to undergo a written job knowledge test and an interview to assess applicants. Anyone is free to apply for the position, and all who apply will be given both the test and the interview. How well each performs on both screening methods determines who is hired. Thus, all applicants have an equal opportunity and the job will be offered following an unbiased assessment.

Affirmative action (AA) focuses on procedures employers use to correct and abolish past discriminatory employment practices against minority group members, women, and those in other groups, while setting goals for hiring and promoting persons from underrepresented groups. AA may be voluntarily undertaken by an employer or court ordered. In our previous example, AA could result if there was a failure to recruit women and minority group members or if the job knowledge test was biased. Then, management would make a good faith effort to meet certain hiring goals, for instance, by improved recruiting.

Quotas are rigid hiring and promotion requirements. In our previous example, a hiring formula would be set that specifies the number or percent of women and minorities to be hired.

These concepts, as applied in the workplace, have raised considerable legal turmoil and controversy over whether in fact they have been successful in correcting discrimination. The issue of "reverse discrimination" has intensified the debate. Court decisions provide guidelines for employers.

Diversity

Diversity in the workforce encompasses many different dimensions, including sex, race, national origin, religion, age, and disability.[5] The workforce, historically dominated by white men, is being increasingly replaced with workers from diverse backgrounds. The 2000 census showed what demographers have long predicted—that the fast-growing Hispanic population would soon become the nation's largest minority group. Numbering about 35 million, at 12.6 percent of the U.S. population of 281 million, these figures are about equal to African-Americans in the United States.[6] The U.S. Bureau of Labor Statistics estimates that, by the year 2005, the U.S. labor force will consist of only 38 percent white, non-Hispanic men.[7] The reasons for this change go beyond affirmative action plans that have brought nontraditional employees into many positions. More than half of the new entrants into the workplace will be women, the average age of employees will climb, immigrant employees will have language and cultural differences, and as companies become more global, there will be an increasing need to respond to the unique needs of individual employees, including their languages, values, and customs. Diversity facilitates tolerance of different behavioral styles and wider views, which can lead to greater responsiveness to diverse customers. The challenge of learning to manage a diverse workforce is an investment in the future.[8]

In August of 2000, the American Society for Industrial Security (ASIS) held a conference on "Women and Minorities in Security." The conference was noteworthy because this field has been dominated by white males since the beginning. The speakers were straightforward with the challenges facing minorities and the security industry. With an increasingly diverse society, recruitment of women and minorities is essential; however, public and media perceptions of security—often in a negative light—makes recruitment difficult. Women have played an increasing role in the industry, but more needs to be done to recruit more women, African-Americans, and Hispanics.[9]

The ASIS is in a key position to take the lead to meet the challenges of diversity in the security industry. Solutions include a recruitment campaign; improved partnering among the ASIS, proprietary and contract security organizations, and colleges and universities; and internships.

The security field can borrow ideas from others. Mentoring programs assign higher-level managers to help lower-level managers understand corporate culture and values and meet senior executives. At Giant Foods, mentoring has lowered turnover of minorities by providing them with resources to solve problems. Toys 'R' Us, like many other companies, has employees attend diversity training to reduce biases and develop skills to manage a diverse workforce. JC Penney monitors high-potential minorities and women employees to ensure they have opportunities for promotion.[10]

Sexual Harassment

The EEOC defines *sexual harassment* as unwelcome sexual conduct that has the purpose or effect of unreasonably interfering with an individual's work performance or creating an intimidating, hostile, or offensive work environment. Although the *Civil Rights Act* was passed in 1964, only during the 1970s did courts begin to recognize sexual harassment as a form of gender discrimination under Title VII. Thereafter, the EEOC issued guidelines for determining what activity is sexual harassment, and these guidelines influence courts.

The two theories upon which an action for sexual harassment may be brought are explained here. *Quid pro quo* involves an employee who is required to engage in sexual activity in exchange for a workplace benefit. For example, a male manager tells his female assistant that he will get her a promotion and raise if she engages in sex with him. A second theory of sexual harassment is *hostile working environment*, which occurs when sexually offensive behavior by one party is unwelcome by another and creates workplace difficulties. Examples include unwelcome suggestive remarks or touching, and posted jokes or photos of a sexual nature.

The following list offers guidance when taking action against the problem of sexual harassment:

1. Ensure that top management takes the lead to establish a zero tolerance policy.
2. Communicate the policy and reporting procedures to all employees, including strong prohibitions against retaliation for reporting.
3. Provide relevant training.
4. Ensure that reported incidents are taken seriously and thoroughly and promptly investigated, and that corrective action is taken if the allegations are true.
5. Ensure that the personnel department is notified about each complaint.
6. Maintain confidentiality, providing information only on a "need to know" basis.

Employers, who are vicariously liable for sexual harassment, must take immediate and appropriate corrective action; otherwise, civil and criminal legal action can be devastating. Under the *Civil Rights Act of 1991,* an employee suing for sexual harassment can ask for up to $300,000 in compensatory and punitive damages and unlimited medical damages, and can request a jury trial. Furthermore, these tort actions may be initiated: assault, battery, intentional infliction of emotional distress, and false imprisonment. In addition, these criminal charges may be filed: assault, battery, and rape.[11]

SCREENING METHODS

Screening methods vary among organizations and depend on such factors as budget, the number of personnel available to investigate applicants, and the types of positions open. Certain employers expend minimal efforts to properly screen, using the excuse that their hands are tied because of legal barriers. Others follow legal guidelines and screen carefully. The EEOC, the Office of Personnel Management, the Department of Justice, and the Department of Labor have adopted and published the *Uniform Guidelines on Employee Selection Procedures*, which is a guide for determining the proper use of tests and other selection procedures for any employment decision such as hiring, promotion, demotion, retention, training, and transfers. These guidelines also contain technical standards and documentation requirements for the validation of selection procedures as described in the *Standards for Educational and Psychological Tests*, prepared by the American Psychological Association and other groups. Courts rely on such guidelines in deciding cases.

The courts also have established screening standards from negligence cases; awards have been made to victims who have sued, claiming the employer was negligent in not conducting a reasonable inquiry into the background of an employee who, for example, had a history of physical violence. The term *reasonable inquiry* has various definitions; however, an employer can take a number of steps to screen applicants.

First, careful planning is required. Input from a competent attorney can strengthen the legality of the screening process. *No single screening tool should be used to assess an applicant. Multiple measures always are best.*

It is important that the job duties and qualifications be clearly defined through a job analysis. Help-wanted advertisements should be worded carefully to attract only those who meet the requirements of the job. This also prevents expensive turnover and charges of discrimination.

To save money, the most expensive screening methods should be performed last. The time and labor spent reading application forms is less expensive than conducting background investigations.

Resumes and Applications

Applications must be carefully studied. Job seekers are notorious for exaggerating and actually lying. The Port Authority of New York and New Jersey did a study by using a questionnaire to ask applicants if they had ever used certain equipment that really did not exist. More than one-third of the applicants said that they had experience with the nonexistent equipment.[12] "Diploma mills," which provide a "degree" for a fee, are another problem. Research in the 1990s showed not only that one-third of resumes were fraudulent, but that the problem was increasing.[13]

Signs of deception on resumes and applications include inconsistencies in verbal and written statements and among background documents. Periods of "self-employment" may be used to hide institutionalization. Not signing an application may be another indicator of deception. Social security numbers are issued by the state, and that can assist in verifying past residence. A thorough background investigation is indispensable to support information presented by the applicant.

Employers are increasingly adding clauses and disclaimers to applications. Clauses include a statement on EEO and AA, employment at will (i.e., employer's decision to terminate employees, which is being challenged in the courts), and the resolution of grievances through arbitration rather than litigation. Disclaimers warn an applicant of refusal to hire or discharge for misstatements or omissions on the application.

The use of the Internet to solicit applications has its advantages and disadvantages. Advantages, when compared to traditional recruitment methods, include the opportunity to attract more applicants from across the country, lower cost, convenience, and speed. Disadvantages include the possibility of screening numerous applications, ignoring other means of recruiting, and hiring too quickly without screening properly.[14]

Interview

When asking the applicant general questions about work experience and education, open-ended questions should be formulated so the interviewee can talk at length. "What were your duties at that job?" elicits more information than short-answer questions requiring yes or no responses. Answers to questions should be compared to the application and resume.

Some employers ask the applicant to complete an application at home to be mailed in before the interview. Before the interview, while the applicant is waiting in an office, he or she is asked to complete another application. Both applications are then compared before the interview for consistency.

The following information concerns questions prohibited during the entire screening process, including the application form. Court rulings under EEO legislation have stressed repeatedly that questions (and tests) must be job related. This legal requirement is known as a *bona fide occupational qualification* (BFOQ).

Questions pertaining to arrest records generally are unlawful. An arrest does not signify guilt. The courts have stated that minority group members have suffered disproportionately more arrests than others. A question that asks about a conviction, however, may be solicited. It is not an absolute bar to employment. Here again, minority group members have disproportionately more convictions. Certain offenses can cause an employer to exclude an applicant, depending on the particular job. Therefore, the question of convictions must be job related (e.g., related to loss prevention) and carefully considered.

Unless a "business necessity" can be shown, questions concerning credit records, charge accounts, and owning one's own home are discriminatory because minority group applicants often are poorer than others. Unless absolutely necessary for a particular job, height, weight, and other physical requirements are discriminatory against certain minority groups (e.g., Latino, Asian, and women applicants often are physically smaller than other applicants).

Other unlawful questions, unless job related, include asking age, sex, color, or race, maiden name of applicant's wife or mother, and membership in organizations that reveal race, religion, or national origin.

The questions that can be asked of an applicant and on an application form, among others, are name, address, telephone number, social security number, past experience and salary, reasons for leaving past jobs, education, convictions, U.S. citizenship, military experience in U.S. forces, and hobbies.

Under the ADA, an employer may ask applicants if they need reasonable accommodations for the hiring process. If the answer is yes, the employer may ask for reasonable documentation concerning the disability. Generally, the employer may not ask whether an applicant will need reasonable accommodations to do the job; however, pre-employment inquiries can be made regarding the ability of the applicant to perform job-related functions.[15]

Extensive research on the interview process shows that without proper care it can be unreliable, low in validity, and biased against certain groups. Research has pointed to concrete steps that can be taken to increase the utility of the personnel selection interview. First, the interview should be structured, standardized, and focused on a small number of goals (e.g., interpersonal style or ability to express oneself). Second, ask questions dealing with specific situations (e.g., "As a security officer, what would you do if you saw a robbery in progress?"). Third, use multiple interviewers and ensure that women and minority group members are represented to include their perspectives.[16]

Validity asks how accurately a test predicts job success. *Reliability* asks if a test is consistent in measuring performance.

Tests

The testing of applicants varies considerably. Here is a summary of various types of tests.

- *Aptitude tests* measure a person's ability (e.g., verbal, numerical, reasoning) to learn and perform a job. Because these tests often contain questions that do not relate to the job, and they may have an adverse impact on the hiring of minority group members, many employers have reduced their use of these tests.
- *Job knowledge tests* are written or oral and measure job-related knowledge. *Proficiency tests* measure how well the applicant can do the work; an example is a typing test for a secretarial position. As with other tests, they must be job related.
- *Personality tests* attempt to measure personality characteristics and categorize applicants by what they are like, such as agreeable and conscientious. When such tests ask job applicants to answer intimate questions, such as their sex practices, class action lawsuits can result. These tests have been criticized for questionable validity and low reliability.
- *Medical examinations* are given to determine whether applicants are physically capable of performing the job. The ADA requires employers to make medical inquiries directly related to the applicant's ability to perform job-related duties and requires employers to make reasonable accommodations to help handicapped individuals to perform the job. This act requires that the medical exam cannot be conducted until after the job offer has been provided to the applicant.

Employers and job applicants are becoming increasingly knowledgeable about the validity and reliability of tests, especially because of the need to eliminate or to detect discrimination. The Buros Institute of Mental Measurement (http://www.unl.edu/buros/) evaluates published tests and acts as a consumers' evaluation service.

- *Honesty tests* are paper-and-pencil tests that measure trustworthiness and attitudes toward honesty. Thousands of companies have used this evaluation tool on millions of workers, and its use is increasing as employers deal with the legal restrictions of the polygraph. These tests have helped employers screen job candidates, and validity and reliability studies have been published in scholarly journals.[17]
- *Drug testing* has grown dramatically in a drug-oriented world. Employers expect workers to perform their jobs free from the influence of intoxicating substances, and accidents must be prevented. The opposing view favors protection from an invasion of an individual's right to privacy. Drug tests vary in terms of cost, quality, and accuracy. A drug test can result in a "false positive," showing that a person tested has used drugs when that is not so. A "false negative" can show that the individual has not used drugs when, in fact, the opposite is true. Another problem with drug testing is cheating. Simply stated, if an observer is not present when a urine sample is requested, a variety of ploys may be used by an abuser to deceive an employer. For example, "clean" urine may be substituted. Such deception is a huge problem. Another strategy of drug testing is to measure drug usage from a sample of a person's hair. Some experts view this method as more accurate than urine sampling. The substance abuse problem is discussed further in Chapter 18.

An employer can be held liable for negligent hiring if an employee causes harm that could have been prevented if the employer had conducted a reasonable background check.

Background Investigations

With restrictions on the use of the polygraph, employers have turned to background investigations to verify job applicant information. This can range from inquiries made by the employer to the use of a private investigator or credit reporting agency.

The Fair Credit Reporting Act (FCRA), enforced by the Federal Trade Commission, is a major law that seeks to protect consumers from abuses of credit reporting agencies while controlling many aspects of background and other types of investigations. (State laws must also be considered.) If a company conducts investigations with in-house investigators, rather than contracting the work to a service firm, the impact of the FCRA may be less burdensome. However, most companies cannot afford in-house investigators.

Under the FCRA, an employer is required to notify a job applicant that a background report will be obtained from an outside firm. The employer must receive written permission from the applicant prior to seeking a report. Some states require that a free copy be provided to the applicant. An employer who takes "adverse action" (e.g., not hiring) against the applicant, based upon the report (credit, criminal, or otherwise), must do the following: notify the applicant about the development, show the applicant the report, provide information on the applicant's rights under the FCRA, and allow the applicant to dispute any inaccurate information in the report with the reporting agency. Following this process, if the employer still takes adverse action, the applicant must be notified of the action, with justification.

The EEOC has issued guidelines to protect applicants against discrimination from background investigations. For example, before an employer makes an adverse decision on hiring or promoting based upon the candidate's personal financial data, the information should be job related, current, and severe. An employer, for instance, may decide not to offer a financial position to a candidate who has serious, current debt. The FCRA prohibits the use of negative information that is older than seven years. Applicants can bring legal action if they are rejected because of a poor credit record, but can show good reasons for their financial problems.[18]

An applicant's criminal history, if any, is a prime concern of employers, especially when the applicant is applying for a loss prevention position. Asking about an applicant's arrest record is generally unlawful, but conviction records legally are obtainable in most jurisdictions; they usually are public records on file at court offices. If an applicant appears to have no convictions, it is possible that the background investigator did not search court records in other jurisdictions where the applicant has lived.

History and Controversy: Polygraph and PSE

Background information on the polygraph and psychological stress evaluator (PSE) will assist the reader in understanding the controversy and subsequent legal restrictions on these devices. In 1895, Cesare Lombroso used the first scientific instrument to detect deception through changes in pulse and blood pressure. In 1921, Dr. John A. Larson developed the polygraph, which measured blood pressure, respiration, and pulse. By 1949, Leonard Keeler added galvanic skin response (i.e., electrical changes on the surface of the skin).

The PSE was developed for the U.S. Army in 1964 by Robert McQuiston, Allan Bell, and Wilson Ford. After it was rejected by the Army, McQuiston patented a civilian version and marketed it to the private sector.

When questions are asked during a polygraph exam, bodily changes are recorded on graph paper. The examiner interprets these readings vis-à-vis questions asked. Persons have been known to try to "fool" the polygraph by biting their tongues or pressing a toe into a thumbtack previously hidden in their shoes. The PSE has a few variations, but basically it records voice stress as questions are asked. There is no hookup, so it can be used covertly.

A disadvantage of the PSE is that only one factor is being recorded, as opposed to the multiple factors of the polygraph. Training for administering and interpreting the PSE is shorter than for the polygraph. The accuracy of either device is subject to considerable debate, especially concerning the PSE. University of Utah research concluded that the polygraph can be over 90 percent accurate.[19] Much depends on the skill of the examiner behind the device. The polygraph has been responsible for eliminating undesirable job applicants, in addition to assisting with criminal and civil cases, but at the same time, abuses have occurred that resulted in the passage of the Employee Polygraph Protection Act.

Employee Polygraph Protection Act of 1988

The Employee Polygraph Protection Act (EPPA) was passed by Congress and signed into law by then-president Ronald Reagan on June 27, 1988. It became effective on December 27. The act prohibits most private employers from using polygraph or "lie detector" tests to screen job applicants and greatly restricts the use of these instruments to test present employees. The EPPA defines the term *lie detector* to include any device that is used to render a diagnostic opinion regarding the honesty of an individual. The congressional Office of Technology Assessment estimated that 2 million polygraph exams had been conducted each year—90 percent by private employers.

The EPPA states that it is unlawful for an employer to directly or indirectly force an employee to submit to a polygraph test. Discrimination against those who refuse to be tested or who file a complaint under the EPPA is prohibited. Employers who violate the EPPA may be assessed a civil penalty up to $10,000 for each violation. In addition, the Secretary of Labor may seek a restraining order enjoining the employer from violating the act. The law provides individuals with the right to sue employers in federal and state courts for employment reinstatement, promotion, and payment of lost wages and benefits.

A few kinds of employees are exempt from the act and can be tested, including employees of:

- National security organizations or defense industries
- Federal, state, and local governments
- Businesses involved with controlled substances
- Certain security service firms, such as armored car or security alarm firms

In addition, a limited exemption exists for any employer who is conducting an ongoing investigation involving economic loss or injury; the suspect employee must have had access to the subject of the investigation, and reasonable suspicion must be present. Considerable justification and documentation is required. Chapter 10 contains proper testing procedures under the EPPA.

Past employment is a crucial area of inquiry because it reveals past job performance. However, human resources offices may be reluctant to supply information because of the potential for defamation suits.

The personal references supplied by the applicant usually are those of people who will make favorable comments about the applicant. If an investigator can obtain additional references from contacting references, more will be learned about the applicant.

Most colleges will verify an applicant's attendance and degree over the telephone. College transcripts can be checked out by mail as long as a copy of the applicant's authorization is enclosed. This conforms to privacy legislation. When educational records are received, the investigator should study characteristics and look for inconsistencies.

The private use of public records is on the increase for background investigations. As we know, conviction records are available in most jurisdictions. Records from state motor vehicle departments can reveal a history of careless driving behavior. A motor vehicle report (MVR) can serve as a cross-check for name, date of birth, and physical description. Federal court records expose violations of federal laws, civil litigation, and bankruptcy. Chapter 10 discusses online databases for acquiring information.

Why do you think there is so much government legal regulation of staffing organizations?

Hire The Right Person, Not the Wrong One!

An error in hiring can bring crime to the workplace, loss of proprietary information, and litigation. Security managers have a duty to work with employers to avoid hiring an employee who:

- Has been convicted of embezzlement, but is handling accounts payable
- Has a history of convictions for computer crimes, but is a corporate IT specialist
- Has a history of convictions for felony drug offenses, robberies, and burglaries, but is working with the cleaning crew
- Has been convicted of securities violations and insider trading, but is working in the corporate public information department
- Has a history of child molestation convictions, but is working in corporate daycare
- Is a convicted rapist, but is working as a security officer escorting female employees to their vehicles at night
- As a temporary employee collecting trash throughout the premises, is really a news reporter seeking a story
- While working in research and development, is really an industrial spy collecting information to sell to a competitor

EMPLOYEE SOCIALIZATION

Socialization, the learning process whereby an employee gains knowledge about the employer and how to become a productive worker, is broader in scope than orientation and training programs. Employers who understand the socialization process are likely to enhance the value of employees to the organization. Furthermore, losses can be reduced as employees adhere to loss prevention strategies. The following emphasizes orientation, training programs, examples set by superiors, and employee needs.

Loss Prevention Orientation for New Employees

When new employees begin to work for an organization, the orientation session plays a significant role in the socialization process. Examples set at the beginning can go a long way in preventing future problems and losses. The orientation program should be designed to acquaint the new employees with the "big picture" of loss prevention. Such discussion can enhance the employee's understanding of the objectives of the loss prevention program, how employees can help, and the benefits to everyone.

Employee Training

In this discussion the focus is on training protection personnel, but the principles that follow can apply to a variety of training programs for a broad spectrum of employees.

Despite the training problems of the security industry, as covered in Chapter 2, increasing numbers of practitioners in the field realize the importance of training. Consequently, training standards and programs constantly are being upgraded. Although training costs money, the investment is well worth it. Training helps to prevent problems such as critical incidents and litigation. Training provides personnel with an improved understanding of what is expected of them, heightens morale and motivation, and reduces disciplinary problems. All these benefits are impossible unless there is management support for training.

Planning Training

Step 1: Training Needs

Several questions need to be answered. Who are the recipients of the training (loss prevention personnel or regular employees; new or experienced employees)? What training programs are available? What deficiencies were noted in employee evaluations? What are the suggestions from supervisors? What are the suggestions from employees? Of particular importance is to conduct a *job and task analysis* to pinpoint the skills required for the job.

Step 2: Budget

Before the training program is prepared, an estimate of money available is necessary, since one cannot spend what one does not have.

Step 3: Behavioral Objectives

Each behavioral objective consists of a statement, usually one sentence, that describes the behavioral changes that the student should undergo because of the training. For example, loss prevention officers must explain how the Fifth Amendment to the Bill of Rights relates to the private sector.

Step 4: Training Program Outline

With the use of the behavioral objectives, an outline is prepared. It can be considered a step-by-step sequence for training.

Step 5: Learning Medium

The method of presentation is described. Various strategies are available, such as lecture, discussion, demonstration, case method, and role playing.

Many training programs use a mixture of techniques. Scenario training, for example, creates workplace situations that trainees will encounter on the job. Initially, managers must determine what types of behavior or performance are desired. Then, the training is designed around such objectives. Several trainees can participate in each scripted scenario, acting as security officers, employees, customers, visitors, and evaluators. As the scenarios change, so should the roles of the trainees. Examples of scenarios are: assisting a visitor who is lost and upset about being late to a meeting; assisting a handicapped person who must deal with an inoperable elevator; barring access to an estranged spouse of an employee; and responding to a report of employee theft. A variation of scenario training is written scenario testing whereby the trainee reads a script and decides what to do and why. As with all training methods, feedback by the instructor is essential so performance can be improved.[20]

Various computer-assisted learning media are available as training aids. Each is characterized by advantages and disadvantages. Whereas the traditional classroom offers an instructor who can provide immediate guidance and feedback to students, computer-assisted, self-paced, and distance learning via the Internet offer a mixture of approaches in providing guidance and feedback to students. How "hands-on" and scenario training are incorporated into the choice of learning medium, plus how simulation relates to the actual job site, should also be considered.[21]

Step 6: Evaluation, Feedback, and Revision

After the training is completed, the students should provide valuable feedback to the instructor. An evaluation questionnaire, completed by students, can guide the instructor in revising the training program. The training is further validated through interviews of participants and supervisors a few months after the training to see if the training helped participants to perform their tasks effectively and to identify topics requiring more or less attention. Audits can be used to further assess the success of training. This can entail observing an employee on the job, checking the quality of written reports, or hiring external investigators to audit the courtesy of employees or perform access penetration tests.

Learning Principles

1. Learning results in a behavioral change. Learning objectives are stated in terms of specific behaviors. When a student is able to perform a task that he or she was unable to perform before a training program, then behavior has changed.
2. Tests are used to measure the changed behavior.
3. If the proper conditions for learning are presented to students, learning will take place. The teacher should help the student to learn by facilitating learning through effective instructional methods.
4. An instructional program should begin with basic introductory information to develop a foundation for advanced information.

5. Feedback, an instructor informing the student whether a response was correct or incorrect, is vital to learning.
6. An instructional program must consider the learner's ability to absorb information.
7. A student will be more receptive to learning if information is job related.
8. Conditioning aids the learning process. Conditioning can be perceived as a method of molding or preparing a student for something through constant practice; for example, repetitive drills so that employees know exactly what to do in case of fire.
9. Increased learning will take place if the practice is spread out over time as opposed to a single, lengthy practice session.
10. Information that is learned and understood is remembered longer than that which is learned by rote.

Wasted Training

In an article in *Administrative Management*, "How Not to Waste Your Training Dollars," Donald J. Tosti declares that "American businesses and government agencies spend about $7 billion a year on training, and by the best estimates half of that amount is wasted."[22] He also states that "the company training instructor who assumes the traditional chalk-in-hand teacher role will have little effect in changing worker behavior."[23] Tosti describes "Seven Deadly Sins of Training," which are still applicable today:

1. Using training to solve motivational problems.
2. Making training more complicated than is necessary.
3. Training personnel at the wrong time, such as training all of an organization's employees for a program that will be instituted in two years.
4. Overtraining, such as instructing retail clerks on the theoretical aspects of their job before explaining important procedural aspects of retailing.
5. Failing to understand the true costs of training.
6. Failing to calculate training on a cost-effective basis. Evaluations of training programs help to predict benefits. Questions of concern are these: Did employees learn and apply the new information? Are losses reduced? Was the training worth the money?
7. Following fads in training.

Think about a training program or course you attended in the past. In what ways could it have been improved?

Examples Set by Superiors

Poor example setting is pervasive in many organizations. All organizations have informal rules that serve as guides to action. These rules often are transmitted to subordinates from superiors. The length of the 15-minute coffee break varies within organizations; the amount of time allowed before an employee is considered late also varies; the number of minor safety violations permitted before strict disciplinary action differs from one organization to another as well as from one superior to another. Clearly, superiors serve as teachers and role models. The actions of superiors greatly affect subordinate performance. Poor supervision results in both low subordinate productivity and losses.

A supervisor can be perceived to be what sociologists call an *agent of socialization*, a person who plays a dominant role in the socialization of an individual. In society, parents, teachers, and clergy are agents of socialization. In a business organization, a supervisor becomes an agent of socialization after establishing a working relationship with a new employee. The superior first makes the new employee feel some degree of belonging, in calming the uneasy new worker. The superior may have to skillfully break down the old methods that the new subordinate may have carried over from a previous job.

Because first impressions are lasting, the initial part of the socialization process is important. A good example must be set in the beginning.

> Based upon your experience, can you think of any poor examples set by superiors in the workplace?

Employee Needs

The way an organization responds to employee needs has an impact not only on the socialization process, but also on losses. When employee needs are met, workers also learn about the employment environment. They learn that management and supervisors care; the employee learns to respect and appreciate the employment environment while helping to reduce losses.

What are employee needs? Psychologist *Abraham Maslow* became famous for designing a "hierarchy of needs" in the early 1950s[24] (see Figure 6-1). Maslow's view is that people are always in a state of want, but what they want depends upon their level within the hierarchy of human needs.

Lower level needs must be satisfied before upper level needs. Maslow's hierarchy of needs follows:

Figure 6–1 Maslow's hierarchy of needs.

Poor Example Set by Ralph Marks, Loss Prevention Manager

The Locost retail store chain emphasized the importance of loss prevention procedures as an aid to increased profits. All employees were expected to adhere to these procedures. The loss prevention manager at each store was expected to reinforce the program. Each store's employees looked to the loss prevention manager for guidance.

At one particular store, Ralph Marks, the loss prevention manager, made a serious mistake. All retail employees were permitted to make purchases and receive a 15 percent discount. Procedures dictated that items bought were to be recorded and then stored under a designated counter until the end of the day. When Ralph Marks bought a stereo for his car, he did not follow the appropriate procedures. He installed the stereo during working hours, which also compounded the poor example. By the end of the working day, all retail employees had seen or heard of this incident. This poor example caused many employees to lose respect for the manager and the loss prevention program.

- *Basic physiological needs.* Survival needs such as food, water, and the elimination of wastes can be satisfied with employer assistance. A well-run company cafeteria and clean lavatories are examples.
- *Safety and security needs.* This need relates to order in one's life. A person needs to feel free from anxiety and fear. Adequate wages, medical insurance, and workplace safety help to satisfy these needs.
- *Societal needs.* The need to be loved and have friends and the need for esteem can be fulfilled by supervisors. A supervisor should praise a

subordinate when appropriate. Employees should receive recognition or awards after completing a good job. Employee socials also are helpful.

- *Esteem and status needs*. A person needs to be competent, to achieve, and to gain approval and respect.
- *Self-actualization needs*. This need is at the top of the hierarchy of needs. It signifies that a person has reached his or her full potential, whether as a janitor, homemaker, doctor, or whatever. An organization and its superiors can do a lot (e.g., training, promotion) in assisting an employee to fulfill this need.

Employees learn which needs are satisfied and which are not. Suppose a workplace has a terrible cafeteria, dirty lavatories, poor wages, limited medical insurance, an inadequate safety program, authoritarian supervisors, and poor training and promotional opportunities. What level of losses would be sustained at this workplace in comparison to another that adhered to Maslow's hierarchy of human needs?

How do you think corporate downsizing affects Maslow's hierarchy of human needs and loss prevention?

Career: Utilities Security

We all enjoy the services offered to us through utilities. When these services are interrupted, our lives become difficult. Utility security specialists are among the many employees of utilities who work to protect these vital services.

Duties: Protect personnel, property, and equipment in the event of crime, disaster, resource shortage, civil disturbance, or war. Maintain 24 hour protection and access controls, operate security systems, investigate, conduct inspections, plan, interface with regulatory agencies, and adhere to state and federal regulations.

Prerequisites: For management, associate degree, but undergraduate degree preferred, 4–8 years of experience, may need special clearance, CPP preferred.

Demographics of typical practitioner: Associate or undergraduate degree; 10–15 years in security; 5–10 years in specialty; $35,000–60,000 yr.; titles: Security Supervisor, Nuclear Security Manager, Security Manager, Risk Manager, Security Director.

Source: American Society for Industrial Security, *Career Opportunities in Security* (Alexandria, VA: ASIS, 1998), p. 17.

Search the Web

Check out the Web site for the Society for Human Resource Management (http://www.shrm.org/). Should a security practitioner join this organization? Why or why not?

Use your favorite search engines to see what types of security training are available on the Web.

Use the Web to check on how the security industry is regulated in your state. What are the requirements for registering, screening, and training security officers in your state?

CASE PROBLEMS

6A. Plan and write a step-by-step screening process for applicants interested in uniformed loss prevention positions. Formulate an application form. Pay particularly close attention to applicable laws.

6B. You are seeking a position as a security officer at a research and development company. Officers at this site wear blazers and focus on access controls and protecting people and information. The job pays well, with opportunity for advancement, so you strive to do your best at each stage of the applicant screening process. You now must complete an assessment center "in-basket" exercise where you are to prioritize the following items, with justification for each, upon reaching the scene of an assault in the parking lot.

A witness to the assault approaches you to offer information.

Someone who is scaling the perimeter fence is screaming for help because of being stuck in the razor ribbon.

An employee approaches you for help because he locked his keys in his car.

You receive a radio transmission from your supervisor who wants to meet with you immediately.

The victim is down and bleeding.

You must complete an incident report for this case.

A car alarm has been activated.

6C. You are a candidate for the position of security manager for a large shopping mall near a major city. The number of candidates has been narrowed to six and the mall human resources manager has decided to use an "in-basket" exercise to further narrow the list of candidates. The "in-basket" exercise consists of a series of memoranda, telephone calls, and radio transmissions that the mall security manager would encounter in the job. Your task is to read all items, set priorities among them, and write what action you would take and the reasoning for your action for each item. The date is September 24. The time to complete this assignment is 60 minutes. It is possible that all candidates will be handed additional memoranda, telephone messages, or radio transmissions during the exercise. A review panel (police captain, firefighter, college educator, and mall security officer) will evaluate each candidate's work without knowing the identity of the writer.[*]

Item 1

TO: Mall Security Manager
FROM: Mall Manager
SUBJECT: Security Seminar
DATE: September 20
Several merchants would like a seminar on security before the busy holiday season. Please get back to me as soon as possible.

Item 2

TO: Mall Security Manager
FROM: Human Resources Manager, Bigmart Department Store
SUBJECT: Selection of Store Detective
DATE: September 24
Please walk over to review the applications for store detective. I have no idea who would be the best one.

Item 3

TELEPHONE MESSAGE: September 21
Mr. John Poston, a mall customer, called again. He is still irate about the damage to his car window when Security Officer Mallory broke into the vehicle after Mr. Poston left his keys in the ignition. Mr. Poston is threatening to sue.

Item 4

TELEPHONE MESSAGE: September 20
Mrs. Johnson, owner of the Befit Health Store, thinks someone is entering her store at night. She is very upset and worried, and wants you to meet her at her store.

Item 5

TO: Mall Security Manager
FROM: Mall Manager

---

[*]Source: Philip P. Purpura, *Retail Security and Shrinkage Protection* (Boston: Butterworth–Heinemann, 1993), pp. 327–329.

SUBJECT: Application Verification
DATE: September 22
The Westwood Mall office called to verify your application for their job opening in security. Are you planning to begin another job? Please let me know immediately. Let's talk.

Item 6

RADIO TRANSMISSION: September 24, 11:15 A.M.
"Four year old boy lost at south end of mall. We have not been able to locate for one hour."

Item 7

TELEPHONE MESSAGE: September 23
Attorney for the plaintiff who was assaulted in the parking lot last month wants you to call him right away.

Item 8

TO: Mall Security Manager
FROM: Mall Manager
SUBJECT: Security/Safety Plan
DATE: September 16
In speaking with other mall managers at a recent seminar, they mentioned their security/safety plans. We probably need to have one, too. Please respond.

Item 9

RADIO TRANSMISSION: September 24, 11:20 A.M.
"Small fire in stock room of Smith's Department Store. We can put it out."

Item 10

TO: Mall Security Manager
FROM: Paula Reed, Security Officer
SUBJECT: Pay Raise
DATE: September 23
I am not pleased about my raise of only $0.15 per hour. I have been doing a good job and I really work hard when we get busy. The male security officers are making much more than my rate per hour. I believe that this difference is because I am a black woman. We have talked about this already, but you haven't done anything about it. I want something done right away or I will take legal action.

Item 11
TELEPHONE MESSAGE: September 22
The manager of Hall Stuart Clothes wants to know why it took so long
for security to respond to a shoplifting incident yesterday.

6D. You are a security manager who has just been given an assignment
by the vice president of human resources to obtain a copy of an e-mail containing racial jokes that has been circulating in the company. She has
received complaints about the e-mail and wants you to bring it to a meeting
to provide input for corrective action. A short time later you obtain the e-
mail, which contains the story of a young man named Boy. One of the sentences states: "I axed my mudder for some money. She had only too bucks
so I axed my fiend, Kenya spare a quarter. He said no so Afro a chair at
him."[25] As the security manager, what do you suggest at the meeting?

THE DECISION FOR "YOU BE THE JUDGE"

Ultimately, no, but the company had to run a gantlet before breaking out
into the clear. There were conflicting judgments at two lower court levels,
but finally a higher court ruled in favor of Hi-Mark. In the end, Zaleszny did
not win anything. This case is based on *Griffiths* v. *CIGN*, 988 F 2nd 457 3rd
Circuit Court (1993). The names in this case have been changed to protect
the privacy of those involved.

Comment

The fact that his company had to go through appeals can give you pause.
You might suppose that simple logic should have upheld Hi-Mark from the
outset. If the company didn't prosecute, how could it be guilty of malicious
prosecution? If the manager who fired Zaleszny didn't know about his EEOC
complaint, how could the firing have been a retaliation for the complaint?
And why didn't these lines of reasoning prevail right away? Because logic
doesn't always prevail in court. Often, other variables are in play, including
the effectiveness with which a case is presented, a jury's understanding of a
judge's instructions, the extent to which all parties understand the relevant
law, and even the personalities in the courtroom.

The two questions that confronted this company can be minefields.
What should you do about prosecution of a crime suspect? Can you safely
fire an employee who has engaged in a protected activity, such as complain-
ing to a federal watchdog agency? Be sure to get a qualified attorney's advice
whenever you face these questions.

NOTES

1. Richard A. Mann and Barry S. Roberts, *Essentials of Business Law*, 7th ed. (Cincinnati, OH: West Pub., 2001), p. 859.
2. John Ivancevich, *Human Resources Management*, 8th ed. (New York: McGraw-Hill, 2001), p. 74.
3. EEOC, *Change Statistics, FY 1992 to FY 2000*. (http//www.eeoc.gov/) (March 19, 2001).
4. Herbert G. Heneman, et al., *Staffing Organization*, 2nd ed. (Middleton, WI: Irwin Pub., 1997), pp. 62–64.
5. Lloyd Byars and Leslie Rue, *Human Resource Management*, 5th ed. (Chicago: Irwin Pub., 1997), p. 8.
6. "Census shows Hispanic, black numbers nearly equal," *USA Today* (http://USA-TODAY.com/) (March 15, 2001).
7. Howard N. Fullerton, Jr., "The American Work Force, 1992-2005: Another Look at the Labor Force," *Monthly Labor Review* (November 1993), pp. 31–40.
8. Byars and Rue, *Human Resource Management*, p. 10.
9. Francis Hamit, "ASIS Confronts a Changing Demographic," *Security Technology & Design* 10 (October 2000), pp. 60–62.
10. Michael Levy and Barton Weitz, *Retailing Management*, 4th ed. (New York: McGraw-Hill, 2001), pp. 313–314.
11. Dawn D. Bennett-Alexander and Laura B. Pincus, *Employment Law for Business* (Chicago: Irwin Pub., 1995), p. 219.
12. "Lying on Job Applications May Be Widespread," *Security* (February 1988), p. 13.
13. Christopher J. Bachler, "Resume Fraud: Lies, Omissions, and Exaggerations," *Personnel Journal* (June 1995), pp. 51–60.
14. "Have You Tried the Internet?" *Security Watch* 2903 (February 1, 2000), pp. 1–2.
15. David Twomey, Marianne Jennings, and Ivan Fox, *Anderson's Business Law and the Regulatory Environment*, 14th ed. (Cincinnati, OH: West Pub., 2001), p. 789.
16. Raymond A. Noe, et al., *Human Resource Management: Gaining a Competitive Advantage* (Chicago: Irwin Pub., 1997), pp. 320–321.
17. Ibid., p. 326.
18. Frederick Giles, "Checking Credit When It's Due," *Security Management* 44 (June 2000), pp. 107–111.
19. U.S. Department of Justice, *Validity and Reliability of Detection of Deception* (Washington, D.C.: U.S. Government Printing Office, 1978), p. 8.
20. Eric Dominguez, "Training That Triumphs," *Security Management* 43 (June 1999), pp. 29–30.
21. Gerald Beckmann, "Security Training: Testing Your Staff's Competency," *Security Technology & Design* 9 (July 1999), pp. 22–28.
22. Donald J. Tosti, "How Not to Waste Your Training Dollars," *Administrative Management* 41, No. 2 (February 1980), p. 44.
23. Ibid., p. 45.
24. Abraham H. Maslow, *Motivation and Personality* (New York: Harper & Row, 1954).
25. Philip Purpura, *Police & Community: Concepts & Cases* (Boston: Allyn & Bacon, 2001), p. 189.

7

Internal Threats and Countermeasures

OBJECTIVES

After studying this chapter the reader will be able to:

1. Describe the broad spectrum of internal threats and the IT threat from within.
2. Explain the internal theft problem.
3. Outline at least five management countermeasures to prevent internal theft.
4. List and explain the steps involved in confronting an employee suspected of internal theft.
5. Explain integration and open architecture.
6. Outline access control methods and systems, including the types of cards used for access.
7. List and describe at least three types of locks.
8. List and describe at least five types of interior intrusion detection sensors.
9. Describe CCTV technology.
10. Explain the characteristics of safes.

Internal loss prevention focuses on threats from inside an organization. Crimes, fires, and accidents are major internal loss problems. Internal threats also include violence in the workplace and theft of proprietary information. Productivity losses illustrate the range of internal losses. Such losses can result from poor plant layout or substance abuse by employees. Other productivity losses result from employees who loaf, arrive at work late, leave early, abuse coffee breaks, socialize excessively, and prolong work to create overtime; these abuses are called *theft of time*. Faulty measuring devices, which may or may not be known to employees, are another cause of losses. Scales or dispensing devices that measure things ranging from truck weight to copper wire length are examples.

We can see that the spectrum of internal threats is broad. Although this chapter focuses on internal theft and associated countermeasures, the strategies covered also apply to many internal and external (e.g., burglary, robbery, espionage) threats.

The IT Threat from Within

Although the media concentrates on a few high-profile outsider cyber-attacks, the greatest threat to corporate information systems is from within. Because news of many insider attacks is not released to the public, the frequency of the following scenario is impossible to gauge: A systems administrator in one hospital learned that she was about to be fired, so she arranged for a "severance package" for herself by encrypting a critical patient database. Her supervisor feared the worst and loss of his job, so in exchange for the decryption key, the manager arranged for a termination "bonus" and an agreement that the hospital would not prosecute.[1]

The dilemma facing the hospital, as to whether to meet the offender's demands or prosecute, can produce interesting debate. How long could the hospital function without the critical patient database? How much time would be required by the criminal justice system to resolve the case? As we know from previous chapters, there are several procedural steps to a criminal case, and the decision to prosecute has its advantages and disadvantages.

Computer industry research shows the average internal attack costs a company $2.7 million, compared with $57,000 for an external attack. Technical solutions alone are not the answer because internal attacks are a *people* problem requiring personnel security solutions. The challenges include the expense of money and time for increased security and the shortage of IT personnel, who may seek a less rigid security environment. Another challenge is the psychological profile (a generalization) of IT employees, who tend to be introverts, prefer to work independently, are less likely to handle work stress in a constructive manner, and may show their disgruntled behavior online rather than in the lunchroom. Conviction checks may be ineffective with IT personnel because their misdeeds are likely to be unrecorded, and as in the case of the hospital systems administrator, unreported. At-risk behaviors, however, can lead to exposure by supervisors and coworkers. Examples include personnel who avoid procedures and hack into a system to fix problems, curious individuals who explore the system while violating security policies, individuals who cause outages to facilitate their own travel or advancement, and those who steal proprietary information to become outside consultants. Another challenge is the frequent physical separation of the IT department from the physical security, legal, and human resources departments. A closer physical presence of other departments can impact personnel issues more intensely.[2]

To personalize the information presented in this chapter, three businesses are described: a retail lumber business (see Figure 7-1), a clothing manufacturing plant (see Figure 7-2), and a research facility (see Figure 7-3). Suppose you are a loss prevention specialist working for a corporation that

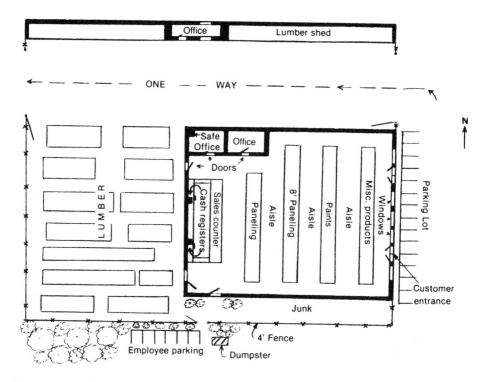

Figure 7–1 Woody's Lumber Company. Woody's Lumber Company has suffered declining profits in recent years. A new manager recently was hired who quickly hired six people to replace the previous crew, which was fired for internal theft. Four additional people were quickly hired for part-time work. The process for conducting business is to have customers park their cars in the front of the store, walk to the sales counter to pay for the desired lumber, receive a pink receipt, drive to the rear of the store, pick up the lumber with the assistance of the yard crew, and then depart through the rear auto exit. At the lumber company, loss prevention is of minimal concern. An inoperable burglar alarm and two fire extinguishers are on the premises.

has just purchased these three businesses. Your supervisor informs you that you are responsible for recommending modifications at these facilities to improve internal loss prevention. First read this chapter, then proceed to the case problem pertaining to these businesses at the end of the chapter.

INTERNAL THEFT

How Serious Is the Problem?

Internal theft also is referred to as employee theft, pilferage, embezzlement, stealing, peculation, and defalcation. *Employee theft* is stealing by employ-

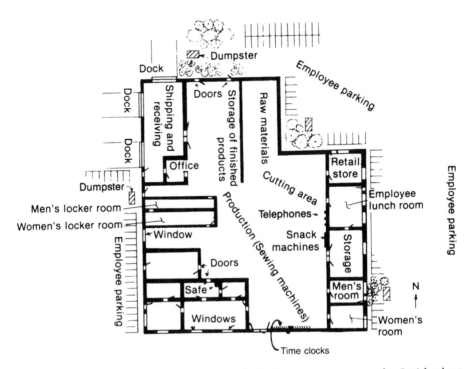

Figure 7–2 Smith Shirt manufacturing plant. In the past two years, the Smith plant has shown declining profits. During this time, managers believed that employee theft might be the cause, but they were unsure of what to do and were worried about additional costs. Employees work one shift from 8 A.M. to 5 P.M. five days per week and are permitted to go to their cars to eat lunch from noon to 1 P.M. A total of 425 employees are divided as follows: 350 sewing machine operators, 15 maintenance personnel, 20 material handlers, 20 miscellaneous workers, 2 retail salespeople, 5 managers, and 13 clerical support staff members. A contract cleanup crew works from 6 to 8 A.M. and from 5 to 7 P.M. on Monday, Wednesday, and Friday; Sunday cleanup is from 1 to 4 P.M. The crew members have their own keys. Garbage dumpster pickup is 7 A.M. and 7 P.M. Monday, Wednesday, and Friday. The plant contains a fire alarm system and four fire extinguishers. One physical inventory is conducted each year.

ees from their employers. *Pilferage* is stealing in small quantities. *Embezzlement* occurs when a person takes money or property that has been entrusted to his or her care; a breach of trust occurs. *Peculation* and *defalcation* are synonyms for embezzlement. Whatever term is used, this problem is an insidious menace to the survival of businesses, institutions, and organizations. This threat is so severe in many workplaces that employees steal anything that is not "nailed down."

The total estimated cost of employee theft varies from one source to another, mainly because theft is defined and data is collected in so many

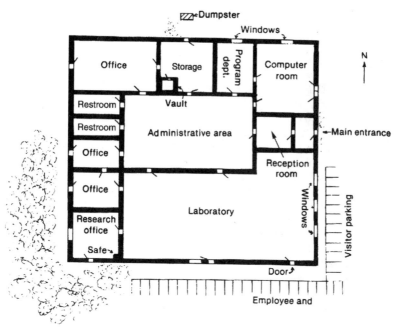

Figure 7–3 Compulab Corporation. Compulab Corporation is a research business with tremendous potential. However, it seems that whenever it produces innovative research results, a competitor claims similar results soon afterward. Compulab employs 33 people, including a research director, 2 assistants, 10 scientist-researchers, 8 computer specialists, and an assortment of office staff. The facility is open 24 hours a day, 7 days per week, and employees work a mixture of shifts each month. Almost every employee has his or her own key for entrance into the building.

different ways. According to the U.S. Chamber of Commerce, 30 percent of business failures result from employee theft with more than $120 billion lost annually to American companies.[3] The Association of Certified Fraud Examiners found that 6 percent of an organization's revenues are lost to employee fraud and abuse, totaling $400 billion annually.[4] However, these figures may be only the tip of the iceberg when direct and indirect costs are combined. Indirect costs can include a slowing of production or an insurance premium hike after a claim. Research by Baker and Westin mentions employee morale and damage to public image as expensive indirect costs following major internal crimes.[5]

Why Do Employees Steal?

There is no one reason why employees steal from their employers. However, two major causes of employee theft are employee personal problems and the environment.

"Let's Not Fire Him for Stealing—He's a Good Employee"

An undercover investigation at Smith's lumberyard #7 revealed that the yard boss, Joe Crate, was stealing. The undercover investigator, Jimmy Wilson, worked at yard #7 and found that Joe was stealing about $80 worth of building products per week. Each evening Joe would hide merchandise near the back gate, and when it was time to close up and lock the gate, he would quickly load his auto, which was conveniently parked nearby.

Before Jimmy was assigned to another yard, he met with a vice president and the manager of yard #7 at company headquarters. During the meeting, Jimmy asked, "Are you going to fire Joe Crate?" The VP stated, "Let's not fire him for stealing—he's a good employee." Then the VP explained: "Joe's salary is $10 per hour, which is equal to $400 per week. If Joe steals about $80 per week, then Joe's salary is about equal to $480 per week. If we hired a carpenter to build the lumber sheds that Joe is building at yard #7, it would cost us almost twice as much." Jimmy could not believe what he was hearing, especially from the VP. He did not say a word and listened to instructions for his next assignment.

What are your views of the way in which internal theft was handled at Smith's lumberyard #7 in the preceding box?

Employee personal problems often affect behavior on the job. Financial troubles, domestic discord, drug abuse, and excessive gambling can contribute to theft. It is inappropriate to state that every employee who has such problems will steal, but during trying times, the pressure to steal may be greater. A wise employer should be alert to troubled employees and suggest referral to an Employee Assistance Program (see Chapter 18).

The environment is perhaps the strongest factor behind internal theft. Politicians, corporate executives, and other "pillars of society" are constantly being found guilty of some form of crime. Inadequate socialization results. In other words, poor examples are set: employees may observe managerial illegalities and then act similarly. In many businesses, so many people are stealing that those who do not steal are the deviants and outcasts; theft becomes normal and honesty becomes abnormal. Some managers believe that employee theft improves morale and makes boring jobs exciting. In many workplaces employees are actually instructed to be dishonest. This can be seen when receiving department workers are told by their supervisor to accept overages during truck deliveries without notifying the vendor.

When employees steal, a hodgepodge of rationalizations (excuses) are mentally reviewed to relieve guilt feelings. Some of these rationalizations are "Everybody does it," "It's a fringe benefit," and "They aren't paying me enough."

Dr. Donald R. Cressey analyzed thousands of offenders to ascertain common factors associated with inside thievery.[6] He found three characteristics that must be present before theft will be committed. Cressey's *employee theft formula* is

Motivation + Opportunity + Rationalization = Theft

Motivation develops from a need for money to finance a debt or a drug problem or to win approval from others. Opportunity occurs at many unprotected locations, such as a loading dock. Rationalizations relieve guilt, as stated already. This formula illustrates the need for security and an honest environment.

Edwin Sutherland, a noted criminologist, offered his theory of *differential association* to explain crime. Simply put, criminal behavior is learned during interaction with others, and a person commits crime because of an excess of definitions favorable to violation of law over definitions unfavorable to violation of law. *The implication of this theory for the workplace is that superiors and colleagues in a company are probably a more important determinant of crime than is the personality of the individual.* A former head of the Securities and Exchange Commission's Division of Enforcement stated bluntly: "Our largest corporations have trained some of our brightest young people to be dishonest."[7]

A study of college student knowledge of how to commit computer crimes found that threat of punishment had little influence on their misdeeds. In this study, the strongest predictor of computer crime was differential association with others who presented definitions favorable to violation of the law.[8]

The implications for security from differential association theory point to the importance of ethical conduct by top management, who should set a good example in the socialization of all employees. Also, since criminal laws can be impotent, preventive security strategies are essential.

How Do Employees Steal?

The methods used to steal from employers are limited by employee imagination. Typically, employees pilfer items by hiding them under their clothing before leaving the workplace. More sophisticated methods involve the careful manipulation of accounting records. Collusion among several employees (and outsiders) is common. The kinds of item to be taken (e.g., tools, a piano, cash) and the obstacles (e.g., loss prevention strategies) dictate the method of theft. A tool can be hidden in a person's pocket or underwear, and a piano might be pilfered piece by piece over a year and then assembled in a home garage. Some employee theft methods follow:

1. Wearing manufactured items while leaving the workplace—for example, wearing pilfered underwear or wearing scrap lead that has been molded to one's body contours
2. Smuggling out pilfered items by placing the item in a lunchbox, pocketbook, bundle of work clothes, radio, umbrella, newspaper, hat, or even one's hair
3. Hiding merchandise in garbage pails, dumpsters, or trash heaps to be retrieved at a later time
4. Returning to the workplace after hours, with a pass key, and helping oneself to goods
5. Truck drivers turning in fictitious bills to employers for fuel and repairs and then splitting the money with truck stops
6. Collusion between truck drivers and receiving personnel
7. Executives padding expense accounts
8. Purchasing agents receiving kickbacks from vendors for buying high-priced goods
9. Retail employees pocketing money from cash sales and not recording the transaction
10. Padding payrolls as to hours and rate of pay
11. Maintaining nonexistent or fired employees on a payroll and then cashing the paychecks
12. Accounts payable employees paying fictitious bills to a bogus account and then cashing the checks for their own use

Possible Indicators of Theft

Certain factors *may* indicate that theft has occurred:

1. Inventory records and physical counts that differ
2. Inaccurate accounting records
3. Mistakes in the shipping and receiving of goods
4. Increasing amounts of raw materials needed to produce a specific quantity of goods
5. Merchandise missing from boxes (e.g., every pallet of 20 boxes of finished goods has at least two boxes short a few items)
6. Merchandise at inappropriate locations (e.g., finished goods hidden near exits)
7. Security devices found to be damaged or inoperable
8. Windows or doors unlocked when they should be locked
9. Workers (e.g., employees, truck drivers, repair personnel) in unauthorized areas

10. Employees who come in early and leave late
11. Employees who eat lunch at their desks and refuse to take vacations
12. Complaints by customers about not having their previous payments credited to their accounts
13. Customers who absolutely have to be served by a particular employee
14. An unsupervised, after-hours cleaning crew with their own keys
15. Employees who are sensitive about routine questions concerning their jobs
16. An employee who is living beyond his or her income level
17. Expense accounts that are outside of the norm

MANAGEMENT COUNTERMEASURES

Management Support

Without management support, efforts to reduce losses are doomed. *A good management team sets both a foundation for strategies and an atmosphere in which theft is not tolerated.* Support for budget requests and appropriate policies and procedures is vital.

Effective Planning and Budgeting

Before implementing measures against internal theft, a thorough analysis of the problem is necessary. What types of losses are occurring, where, by whom, when, and why?

Internal and External Relations

Good internal and external relations can play a role in preventing employee theft. Loss prevention practitioners who show appropriate courtesy, demeanor, and appearance are respected by employees. Prompt investigations of incidents indicate that losses are a major concern.

With a heightened prevention atmosphere within a workplace, an external reputation is sure to follow. Outside people with ulterior motives will think twice before applying for a job.

Job Applicant Screening and Employee Socialization

The screening of job applicants from full-time to part-time and temporary workers is a major theft-prevention technique. Whatever steps are taken, an atmosphere of loss prevention should exist from every applicant's initial contact.

Accountability, Accounting, and Auditing

Accountability defines a responsibility for and a description of something. For example, John Smith is responsible (i.e., is held accountable) for all finished products in a plant, and he maintains accurate records (i.e., a description) of what is in stock. *Accounting* is concerned with recording, sorting, summarizing, reporting, and interpreting business data. *Auditing* is an examination or check of a system to uncover deviations. Personnel audit physical security by checking alarms, CCTV, and so on. An auditor audits the accounting records of a company to see if the records are reliable and to make sure embezzlement has not occurred.

Policy and Procedural Controls

These controls coincide with accountability, accounting, and auditing. In each of these three functions, policies and procedures are dictated to employees through manuals and memos. *Policies* are management tools that control employee decision making and reflect the goals and objectives of management. *Procedures* guide action to fulfill the requirements of policies.

As an example, a company policy states that, before trash is taken to outside dumpsters, a loss prevention officer must be present to check for stolen items. Procedures point out that to conform to this policy the head of the cleaning crew must call the loss prevention office and wait for an officer to arrive before transporting the trash outside.

Signs

Placing messages about loss prevention on the premises is another method. The message must be brief, to the point, and in languages for diverse readers. An example of a message is "Let's all work together to reduce losses and save jobs."

Toll-Free Number and Reward System

Numerous organizations have established a toll-free number to facilitate ease of loss reporting. A company Web site is another avenue to facilitate loss reporting. A reward system is a strategy to reinforce reporting. One method employed is to provide the informant with a secret number that is required to pick up reward money at a bank at a time convenient to the caller, who is encouraged to send a substitute to strengthen anonymity.

Investigation

Employee thieves often are familiar with the ins and outs of an organization's operation and can easily conceal theft. In addition, a thorough knowledge of the loss prevention program is common to employee thieves. Consequently, an undercover investigation is an effective method to outwit and expose crafty employee thieves and their conspirators.

Property Losses and Theft Detection

To remedy property or tool losses within a firm, three recommendations are (1) set up an inventory system, (2) mark property, and (3) use metal detectors. An *inventory system* maintains accountability for property and tools. When employees borrow or use equipment or tools a record is kept of the item, its serial number, the employee's name, and the date. On return of the item, a notation is made, including the date, by both the clerk and the user.

Marking property (e.g., tools, computers, furniture) serves several useful purposes. When property is marked with a serial number, or a firm's name is etched with an engraving tool, thieves are deterred because the property can be identified if the thief is caught. Publicizing the marking of property reinforces the deterrent effect.

Fluorescent substances can be used to mark property. An ultraviolet light is necessary to view these invisible marks, which emerge as a surprise to the offender.

Organizations sometimes experience the theft of petty cash. To expose such theft, fluorescent substances, in the form of powder, crayon, or liquid, are used to mark money. The typical scenario involves a few suspects who are the only people with access to petty cash after hours. Before these after-hour employees arrive, the investigator handling the case places bills previously dusted with invisible fluorescent powder in envelopes at petty cash locations. The bills even can be written on with the invisible fluorescent crayon. Statements such as "marked money" can be used to identify the bills under ultraviolet light. Serial numbers from the bills are recorded and retained by the investigator. Before the employees are scheduled to leave, the "planted" bills are checked. If the bills are missing, then the employees' hands are checked under an ultraviolet light. Glowing hands expose the thief, and identification of the marked money carried by the individual strengthens the case. The marked money must be placed in an envelope because the fluorescent powder may transfer to other objects and onto an honest person's hands. A wrongful arrest can lead to a false-arrest suit. A check of a suspect's bills, for the marked money, helps avoid this problem. Many cleaning fluids appear orange under an ultraviolet light. The investigator should analyze all cleaning fluids on the premises and select a fluorescent color that is different from the cleaning substances. The use of a pinhole lens camera for covert surveillance is another investigative technique covered later in this chapter.

Walk-through *metal detectors*, similar to those at airports, are useful at employee exits to deter thefts of metal objects and to identify employee thieves. Such detectors also uncover weapons being brought into an area. Handheld metal detectors are also helpful.

Insurance, Bonding

If insurance is the prime bulwark against losses, premiums are likely to skyrocket and become too expensive. For this reason, *insurance is best utilized as a supplement to other methods of loss prevention that may fail.* Fidelity bonding is a type of employee honesty insurance for employees who handle cash and perform other financial activities. Bonding deters job applicants and employees with evil motives. Some companies have employees complete bonding applications but do not actually obtain the bond.

Confrontation with the Employee Suspect

Care must be exercised when confronting an employee suspect. The following recommendations, in conjunction with good legal assistance, can produce a strong case. The list of steps presents a cautious approach. Many locations require approval of management before an arrest.

1. Never accuse anyone unless absolutely certain of the theft.
2. Theft should be observed by a reliable person. Do not rely on hearsay.
3. Make sure you can show intent: the item stolen is owned by the organization, and it was removed from the premises by the person confronted.

In steps 4 through 14 an arrest has not been made.

4. *Ask* the suspect to come to the office for an interview. Employees do not have a right to have an attorney present during one of these employment meetings. If the person is a union employee and requests a union representative, comply with the request.[9]
5. Without accusing the employee, he or she can be told: "Some disturbing information has surfaced and we want you to provide an explanation."
6. Maintain accurate records of everything. These records may become an essential part of criminal or civil action.
7. Never threaten a suspect.
8. Never detain the suspect if the person wants to leave. Interview for less than one hour.
9. Never touch the suspect or reach into the suspect's pockets.
10. *Request permission* to search the suspect's belongings. If left alone in a room under surveillance, the suspect may take the item concealed on his or her person and hide it in the room. This approach avoids a search.
11. Have a witness present at all times. If the suspect is female and you are male, have another woman present.
12. If permissible under the Employee Polygraph Protection Act of 1988, ask the suspect to volunteer for a polygraph test and have the suspect sign a statement of voluntariness. Follow EPPA guidelines.
13. If verbal admission or confession is made by suspect, have him or her write it out, and have everyone present sign it.
14. *Ask* the suspect to sign a statement stipulating that no force or threats were applied.
15. For the uncooperative suspect, or if prosecution is favored, call the public police, but first be sure you have sound evidence as in step 3.
16. Do not accept payment for stolen property, because it can be construed as a bribe and it may interfere with a bond. Let the court determine restitution.
17. Handle juveniles differently from adults; consult the public police.
18. When in doubt, consult an attorney.

Prosecution

Many feel strongly that prosecution is a deterrent, whereas others maintain that it hurts morale and public relations and is not cost effective. Whatever management decides, it is imperative that an incident of theft be given considerable attention so that employees realize that a serious act has taken place. Establish a written policy that is fair and applied uniformly.

Research

Although employee theft is a significant national problem, limited research is available. One such research project was conducted by the University of Minnesota and the American Management Association with funds from the U.S. Department of Justice.[10] Thirty-five corporations including 4,985 employee respondents anonymously provided data. Conclusions from this research report that deserve further study are the following:

1. In the three industries studied (retail stores, electronic manufacturers, and hospitals), employees most likely to be involved in theft constitute a significant portion of the workforce: salespersons, engineers, and nurses.
2. The dissatisfied employee was found more frequently to be involved in theft.
3. The most consistent predictor of theft involvement was the employee's perceived chance of being caught.
4. Theft decreased when a negative reaction by management and coworkers increased.
5. Informal coworker sanctions are twice as influential in changing behavior as formal management responses.
6. Prevention measures have an effect on theft.
7. Those companies with a clearly defined antitheft policy had a lower incidence of theft.
8. Theft can be lowered by communicating antitheft policies to employees (e.g., through signs or memos).
9. A lesser degree of theft was found in businesses that had theft-prevention strategies within the inventory system.
10. Pre-employment screening deters theft.
11. Lower levels of theft can be achieved by instituting several strategies at once.

PHYSICAL SECURITY COUNTERMEASURES

What Is Integration and Open Architecture?

The physical security strategies covered in subsequent pages are being increasingly combined into what is called integrated systems. "An *integrated system* is the control and operation by a single operator of multiple systems whose perception is that only a single system is performing all functions."[11] These computer-based systems include access controls, alarm monitoring, CCTV, electronic article surveillance, fire protection and safety systems, HVAC, environmental monitoring, radio and video media, intercom, point-of-sale transactions, and inventory control. Such systems are installed within facilities worldwide, controlled and monitored by operators and management at a centralized workstation or from remote locations.

The benefits of integrated systems include lower costs, a reduction in staff, improved efficiency, centralization, and reduced travel and time costs. For example, a manufacturing executive at corporate headquarters can monitor a branch plant's operations, production, inventory, sales, and loss prevention. Likewise, a retail executive at headquarters can watch the sales floor, special displays, point-of-sale transactions, customer behavior, inventory, shrinkage, and loss prevention. *These "visits" to worldwide locations are conducted without leaving the office!*

Integration requires careful planning and clear answers to many questions, such as the following:

- Will the integrated system truly cost less and be easier to operate and maintain than separate systems? Obtain separate quotations on integrated and interconnected systems.
- Does the supplier truly have expertise across all of the applications?
- Is the integration software listed or approved by a third-party testing agency such as Underwriters Laboratories?
- Do authorities prohibit integration of certain systems? Some fire departments prohibit integrating fire alarm systems with other systems.[12]

Robert Pearson writes:

> When attending a conference or trade show, it becomes obvious that every vendor and manufacturer claims to have the "total integrated solution." It would appear that one would only need to place an order at any number of display booths and all the security problems at a user's facility would simply vanish. The vendors and manufacturers freely use terms such as integrated systems, enterprise systems and digital solutions in an effort to convince end users to purchase systems and components.[13]

Pearson goes on to describe a typical security alarm system as composed of sensors which connect to a data-gathering panel connected to a computer at the security control center. Integration would mean that sensors, card readers, and other functions would connect to the same data-gathering panel which reports to the same computer. Which multiple functions are integrated depends on the manufacturer. Some manufacturers began with energy management and added security alarm systems in later years; others began with security alarm systems and added access control. Pearson points out that integration is not easy to define because, for example, a question surfaces as to where separate functions come together. Different data-gathering units typically do not connect to a single computer; one reason for this is because there is no standard protocol among manufacturers' data-gathering systems. Thus, integrating functions among different manufacturers via a single computer is often challenging and produces various approaches. However, integration firms exist that specialize in application specific software that combine systems for a specific client.[14]

Besides integration, another term used loosely in the security industry is *open architecture*. It refers to the building of hardware and software whose specifications are public. "This includes officially approved standards as well as privately designed architectures whose specifications are made public by the designers. The opposite of open is closed or proprietary. *The great advantage of open architecture is that anyone can design add-on products for it.* By making an architecture public, however, manufacturers allow others to duplicate its product." To illustrate, *Windows* is closed and many lawsuits have been filed over clones. Linux, on the other hand, is open because its source code is available to the public for free.[15] Robert Pearson writes: "By standing back and looking at the entire system from the security control center to the door sensor it is obvious that there is no security system manufacturer that has a totally open architecture."[16] David Swartz notes that the bottom line is that field security hardware is not interchangeable from one manufacturer to the next. As a result, most systems available today preclude the customer from (1) switching to more advanced products; (2) integrating products from other vendors; or (3) choosing the best product.[17] However, Pearson adds that if security systems used open architecture, safeguards would have to be added to prevent compromise. Today, standard operating systems, proprietary application programs, and data-gathering unit protocols that are proprietary combine to provide protection for the end user.[18]

James Coleman describes trends that help us to understand how physical security is developing. He sees standardizing on a common operating system, something often insisted upon by IT personnel to simplify support requirements. Microsoft NT is the choice of many organizations, with Linux being used by others. Coleman notes that every major access control manufacturer has responded to this trend by developing an NT-based product. Such products are becoming increasingly feature rich with improved performance with each new release and the ability to integrate new products, such as asset tracking. Another trend is how security devices communicate with each other. For many years, dedicated wiring has been used to connect security components. With computer networks becoming standard infrastructure in offices and plants, they are being used to connect portions of security systems.[19]

Access Controls

Access controls regulate people, vehicles, and items during movement into, out of, and within a building or facility. With regulation, assets are easier to protect. If a truck can enter a business facility easily, back up to the shipping dock so that the truck driver can load valuable cargo illegally, and then drive away, that business cannot last long. But if the truck has to stop at the facility's front gate, where a uniformed officer issues a pass and records the license and other information, and appropriate paperwork is exchanged at the shipping dock under the watchful eyes of another officer who restricts the driver's access into the facility, then these controls can prevent losses.

Access controls are vital for the everyday movement of employees, customers, vendors, service people, contractors, and government inspectors. Any of these people can be someone who would steal. In addition to merchandise, proprietary information must be protected.

> At one corporation a security officer permitted two salespeople from another company to enter a restricted area involved in new product development. The officer was fired.

Access control varies from simple to complex. A simple setup includes locks and keys, officers checking identification badges, and written logs of entries and exits. More complex systems use access cards that activate electronic locking devices while a CCTV system observes and records the entry. A prime factor influencing the kind of system employed is need. A research laboratory developing a new product requires strict access controls, whereas a retail business would require minimal controls.

Controlling Employee Traffic

The fewest entrances and exits is best. This permits officers to observe people entering and departing. If possible, employees should be routed to the exit closest to the workplace away from valuable assets.

Unauthorized exits locked from within create a hazard in case of fire or other emergency. To ensure safety yet fewer losses, emergency exit alarms on each locked door are a worthwhile investment. These devices enable quick exit, or a short delay, when pressure is placed against a horizontal bar that is secured across the door. An alarm is sounded when these doors are activated, which discourages unauthorized use.

Searching Employees

Management can provide in the contract of employment that reasonable detentions are permissible, that reasonable searches may be made to protect people and company assets, and that searches may be made at any time of desks, lockers, containers carried by employees and vehicles.[20] Case law has permitted an employer to use a duplicate key, known to the employee, to enter a locker at will. On the other hand, an employee who uses a personal lock has a greater expectation of privacy, barring a written condition of employment to the contrary that includes forced entry. When a desk is assigned to a specific employee, an expectation of privacy exists, unless a contract states otherwise. If employees jointly have access to a desk to obtain items, no privacy exists.[21]

Policies and procedures on searches should consider input from management, an attorney, employees, and a union if on the premises. Also consider business necessity, what is subject to search, signed authorization from each employee, signs at the perimeter and in the workplace, and searches of visitors and others.

Should management and security have the right to search employees and others on the premises? Why or why not?

Visitors

Visitors include customers, salespeople, vendors, service people, contractors, and government employees. A variety of techniques are applicable to visitor access control. An appointment system enables preparation for visitors. When visitors arrive without an appointment, the person at reception should lead them to a waiting room. Whatever the reason for the visit, the shortest route to specific destinations, away from valuable assets and dangerous conditions, can avert theft and injuries. Lending special equipment, such as a helmet, may be necessary. A record or log of visits is wise. Relevant information would be name of the visitor, date of visit, time entering and leaving, purpose, specific location visited, name of employee escorting visitor, and temporary badge number. These records aid investigators. Whenever possible, procedures should minimize employee–visitor contact. This is especially important in the shipping and receiving department, where truck drivers may become friendly with employees and conspiracies may evolve. When telephones, restrooms, and vending machines are scattered throughout a plant, truck drivers and other visitors who are permitted easy access may actually steal the place blind. These services should be located at the shipping and receiving dock and access to outsiders should be limited.

Controlling the Movement of Packages and Property

The movement of packages and property also must be subject to access controls. Some locations require precautions against packaged bombs, letter bombs, and other hazards. Clear policies and procedures are needed for incoming and outgoing items. To counter employee theft, outgoing items require both scrutiny and accountability. Uniformed officers can check outgoing items while a property pass system service the accountability function.

Employee Identification System

The use of an employee identification (card or badge) system will depend on the number of employees that must be accounted for and recognized by other employees. An ID system not only prevents unauthorized people from entering a facility but also deters unauthorized employees from entering restricted areas. For the system to operate efficiently, clear policies should state the use of ID cards, where and when the cards are to be displayed on the person, who should collect cards from employees who quit or are fired, and the penalties for noncompliance. A lost or stolen card should be reported so that the proper information reaches all interested personnel. Sometimes ID systems become a joke and employees refuse to wear the badges, or they decorate them or wear them in odd locations on their persons. To sustain an ID system, proper socialization is essential.

Simple ID cards contain employer and employee names. A more complex system would include an array of information: name, signature, address, employee number, physical characteristics (e.g., height, weight, hair and eye colors), validation date, authorized signature, location of work assignment, thumbprint, and color photo.

Lamination discourages card tampering: if an attempt is made to alter the card, it will be disfigured. To laminate a card, a paper ID card is inserted into a plastic case and then placed in a laminating machine that bonds a clear plastic coating over the card.

Automatic Access Control

Keys are difficult to control and easy to duplicate, so there are limitations to the lock-and-key method of access control. Because of these problems, the need for improved access control, and technological innovations, a huge market has been created for electronic card access control systems. These systems are flexible. Unauthorized duplication of cards can be difficult, and personnel (i.e., an officer at each entrance) costs are saved. The card contains coded information "read" by the system for access or denial.

Before an automatic access control system is implemented, several considerations are necessary. *Safety must be a prime factor to ensure quick exit in case of emergency.* Another consideration deals with the adaptability of the system to the type of door presently in use. Can the system accommodate all traffic requirements? How many entrances and exits must be controlled? Will there be an annoying waiting period for those who want to gain access? Are additions to the system possible? What if the system breaks down? Is a backup source of power available (e.g., generators)?

Tailgating is another concern. This is when an authorized user lets in an unauthorized user. To thwart this problem, a security officer can be assigned to each access point, but this approach is expensive when compared to applying CCTV, revolving doors, or turnstiles. Revolving doors can be expensive initially and they are not an approved fire exit. Optical turnstiles contain invisible infrared beams to count people entering to control tailgating.

A summary of cards used in card access systems follows:

- *Magnetic stripe cards* are plastic, laminated cards (like credit cards) that have a magnetic stripe along one edge onto which a code is printed. When the card is inserted, the magnetically encoded data is compared to data stored in a computer and access is granted on verification.
- *Magnetic dot cards* contain magnetic material, often barium ferrite, laminated between plastic layers. The dots create a magnetic pattern that activates internal sensors in a card reader.
- *Weigand cards* employ a coded pattern on a magnetized wire within the card to generate a code number. To gain access, the card is passed through a sensing reader.
- *Bar-coded cards* contain an array of tiny vertical lines that can be visible and vulnerable to photocopying, or invisible and read by an infrared reader.
- *Proximity cards* need not be inserted into a reader but placed in its "proximity." A code is sent via radio frequency, magnetic field, or microchip-tuned circuit.
- *Smart cards* contain an integrated circuit chip within the plastic that serves as a miniature computer as it records and stores information and personal identification codes in its memory. Security is increased because information is held in the card, rather than the reader. These cards permit a host of activities from access control to making purchases, while almost eliminating the need for keys or cash.

Access card systems vary in terms of advantages, disadvantages, and costs. Each type of card can be duplicated with a sufficient amount of knowledge, time, and equipment. A magnetic stripe is easy to duplicate. A piece of cardboard with a properly encoded magnetic stripe functions with equal efficiency. Magnetic dot cards are vulnerable to deciphering. Although bar-coded cards also are easy to duplicate, they can be made more secure by covering the code with an opaque patch, which prevents photocopying. Many software programs are available that can generate bar codes, so fully concealing the code adds more security. Weigand and proximity cards are more difficult to duplicate but higher in cost. The Weigand card has the disadvantage of wear and tear on the card that passes through a slot for access. Proximity cards have the advantage of the sensing element being concealed in a wall, and the card typically can be read without removing it from a pocket. Smart cards are expensive, but they can be combined with other card systems; also, they are convenient because of the capability of loading and updating the card applications over the Web.[22]

Biometric security systems have been praised as a major advance in access control. These systems verify an individual's identity through fingerprint scan, hand scan (hand geometry) (see Figure 7-4), iris scan (the iris is the colored part around the pupil of the eye), retina scan (the retina is the sensory membrane lining the eye and receiving the image formed by the lens), voice patterns, physical action of writing, and facial scan. The biometric leaders are fingerprint, hand, and iris, which offer the best balance of accuracy, reliability, and cost.[23] Research continues to improve biometrics. Voice and writing are being refined. In the near term we will not see facial scan pick a known terrorist out of a crowd, but the technology is evolving. At this time facial scan is unreliable with crowds because digitized photos shot at angles or in poor light can be flawed in comparison to mug shots.[24]

Basically, biometric systems operate by storing identifying information (e.g., fingerprints, photos) in a computer to be compared with information presented by a subject requesting access. The applications are endless: doors, computers, vehicles, and so on. Although biometric systems have been touted as being invincible, no security is foolproof, as illustrated by terrorists who cut off the thumb of a bank manager to gain entry through a fingerprint-based access control system.

Access controls often use multiple technologies. For example, magnetic-stripe and smart-card technologies can complement each other on a single card. One location may require a card and a personal identification number, or PIN (see Figure 7-5), whereas another requires scanning a finger

Figure 7-4 Verifying identity through hand geometry. Courtesy: HID Corporation.

Figure 7–5   Card reader and key pad. Courtesy: Diebold, Inc.

and a PIN. Many systems feature a distress code that can be entered if someone is being victimized. Another feature is an alarm that sounds during unauthorized attempted entry. Access systems can be programmed to allow select access according to time, day, and location. The logging capabilities are another feature to ascertain personnel location by time, date, and the resources expended (e.g., computer time, parking space, cafeteria).

We are seeing an increasing merger of card access systems and biometric technology, and thus, missing or stolen cards are less of a concern. We will see more point-of-sale readers that accept biometric samples for check cashing, credit cards, and other transactions. The use of biometric systems will become universal—banking, correctional facilities, welfare control programs, and so forth.

Locks and Keys

The basic purpose of a lock-and-key system is to hinder unauthorized entry. Attempts to enter a secure location usually are made at a window or door to a building or at a door somewhere within a building. Consequently, locks deter unauthorized access from outsiders and insiders. *Many see a lock only as a delaying device that is valued by the amount of time needed to defeat it.*

Figure 7–6   Deadbolt lock.

Almost all locking devices are operated by a key, numerical combination, card, or electricity. Most key-operated locks (except padlocks) use a bolt or latch. The *bolt (or deadbolt)* extends from a door lock into a bolt receptacle within the door frame (see Figure 7-6). Authorized entry is made by using an appropriate key to manually move the bolt into the door lock. *Latches* are spring loaded and less secure than a bolt. They are cut on an angle to permit them to slide right into the strike when the door is closed (see Figure 7-7). Unless the latch is equipped with a locking bar (deadlatch), a credit card or knife can be used to push the latch back to open the door.

The *cylinder* part of a lock contains the keyway, pins, and other mechanisms that permit the bolt or latch to be moved by a key for access (see Figure 7-8). Double-cylinder locks, in which a cylinder is located on each side of a door, are a popular form of added security as compared to single-cylinder locks. *Double-cylinder locks require a key for both sides* (see Figure 7-6). With a single-cylinder lock, a thief may be able to break glass or remove a wood panel and then reach inside to turn the knob to release the lock. For safety's sake, locations that use double-cylinder locks must prepare for emergency escape by having a key readily available.

Key-in-knob locks are used universally, but are being replaced by key-in-the-lever locks (see Figure 7-9) to be ADA compliant. As the name implies, the keyway is in the knob or lever. Most contain a keyway on the outside and a button on the insider for locking from within.

Entrances for Handicapped

The Internal Revenue Service offers a tax credit to eligible businesses that comply with provisions of the ADA to remove barriers and promote access for individuals with disabilities. The door hardware industry offers several

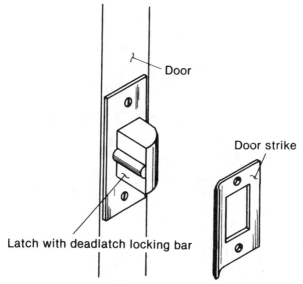

Figure 7–7 Latch and door strike.

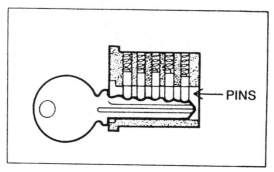

Figure 7–8 Cylinder.

products and solutions to aid the disabled (see Figure 7-10). Electrified door hardware such as magnetic locks and electromechanical locks retracts the latch when energized.

Attacks and Hardware

There are several ways to attack locks. Probably one of the simplest techniques, as stated earlier, is to force a credit card or knife between the door frame (jamb) and the door near the lock to release the latch, which is easily defeated. But, when a deadlatch or bolt is part of the locking mechanism, more forceful methods are needed. In one method, called *springing the door*, a screwdriver or crowbar is placed between the door and the door frame so that the bolt extending from the door lock into the bolt receptacle

Figure 7-9 Mechanical lock with lever requiring no wiring, electronics, or batteries. Courtesy: Ilco Unican.

can be pried out, enabling the door to swing open. This type of attack can be difficult to detect (see Figure 7-11). A 1-inch bolt will hinder this attack.

In *jamb peeling*, another method of attack, a crowbar is used to peel at the door frame near the bolt receptacle so that the door is not stopped from swinging open. Strong hardware for the door frame is helpful. In *sawing the bolt*, a hacksaw is applied between the door and the door frame, similar to the placement of the screwdriver in Figure 7-11. Here again, strong hardware, such as a metal bolt composed of an alloy capable of withstanding a saw blade, will impede attacks. Some offenders use the *cylinder-pulling technique*: the cylinder on the door is actually ripped out with a set of durable pliers or tongs. A circular steel guard surrounding the cylinder (see Figure 7-11) will frustrate the attacker. Offenders also are known to use automobile jacks to pressure door frames away from a door.

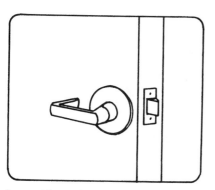

Lever trim reduces force required to unlatch a door.

Push/Pull Latch

Push/Pull latches are popular on institutional doors because of ease of operation.

Proximity Card

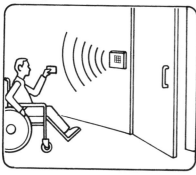

Proximity card reader requires only close presence of the user's card to activate door's automatic opener.

Presence detectors are popular with automatic exit doors and require no physical action.

Figure 7–10   Entrances for handicapped. Courtesy: Von Duprin Division of Ingersoll-Rand Company.

Both high-quality hardware and construction will impede attacks, but the door itself must not be forgotten. If a wood door is only 1/4-inch thick, even though a strong lock is attached, the offender may simply break through the door. A solid wood door 1-3/4 inches thick or a metal door are worthwhile investments. Wood door frames at least 2 inches thick provide durable protection. When a hollow steel frame is used, the hollow area can be filled with cement to resist crushing near the bolt receptacle. An L-shaped piece of iron secured with one-way screws will deter attacks near the bolt receptacle for doors swinging in (see Figure 7-12). When a padlock

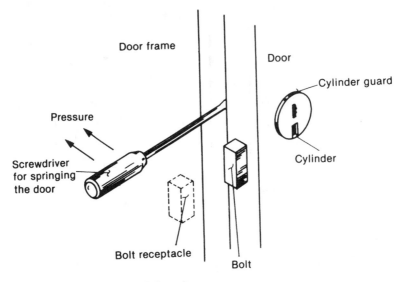

Figure 7–11   Deadbolt lock and door frame.

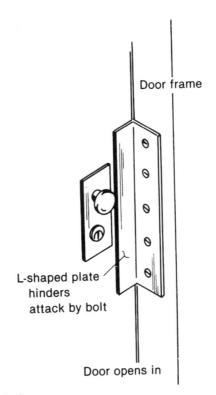

Figure 7–12   L-shaped plate.

is used in conjunction with a safety hasp, the hasp must be installed correctly so that the screws are not exposed (see Figure 7-13).

Many attacks are by forced entry, which is easier to detect than when the use of force is minimal. Lock picking is one technique needing a minimum amount of force. It is used infrequently because of the expertise required. *Lock picking* is accomplished by inserting a tension wrench (an L-shaped piece of metal) into the cylinder and applying tension while using metal picks to align the pins in the cylinder as a key would to release the lock (see Figure 7-8). The greater the number of pins the more difficult it is to align them. A cylinder should have at least six pins.

A more difficult attack utilizes a blank key, matches, and a file. The blank key is placed over a lighted match until carbon is produced on the key. Then the key is inserted into the cylinder. The locations where the pins have scraped away the carbon signifies where to file. Needless to say, this method is time consuming and calls for repeated trials.

After gaining access, a professional burglar will employ some tricks to make sure nobody enters while he or she is busy. This is accomplished, for instance, by inserting a pin or obstacle in the keyway and locking the door from the inside.

Whatever hardware is used, the longer it takes to attack a lock, the greater is the danger for the offender. Six or more pins and pick-resistant, impression-resistant cylinders inhibit unauthorized access. One further

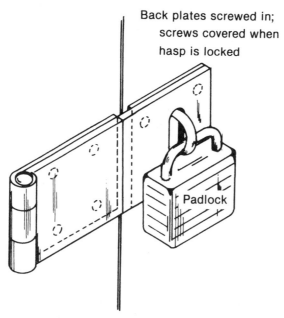

Back plates screwed in;
screws covered when
hasp is locked

Padlock

Figure 7–13   Safety hasp.

point: most burglary insurance policies state that there must be visible signs of forced entry to support a claim.

Other methods of entry may be used by offenders. A thief may simply use a stolen key or a key borrowed from another person. Unfortunately, intruders often enter restricted areas because somebody forgot to use a locking device. This mistake renders the most complex locks useless. *Padlock substitution* is a technique whereby an unlocked padlock is replaced with the thief's similar padlock. When the opportunity is ripe, the thief opens his or her lock, enters, and then replaces the original lock. Therefore, all padlocks should be locked even when not in use. The methods of defeating lock-and-key systems do not stop here. Innovative thieves and various kinds of locks and keys create a hodgepodge of methods that loss prevention practitioners should understand.

Kinds of Locks

Volumes have been written about locks. The following briefly summarizes the common kinds of locks.

- *Warded (or skeleton key tumbler) lock.* This older kind of lock is disengaged when a skeleton key makes direct contact with a bolt and slides it back into the door. It is an easy lock to pick. A strong piece of L-shaped wire can be inserted into the keyway to move the bolt. Warded locks are still in use in many older buildings and are recognized by a keyway that permits seeing through. Locks on handcuffs are of the warded kind and can be defeated by a knowledgeable offender.
- *Disc tumbler (or wafer tumbler) lock.* Originally designed for the automobile industry, its use has expanded to desks, cabinets, files, and padlocks. The operation of this lock entails spring-loaded flat metal discs, instead of pins, that align when the proper key is used. These locks are mass produced, inexpensive, and have a short life expectancy. More security is offered than a warded lock can provide, but disc tumbler locks are subject to defeat by improper keys or being jimmied.
- *Pin tumbler lock.* Invented by Linus Yale in 1844, the pin tumbler lock is used widely in industry and residences (see Figure 7-8). Its security surpasses that of the warded and disc tumbler kinds.
- *Lever lock.* Lever locks vary widely. Basically, these locks disengage when tumblers are aligned by the proper key. Those found in cabinets, chests, and desks often provide minimal security, whereas those found in bank safe deposit boxes are more complex and provide greater security. The better quality lever lock offers more security than the best pin tumbler lock.
- *Combination lock.* This lock requires manipulating a numbered dial(s) to gain access. Combination locks usually have three or four dials that must be aligned in the correct order for entrance. These locks provide greater security than key locks because a limited number of people

probably will know the lock combination, keys are unnecessary, and lock picking is obviated. They are used for safes, bank vaults, and high-security filing cabinets. With older combination locks, skillful burglars are able actually to listen to the locking mechanism to open the lock; more advanced mechanisms have reduced this weakness. A serious vulnerability results when an offender watches the opening of a combination lock either with binoculars or a telescope. Retailers sometimes place combination safes near the front door for viewing by patrolling police; however, unless the retailer uses his or her body to block the dial from viewing, losses may result. This same weakness exists where access is permitted by typing a secret code into a keyboard for access to a parking lot, doorway, or secure area.

- *Combination padlock.* This lock is similar in operation to a combination lock. It is used on employee or student lockers and in conjunction with safety hasps or chains. Some of these locks have a keyway so they can be opened with a key.
- *Padlock.* Requiring a key, this lock is used on lockers or in conjunction with hasps or chains. Numerous kinds of construction are possible, each affording differing levels of protection. Low-security padlocks contain warded locks, whereas more secure ones have disc tumbler, pin tumbler, or lever characteristics. Serial numbers on padlocks are a security hazard similar to combination padlocks.

Other kinds of locks include devices that have a bolt that locks vertically instead of horizontally. Emergency exit locks with alarms or "panic alarms" enable quick exit in emergencies while deterring unauthorized door use. Sequence locking devices require locking the doors in a predetermined order; this ensures that all doors are locked because the outer doors will not lock until the inner doors are locked.

The use of *interchangeable core locks* is a quick method to deal with the theft, duplication, or loss of keys. Using a special control key, one core (that part containing the keyway) is simply replaced by another. A different key then is needed to operate the lock. This system, although more expensive initially, minimizes the need for a locksmith or the complete changing of locks.

Automatic locking and unlocking devices also are a part of the broad spectrum of methods to control access. Digital locking systems open doors when a particular numbered combination is typed. If the wrong number is typed, an alarm is sounded. Combinations can be changed when necessary. *Electromagnetic locks* use magnetism, electricity, and a metal plate around doors to hold doors closed. When the electricity is turned off, the door can be opened. Remote locks enable opening a door electronically from a remote location. Before releasing the door lock, an officer seated in front of a console identifies an individual at a door by use of CCTV and a two-way intercom.

Trends taking place with locks and keys include increasing use of electronics and microchip technology. For example, hybrids have been developed whereby a key can serve as a standard hardware key in one door and an electronic key in another door. Manufacturers also offer mechanical locks and keys with microchip technology to produce an intelligent system that can provide an audit trail. Such systems are self-contained on a door and use a common watch-type battery. A key collection device is used to retrieve data. As electronic devices get smaller, we will see more of them being merged with mechanical locks. Another trend is electronic locks on the perimeter and hardware locks on inner doors.[25] The American National Standards Institute (ANSI) (www.ansi.org) offers standards for locks that are followed by manufacturers.

Master Key Systems

In most instances, a lock accepts only one key that has been cut to fit it. A lock that has been altered to permit access by two or more keys has been *master keyed*. The master key system allows a number of locks to be opened by the master key. This system should be confined to high-quality hardware utilizing pin tumbler locks. A disadvantage of the master key system is that if the master key is lost or stolen, security is compromised.

A *change key* fits one lock. A *submaster key* will open all locks in, for instance, a wing of a building. The *master key* opens locks covered by two or more submaster systems.

As a security manager, how do you solve the following problem? Because of employees who quit, were laid off, or fired, many keys are not being returned and concern is being expressed by remaining employees about their safety.

Key Control

Without adequate key control, locks are useless and losses are likely to climb. Accountability and proper records are necessary. Keys should be marked with a code to identify the corresponding lock; the code is interpreted via a record stored in a safe place. A key should never be marked, *Key for room XYZ*. When not in use, keys should be positioned on hooks in a locked key cabinet or vault. The name of the employee, date, and key code are vital records to maintain when a key is issued. These records require continuous updating. Employee turnover is one reason why precise records are vital. Departing employees will return keys (and other valuables) if their final paycheck is withheld. Policies should state that reporting a lost key will not result in punitive action; an investigation and a report will strengthen key control. If key audits check periodically on who has what key, control is further reinforced. To hinder duplication of keys, "do not duplicate" may be stamped on keys, and company policy can clearly state that key duplication will result in dismissal. Lock changes are wise every eight months and sometimes at shorter intervals on an irregular basis. Key control also is important for vehicles such as autos, trucks, and forklifts.

Even the most thorough system of key control is not foolproof. An offender may quickly press a borrowed key into a bar of soap to use as a guide for duplication. A very intelligent offender may even memorize the cuts on a key for subsequent duplication.

> Although card access systems are used universally, locks and keys are still used to protect a variety of assets.

Intrusion Detection Systems

An *intrusion detection system* detects and reports an event or stimulus within its detection area. A response to rectify the reported problem is essential. The emphasis here is on interior sensors. Sensors appropriate for perimeter protection are stressed in Chapter 8.

What are the basic components of an intrusion detection system? Three fundamental components are sensor, control unit, and annunciator. *Sensors* detect intrusion by, for example, heat or movement of a human. The *control unit* receives the alarm notification from the sensor and then activates a silent alarm or *annunciator* (e.g., a bell or siren), which usually produces a human response.

Interior Sensors

A *balanced magnetic switch* consists of a switch mounted to a door (or window) frame and a magnet mounted to a moveable door or window. When the door is closed, the magnet holds the switch closed to complete a circuit. An alarm is triggered when the door is opened and the circuit is interrupted. An ordinary magnetic switch is similar to the balanced type, except that it is simpler, is less expensive, and provides a lower level of security. Switches provide good protection against opening a door; however, an offender may cut through a door or glass. (Chapter 8 provides illustrations of switch sensors.)

Mechanical contact switches contain a pushbutton-actuated switch that is recessed into a surface. An item is placed on it that depresses the switch, completing the alarm circuit. Lifting the item interrupts the circuit and signals an alarm.

Pressure-sensitive mats contain two layers of metal strips or screen wire separated by sections of foam rubber or other flexible material. When pressure is applied, as by a person walking on the mat, both layers meet and complete an electrical contact to signal an alarm. These mats are applied as internal traps at doors, windows, and main traffic points, as well as near valuable assets. The cost is low and these mats are difficult to detect. If the mat is detected by the offender, he or she can walk around it.

Grid wire sensors are made of fine insulated wire attached to protected surfaces in a grid pattern consisting of two circuits, one running vertical, the other horizontal, and each overlapping the other. An interruption in either circuit signals an alarm. This type of sensor is applied to grill work, screens, walls, floors, ceilings, doors, and other locations. Although these sensors are difficult for an offender to spot, they are expensive to install and an offender can jump the circuit.

Trip wire sensors use a spring-loaded switch attached to a wire stretched across a protected area. An intruder "trips" the alarm (i.e., opens the circuit) when the wire is pulled loose from the switch. These sensors are often applied to ducts, but can be applied to other locations. If the sensor is spotted by an offender, he or she may be able to circumvent it.

Vibration sensors detect low-frequency energy resulting from the force applied in an attack on a structure (see Figure 7-14). These sensors are applied to walls, floors, and ceilings. Various sensor models require proper selection.

Capacitance sensors create an electrical field around metallic objects that, when disturbed, signals an alarm (see Figure 7-15). These sensors are applied to safes, file cabinets, grills at openings (e.g., windows), and other metal objects. One sensor can protect many objects; however, it is subject to defeat by using insulation (e.g., heavy gloves).

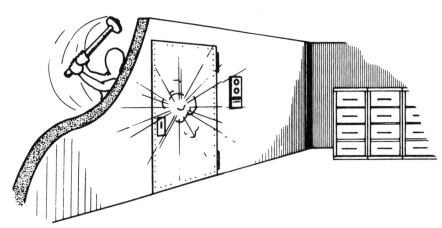

Figure 7–14   Vibration sensor.

Figure 7–15   Capacitance sensor.

Infrared photoelectric beam sensors activate an alarm when an invisible infrared beam of light is interrupted (see Figure 7-16). If the system is detected, an offender may jump over or crawl under the beam to defeat it.

Ultrasonic motion detectors create a pattern of inaudible sound waves that are transmitted into an area and monitored by a receiver. These detectors operate on the *Doppler effect*, which is the change in frequency that results from the motion of an intruder. These detectors are installed on

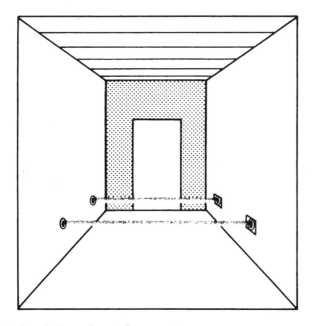

Figure 7–16   Infrared photoelectric beam system.

walls or ceilings or used covertly (i.e., disguised within another object). They are subject to nuisance alarms from high-pitched noises or air currents and can be defeated by objects blocking the sensor or by fast or slow movement. This detector has been labeled as obsolete because of false alarms.

Microwave motion detectors operate on the Doppler frequency-shift principle. An energy field is transmitted into an area and monitored for a change in its pattern and frequency, which results in an alarm. Because microwave energy penetrates a variety of construction materials, care is required for placement and aiming. However, this can be an advantage in protecting multiple rooms and large areas with one sensor. These sensors can be defeated (like ultrasonic ones) by objects blocking the sensor or by fast or slow movement.

Passive infrared intrusion sensors (PIR) are passive in that they do not transmit a signal for an intruder to disturb. Rather, moving infrared radiation (from a person) is detected against the radiation environment of a room. When an intruder enters the room, the level of infrared energy changes and an alarm is activated. Although the PIR is not subject to as many nuisance alarms as ultrasonic and microwave detectors, it should not be aimed at sources of heat or surfaces that can reflect energy. The PIR can be defeated by blocking the sensor so it cannot pick up heat.

Passive audio detectors listen for noise created by intruders. Various models filter out naturally occurring noises not indicating forced entry. These detectors can use public address system speakers in buildings, which can act as microphones to listen to intruders. The actual conversation of intruders can be picked up and recorded by these systems. To enhance this system, CCTV can provide visual verification of an alarm condition, video in real time, and still images digitally to security or police, and evidence. The audio also can be two-way, enabling security to warn the intruders. *Such audiovisual systems must be applied with extreme care to protect privacy, confidentiality, and sensitive information, and to avoid violating state and federal wiretapping laws.*

Fiber optics is growing in popularity for intrusion detection and for transmission of alarm signals. It involves the transportation of information via guided light waves in an optical fiber. This sensor can be attached to or inserted in many things requiring protection. When stress is applied to the fiber optic cable, an infrared light pulsing through the cable reacts to the stress and signals an alarm.

Intrusion detection systems only *detect* and *report* an alarm condition. These systems do not stop or apprehend an intruder.

Trends

Two types of sensor technologies often are applied to a location to reduce false alarms, prevent defeat techniques, or fulfill unique needs. The combination of microwave and passive infrared sensors is a popular example of applying *dual technologies*. Reporting can be designed so an alarm is signaled when both sensors detect an intrusion (to reduce false alarms) or when either sensor detects an intrusion. Sensors are also becoming "smarter" by sending sensor data to a control panel or computer, distinguishing between humans and animals, and activating a trouble output if the sensor lens is blocked. *Supervised wireless sensors* have become a major advancement because sensors can be placed at the best location without the expense of running a wire; these sensors are constantly monitored for integrity of the radio frequency link between the sensor and panel, status of the battery, and whether the sensor is functioning normally.[26]

Operational Zoning

Operational zoning means that the building being protected has a segmented alarm system, whereby the alarm can be turned on and off within particular zones depending on usage (see Figure 7-17). For example, if an early morning cleaning crew is in the north end of a plant, then that alarm is turned off while other zones still have the alarm on. Furthermore, zoning helps to pinpoint where an intrusion has occurred.

Alarm Monitoring

Today, many entities have an alarm system that is monitored by an in-house station (e.g., a console at a secure location) or from a central station (contract service) located off the premises. These services easily can supply reports of unusual openings and closings, as well as those of the regular routine. Chapter 8 covers alarm signaling systems.

Closed-Circuit Television

Closed-circuit television, or CCTV (see Figure 7-18), assists in deterrence, surveillance, apprehension, and prosecution. Although it may be costly initially, CCTV reduces personnel costs because it allows the viewing of multiple locations by one person. A simple *CCTV system* consists of a television camera, monitor (TV), and cable. The camera and monitor are plugged in, and the cable is connected between them before both are turned on. An extensive system would have numerous cameras strategically located.

For instance, throughout a manufacturing plant, personnel seated in front of a console of monitors could view the targets of many cameras. Accessories include zoom lenses, remote pan (i.e., side-to-side movement), and tilt (i.e., up-and-down movement) mechanisms that enable viewing

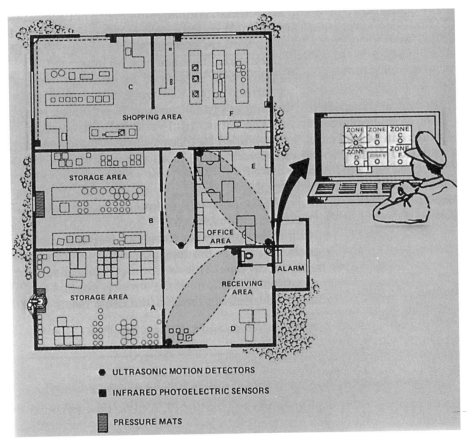

Figure 7–17 Floor plan with sensors.

mobility and opportunities to obtain a close look at any suspicious activity. Low-light-level equipment permits viewing when limited light is present.

Several methods can be applied to transmit the camera image to the monitor: coaxial cable, fiber optics, microwave, radio frequency, telephone lines, and the Internet. Furthermore, it will be common to see video images on personal digital assistants and cell phones. What we have is the opportunity (as with other electronic security systems) for, say, an executive in New York to monitor inside a business in Hong Kong.

Changing technology has brought about the *charged coupled device* (CCD) or *"chip" camera*, a small, photosensitive, solid-state unit designed to replace the tube in the closed-circuit camera. CCD technology is found in camcorders. CCD cameras have certain advantages over tube cameras: CCD cameras are more adaptable to a variety of circumstances, they have a longer life expectancy, "ghosting" (i.e., people appearing transparent) is less of a problem, there is less intolerance to light, less power is required, and less

Figure 7–18 Closed-circuit television (CCTV) sign. Camera at top.

heat is produced, thereby requiring less ventilation and permitting installation in more locations.

Cameras commonly are placed at access points, passageways, shipping and receiving docks, merchandise storage areas, cashier locations, parts departments, computer rooms, and overlooking files, safes, vaults, and production lines. Wherever cameras are located, careful planning is essential to avoid harming employee morale. Constant monitoring of a CCTV system ensures its loss prevention capabilities. Personnel that are not rotated periodically become fatigued from watching too much TV. This is a serious problem that is often overlooked. Regular employees may "test" the monitoring of the system by placing a bag or rag over a camera or even spraying the lens with paint. If employees see that there is no response, CCTV becomes a hoax. The use of dummy cameras is not recommended because, when employees discover the dummy, loss prevention appears to be a deceitful farce.

The newer *digital systems* or the older *video cassette recorder (VCR) systems*, combined with a CCTV system, permit recording of visual evidence. This is helpful in the prosecution of offenders and may be used in court. Further, if an employee violates policies and procedures and is disciplined, a recording is helpful for arbitration hearings or litigation. The time and date of the recording, shown on the video, strengthens the case.

VCRs generally record for two, four, or six hours. *Time-lapse recorders* (i.e., single frames of video are stored at intervals over an extended period of time) have total recording time of up to several hundred hours, plus an alarm mode in which the recorder reverts to real time when an alarm condition exists. Real-time setting records 30 frames a second; time-lapse video may record between 1 frame a second and 1 frame every 8 seconds.

Time-lapse recorder features include a quick search for alarm conditions during playback, the playing of recorded video frames according to the input of time by the user, and the interface with other security systems such as access controls to ensure a video record of all people entering and departing.

CCTV capabilities can be enhanced by using a video motion detector. A *video motion detector* operates by sending, from a camera, a static (i.e., having no motion) picture to a memory evaluator. Any change in the picture, such as movement, activates an alarm. These systems assist security officers in reacting to threats.

Increasing "intelligence" is being built into CCTV-computer-based systems. *Multiplex* means sending many signals over one communications channel. *Video multiplex systems* minimize the number of monitors security personnel must watch by allowing up to 16 cameras to be viewed at the same time on one video screen. The pictures are compressed, but a full view is seen of each picture. If an alarm occurs, a full screen can be brought up. The *digital multiplex recorder* enables users to record events without a time-lapse recorder, directly to a hard drive, reducing storage space. The images are collected digitally, which improves video quality and permits fast storage and retrieval of information, while avoiding tape degradation. This technology facilitates the move from video monitors to computer monitors, and we are seeing increasing use of security video at the desktop computer and remote monitoring (e.g., watching a business from many miles away).

CCTV technology called *intelligent surveillance* has further reduced the problem of real-time monitoring of dozens of cameras, which is beyond human capacity. Based on machine vision technology, these computerized systems digitize video images and, through specially designed software, automatically identify targets and track people or vehicles. The system alerts security through voice annunciation, the live video is called to the screen, and the video images are filed to a disk.[27]

The extent of the use of hidden surveillance cameras is difficult to measure, especially because many individuals are unaware of the existence of these cameras in workplaces. Pinhole lenses are a popular component of hidden surveillance cameras. They get their name from the outer opening of the lens, which is 1/8 to 1/4 inch in diameter and difficult to spot. Cameras are hidden in almost any location, such as clocks, file cabinets, computers, sprinkler heads, and mannequins.

Security Officers

When supervised, uniformed officers patrol on foot inside a facility—through production, storage, shipping, receiving, office, and sales floor areas—an enhanced loss prevention atmosphere prevails. Unpredictable and irregular patrols can play an important role in deterring employee theft (among other losses). A properly trained officer looks for deviations, such as merchandise stored or hidden in unusual places, and tampered devices (e.g., locks, alarms, and CCTV). Thoroughly searching trash containers deters employees from hiding items in that popular spot. Losses also are hindered when officers identify and check people, items, and vehicles at access points.

Safes, Vaults, and File Cabinets

Protective containers (see Figure 7-19) secure valuable items (e.g., cash, confidential information). These devices generally are designed to withstand

Figure 7–19   Safe with electronic lock. Courtesy: Sargent & Greenleaf, Inc.

losses from fire or burglary. Specifications vary and an assessment of need should be carefully planned. Management frequently is shocked when a fire-resistive safe in which valuable items are "secured" enables a burglar to gain entry because the safe was designed only for fire. The classic *fire-resistive (or record) safe* has a square (or rectangular) door and thin steel walls that contain insulation. During assembly, wet insulation is poured between the steel walls; when the mixture dries, moisture remains. During a fire, the insulation creates steam that cools the safe below 350°F (the flash point of paper) for a specified time. Record safes for computer tapes and disks require better protection because damage occurs at 150°F and these records are more vulnerable to humidity. Fire safes are able to withstand one fire; thereafter, the insulation is useless.

The classic *burglary-resistive (or money) safe* has a thick, round door and thick walls. Round doors were thought to enhance resistance, but today many newer burglary-resistive safes have square or rectangular doors. The burglary-resistive safe is more costly than the fire-resistive safe.

Ratings

Better quality safes have the UL (Underwriters Laboratory, a nonprofit testing organization) rating (see Table 7-1). This means that manufacturers have submitted safes for testing by UL. These tests determine the fire- or burglary-resistive properties of safes. For example, a fire-resistive container with a UL rating of 350-4 can withstand *external* temperatures to 2000°F for four hours while the *internal* temperature will not exceed 350°F. The UL test actually involves placing a safe in an increasingly hot furnace to simulate a fire. An explosion impact test requires another safe of the same model to be placed in a preheated (2000°F) furnace for half an hour. Then the heat is lowered slightly for another half hour before the safe is dropped 30 feet onto rubble. If the safe is still intact, it is returned to the furnace for an hour at 1700°F before it is allowed to cool so that the papers inside can be checked for damage. In reference to burglary-resistive containers, a UL rating of TL-15, for example, signifies weight of at least 750 pounds and resistance to an attack on its door by common tools for a minimum of 15 minutes. UL-rated burglary-resistive safes also contain UL-listed combination locks and other UL-listed components. UL is constantly toughening its standards. When selecting a safe, consider recommendations from insurance companies and peers, whether or not safe company employees are bonded, and how long the company has been in business.

Attacks

Before a skilled burglar attacks a safe, he or she studies the methods used to protect it. Inside information (e.g., a safe's combination) is valuable, and scores of employees and former employees of attacked firms have been implicated in burglaries. Listed next are major attack techniques of two types: with force and without force.

Table 7-1   UL Listed Safes

Class	Resistance to attack	Attack time	Description
Fire			
350-*	Not tested	N/A	For paper and document storage
150-*	Not tested	N/A	For storage of magnetic computer tapes and photographic film
125-*	Not tested	N/A	For storage of flexible disks
Burglary			
TL-15	Door or front face	15 min	Resists against entry by common mechanical and electrical tools or combination of these means, Group 2, 1, or 1R combination lock.**
TL-15X6	6 sides	15 min	Same as above
TRTL-15X6	6 sides	15 min	Resists against entry by common mechanical, electrical tools and cutting torches or combination of each, Group 1 or 1R combination lock.**
TL-30	Door or front face	30 min	Same tools as TL-15, Group 1 or 1R combination lock.**
TL-30X6	6 sides	30 min	Same tools as TL-15, Group 2, 1 or 1R combination lock.**
TRTL-30	Door or front face	30 min	Same tools as TRTL 15X6, Group 1 or 1R combination lock, encased in a minimum 3" of concrete or in a larger safe or container.**
TRTL-30X6	6 sides	30 min	Same tools as TRTL 15X6, Group 1 or 1R combination lock.**
TRTL-60X6	6 sides	60 min	Same tools as TRTL-15, Group 1 or 1R combination lock, minimum weight 750 lbs., body 1" thick solid open hearth steel.
TXTL-60X6	6 sides	60 min	Same tools as TRTL-15 + up to 8 oz. of nitroglycerine with a maximum of 4 oz., per test, Group 1 or 1R combination lock, minimum weight 1000 lbs., wall thickness not specified.

*Hour rating 4, 2, or 1. Before inside temperature reaches 125, 150, or 350°F as shown by class designation.
**Minimum weight 750 lbs., body 1" steel, minimum tensile strength of 50,000 PSI.

Combination Locks (These products are tested in accordance with UL 768)

Group 1. Highly resistant to expert or professional manipulation. Used in safes designated as TRTL-15X6, TRTL-30, TRTL-30X6, TRTL-60X6, and TXTL-60X6.

Group 1R. These locks meet all of the requirements of Group 1 and are resistant against radiological methods of manipulation.

Group M. Moderate resistant to skilled manipulation, these are found in TL-15, TL-15X6, TL-30, and TL-30X6 safes, ATM safes, gun safes, and fire-rated record containers.

Group 2. Resistant to semiskilled manipulation, these locks are found in non-Listed safes, insulated record containers, and residential security containers.

Source: Correspondence (March 12, 2001) with UL, 1285 Walt Whitman Rd., Melville, NY 11747.

Attack methods using force include:

- *Rip or peel.* Most common, the method is used on fire-resistive safes that have lightweight metal. Like opening a can of sardines, the metal is ripped from a corner. The peel technique requires an offender to pry along the edge of the door to reach the lock.
- *Punch.* The combination dial is broken off with a hammer. A punch is placed on the exposed spindle, which is hammered back to enable breakage of the lock box. The handle then is used to open the door. The method is effective against older safes.
- *Chop.* This is the attack of a fire-resistive safe from underneath. The safe is tipped over and hit with an ax or hammer to create a hole.
- *Drill.* A skillful burglar drills into the door to expose the lock mechanism; the lock tumblers are aligned manually to open the door.
- *Torch.* The method is used against burglar-resistive safes. An oxygen-acetylene cutting torch melts the steel. The equipment is brought to the safe, or the offender uses equipment from the scene.
- *Carry away.* The offender removes the safe from the premises and attacks it in a convenient place.

Attack methods using no force include:

- *Office search.* Simply, the offender finds the safe combination in a hiding place (e.g., taped under a desk drawer).
- *Manipulation.* The offender opens a safe without knowing the combination by using sight, sound, and touch—a rare skill. Sometimes the thief is lucky and opens a safe by using numbers similar to an owner's birth date, home address, or telephone number.
- *Observation.* An offender views the opening of a safe from across the street with the assistance of binoculars or a telescope. To thwart this, the numbers should be on the top edge of the dial, rather than on the face of the dial.
- *Day combination.* For convenience, during the day, the dial is not completely turned each time an employee finishes using the safe. This facilitates an opportunity for quick access. An offender often manipulates the dial in case the day combination is still in effect.
- *X-ray equipment.* Metallurgical X-ray equipment is used to photograph the combination of the safe. White spots appear on the picture that help to identify the numerical combination. The equipment is cumbersome, and the technique is rare.

The following measures are recommended to fortify the security of safes and other containers:

1. Utilize alarms (e.g., capacitance and vibration), CCTV, and adequate lighting.

2. Locate the safe in a well-lighted spot near a window where police or pedestrians can see it. Hiding the safe gives the burglar better working conditions.

3. Secure the safe to the building so it is not stolen. (This also applies to cash registers that may be stolen in broad daylight.) Bolt the safe to the foundation or secure it in a cement floor. Remove any wheels or casters.

4. Do not give the burglar an opportunity to use any tools on the premises; hide or secure all potential tools. A ladder or torch on the premises can be used.

5. A time lock permits the safe to be opened only at select times. This hinders access even if the combination is known. A delayed-action lock provides an automatic waiting period (e.g., 15 minutes) from combination use to the time the lock mechanism activates. A silent signal lock triggers an alarm when a special combination is used to open a safe.

6. At the end of the day, turn the dial several times in the same direction.

7. A written combination is risky. Change the factory combination as soon as possible. When an employee leaves who knows the combination, change it.

8. Maintain limited valuables in the safe through frequent banking.

9. Select a safe with its UL rating marked on the inside. If a burglar identifies the rating on the outside, an attack is made easier.

Vaults

A walk-in vault is actually a large safe; it is subject to similar vulnerabilities from fire and attack. Because a walk-in vault is so large and expensive, typically only the door is made of steel, and the rest of the vault is composed of reinforced concrete. Vaults are heavy enough to require special support within a building. They commonly are constructed at ground level to avoid stress on a building.

File Cabinets

According to Richard Healy, "There is a correlation between fire damage and business failure. Statistics seem to indicate that almost half of the companies that lose their records are forced out of business."[28] Records help to support losses during insurance claims. Some vital records are accounts receivable, inventory lists, legal documents, contracts, research and development, and personnel data.

File cabinets that are insulated and lockable can provide fair protection against fire and burglary. The cost is substantially lower than that of a safe or vault, but valuable records demanding increased safety should be placed in a safe or vault, or stored off-site. Special computer safes are designed to protect against forced entry, fire, and moisture that destroys computer media.

Search the Web

Use your favorite search engines to see what vendors have to offer and prices for the following products: access control systems, locks, closed-circuit television, and safes.

CASE PROBLEMS

7A. Consult the floor plans for Woody's Lumber Company, the Smith Shirt manufacturing plant, and Compulab Corporation (Figures 7-1, 7-2, and 7-3). Draw up a priority list of ten loss prevention strategies for each company, which you think would best solve the internal loss problems. Why did you select as top priorities your first three strategies on each list?

7B. As a corporate security manager you learn that an IT specialist at the same company is extremely upset because he did not receive a promotion and raise he was expecting. This very intelligent, single, young man told his supervisor that he will get back at the company for the injustice before he quits. What do you do?

7C. You are a security officer at a manufacturing plant where an employee informs you about observing another employee hiding company property near a back door. You check the area near the door and find company property under boxes. What action do you take?

7D. As a security officer you learn that officers on your shift, and your immediate supervisor, have secretly installed, without authorization, a pinhole lens camera in the women's restroom. You refuse to be involved in peeping. The officers have been your friends since high school and you socialize with them when off duty. One day the corporate security manager summons you to her office and questions you concerning the whereabouts of the pinhole lens camera. What do you say?

NOTES

1. Eric Shaw, Jerrold Post, and Keven Ruby, "Managing the Threat from Within," *Information Security* 3 (July 2000), p. 62.
2. Ibid., pp. 62–66.
3. "Background Checks Provide Means to Combat Employee Theft," *Access Control & Security Systems Integration* 43 (December 2000), p. 8.
4. John Conley, "Knocking the Starch Out of White Collar Crime," *Risk Management* 47 (November 2000), p. 14.
5. Michael A. Baker, Alan F. Westin, and U.S. Department of Justice, *Employer Perceptions of Workplace Crime* (Washington, D.C.: U.S. Government Printing Office, 1987), p. 12.

6. Banning K. Lary, "Thievery on the Inside," *Security Management* (May 1988), p. 81.
7. John Conklin, *Criminology*, 7th ed. (Boston: Allyn & Bacon, 2001), pp. 278–279.
8. William Skinner and Anne Fream, "A Social Learning Theory Analysis of Computer Crime among College Students," *Journal of Research in Crime and Delinquency* 34 (November 1997), pp. 495–518.
9. Gillian Flynn, "Legal Insight," *Personnel Journal* (April 1995), pp. 158–166.
10. John P. Clark and Richard C. Hollinger, "Theft by Employees," *Security Management* 24 (September 1980), p. 106.
11. James Keener, "Integrated Systems: What They Are and Where They Are Heading," *Security Technology and Design* (May 1994), pp. 6–9.
12. "Hard Questions to Ask in Integration Projects," *Security* (August 1996), p. 54.
13. Robert Pearson, "Integration vs. Interconnection: It's a Matter of Semantics," *Security Technology & Design* 11 (November 2000), p. 20.
14. Ibid., pp. 20–26.
15. "Open Architecture." <webopedia,internet.com> (March 28, 2001).
16. Robert Pearson, "Open Systems Architecture: Are We There Yet," *Security Technology & Design* 11 (January 2001), p. 16.
17. David Swartz, "Open Architecture Systems: The Future of Security Management," *Security Technology & Design* 9 (December 1999), p. 24.
18. Pearson, "Open Systems Architecture," p. 16.
19. James Coleman, "Trends in Security Systems Integration," *Security Technology & Design* 10 (August 2000), pp. 38–44.
20. Fred Inbau, Bernard Farber, and David Arnold, *Protective Security Law*, 2nd ed. (Boston: Butterworth–Heinemann, 1996), p. 68.
21. Ibid., p. 47.
22. David Gersh, "Untouchable Value," *iSecurity* (November 2000), p. 18. Joseph A. Barry, "Don't Always Play the Cards You Are Dealt," *Security Technology and Design* (July-August 1993), p. 75. Bud Toye, "Bar-Coded Security ID Cards Efficient and Easy," *Access Control* (March 1996), p. 23.
23. John Strauchs, "Which Way to Better Controls?" *Security Management* 45 (January 2001), p. 97.
24. Steve Lasky, "Can I Get a Witness?" *Security Technology & Design* 11 (February 2001), p. 4.
25. "Door Hardware/Electronic Audit Trail" Van Lock Co. (http://www.vanlock.com; April 1, 2001). And, "In Electronic Age Even Keys, Locks Are Going High-Tech," *Security* 37 (January 2000), p. 53.
26. Tim O'Leary, "New Innovations in Motion Detectors," *Security Technology & Design* 9 (November 1999), pp. 36–48.
27. Robin Thompson, "Intelligent Surveillance Provides Security Uplift," *National Defense* (May–June 1997), p. 52.
28. Richard J. Healy, *Design for Security* (New York: John Wiley & Sons, 1968), p. 174.

8

External Threats and Countermeasures

OBJECTIVES

After studying this chapter the reader will be able to:

1. List and define the five "Ds" of security.
2. Explain how environmental design can enhance security.
3. Discuss perimeter security and list and define five types of barriers.
4. Explain window and door protection.
5. Discuss the application of intrusion detection systems to perimeter protection.
6. List and explain at least four types of alarm signaling systems.
7. Explain lighting illumination and at least five types of lamps.
8. Discuss parking lot and vehicle controls.
9. Explain the deployment and monitoring of security officers.
10. Discuss the use of protective dogs.

External loss prevention focuses on threats from outside an organization. This chapter concentrates on countermeasures to impede unauthorized access from outsiders. If unauthorized access can be accomplished, numerous losses are possible from such crimes as assault, burglary, robbery, vandalism, arson, and espionage. Naturally, these offenses may be committed by employees as well as outsiders or a conspiracy of both. Outsiders can gain legitimate access if they are customers, repair personnel, and so on. Internal and external countermeasures play an interdependent role in minimizing losses; a clear-cut division between internal and external countermeasures is not possible because of this intertwined relationship.

The IT perspective is important to produce comprehensive security. IT specialists use terms such as "denial of access" and "intrusion detection," as do physical security specialists; however, IT specialists apply these terms to the protection of information systems. As IT and physical security specialists learn from each other, a host of protection methods will improve, examples being integration of systems, investigations, and disaster planning. Chapter 16 covers IT security.

Many organizations have developed formidable perimeter security to prevent unauthorized entry, while not realizing that the greatest threat is from within.

METHODS OF UNAUTHORIZED ENTRY

A good way to begin thinking about how to deter unauthorized entry is to study the methods used by offenders. The characteristics of patrols, fences, sensors, locks, windows, doors, and the like are studied by both management (to hinder penetration) and offenders (to succeed in gaining access). By placing yourself in the position of an offender (i.e., *think like a thief*) and then that of a loss prevention manager, you can see, while studying Woody's Lumber Company, the Smith Shirt manufacturing plant, and Compulab Corporation (discussed in Chapter 7), that a combination of both perspectives aids in the designing of defenses. (Such planning is requested in a case problem at the end of this chapter.)

Forced entry is a common method used to gain unauthorized access. Windows and doors are especially vulnerable to forced entry. Offenders repeatedly break or cut glass (with a glass cutter) on a window or door and then reach inside to release a lock or latch. To stop the glass from falling and making noise, a suction cup or tape is used to remove or hold the broken glass together. Retail stores may be subject to *smash and grab attacks*: a store display window is smashed, merchandise is quickly grabbed, and the thief immediately flees. A complex lock may be rendered useless if the offender is able to go through a thin door by using a hammer, chisel, and saw. Forced entry also may be attempted through walls, floors, ceilings, skylights, utility tunnels, sewer or storm drains, and ventilation vents or ducts.

Even though an attempted intrusion may be unsuccessful, losses inevitably result from damaged construction and locks. But, if offenders can be convinced that security is a discouraging obstacle, attempts will decline. This is accomplished through signs informing people about the extent of the security features such as patrols, sensors, and CCTV.

Unauthorized access also can be accomplished *without force*. Wherever a lock is supposed to be used, if it is not locked properly, access is possible. Windows or doors left unlocked are a surprisingly common occurrence. Lock picking or possession of a stolen key or computerized access card renders force unnecessary. Dishonest employees are known to assist criminals by unlocking locks, windows, or doors and by providing keys and technical information. Offenders sometimes hide inside a building until closing and then break out following an assault or theft. Tailgating is a method whereby an intruder blends into a group of entering employees. These sly methods of gaining entry are often referred to as *surreptitious entry.*

COUNTERMEASURES

Countermeasures for external (and internal) threats can be conceptualized around the five Ds:

- *Deter:* The mere presence of physical security can dissuade offenders from committing criminal acts. The impact of physical security can be enhanced through an *aura of security.* An aura is a distinctive atmosphere surrounding something. Supportive management and security personnel should work to produce a professional security image. They should remain mum on such topics as the number and types of intrusion detection sensors on the premises and security system weaknesses. Security patrols should be unpredictable and never routine. Signs help to project an aura of security by stating, for example: PREMISES PROTECTED BY HIGH-TECH REDUNDANT SECURITY. Such signs can be placed along a perimeter and near openings to buildings. The aura of security strives to produce a strong psychological deterrent so offenders will consider the success of a crime to be unlikely. It is important to note that no guarantees come with deterrence. (Criminal justice policies are in serious trouble because deterrence is faulty; criminals continue to commit crimes even while facing long sentences.) In the security realm, deterrence must be backed up with the following four "Ds."
- *Detect*: Offenders should be detected and their location pinpointed as soon as they step onto the premises or commit a violation on the premises. This can be accomplished through observation, CCTV, intrusion sensors, duress alarms, weapons screenings, protective dogs, and hotlines.
- *Delay*: Security is often measured by the time it takes to get through it. *Redundant* (e.g., two fences; two types of intrusion sensors) and *layered* (e.g., perimeter fence, strong doors at buildings) security creates a time delay. Thus, the offender may become frustrated and decide to depart, or the delay may provide time for a response force to arrive to make an apprehension. The retail chapter covers the danger of a delay during a robbery.
- *Deny*: Strong physical security, often called "target hardening," can deny access. A steel door and a safe are examples. Frequent bank

deposits of cash and other valuables extend the opportunity to deny the offender success.

- *Destroy*: When you believe your life or another's will be taken, you are legally permitted to use deadly force. An asset (e.g., proprietary information on a computer disk) may require destruction before it falls into the wrong hands.

Which "D" do you view as most important? Which "D" do you view as least important? Explain your answers.

Construction and Environmental Security Design

When planning a new facility, the need for a coordinated effort by architects, fire protection and safety engineers, loss prevention practitioners, and local police and fire officials cannot be overstated. Further, money is saved when security and safety are planned before actual construction rather than accomplished by modifying the building later.

Years ago, when buildings were designed, loss prevention features were an even smaller part of the planning process than today. Older buildings often have the original warded-type locks that are easy to defeat. Before air conditioning came into widespread use, numerous windows were required for proper ventilation, providing thieves with many entry points. Today's buildings also present problems. For example, ceilings are constructed of suspended ceiling tile with spaces above the tile that enable access by simply pushing up the tile. Once above the tiles, a person can crawl to other rooms on the same floor. Roof access from neighboring buildings is a common problem for both old and new buildings. Many of these weak points are corrected by adequate hardware such as locks on roof doors, and by alarms.

Architects are playing an increasing role in designing crime prevention into building plans. *Environmental security design* includes natural and electronic surveillance of walkways and parking lots, windows and landscaping that enhance visibility, improved lighting, and other architectural designs that promote crime prevention. Additionally, dense shrubbery can be cut to reduce hiding places and grid streets can be turned into cul-de-sacs by using barricades to reduce ease of escape.

During the late 1960s and early 1970s, *Oscar Newman* conducted innovative research into the relationship between architectural design and crime prevention that developed into the concept of *defensible space*.[1] He studied more than 100 housing projects and identified design elements that inhibit crime. For instance, Newman favored the creation of surveillance opportunities through windows for residents and the recognition that the neighborhood surrounding the residential setting influences safety. An essential part of defensible space is to create designs that change residents' use of public places while reducing fear of crime; this is hoped to have a snowballing effect. Oscar Newman found that physical design features of public housing affect both the rates of victimization of residents and their perception of security. Crime prevention through environmental design (CPTED) is applicable not only to public housing but also to businesses, industries, public buildings, transportation systems, and schools, among others. In the past, the U.S. Department of Justice has funded CPTED programs in several cities.

An illustration of how CPTED is applied can be seen with the design of Marriott hotels. To make offenders as visible as possible, traffic is directed toward the front of hotels. Lobbies are designed so that people walking to guest rooms or elevators must pass the front desk. On the outside, hedges are emphasized to produce a psychological barrier that is more appealing than a fence. Pathways are well lit and guide guests away from isolated areas. Parking lots are characterized by lighting, clear lines of sight, and access control. Walls of the garage are painted white to enhance lighting. On the inside of hotels, the swimming pool, exercise room, vending and laundry areas have glass doors and walls to permit maximum witness potential. One application of CCTV is to aim cameras at persons standing at the lobby desk and install the monitor in plain view. Since people can see themselves, robberies have declined. CPTED enhances traditional security methods such as patrolling officers and emergency call boxes.[2]

Today, research continues on how the physical environment influences behavior. Offenders may decide whether or not to commit a crime at a location after they determine the following:

1. How easy will it be to enter?
2. How visible, attractive, or vulnerable do targets appear?
3. What are the chances of being seen?
4. If seen, will the people in the area do something about it?
5. Is there a quick, direct route from the location?[3]

Perimeter Security

Perimeter means outer boundary, and it is often the property line and the first line of defense against unauthorized access (see Figure 8-1). Building access points such as doors and windows also are considered part of perimeter defenses at many locations. Typical perimeter security begins with a fence and gate and may include multiple security methods (e.g., card access, locks, sensors, lighting, CCTV, and patrols) to increase protection (see Figure 8-2). The following variables assist in the design of perimeter security:

Figure 8–1 Perimeter security. Courtesy of Wackenhut Corporation. Photo by Ed Burns.

1. Whatever perimeter security methods are planned, they should inter-relate with the total loss prevention program.
2. Perimeter security needs to be cost effective. When plans are presented, management is sure to ask: "What type of return will we have on such an investment?"
3. Although the least number of entrances strengthens perimeter security, the plan must not interfere with normal business and emergency situations.
4. Perimeter security has a psychological impact on potential intruders. It signals a warning to outsiders that steps have been taken to block intrusions. Offenders actually "shop" for vulnerable businesses.
5. Even though a property line may be well protected, the possibility of unauthorized entry cannot be totally eliminated. For example, a fence can be breached by going over, under, or through it.
6. Penetration of a perimeter is possible from within. Merchandise may be thrown over a fence or out of a window. A variety of things are subject to smuggling by persons walking or using a vehicle while exiting through a perimeter.
7. The perimeter of a building, especially in urban areas, often is the building's walls. A thief may enter through a wall from an adjoining building.
8. To permit an unobstructed view, both sides of a perimeter should be kept clear of vehicles, equipment, and vegetation. This allows for what is known as *clear zones*.

Figure 8–2   Multiple security methods increase protection.

9. Consider integrating perimeter intrusion sensors with landscape sprin-
    kler systems. Trespassers, protesters, and other intruders will be dis-
    couraged, plus, when wet, they are easier to find and identify.
10. Perimeter security methods are exposed to a hostile outdoor environ-
    ment not found indoors. Adequate clothing and shelter are necessary
    for personnel. The selection of proper security systems prevents false
    alarms from animals, vehicle vibrations, and adverse weather.
11. Perimeter security should be inspected periodically.

International Perspective: Physical Security Proves Its Value[4]

Forty hooded demonstrators seemed to have appeared out of nowhere at the front gate of the breeding farm in the English countryside, where a pharmaceutical giant breeds animals for government-mandated testing of new medicines. A video recording of the incident shows protesters rocking the perimeter fence and harassing employees. What follows here is a description of how this business responded to its protection needs.

For simplicity's sake we will refer to this actual company as "PC" for pharmaceutical company. One threat facing the PC was the fifty or so incidents from animal activists in one year. Consequently, protection against sabotage, terrorism, and infiltration by animal rights activists became top priorities. Measures included physical security and access control, internal theft countermeasures, information safeguards, and bomb threat response. Protection was afforded not only to 2,000 scientists, support personnel, intellectual property, and physical assets, but also to the company image.

The PC favors a layered approach to physical security, which begins with strong perimeter protection. At the breeding farm a seven-foot-high fence bounds the site and security officers monitor the farm from a gatehouse which doubles as a control room for intrusion and fire detection and CCTV. Because no police are nearby, a PC facility twelve miles away provides backup. The PC's response to protestors is low-key in part because in England simple trespass is a civil, not a criminal, matter. Protestors, even if verbally abusive, can only be arrested if they are violent; then police will make the arrests. Protestors generally want media attention so they usually surrender to security when found on the premises. They know they will not be arrested and no civil action will be initiated.

At another PC facility, security integration is shown through CCTV cameras, mounted every 75 yards along the perimeter, that work with video motion detection and infrared sensors. Although continuous recording occurs, when motion is detected the action appears on a monitor for evaluation in the control room. This facility requires vehicles to pass through a raising-arm barrier. Pedestrians must register at a gatehouse and employees use their Wiegand access control cards as they pass through a full-height, antipassback turnstile. Doors are alarmed and windows are treated with anti-bandit glazing to delay an offender.

To reduce internal theft from employees and contractors, personnel are reminded of their responsibility to secure valuables, vulnerable areas have restricted access, doors are kept locked, and a crime prevention day is held. Information is protected through an awareness course, security bulletins, secure fax and videoconferencing facilities, a high priority on computer security, technical surveillance sweeps, and tours under close controls.

The animal activist threat is handled through counterintelligence (i.e., a database of information), vetting (i.e., examination of all personnel to prevent infiltration or the planting of devices to collect information), and public relations (i.e., outreach to explain the importance of research with animals). To deal with bomb threats, PC facilities are too large for a dedicated team to conduct a search, so each employee is responsible for checking for anything unusual in their work area. Also, all incoming mail passes through an X-ray scanner. One lesson from all this protection is that losses can be much more expensive than security.

Barriers

Post and Kingsbury state that "the physical security process utilizes a number of barrier systems, all of which serve specific needs. These systems include natural, structural, human, animals, and energy barriers."[5] *Natural barriers* are rivers, hills, cliffs, mountains, foliage, and other features difficult to overcome. Fences, walls, doors, and the architectural arrangement of buildings are *structural barriers. Human barriers* include security officers who scrutinize people, vehicles, and things entering and leaving a facility. The typical *animal barrier* is a dog. *Energy barriers* include protective lighting and intrusion sensors.

The most common type of barrier is a *chain-link fence* topped with barbed wire. A search of the Web (http://www.techstreet.com/) shows many industry standards for fences from ASTM, UL, ISO, and other groups from the United States and overseas. (See Chapter 3 for these organizations.) An example of a fence standard is ASTM F1043-00, Standard Specification for Strength and Protective Coatings on Metal Industrial Chain Link Fence Framework. This standard covers fences up to 12 feet with post spacing not to exceed 10 feet.

One advantage of chain-link fencing is that it allows observation from both sides: a private security officer looking out and a public police officer looking in. Foliage and decorative plastic woven through the fence can reduce visibility and aid offenders. Opposition to chain-link fencing sometimes develops because management wants to avoid an institutional-looking environment. Hedges are an alternative.

It is advisable that the chain-link fence be made of at least 9-gauge or heavier wire with 2" × 2" diamond-shaped mesh. It should be at least 7 feet high. Its posts should be set in concrete and spaced no more than 10 feet apart. The bottom should be within 2 inches of hard ground; if the ground is soft, the fence can become more secure if extended a few inches below the ground. Recommended at the top is a *top guard*: supporting arms about 1 or

2 feet long containing three or four strands of taut barbed wire 6 inches apart and facing outward at 45 degrees.

Barbed wire fences are less effective and used less frequently than chain-link fences. Each strand of barbed wire is constructed of two 12-gauge wires twisted and barbed every 4 inches. For adequate protection, vertical support posts are placed 6 feet apart, and the parallel strands of barbed wire are from 2 to 6 inches apart. A good height is 8 feet.

Concertina fences consist of coils of steel razor wire clipped together to form cylinders weighing about 55 pounds. Each cylinder is stretched to form a coil-type barrier 3 feet high and 50 feet long. The ends of each 50-foot coil need to be clipped to the next coil to obviate movement. Stakes also stabilize these fences. This fence was developed by the military to act as a quickly constructed barrier. When one coil is placed on another, they create a 6-foot-high barrier. One coil placed on two as a base provides a pyramid-like barrier that is difficult to penetrate. Concertina fences are especially helpful for quick temporary repairs to damaged fences.

Razor ribbon or *coiled barbed tape* are increasing in popularity. They are similar to concertina fencing in many ways. Every few inches along the coil are sharp spikes, looking something like a sharpened bow tie.

Gates are necessary for traffic through fences. The fewer gates, the better because, like windows and doors, they are weak points along a perimeter. Gates usually are secured with a chain and padlock. Uniformed officers stationed at each gate and fence opening increase security while enabling the observation of people and vehicles.

Vehicle barriers control traffic and stop vehicles from penetrating a perimeter. The problems of drive-by shootings and vehicle bombs have resulted in greater use of vehicle barriers. These barriers are assigned government-certified ratings based on the level of protection; however, rating systems vary among government agencies. One agency, for example, tests barriers against 15,000-pound trucks traveling up to 50 miles per hour, while another agency tests 10,000-pound trucks traveling the same speed. *Passive vehicle barriers* are fixed and include decorative bollards, large concrete planters, specially engineered and anchored park benches, hardened fencing, fence cabling, and trees. *Active vehicle barriers* are used at entrances and include gates, barrier arms, and pop-up type systems that are set underground and, when activated, spring up to block a vehicle.[6] As we know, no security method is foolproof, and careful security planning is vital. In 1997, to protest government policy, the environmental group Greenpeace penetrated government security in Washington, D.C., and dumped four tons of coal outside the Capitol building. The driver of the truck drove the wrong way up a one-way drive leading to the building!

Walls are costly and a substitute for fences when management is against the use of a wire fence. Attractive walls can be designed to produce security equal to fences while blending into surrounding architecture. Walls are made from a variety of materials: bricks, concrete blocks, stones, or cement. Depending on design, the top of walls 6 or 7 feet high may contain barbed wire, spikes, or broken glass set in cement. Offenders often avoid injury by throwing a blanket or jacket over the top of the wall (or fence) before scaling it. Many jurisdictions prohibit ominous features at the top of barriers. Check local ordinances. An advantage of a wall is that outsiders are hindered from observing inside. However, observation by public police during patrols also is hindered; this can benefit an intruder.

Hedges or shrubbery are useful as barriers. Thorny shrubs have a deterrent value. These include holly, barberry, and multiflora rose bushes, all of which require a lot of watering. The privet hedge grows almost anywhere and requires minimal care. A combination of hedge and fence is useful. Hedges should be less than 3 feet high and placed on the inside to avoid injury to those passing by and to create an added obstacle for someone attempting to scale the fence. Any plants that are large and placed too close to buildings and other locations provide a climbing tool, cover for thieves, and a hiding place for stolen goods.

Municipal codes restrict the heights of fences, walls, and hedges to maintain an attractive environment devoid of threatening-looking barriers. Certain kinds of barriers may be prohibited to ensure conformity. Planning should encompass research of local standards.

The following list can help a security manager eliminate weak points along a perimeter or barrier.

1. Utility poles, trees, boxes, pallets, forklifts, tools, and other objects outside of a building can be used to scale a barrier.
2. Ladders left outside are a burglar's delight. Stationary ladders are made less accessible via a steel cage with a locked door.
3. A *common wall* is shared by two separate entities. Thieves may lease and occupy or just enter the adjoining building or room and then hammer through the common wall.
4. A roof is easy to penetrate. A few tools, such as a drill and saw, enable offenders to actually cut through the roof. Because lighting, alarms, and patrols rarely involve the roof, this weakness is attractive to thieves. A rope ladder often is employed to descend from the roof, or a forklift might be used to lift items to the roof. Vehicle keys should be hidden and other precautions taken. Alarms, lights, patrols, and a roof fence to hinder access from an adjoining building's roof deter burglars.
5. Roof hatches, skylights, basement windows, air-conditioning and other vent and duct systems, crawl spaces between floors and under buildings, fire escapes, and utility covers may need a combination of locks, alarms, steel bars, heavy mesh, fences, and inspections. A widely favored standard is that any opening greater than 96 square inches requires increased protection.

Windows

Glazing

Glass can be designed to block penetration of bullets, defeat attempted forced entry, remain intact following an explosion, and protect against electronic eavesdropping. The Web shows many standards for glazing from the American Architectural Manufacturers Association (AAMA), ANSI, UL, ASTM, Consumer Product Safety Commission, ISO, and overseas groups. Security glazing should be evaluated on comparative testing to an established national consensus standard such as ASTM F1233(8), Standard Test Method for Security Glazing Materials and Systems. Important issues for glazing include product life cycle, durability, installation, maintenance, and framing.[7]

Underwriters Laboratories classifies *bullet-resistant windows* into eight protection levels, with levels 1 to 3 rated against handguns and 4 to 8 rated against rifles. Level 4 or higher windows usually are applied by government agencies and the military. Protective windows are made of either glass or plastic or mixtures of each.

Laminated glass absorbs a bullet as it passes through various glass layers. The advantage of glass is in its maintenance: easy to clean and less likely to scratch than plastic. It is less expensive per square foot than plastic, but heavier, which requires more workers and stronger frames. Glass has a tendency to spall (i.e., chip) when hit by a bullet. UL752-listed glass holds up to three shots, then it begins to shatter from subsequent shots.

Two types of plastic used in windows are acrylic and polycarbonate. Both vary in thickness and are lighter and more easily scratched than glass. *Acrylic windows* are clear and monolithic, whereas glass and polycarbonate windows are laminates consisting of layers of material bonded one on top of another. Acrylic will deflect bullets and hold together under sustained hits. Some spalling may occur. *Polycarbonate windows* are stronger than acrylics against high-powered weapons. In addition to protective windows, wall armor is important because employees often duck below a window during a shooting. These steel or fiberglass plates also are rated.[8]

Burglar-resistant windows are rated (UL 972, Burglary Resisting Glazing Material), available in acrylic and polycarbonate materials, and protect against hammers, flame, "smash and grab," and other attacks. Combined bullet- and burglar-resistant windows are available. Although window protection is an expense that may be difficult to justify, insurers offer discounts on insurance premiums for such installations.

Following the Oklahoma City bombing, considerable interest focused on the vulnerability of flying glass due not only to explosions, but also to accidents or natural disasters. Experts report that 75 percent of all damage and injury from bomb blasts results from flying and falling glass. Vendors sell shatter-resistant film to reduce this problem. Conversely, a report on the 1993 World Trade Center bombing in New York City claimed that the destroyed windows permitted deadly gases to escape from the building, enabling occupants to survive. Because of this controversy, the U.S. Army

Corps of Engineers is studying how different types of materials perform during bomb blasts. No federal standards currently exist.[9]

Electronic security glazing, containing metalized fabrics, can prevent electromagnetic signals inside a location from being intercepted from outside, while also protecting a facility from external electromagnetic radiation interference from outside sources. Standards for this type of glazing are from the National Security Agency, NSA 65-8.

Window Protection

Covering windows with grating or security screens is an additional step to impede entrance by an intruder or items being thrown out by a dishonest employee. Window grating consists of metal bars constructed across windows. These bars run horizontally and vertically to produce an effective form of protection. Although these bars are not aesthetically pleasing, they can be purchased with attractive ornamental designs. Security screens are composed of steel or stainless steel wire (mesh) welded to a frame. Screens have some distinct advantages over window grating. Employees can pass pilfered items through window bars more easily than through a screen. Security screens look like ordinary screens, but they are much heavier in construction and can stop rocks and other objects.

When planning window protection, one must consider the need for emergency escape and ventilation. To ensure safety, certain windows can be targeted for the dismantling of window protection during business hours.

Window Locks

Businesses and institutions often contain windows that do not open. For windows that do open, a latch or lock on the inside provides some protection. The double-hung window, often applied at residences, is explained here as a foundation for window protection. It consists of top and bottom windows that are raised and lowered for user convenience. When the top window is pushed up and the bottom window pushed down, a sash lock containing a curved turn knob locks both parts of the whole window in place (see Figure 8-3). By inserting a knife under the sash lock where both window sections meet, a burglar can jimmy the latch out of its catch. If an offender breaks the glass, the sash lock can be unlocked by reaching inside. With such simple techniques known to burglars, more complicated defenses are necessary. Nails can be used to facilitate a quick escape while maintaining good window security: one drills a downward-sloping hole into the right and left sides of the window frame where the top and bottom window halves overlap and inserts nails that are thinner and longer than the holes. This enables the nails to be quickly removed during an emergency escape. If a burglar attacks the window, he or she cannot find or remove the nails (see Figure 8-3). Another method is to attach a window lock requiring a key (see Figure 8-3). These locks are capable of securing a window in a closed or slightly opened position. This can be done with the nail (and several holes) as well. The key should be hidden near the window in case of emergency.

Problems

Solutions

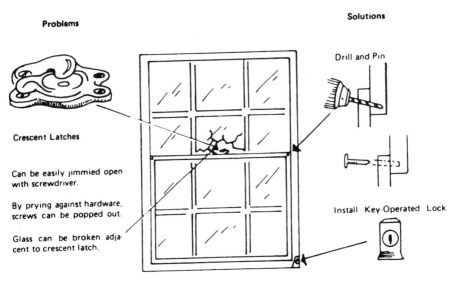

Crescent Latches

Can be easily jimmied open with screwdriver.

By prying against hardware, screws can be popped out.

Glass can be broken adjacent to crescent latch.

Drill and Pin

Install Key-Operated Lock

Figure 8–3 Double-hung window (view from inside).

Electronic Protection for Windows

Four categories of electronic protection for windows are foil, vibration, glass-breakage, and contact-switch sensors. *Window foil*, which has lost much of its popularity, consists of lead foil tape less than 1 inch wide and paper thin that is applied right on the glass near the edges of a window. In the nonalarm state, electricity passes through the foil to form a closed circuit. When the foil is broken, an alarm is sounded. Window foil is inexpensive and easy to maintain. One disadvantage is that a burglar may cut the glass without disturbing the foil. *Vibration sensors* respond to vibration or shock. They are attached right on the glass or window frame. These sensors are noted for their low false alarm rate and are applicable to fences, walls, and valuable artwork, among other things. *Glass-breakage sensors* react to glass breaking. A sensor the size of a large coin is placed directly on the glass and can detect glass breakage several feet away. Some types operate via a tuning fork, which is tuned to the frequency produced by glass breaking. Others employ a microphone and electric amplifier. *Contact switches* activate an alarm when opening the window interrupts the contact. (In Figure 8-4, this sensor protects a door.)

Additional ideas for window protection follow:

1. A strong window frame fastened to a building prevents prying and removal of the entire window.
2. First floor windows are especially vulnerable to penetration and require increased protection.
3. Consider tinting windows to hinder observation by offenders.
4. Windows (and other openings) no longer used can be bricked.

Figure 8–4   Switch sensors have electrical contacts that make or break an electrical circuit in response to a physical movement.

5. Expensive items left near windows invite trouble.
6. Cleaning windows and windowsills periodically increases the chances of obtaining clear fingerprints in the event of an attack.

Doors

Many standards apply to doors from the AAMA, ANSI, ASTM, National Association of Architectural Metal Manufacturers (NAAMM), NFPA, Steel Door Institute (SDI), UL, and ISO. Also, other countries have standards.

Doors having fire ratings require certain frame and hardware requirements. Decisions on the type of lock and whether electronic access will be applied also affect hardware. Decisions on doors are especially crucial because of their daily use and the potential for satisfying or enraging users and management.[10]

Businesses and institutions generally use aluminum doors. Composed of an aluminum frame, most of the door is covered by glass. Without adequate protection, the glass is vulnerable, and prying the weak aluminum is not difficult. The all-metal door improves protection at the expense of attractiveness.

Hollow-core doors render complex locks useless because an offender can punch right through the door. Thin wood panels or glass on the door are additional weak points. More expensive, *solid-core doors* are stronger; they are made of solid wood (over an inch thick) without the use of weak fillers. To reinforce hollow-core or solid-core doors, one can attach 16-gauge steel sheets, via one-way screws.

Intruding Neighbors

The Finch Brothers Supermarket Company maintained a busy warehouse stocked with hundreds of different items for local Finch supermarkets. The company leased the large warehouse to accommodate the increasing number of supermarkets. After 18 months at this location, managers were stumped as to why shrinkage was over 4 percent. Several precautions were taken to avert losses: perimeter security consisted of intrusion sensors, lighting, and a security officer. A perpetual inventory was maintained.

Eventually, Finch's loss prevention manager's job was on the line, so he began a secret, painstaking, and continuous surveillance of the warehouse at night. After an agonizing week went by, he made an astonishing discovery. A printing company building next door was only 7 feet away from the warehouse and printing company employees on the late shift were able to slide a 12' by 16" by 2" board from a third-story window to a window of the same height at the warehouse. Within 30 minutes, the group of thieves hauled and threw many burlap sacks of items from one building to another. With a sophisticated camera, the manager snapped several pictures. Police were later notified and arrests made.

The thieves confessed that, when they worked the 11 P.M. to 8 A.M. shift, they stole merchandise from the warehouse. They stated that a maintenance man, who visited the warehouse each day, left the window open so the board could be slipped in. They added that dim lighting and the fact that intrusion sensors existed on the first floor only were factors that aided their crimes.

Whenever possible, door hinges should be placed on the inside. Door hinges that face outside enable easy entry. By using a screwdriver and hammer, one can raise the pins out of the hinges to enable the door to be lifted away. To protect the hinge pins, it is a good idea to weld them so they cannot be removed in this manner. Another form of protection is to remove two screws on opposite sides of the hinge, insert a pin or screw on the jamb side of the hinge so that it protrudes about half an inch, and then drill a hole in the opposite hole to fit the pin when the door is closed. With this method on both top and bottom hinges, even if the hinge pins are removed, the door will not fall off the hinges (see Figure 8-5).

Contact switches applied to doors offer electronic protection. Greater protection is provided when contact switches are recessed in the edges of the door and frame. Other kinds of electronic sensors applied at doors include vibration sensors, pressure mats, and various types of motion detectors aimed in the area of the door.

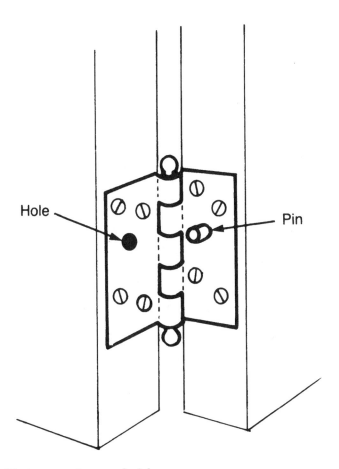

Figure 8–5   Pin to prevent removal of door.

More hints for door security follow:

1. Doors (and windows) are afforded extra protection at night by chain closures. These frequently are seen covering storefronts in malls and in high-crime neighborhoods.
2. To block "hide-in" burglars (those who hide in a building until after closing) from easy exit, require that openings such as doors and windows have a key-operated lock on the inside as well as on the outside.
3. Almost all fire departments are equipped with power saws that cut through door locks and bolts in case of fire. Many firefighters can gain easy access to local buildings because building owners have provided keys that are located in fire trucks. Although this creates a security hazard, losses can be reduced in case of fire.
4. All doors need protection, including garage, sliding, overhead, chain-operated, and electric doors.

Intrusion Detection Systems

Standards for intrusion alarm systems are from UL, the Institute of Electrical and Electronics Engineers (IEEE), and ISO, plus other groups in the United States and overseas. UL, for example, "lists" installation companies who are authorized to issue UL Certificates on each installation. This means that the installer conforms to maintenance and testing as required by UL which conducts unannounced inspections.

Table 8-1 describes intrusion detection systems. These systems have gone through several generations leading to improved performance.[11] Not in the table is *magnetic field*, which consists of a series of buried wire loops or coils. Metal objects moving over the sensor induce a current and signal an alarm. Research shows that the vulnerability to defeat (VD) for magnetic field, infrared photo beam, and taut wire systems is high. Microwave, electric field, fence disturbance, seismic sensor cable, and video motion systems all have a medium VD. The VD for ported coaxial cable systems is low. Visible sensors are relatively easy to defeat but cost effective for low-security applications. Multiple sensors, and especially covert sensors, provide a higher level of protection.[12]

Fiber optics is a growing choice for intrusion detection and transmission. *Fiber optics* refers to the transportation of data by way of guided light waves in an optical fiber. This differs from the conventional transmission of electrical energy in copper wires. Fiber optic applications include video, voice, and data communications. Fiber optic data transmission is more secure and less subject to interference than older methods.

Fiber optic perimeter protection can take the form of a fiber optic net installed on a fence. When an intruder applies stress on the cable, an infrared light source pulsing through the system notes the stress or break and activates an alarm. Optical fibers can be attached to or inserted within numerous items to signal an alarm, including razor ribbon, security grills, windows, and doors, and it can protect valuable assets such as computers.

No one technology is perfect; many protection programs rely on dual technology to strengthen intrusion detection. When selecting a system, it is wise to remember that manufacturers' claims often are based on perfect weather. Security decision makers must clearly understand the advantages and disadvantages of each type of system under a variety of conditions.

Applications

Intrusion detection systems can be classified according to the kind of protection provided. There are three basic kinds of protection: point, area, and perimeter. *Point protection* (see Figure 8-6) signals an alarm when an intrusion is made at a special location. It is also referred to as *spot* or *object protection*. Files, safes, vaults, jewelry counters, and artworks are targets for point protection. Capacitance and vibration systems provide point protection and are installed right on the object. These systems often are used as a backup after a burglar has succeeded in gaining access. *Area protection* (see Figure 8-7) detects an intruder in a selected area such as a main aisle in a building or at a strategic passageway. Ultrasonic, microwave, and infrared systems are applicable to area protection. *Perimeter protection* (see Figure 8-8) focuses on the outer boundary of the premises. If doors and windows

Figure 8–6   Point protection.

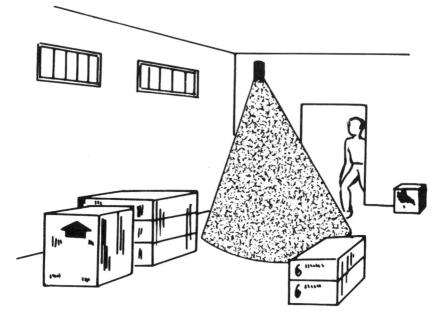

Figure 8–7   Area protection.

Figure 8–8   Perimeter protection.

are part of the perimeter, then contact switches, vibration detectors, and other devices are applicable.

Control Unit

As described in Chapter 7, intrusion detection systems contain three major components: once a *sensor* detects an intruder, a *control unit* receives this information and activates an *annunciator* (e.g., noise or light) to summon security or police. Figure 8-9 shows a control unit with user instructions.

Alarm Signaling Systems

Alarm signaling systems transmit data from a protected area to an annunciation system. Local ordinances and codes may restrict certain systems,

Figure 8–9 Alarm control unit with user instructions.

Table 8-1 Types of Intrusion Alarm Systems*

System	Graphic Idea	Concept	Advantages	Disadvantages
Motion detection				
Fence-mounted sensor		Detection depends on movement of fence	Ease of installation; early detection on interior fence; relatively inexpensive; requires little space; follows terrain easily	Frequent false alarms (weather and birds); conduit breakage; dependent on quality, rigidity of fence, and type of installation
Seismic sensor cable (buried)		Detection depends on ground movement (intruder walking over buried movement sensors, or other seismic disturbances)	Good for any site shape, uneven terrain; early warning; good in warm climate with little rain	False alarms from ground vibrations (vehicles, thunderstorms, heavy snow); not recommended for heavy snow regions; difficult installation and maintenance
Balanced capacitance		Detection depends on touching of cable, interfering with balance of cable	Few false alarms; good for selected areas of fence, rooftops, curves, corners, any terrain	Not to be used independently; for selected areas only
Taut wire		Detection depends on deflecting, stretching, or releasing the tension of wire that triggers alarming mechanism	Good for any terrain or shape; can be used as interior fence; extremely low false alarm rates	Relatively expensive; possible false alarms from snow, ice, birds, etc.; temperature changes require adjustments
Energy field				
Microwave sensor		Based on line of sight; detection depends on intrusion into volumetric area above ground between transmitter and receiver	Does not require a great deal of maintenance	Not good on hilly or heavily contoured terrain; costly installation; potential false alarms caused by weather (snow, ice, wind, and rain); vegetation must be removed

208

Table 8-1 Types of Intrusion Alarm Systems*

System	Graphic Idea	Concept	Advantages	Disadvantages
Energy Field				
Infrared photo beam sensor		Based on line of sight; detection depends on intrusion into beam(s) stacked vertically above ground	Good for short distances, building walls, and sally ports	Distances between transmitter and receiver must be short, requiring more intervals; potential false alarms by animals and weather conditions (fog, dust, snow); voltage surges
Ported coaxial cable		Detection depends on interruption of field in terms of mass, velocity, and length of time	Adaptable to most terrains	False alarms caused by heavy rain (pooling of water), high winds, tree roots; relatively expensive installation and maintenance
Video motion detection		Detection depends on change in video-monitor signal	Good for enhancing another system; good for covering weak spots	Lighting is a problem
Electric field sensor		Detection depends on penetration of volumetric field created by field wires and sensor wires	Good on hilly or heavily contoured terrain; can be freestanding or fence-mounted	Requires more maintenance; sensor wires must be replaced every 3 years; vegetation must be controlled

*Sources: Information from New York State Department of Corrections, Pennsylvania Department of Corrections, South Carolina Department of Corrections, and Federal Bureau of Prisons. Reproduced from U.S. Dept. of Justice, National Institute of Justice, *Stopping Escapes: Perimeter Security* (U.S. Government Printing Office, August 1987), p. 6.

designate to whom the alarm may be transmitted, or limit the length of time the alarm is permitted to sound.

Local alarm systems notify, by sound or lights, people in the hearing or seeing range of the signal. This includes the intruder, who may flee. Typically, a bell rings outside of a building. Often, local alarms produce no response—in urban areas responsible action may not be taken, and in rural areas nobody may hear the alarm. These alarms are less expensive than other signaling systems but are easily defeated. If a local alarm is used during a robbery, people may be harmed.

A central station alarm system receives intrusion or fire signals or both at a computer console located and monitored a distance away from the protected location. When an alarm signal is received, central station personnel contact police, firefighters, or other responders. Central station services employ sales, installation, service, monitoring, and response personnel. Proprietary monitoring systems are similar to central station systems, except that the former does the monitoring and the system is operated by the proprietary organization. Resources for central station design are available from UL, NFPA, and the Security Industry Association.[13]

A variety of data transmission systems are utilized to signal an alarm.[14] Telephone lines have been used for many years. Here, the earlier technology is covered first before the more modern technology.

Automatic telephone dialer systems are of two kinds: tape dialer and digital dialer. Tape dialer systems seldom are used today. They deliver a prerecorded or coded message to an interested party (e.g., central station, police department) after that party answers the telephone. Digital dialers do not use a recorded tape message; coded electronic pulses are transmitted, and an electronic terminal decodes the message onto a panel or teletype.

With direct connect systems the intrusion device is connected by wire directly to an alarm receiver located on the premises, at a police station, or some other location. Local ordinances may not permit direct reporting to police stations. A variation of this method is the "buddy" alarm system, in which the alarm signal is transmitted via direct wire to a neighbor, who calls the police. These systems usually are silent alarms.

Radio frequency (RF) and microwave data transmission systems often are applied where telephone lines are not available or where hardwire lines are not practical. The components include transmitter, receiver, repeaters to extend range, battery backup, and solar power.

Fiber optic data transmission systems, as discussed earlier, transport data by way of light waves within a thin glass fiber. These cables are either underground or above ground. The components include transmitter, receiver, repeaters, battery backup, and solar power. Fiber optic systems often support computer-based multiplex data communications systems and are more secure than direct wire.

Signals should be backed up by multiple technologies. Options for off-site transmission of activity include satellite, LAN, WAN, cellular, and the

Internet. Cellular is especially useful for backup since it is more likely to remain in operation in certain disasters.[15]

Among the advances in alarm monitoring is remote programming. By this method, a central station can perform a variety of functions without ever visiting the site. Capabilities include system arming and disarming, unlocking doors, diagnostics and corrections, and, with access systems, adding or deleting cards.

Alarm systems also may be multiplexed or integrated. *Multiplexing* is a method of transmitting multiple information signals over a single communications channel. This single communications channel reduces line requirements by allowing signal transmission from many protected facilities. Two other advantages are that more detailed information can be transmitted, such as telling which detector is in an alarm state, and transmission line security is enhanced through the use of encoding. *Integrated systems*, as covered in Chapter 7, combine multiple systems (e.g., alarm monitoring, access controls, and CCTV).

CCTV

Closed-circuit television allows one person to view several locations. This is a distinct advantage when protecting the boundaries of a facility, because it reduces personnel costs.

Television programs and movies sometimes portray an intruder penetrating a perimeter barrier by breaking through when a CCTV camera had momentarily rotated to another location. Usually the camera just misses the intruder by returning to the entry point right after the intruder gains access. Such a possibility can be averted via overlapping camera coverage. If cameras are capable of viewing other cameras, personnel can check on viewing obstructions, sabotage, vandalism, or other problems. Tamper-proof housings will impede those interested in disabling cameras. Different models are resistant to bullets, explosion, dust, and severe weather. Housings are manufactured with heaters, defrosters, windshield wipers, washers, and sun shields. Low-light-level cameras provide the means to view outside when very little light is available. When no visible light is available, an infrared illuminator creates light, invisible to the naked eye, but visible to infrared-sensitive cameras. Another option is thermal imaging cameras, which sense heat and are especially helpful to spot intruders in darkness, fog, smoke, and foliage.[16]

An essential aspect of CCTV is proper monitoring. To reduce fatigue and ensure good-quality viewing, it is a good idea to rotate personnel every two hours if possible, limit TV monitors to fewer than 10, arrange the monitors in a curved configuration in front of the viewer, control the lighting over the console to avoid glare on the monitor screens or tilt the monitors if necessary, place the monitors in an order that permits easy recognition of camera locations, provide a swivel chair that hampers the opportunity for sleeping, and assign tasks to the viewer (e.g., communications, logging). The previous chapter covers technology that has enhanced CCTV systems.

Lighting

From a business perspective, lighting can be justified because it improves sales by making a business and merchandise more attractive, promotes safety and prevents lawsuits, improves employee morale and productivity, and enhances the value of real estate. From a security perspective, two major purposes of lighting are *to create a psychological deterrent to intrusion* and *to enable detection.* Good lighting is considered such an effective crime control method that the law, in many locales, requires buildings to maintain adequate lighting.

One way to analyze lighting deficiencies is to go to the building at night and study the possible methods of entry and areas where inadequate lighting will aid a burglar. Before the visit, one should contract local police as a precaution against mistaken identity and to recruit their assistance in spotting weak points in lighting.

Negligence Caused by Lighting Deficiency

Entities have an obligation to create a safe environment through lighting. In addition to moral and societal obligations, legal responsibilities are illustrated in the Illinois case of *Fancil v. Q.S.E. Foods, Inc.* In this case, a police officer's widow won a wrongful death suit because a store owner had disconnected his back-door light even though the location had been burglarized several times and the owner was aware that local police checked the business during the evenings. A burglar hidden in a dark area shot the officer. The court found the store owner guilty of negligence through his failure to provide adequate lighting.[17]

What lighting level will aid an intruder? Most people believe that under conditions of darkness a criminal can safely commit a crime. But this view may be faulty, in that one generally cannot work in the dark. Three possible levels of light are *bright light, darkness,* and *dim light.* Bright light affords an offender plenty of light to work but enables easy observation by others; it will deter crime. Without light—in darkness—a burglar finds that he or she cannot see to jimmy a door lock, release a latch, or whatever work is necessary to gain access. However, dim light provides just enough light to break and enter while hindering observation by authorities. Support for this view was shown in a study of crimes during full-moon phases, when dim light was produced. This study examined the records of 972 police shifts at three police agencies, for a two-year period, to compare nine different crimes during full-moon and non-full-moon phases. Only one crime, breaking and entering, was greater during full-moon phases.[18]

Although much case law supports lighting as an indicator of efforts to provide a safe environment, security specialists are questioning conventional wisdom about lighting.[19] Because so much nighttime lighting goes unused, should it be reduced or turned off? Does an offender look more suspicious under a light or in the dark with a flashlight? Should greater use be made of motion-activated lighting? How would these approaches affect safety and cost-effectiveness? These questions are ripe for research.

What are your views on nighttime lighting? Should certain locations turn it off?

Illumination[20]

Lumens (of light output) per watt (of power input) is a measure of lamp efficiency. Initial lumens-per-watt data are based on the light output of lamps when new; however, light output declines with use. *Illuminance* is the intensity of light falling on a surface, measured in foot-candles (English units) or lux (metric units). The *foot-candle* (FC) is a measure of how bright the light is when it reaches one foot from the source. One lux equals 0.0929 FC. The light provided by direct sunlight on a clear day is about 10,000 FC, an overcast day would yield about 100 FC, and a full moon about 0.01 FC. A sample of outdoor lighting illuminances recommended by the Illuminating Engineering Society of North American are as follows: self-parking area, 1 FC; attendant parking area, 2 FC; covered parking area, 5 FC; active pedestrian entrance, 5 FC; building surroundings, 1 FC. It generally is recommended that gates and doors, where identification of persons and things takes place, should have at least 2 FC. An office should have a light level of about 50 FC.

Care should be exercised when studying FC. Are they horizontal or vertical? Horizontal illuminance may not aid in the visibility of vertical objects such as signs and keyholes. (The preceding FC are horizontal.) FC vary depending on the distance from the lamp and the angle. If you hold a light meter horizontally, it often gives a different reading than if you hold it vertically. Are the FC initial or maintained? Maintenance and bulb replacement ensure high-quality lighting.

Lamps[21]

The following lamps are applied outdoors:

- *Incandescent* lamps are commonly found at residences. Passing electrical current through a tungsten wire that becomes white-hot produces light. These lamps produce 10 to 20 lumens per watt, are the least efficient and most expensive to operate, and have a short lifetime of from 1,000 to 2,000 hours.

- *Halogen* and *quartz halogen* lamps are incandescent bulbs filled with halogen gas (like sealed-beam auto headlights) and provide about 25 percent better efficiency and life than ordinary incandescent bulbs.
- *Fluorescent* lamps pass electricity through a gas enclosed in a glass tube to produce light, producing 40 to 80 lumens per watt. They create twice the light and less than half the heat of an incandescent bulb of equal wattage and cost 5 to 10 times as much. Fluorescent lamps do not provide high levels of light output. The lifetime is 10,000 to 15,000 hours. They are not used extensively outdoors, except for signage.
- *Mercury vapor* lamps also pass electricity through a gas. The yield is 30 to 60 lumens per watt and the life is about 20,000 hours.
- *Metal halide* lamps are also of the gaseous type. The yield is 80 to 100 lumens per watt, and the life is about 10,000 hours. They often are used at sports stadiums because they imitate daylight conditions and colors appear natural. Consequently, these lamps complement CCTV systems, but they are the most expensive light to install and maintain.
- *High-pressure sodium* lamps are gaseous, yield about 100 lumens per watt, have a life of about 20,000 hours, and are energy efficient. These lamps are often applied on streets and parking lots, cut through fog, and are designed to allow the eyes to see more detail at greater distances.
- *Low-pressure sodium* lamps are gaseous, produce 150 lumens per watt, have a life of about 15,000 hours, and are even more efficient than high-pressure sodium. These lamps are expensive to maintain.

Each type of lamp has a different *color rendition*, which is the way a lamp's output affects human perceptions of color. Incandescent, fluorescent, and certain types of metal halide lamps provide excellent color rendition. Mercury vapor lamps provide good color rendition but are heavy on the blue. High-pressure sodium lamps, which are used extensively outdoors, provide poor color rendition, making things look yellow. Low-pressure sodium lamps make color unrecognizable and produce a yellow-gray color on objects. People find sodium vapor lamps, sometimes called *anticrime lights*, to be harsh because they produce a strange yellow haze. Claims are made that this lighting conflicts with aesthetic values and that it affects sleeping habits. In many instances, when people park their vehicles in a parking lot during the day and return to find their vehicle at night, they are often unable to locate it because of poor color rendition from sodium lamps; some report their vehicles as being stolen. Another problem is the inability of witnesses to describe offenders accurately.

Mercury vapor, metal halide, and high-pressure sodium take several minutes to produce full light output. If they are turned off, even more time is required to reach full output because they first have to cool down. This may not be acceptable for certain security applications. Incandescent, halogen, and quartz halogen have the advantage of instant light once electricity is turned on. Manufacturers can provide information on a host of lamp characteristics including the "strike" and "restrike" time.

The following three sources provide additional information on lighting:

- *National Lighting Bureau* (http://www.nlb.org/): Publications.
- *Illuminating Engineering Society of North America* (http://www.iesna.org/): Technical materials and services; recommended practices and standards; many members are engineers.
- *International Association of Lighting Management Companies* (http://www.nalmco.org/): Seminars, training, and certification programs.

Lighting Equipment

Incandescent or gaseous discharge lamps are used in street lights. Fresnel lights have a wide flat beam that is directed outward to protect a perimeter, glaring in the faces of those approaching. A floodlight "floods" an area with a beam of light, resulting in considerable glare. Floodlights are stationary, although the light beams can be aimed to select positions. The following strategies reinforce good lighting:

1. Locate perimeter lighting to allow illumination of both sides of the barrier.
2. Direct lights down and away from a facility to create glare for an intruder. Make sure the directed lighting does not hinder observation by patrolling officers.
3. Do not leave dark spaces between lighted areas for burglars to move within. Design lighting to permit overlapping illumination.
4. Protect the lighting system: locate lighting inside the barrier, install protective covers over lamps, mount lamps on high poles, bury power lines, and protect switch boxes.
5. Photoelectric cells will enable lights to go on and off automatically in response to natural light. Manual operation is helpful as a backup.
6. Consider motion-activated lighting for external and internal areas.
7. If lighting is required in the vicinity of navigable waters, contact the U.S. Coast Guard.
8. Try not to disturb neighbors by intense lighting.
9. Maintain a supply of portable, emergency lights and auxiliary power in the event of a power failure.
10. Good interior lighting also deters burglars. Locating lights over safes, expensive merchandise, and other valuables and having large clear windows (especially in retail establishments) lets passing patrol officers see in.
11. If necessary, join other business owners to petition local government to install improved street lighting.

Parking Lot and Vehicle Controls

In the previous chapter, considerable attention focused on access controls. This chapter stresses parking lot and vehicle controls as integral components of access controls.

A well-designed parking lot is a chief prerequisite to construction. Space usually is limited, and the layout of parking spaces and traffic lanes demands care. Employee access control to a building is easier when a parking lot is on one side of a building rather than surrounding the building. Vehicles should be parked away from shipping and receiving docks, garbage dumpsters, and other crime-prone locations.

Executives and other employees should have permanent parking stickers, whereas visitors, delivery people, and service groups should be given a temporary pass to be displayed on the windshield. Stickers and passes allow uniformed officers to locate unauthorized vehicles.

Parking lots are more secure when these specific strategies are applied: security patrols, panic buttons and emergency phones, lighting, and CCTV.[22] Assault, rape, robbery, and larceny committed in parking areas can harm morale and create lawsuits, unless employees (and customers) are protected. Hospitals, for example, supply an escort for nurses who walk to their vehicles after late shifts. Employee education about personal safety, locking vehicles, and additional precautions will cut losses. Furthermore, the threat of drive-by shootings and vehicle bombs may necessitate vehicle barriers as discussed earlier in the chapter.

Certain types of equipment can aid a parking lot safety program. Cushman patrol vehicles, capable of traveling through narrow passageways, increase patrol mobility. Bicycles are another option. Security booths (unfortunately called *guard shacks* at times) are useful as command posts in parking lots.

Security Officers

Officers normally are assigned to stationary (fixed) posts or to patrol. A *stationary post* is at a door or gate where people, vehicles, and objects are observed and inspected. Stationary posts also involve directing traffic or duty at a command post where communications, CCTV, and alarms are monitored. *Foot or vehicle patrols* conducted throughout the premises and along perimeters identify irregularities while deterring offenders. Examples of unusual or harmful conditions that should be reported are damaged security devices, holes in perimeter fences or other evidence of intrusion, hidden merchandise, unattended vehicles parked inappropriately, keys left in vehicles, employees sleeping in vehicles or using drugs, blocked fire exits, cigarette butts in no-smoking areas, accumulations of trash, and odors from fuels or other combustibles. In contrast to public police officers, private security officers act in primarily a preventive role and *observe and report*.

Before security officers are employed, far-sighted planning ensures optimum effectiveness of this service. What are the unique characteristics of the location? What assets need protection? How many hours per day is the facility open? How many employees? How many visitors and vehicles are admitted daily? What are the particular vulnerabilities? How will security officers interact with other loss prevention measures?

Security officers are expensive. Wages, insurance, uniforms, equipment, and training add up to a hefty sum per officer per year. If each officer costs $30,000 per year for a proprietary force and 5 officers are required for the premises at all times, to maintain all shifts 7 days per week requires approximately 20 officers. The cost would be about $600,000 per year. To reduce costs, many companies switch to contract security services and/or consider technological solutions.

Several specific steps can be taken to improve the effectiveness of officers. Three of the most critical are *careful applicant screening, sound training*, and *proper supervision*. Management should ensure that officers know what is expected of them. Policies, procedures, and day-to-day duties are communicated via verbal orders, memos, and training programs. Policies should ensure that supervisors check on officers every hour. Irregular, unpredictable patrols hinder offenders. Rotating officers reduces fatigue while familiarizing them with a variety of duties. Providing inspection lists for adverse conditions will keep them mentally alert. The formal list should be returned with a daily report. Courtesy and a sharp appearance command respect from employees and visitors.

Monitoring Officers

Historically, *watch clocks* have been used to monitor officer patrols along preplanned routes. The officer on patrol carried this older technology, consisting of a timepiece that contained a paper tape or disc divided into time segments. A watch clock was operated by an officer via keys mounted in walls at specific locations along a patrol route. These keys were often within metal boxes and chained to walls. When inserted into the watch clock, the key made an impression in the form of a number on the tape or disc. Supervisors could examine this to see whether the officer visited each key location and completed the scheduled route. Keys were located at vulnerable locations (e.g., entry points, flammable storage areas). Good supervision prevented officers from disconnecting all the keys at the beginning of the shift, bringing them to one location for use in the watch clock (and, thus, avoiding an hourly tour), and returning the keys at the end of the shift.

Automatic monitoring systems are another way to monitor patrols and keep records. Key stations are visited according to a preplanned time schedule and route. If an officer does not visit a key station within a specific time period, a central monitoring station receives a transmitted signal, and if contact cannot be made, personnel are dispatched.

Bar-code or *touch button* technology provides other avenues for monitoring patrols. A security officer carries a wand that makes contact with a bar code or touch button to record data that is later downloaded into a computer. Bar codes or buttons are affixed at vulnerable locations for a swipe by the wand to record the visit by the officer, who can also swipe bar codes or buttons carried by the officer that represent various conditions (e.g., fire extinguisher needs recharging). Supervision of these systems ensures that officers are patrolling properly and conditions are being reported.[23] To improve the efficiency of security officers, a wireless tablet PC (see Figure 8-10) enables an officer to leave a monitoring post and take the workstation with him or her. If, for example, an officer must leave a control center to investigate an incident, the officer can bring the tablet PC and continue to watch CCTV, monitor alarms, and open doors for employee access.

Figure 8–10   The tablet PC is a mobile workstation enabling a security officer to leave a post and do many things mobile that are done from a desktop PC, such as view CCTV, monitor alarms, and open doors. Courtesy: Hirsch Electronics, Santa Ana, CA.

Lower burglary and fire insurance premiums are possible through the use of monitored patrols. Insurance personnel may subject records to inspection.

Contraband Detection

Contraband is an item that is illegal to possess or prohibited from being brought into a specific area. Examples are weapons, illegal drugs, and explosives. *Security officers play a crucial role in spotting contraband* at businesses, schools, airports, courthouses, and many other locations. They use special devices to locate contraband, and *these expensive devices are as good as the personnel behind them.* Here is an overview of these devices.[24]

- *Metal detectors* transmit a magnetic field that is disturbed by a metallic object, which sets off a light or audio signal. Two types of metal detectors are handheld and walk-through. False alarms are a common problem.
- *X-ray scanners* use pulsed energy to penetrate objects that are shown on a color monitor. Drugs, plastic explosives, and firearms with plastic parts are difficult to identify with this method of detection.
- *Dual-energy systems* use X-rays at different energy levels to classify objects as organic, inorganic, or mixed. Colors are assigned to each classification to help spot contraband. When color and shape are observed, these systems are good at detecting explosives since most are organic.
- *Computed tomography scanners* are like CAT scanners used in hospitals. An X-ray source is spun around an object taking slice pictures that show on a computer. Although this device is expensive, detection of items is good.

Armed versus Unarmed Officers

The question of whether to arm officers is controversial. Probably the best way to answer this question is to study the nature of the particular officer's assignment. If violence is likely, then officers should be armed. Officers assigned to locations where violent crimes are unlikely do not need firearms which, if worn by officers, could be offensive. The trend is toward unarmed officers because of liability issues.

If weapons are issued to officers, proper selection of officers and training are of the utmost importance. Instructions on the use of force and firearms safety, as well as practice on the firing range every four months, will reduce the chances of accidents, mistakes, and costly lawsuits.

Communications and the Control Center

As emergency personnel know, the ability to communicate over distance is indispensable. Every officer should be equipped with a portable two-way radio; this communication aid permits officers to summon assistance and notify superiors about hazards and impending disasters. Usually, officers on assignment communicate with a control center that is the hub of the loss prevention program. The control center is the appropriate site for a console containing alarm indicators, CCTV monitors, door controls, the public address system, and an assortment of other components for communication and loss prevention (see Figure 8-11). Because personnel will seek guidance from the control center in the event of an emergency, that center must be secure and operational at all times. A trend today is automated response systems programmed into the control center because so many decisions and actions are required for each type of emergency.[25] The control center is under increased protection against forced entry, tampering, or disasters when it contains a locked door, is located in a basement or underground, and is constructed of fire-resistant materials. An automatic, remotely operated lock, released by the console operator after identifying the caller, also enhances security. Bullet-resistant glass is wise for high-crime locations. Whoever designs the control center should be well versed in ergonomics, which deals with the efficient and safe partnership between people and machines.

Protective Dogs

Classified as an animal barrier, a dog can strengthen security around a protected location. An *alarm dog* patrols inside a fenced area or building and

Figure 8–11   Security officer at console managing access control, CCTV, alarm monitoring, and video imaging. Courtesy: Diebold, Inc.

barks at the approach of a stranger, but makes no attempt to attack. These dogs retreat when threatened but continue to bark. Such barking may become so alarming to an intruder that he or she will flee. A *guard or attack dog* is similar to an alarm dog with an added feature of attacking the intruder. To minimize the possibility of a lawsuit, these dogs should be selectively applied and adequately fenced in, and warning signs should be posted. An experienced person on call at all times is needed to respond to emergencies. Another type of attack dog is the *sentry dog*. This dog is kept on a leash and responds to commands while patrolling with a uniformed officer. The advantages are numerous These animals protect officers. Their keen sense of hearing and smell is a tremendous asset when trying to locate a hidden burglar (or explosives or drugs). Dogs can discern the slightest perspiration from people under stress, enabling the dog to sense individuals who are afraid of them. An ingredient in stress perspiration irritates dogs, which makes frightened persons more susceptible to attack. When an "attack" command is given, a German shepherd has enough strength in its jaws to break a person's arm.

In addition to the possibility of a lawsuit if a dog attacks someone, there are other disadvantages to the use of dogs. If a proprietary dog is part of the protective team, personnel and kennel facilities are needed to care for the dogs. These costs and others include the purchase of dogs and their training, medical care, and food. Using a contract service would probably be more feasible. Another disadvantage is the possibility that dogs may be poisoned, anesthetized, or killed. A burglar also may befriend a dog. Dogs should be taught to accept food only from the handler. Neighbors near the protected premises often find dogs noisy or may perceive them as offensive for other reasons.

Which strategies do you view as affording the best protection against unauthorized entry? Support your answer.

International Perspective: UN Efforts at Global Crime Prevention

In 1951, the United Nations established the Ad Hoc Advisory Committee of Experts to advise the UN on crime matters. In 1971, the group's name changed to the Committee on Crime Prevention and Control.

Several strategies are employed by the UN to prevent crime and improve justice. The UN fosters UN norms in national legislation, conducts research, and provides technical expertise to countries. Every five years since 1955, the UN has held a congress on crime issues, where successful policies and strategies are shared.[26]

In light of the crime problem, the UN asked its member states to prepare an inventory of crime prevention measures so the information can be published and shared worldwide. The inventory focuses on four sections:

- *Crime prevention through social measures.* This approach tackles the root causes of crime and works to improve the family, schools, activities for youth, employment, and health.
- *Situational crime prevention.* These measures involve the management, design, or manipulation of the environment to reduce opportunities for criminal behavior and increase the risk for the offender. Specific strategies include hardening the target through security surveys, building and design codes, publicity and awareness campaigns, and insurance incentives to install physical security. Additional measures are marking property, natural surveillance (i.e., designing the inside and outside of buildings so people can more easily observe others), Neighborhood Watch, and citizen patrols.
- *Community crime prevention.* This approach recognizes that physical security should be part of a broader, community-based response to crime. Community policing and multiagency cooperation are also a part of this approach.
- *Planning, implementation, and evaluation of crime prevention.* The first step in this approach is an analysis of crime and victimization. Compiling and analyzing the location and nature of offenses and many other characteristics of crime enhance crime prevention planning and implementation. Evaluation assesses whether preventive measures were successful.[27]

In essence, crime is a global problem and many of the crime prevention methods employed in the United States also are employed overseas. The UN is asking member nations to compile and share their ideas on how best to reduce crime.

Search the Web

Use your favorite search engines to see what vendors have to offer and prices for the following: fences, window protection or glazing, door protection, intrusion detection systems, security lighting, and protective dogs.

CASE PROBLEMS

8A. Study the characteristics of Woody's Lumber Company, the Smith Shirt manufacturing plant, and Compulab Corporation (Figures 7-1, 7-2, and 7-3). Establish a priority list of what you think are the ten most important countermeasures for each location to prevent unauthorized entry. Why did you select as top priorities your first three strategies from each list?

8B. As a security manager for a corporation, you made several written recommendations to management to improve perimeter security at corporate headquarters located in a suburban environment. Management rejected your plans because "headquarters will look like a prison." What measures can you include in your new plan that provide security and are aesthetically pleasing?

8C. As a newly hired security manager for an office building, a site for research and development, you are faced with three immediate challenges: (1) some employees are not wearing required ID badges from when they first enter the building to when they depart; (2) during off-hours there are too many security system false alarms; and (3) public police are responding to about half of these alarms. What do you do?

8D. You are a physical security specialist for a corporation with locations worldwide. Your next big assignment from your supervisor, the VP of Loss Prevention, is to work with a corporate IT specialist to apply Internet technology to the integration of access controls, intrusion detection, and CCTV systems. Basically, the VP wants to "visit" all corporate locations from her office. The IT specialist that you must work with constantly complains, feels that the corporate IT infrastructure has reached its maximum capacity, and seems to be distrustful of loss prevention personnel. How do you gain his cooperation, promote harmony, and get the job done?

NOTES

1. Oscar Newman, *Defensible Space* (New York: Macmillan, 1972).
2. Patrick M. Murphy, "Grounds for Protection," *Security Management* 44 (October 2000), pp. 84–88.
3. Ralph B. Taylor and Adele V. Harrell, *Physical Environment and Crime* (Washington, D.C.: National Institute of Justice, May 1996), pp. 1–32.
4. Michael Gips, "A Pharmacopoeia of Protection," *Security Management* 43 (March 1999), pp. 42–50.
5. Richard S. Post and Arthur A. Kingsbury, *Security Administration: An Introduction*, 3rd ed. (Springfield, IL: Charles C. Thomas Publishing Co., 1977), pp. 502–503.
6. Tim True, "Raising the Ramparts," *Security Management* (October 1996), pp. 49–53.
7. Saflex, Inc., *Introduction to Security Glazing* (http://www.saflex.com/; April 7, 2001).
8. Sharon Durst, "Dodging the Bullet," *Security Management* (October 1996), pp. 55–58.
9. "Framing the Debate on Window Safety," *Security Management* (August 1996), pp. 13. And, Saflex, Inc., "Applications/Security" (April 7, 2001).
10. Jeff Schumacher, "How to Resolve Conflict with Proper Systems Integration," *Security Technology & Design* 10 (October 2000), p. 40.
11. Paul Trouten, "Improving Perimeter Security with Digital Signal Processing," *Security Technology & Design* 10 (June 2000), pp. 68–72. Also, http://www.senstarstellar.com/ (April 7, 2001).

12. Ronald W. Clifton and Martin L. Vitch, "Getting a Sense for Danger," *Security Management* (February 1997), pp. 57–61.
13. David Patterson, "How Smart Is Your Setup?" *Security Management* 44 (March 2000), p. 80.
14. See Robert L. Barnard, *Intrusion Detection Systems*, 2nd ed. (Boston: Butterworth–Heinemann, 1988).
15. Tim O'Leary, "The Real Deal in Perimeter Security," *Security Technology & Design* 10 (January 2000), p. 75. And, Steve Keller, "Framing an Alarm Design," *Security Management* 44 (January 2000), p. 133.
16. "Guard Perimeters with Thermal Cameras," *Security Watch* 2914 (July 15, 2000), p. 7.
17. U.S. Department of Justice, *Report of the Task Force on Private Security* (Washington, D.C.: U.S. Government Printing Office, 1976), p. 183.
18. Philip Purpura, "Police Activity and the Full Moon," *Journal of Police Science and Administration* 7, no. 3 (September 1979), p. 350.
19. Henri Berube, "New Notions of Night Light," *Security Management* (December 1994), pp. 29–33.
20. National Lighting Bureau, *Lighting for Safety and Security* (Washington, D.C.: National Lighting Bureau, n.d.), pp. 1–36; Mary S. Smith, *Crime Prevention Through Environmental Design in Parking Facilities* (Washington, D.C.: National Institute of Justice, April 1996), pp. 1–4; Dan M. Bowers, "Let There Be Light," *Security Management* (September 1995), pp. 103–111; Douglas R. Kunze and John Schiefer, "An Illuminating Look at Light," *Security Management* (September 1995), pp. 113–116.
21. Ibid.
22. Howard Moster and Ann Longmore-Etheridge, "A Good Parking Space," *Security Management* 44 (October 2000), pp. 62–68.
23. Louise Arnheim, "A Tour of Guard Patrol Systems," *Security Management* (November 1999), pp. 48–58.
24. "Scanning for Trouble," *Security Watch* 2908 (April 15, 2000), pp. 1–3.
25. Patterson, pp. 76–81.
26. United Nations, "Work of the United Nations in Crime Prevention and Criminal Justice," *Crime Prevention and Criminal Justice* (June 1993), pp. 1–19.
27. Eighth United Nations Congress on the Prevention of Crime and the Treatment of Offenders, *Inventory of Comprehensive Crime Prevention Measures* (Havana, Cuba, September 1990).

9

Services and Systems: Methods Toward Wise Purchasing Decisions

OBJECTIVES

After studying this chapter the reader will be able to:

1. Discuss the dangers when purchasing security/loss prevention services and systems.
2. List five specific purchasing rules and seven sources of information.
3. List guidelines and inquisitive questions that improve purchasing decisions when obtaining security services.
4. List guidelines and inquisitive questions that improve purchasing decisions when obtaining security systems.
5. Explain outsourcing.

One topic often neglected in the security literature focuses on how to make wise purchasing decisions when obtaining security services and systems. The best security plans are useless when poor purchasing decisions are made to implement those plans. *Services* include activities performed by personnel to further the goals of security and loss prevention. Security officers represent a large part of available services. *Systems* include manufactured items that increase security. This chapter emphasizes security services and systems, keeping in mind the understanding that fire protection and safety are integral components of an effective loss prevention program.

Most business executives and institutional administrators do not know how to select security services or systems or even what questions to ask vendors. Frequently, money is wasted and the results after the purchases are made are disappointing. A specialist in the field who is not a salesperson can improve decision making.

During their careers loss prevention practitioners are most likely to purchase all kinds of services and systems. Purchasing decisions have a definite impact on career opportunities and on the success of loss prevention programs. Care is required during decision making to obtain the best services and systems for the money at hand. This task is difficult when one is confronted with a multitude of salespeople and a varied market that is taking in billions of dollars per year.

THE DANGERS OF PURCHASING

Suppliers of services and systems are not immune to the temptation of unethical and illegal activities for profit. Vendors (sellers) have been known to misrepresent information, exaggerate, lie, and fail to deliver what was promised. The rotten-apple syndrome is prevalent in this industry just as it is in other facets of life—there are unscrupulous vendors as well as honest ones.

A U.S. Department of Justice publication, *Private Police in the United States: Findings and Recommendations*, states:

> On the basis of regulatory-agency reports of the number of complaints filed and the reasons for licenses being suspended and revoked, and on the basis of impressions gleaned from security executives, we conclude that substantial dishonesty and poor business practices exist. The former entails common crimes by some security employees and employers, including burglary, robbery, theft, and extortion. The latter include franchising licenses, operating without a license, failure to perform services paid for, misrepresenting price or service to be performed, and negligence in performing security duties.[1]

Purchasers of security officer services may be billed for hours not worked. Because this service industry is so competitive, some companies bid very low, knowing that they will have to bill the client for phantom services (services not rendered) to make a profit. Other companies lie to clients about training and experience. Promised supervision may not take place. Liability insurance coverage may be exaggerated or nonexistent. Investigative companies that conduct overt and undercover investigations are known to deceive clients about excessive losses through scary weekly reports in order to lengthen investigations and thereby reap greater profits.

Techniques employed by people selling systems include selling unneeded equipment. Alarm systems composed of outdated technology, which are overstocked at warehouses, are pushed on buyers who do not realize that burglars can easily defeat these systems. Salespeople conveniently delete information concerning extra personnel needed, additional hardware required, software problems, and expensive maintenance. Vendors sell technology that makes customers think they are monitoring remotely, but with real-time delay, it is not so. Demo videos are sent to prospective buyers with systems operating under ideal conditions (e.g., perfect weather and lighting).[2] *One specific tactic involves reinforcing the purchaser's fear.* Crime, fire, and accident dangers are intertwined within high-pressure sales pitches.

Most salespeople are not dishonest. Many vendors adhere to ethical conduct. The point of the industry criticism is that the buyer should be aware of these practices when confronted with a purchasing decision.

The *Report of the Task Force on Private Security* and the first Hallcrest report stated several recommendations for improving the industry with the consumer in mind. For example, both reports favor certified training for alarm service personnel.[3]

The following five cardinal rules, designed with the consumer in mind, can put the buyer on the road toward making wise purchasing decisions:

1. Buyer beware.
2. Properly evaluate the needs of the organization to be protected.
3. Acquire information and know the state of the art.
4. Analyze the advantages and disadvantages of each service or system. Apply critical thinking skills.
5. Avoid panic buying.

A survey of the premises will assist the buyer in pinpointing weaknesses and evaluating needs. If the buyer has a list of weaknesses and needs, the salesperson will be hindered from influencing the buyer into purchasing something unnecessary. *To acquire information about services and systems, seven beneficial sources are the Web, trade publications, peers, salespeople, consultants, seminars, and courses.*

Is the security industry the only industry where the buyer should beware? Support your answer.

PURCHASING SECURITY SERVICES

Questions When Considering Contract Security Officers

1. Does the company conform to state and local regulatory law, such as registration, licensing, training, and bonding?
2. What is the contract company's liability and other insurance coverage? Request copies of policies. Are there any lawsuits pending against the company?
3. Have there been any EEO complaints against the company?
4. What is the company's Dun and Bradstreet financial rating?
5. Is the company willing to customize service for client company needs?
6. Does the company have the ability to provide extra officers?
7. Can the company perform expanded services, such as investigations?

8. Have you been invited to visit the company's offices?
9. Have you read the employment application form and company publications (e.g., orders, regulations, training literature)?
10. What type of background screening is employed for applicants? Can you set up an agreement whereby your company interviews officers before assignment? Do you require personnel folders to help you select the best candidates?
11. How often during a shift does a supervisor visit?
12. How does the company ensure the honesty of its officers?
13. How are disciplinary problems handled?
14. In general, how is morale? What is the turnover rate?
15. What is the extent of training?
16. What equipment is supplied to officers?
17. What are the pay scales and benefits?
18. What is the wage-to-rate ratio? This shows the portion of the total rate received by each officer.

Many security firms draft their contracts so that much of the risk is on the customer. An attorney should review contracts and negotiate changes. It is important that both parties know the amount of duty the security company is agreeing to. The contract should specify number of officers and hours, location of officers, and equipment. If, for example, an assault takes place on the tenth floor of a building, the security company may go back to the contract and read that an officer was assigned only to the lobby and that more services were available, but the client refused them.[4]

When dealing with contract companies, it is good to know the views of these business people: many of the managers in contract guard companies refer to their vocation as a "nickel-and-dime-business" with a "never-ending turnover of bodies." The former comment refers to the awarding of contracts by clients based on slim differences in bids. The latter comment refers to the high turnover of officers because of low wages.

International Perspective: Are China's Private Security Services Superior to Those of the United States?[5]

Security service companies (SSCs) are crime control organizations set up in post-Mao China. They perform security services similar to those in the United States.

As foreign investments increased in China, several questions evolved concerning the security of businesses. Foreign companies refused to have a police-controlled security force inside their companies. At the same time, Chinese police will not allow private security forces controlled by foreign owners. This dilemma led to the SSC, a buffer in which foreign managers feel comfortable and the police retain a certain amount of control.

The SSC is characterized by the following:

- The SSC concept has spread throughout China. The services offered depend on the contract with the client and include gate keeping, patrol, fire protection, escort for valuables, and selling security equipment.
- SSC security officers are equipped with uniforms, a badge and ID, "non-offensive tools," and cars. They search, detain, and arrest.
- It is an independent organization whose managers assume responsibility for profit and loss.
- It works on a fee-for-service design by contracting with clients.
- Each SSC must be approved by the government and police and issued a license, and its service fees are controlled by a government agency.
- The police play a heavy role in SSC organization, management, screening of security officers, and training. The SSC leaders are civilians, often retired police or police demobilized for SSC service. The police also control the profits of the SSC.
- Proponents of the SSC claim that crime is a growing problem that community crime control and police are not able to curb and SSC profits can be diverted to public crime control programs.
- Detractors claim that pay for service in public security is an illicit levy.
- One problem is that many nonprofit security forces have changed their names to SSC to make a profit, and this leads to disorganization of community crime prevention. Some SSCs sell nonsecurity merchandise and use their licenses to run other businesses.
- Security services in Western societies are characterized by low pay, high turnover, and difficulty in justifying high-quality training. The SSC pays a stable income, has lower turnover, and requires from one to three months of training.

Do you view China's private security services as superior to those of the United States? Support your answer.

Contract Undercover Investigators

A common scenario in businesses is the panic atmosphere after the discovery of a high inventory-shrinkage statistic following an inventory. When this happens, management wants immediate action even when it is predisposed to avoid panic buying. Management often recruits an outside firm specializing in undercover investigations. The undercover investigator secretly infiltrates employee informal groups, as a regular employee, to gather information about losses.

With an understanding of how contract undercover investigation services operate, the client will obtain better results. When speaking to a service representative, the client needs to find out the cost and probable length of the investigation. These investigations last from six to eight weeks but may require months to yield success. The cost varies from $1,500 to $2,000 per week.[6] The client should ask the representative about the backgrounds of investigators, selection methods (for employment and assignment), training, and supervision. Are investigators bonded? Proof should be provided. Are they prepared to testify in court, if necessary? How many reports will the client receive each week? Undercover investigators send reports to their immediate supervisor, who edits them before sending a report to the client. The reporting phase of the investigation is when unscrupulous activity by the service company may take place. Supervisors are known to withhold from clients good information to submit later during "dry weeks," when no substantial information is uncovered. Frightening reports about losses can scare clients into paying for unnecessarily lengthy investigations. When clients become impatient and ask why the investigation is taking so long, sometimes the service company's response is that "a break in the case is right around the corner and we just need a few more weeks." If put under excessive pressure by supervisors, investigators may succumb to exaggerated reports and may even invent information. Although these practices produce a negative image of undercover investigative services, not all of these companies are unethical. Undercover investigations are a widely used and effective method to combat losses.

Consultants

Why would an executive require the services of a loss prevention consultant? Two major reasons are that (1) the executive lacks knowledge about loss prevention and there is an absence of a proprietary loss prevention practitioner or (2) the executive is a loss prevention practitioner but lacks expertise in a specialized field.

A consultant is commonly called in when a loss problem needs to be corrected—for instance, a baffling shrinkage problem, the loss of trade secrets, or numerous workplace accidents. Consultants also can be a tremendous asset when an organization is contemplating a loss prevention program for the first time or when an established program suffers from morale or training problems. New ideas can stimulate greater efficiency and effectiveness. Consultants can act as a company's representative in negotiating contract services and purchasing systems.

Executives sometimes refrain from hiring a consultant because they feel that it will reflect adversely on their ability. A consultant can be a cost-effective investment, but the buyer must beware.

The client interested in a successful consulting experience will be involved in three specific phases: (1) selection, (2) direction, and (3) evaluation. The objective of the selection phase is to contact the most appropriate person for the job. The executive must first *clearly define the problem* and then search for the individual with the required background.

Select a consultant who is independent, that is, not affiliated with any particular service or system. Also, ask how much money and time are required to complete the work.

In the second phase, the client assists the consultant in becoming familiar with the business and the problem. The consultant is introduced to select personnel. A tour of the premises is another part of what is known as the startup time, which can easily consume a day. The consultant will be preoccupied with collecting information via interviews, observation, and records. Many questions will be asked by the consultant. A previously prepared survey or checklist form is brought by the consultant as a reminder of what specific questions to ask or areas to check. Clients may request a one-day survey followed by verbal advice, whereas other assignments may last for weeks, months, or years.

When sufficient information has been collected, and the consultant has a good grasp of the problem and possible solutions, he or she presents a report of findings and recommendations to the client. Naturally, the consultant is in an advisory capacity and the executives in charge have the authority and must accept the responsibility of instituting the recommendations.

The third and final phase for the client pertains to evaluating the consultant. A standard personnel evaluation form provides several relevant questions (e.g., works well with others, is flexible, communicates clearly). But the primary question is this: was the problem uncovered and satisfactorily remedied?

Certified Protection Professional

Most states have no regulation for security and loss prevention consultants. When registration or licensing is required, it often is accomplished via the laws regulating security officers and private investigators. With such minimal controls, almost anybody can call himself or herself a consultant. Hence, charlatans appear who tarnish the field and create a bad image that reflects on competent professionals.

In light of the scarcity of regulations or standards for loss prevention consultants and managers and to reinforce professionalism in this field, the American Society for Industrial Security (ASIS; http://www.asisonline.org/) created the Certified Protection Professional program in 1972. To qualify for CPP certification, the applicant must meet certain education and experience requirements, affirm adherence to the CPP Code of Professional Responsibility, receive endorsement by a person certified as a CPP, and achieve a passing grade on the written examination.

In addition to ASIS CPPs as a source of consultants, another source, although small, is the International Association of Professional Security

Consultants (IAPSC; http://www.iapsc.org/), founded in 1984. Members of this professional association are required to have education and experience, and the CPP is accepted as a component of the qualifications for membership. Like ASIS, the IAPSC requires its members to adhere to a code of ethics.

> What are the benefits of obtaining the Certified Protection Professional designation?

PURCHASING SECURITY SYSTEMS

Besides the seven sources of information stated earlier in the chapter for acquiring information on services and systems, the National Burglar and Fire Alarm Association (NBFAA; http://www.alarm.org/) provides additional assistance. The NBFAA is a nonprofit association that promotes professionalism in the industry and offers consumer information through its Web site. The NBFAA has published a consumer guide, *Considerations When Looking for a Burglar Alarm System*. This pamphlet recommends conducting a security survey to determine needs; locating a reputable alarm company by contacting local police, UL, or the NBFAA; checking local laws on requirements for alarm systems; studying the contract; and training employees on how to properly use the system.[7]

> ### You Be the Judge*
>
> Carl Simpson, the security director at Southeast Tool Company, was fighting mad. The plant had been burglarized again, but that was nothing new. What had him angry was that the alarm system the company had leased recently had failed to detect the intrusion.
>
> "Get Security Systems International on the phone," snapped Simpson at his secretary.
>
> Once SSI came on the line, Simpson began his attack: "We had $135,000 worth of precision machine tools stolen last night, and your people are responsible. According to our contract, you're supposed to make sure this alarm system works. It doesn't, so your company had better come up with $135,000."
>
> The manager of SSI just laughed. "Calm down and reread your contract," he said. "It has what's called an exculpatory clause, which says that SSI is not responsible for any loss caused by burglary."
>
> "But this was your fault!" Simpson cried.
>
> "It doesn't matter," replied the manager. "The clause covers us even if we're negligent." He chuckled, "I can tell you've never dealt with a burglar alarm company before. Almost all alarm contracts have an exculpatory clause in them."

But Simpson refused to give up without a fight. He had Southeast sue SSI for breach of contract, breach of warranty, and negligence, despite the exculpatory clause in the contract. "It's not fair," Simpson argued. "When we contracted with SSI we put the safety of our company in their hands. They took on the responsibility, and they shouldn't be able to use a catch-all clause to escape liability for their negligence."

Did the court agree?

Make your decision; then turn to the end of the chapter for the court's decision.

*Reprinted with permission from *Security Management—Plant and Property Protection*, a publication of Bureau of Business Practice, Inc., 24 Rope Ferry Road, Waterford, CT 06386.

Questions When Considering a Security System

1. What can the product do?
2. What is the *total cost* of the product, including installation, additional personnel, training, maintenance, finance charges, and so on? When the purchaser buys in large volume, the greater profit for the vendor may result in lower prices.
3. Is the total price competitive with other vendors?
4. Can the product adapt to new technological developments? What modifications are possible? Costs?
5. How long will it take for the product to be installed and become operational? If the manufacturer contracts the installation to a subcontractor, how are standards maintained and inspections conducted, and what are the related stipulations in the contract?
6. What is the product life?
7. What does the warranty cover?
8. What maintenance is required and by whom? Since a system is useless when it fails and is not repaired, is preventive maintenance and emergency maintenance part of the contract?
9. Have we checked the company's Dun and Bradstreet rating?
10. Does the vendor have appropriate business licenses? Does the vendor conform to applicable state laws requiring training or registration?
11. Is the vendor a member of trade associations that help members stay current on new technology and product developments?
12. What is the background of personnel involved with the product? Are professional engineers employed? Is electrical work done by licensed contractors?
13. Have we requested references from the vendor from current users of the same product? Have we followed up on those references?

14. Does the manufacturer freely release information about its product to outsiders? (Offenders are known to pose as writers, reporters, or customers to acquire system information.)
15. Have the product and its components been evaluated by an independent testing organization? If applicable, does it meet NFPA standards?
16. How will the system be evaluated? Can security personnel, in a controlled test, "trip" a sensor to ensure reliability?

OUTSOURCING

Outsourcing is purchasing from outside companies services that were previously performed in-house. In *Business at the Speed of Thought*, Bill Gates writes: "An important reengineering principle is that companies should focus on their core business and outsource everything else." Internet connectivity has produced a global economy with intense competition requiring management to concentrate on new challenges and opportunities or be left behind. For success and profit, management is learning that they must focus on what the company does best and outsource support functions. Outsourcing improves a company's focus, frees internal resources for other purposes, reduces costs, and shares risks. Consequently, activities that do not contribute directly to the bottom line and are part of "the cost of doing business" are ripe targets for outsourcing. Examples are human resources, risk management, environmental management, safety, and security.[8]

Here we consider some outsourcing decisions. A frequent outsourcing decision concerns choosing between in-house and contract security officer services. Consider the following generalized advantages and disadvantages. With in-house, the advantages are lower turnover and increased control over hiring, training, and quality. Plus, officers often have greater loyalty and are familiar with unique needs. The disadvantages are costs (e.g., social security and insurance) and total responsibility for security. With contract services, the advantages are lower costs, fewer human resources duties, and shared responsibility. The disadvantages are less direct control and less impact on hiring and loyalty. It is not uncommon for a contract security officer to work for months without the client knowing that the officer has a felony record. One solution is for the contractor to maintain a personnel folder on-site for each officer and for it to contain a copy of the application, background check, training, and regulatory papers.[9]

Another outsourcing decision involves choosing between in-house and off-site monitoring of intrusion detection systems. In-house costs are leasing or purchasing of the intrusion detection system, capital expenses for the monitoring system and emergency backup system, capital expenses for power backup, staff and training, maintenance contract, monthly expenses for phone lines, and overhead for maintaining the monitoring site. When contracting with an outside firm, the costs include leasing or purchasing of the intrusion detection system, monitoring service, maintenance, phone lines, and reports of system activity. For a card access system, the types of costs would show several similarities. Cost per access card would be another consideration.[10]

Outsourcing may include hiring a systems integrator. As covered earlier in this book, selecting the best integrator is a crucial and tricky process. Seek evidence of financial stability and insurance bonding and a close relationship between the integrator and manufacturers. Also, visit customers of the integrator, seek an open architecture, and get IT personnel involved.

In the IT sphere, "managed security" is a growing trend involving outsourcing of security technologies, infrastructure, and services. Many companies with in-house staff simply cannot keep up with all the pressing IT security issues.[11] But before outsourcing IT security, thoroughly investigate several important questions such as: Who will be responsible for financial losses caused by the exploitation of IT resources? What is the financial health of the outsourcer? Are clients satisfied with the outsourcer?[12]

Is outsourcing a good or bad idea? Justify your answer.

Career: Security Sales

Selling can be stimulating, challenging, and financially rewarding. The growth of the security industry has been meteoric and there is no leveling off in sight. Constantly evolving security services and technology and an increase in the number of related companies have resulted in numerous career opportunities.

Duties: Entry level includes making sales calls, handling advertising queries, staffing and organizing trade show booths, demonstrating products, and formulating proposals. In addition, management responsibilities include developing marketing plans and directing sales personnel.

Prerequisites: A broad-based education in business, engineering, or marketing. For management, an undergraduate degree, 15 years of experience, and CPP preferred.

Demographics of typical practitioner: Undergraduate degree; 15 years in security; 10 years in specialty; salary $40,000–100,000 yr.; titles: Sales Associate, Sales Manager, and Vice President.

Source: American Society for Industrial Security, *Career Opportunities in Security* (Alexandria, VA: ASIS, 1998), p. 15.

Search the Web

Use your favorite search engines to view what is online for "security services" and "security systems."

Research the Certified Protection Professional program of the American Society for Industrial Security at http://www.asisonline.org/.

Search for consumer information from the Web site of the National Burglar and Fire Alarm Association at http://www.alarm.org/.

CASE PROBLEM

9A. Select a specific security service or system. Study the state of the art. Then, list in order of priority, ten questions you would ask vendors. Explain why the first three questions are placed at the top of the list.

THE DECISION FOR "YOU BE THE JUDGE"

The court did not agree with Simpson's reasoning and dismissed Southeast's lawsuit against SSI. The court held that the clause was valid and clear in totally absolving SSI from liability for the burglary. If your company has leased a burglar alarm system, check the contract to see if it has an exculpatory clause. If it does, take heart. Not all courts have upheld the validity of such clauses in all circumstances. Check with your company's lawyer to find out where your state courts stand on this issue.

This case is based on *L. Luria & Son v. Alarmtech International*, 384 So2d 947. The names in this case have been changed to protect the privacy of those involved.

NOTES

1. U.S. Department of Justice, *Private Police in the United States: Findings and Recommendations*, Vol. 1 (Washington, D.C.: U.S. Government Printing Office, 1972), p. 59.
2. John Strauchs, "Which Way to Better Controls?" *Security Management* 45 (January 2001), p. 98.
3. U.S. Department of Justice, *Report of the Task Force on Private Security* (Washington, D.C.: U.S. Government Printing Office, 1976), pp. 146–147. And, U.S. Department of Justice, National Institute of Justice, *Crime and Protection in America (Executive Summary of the Hallcrest Report)* (Washington, D.C.: U.S. Government Printing Office, 1985), p. 71.

4. John P. Finnerty, "Who's Liable, the Security Firm or You?" *Risk Management Advisor* (May 1996), pp. 4–7.
5. Hualing Fu, "The Security Service Company in China," *Journal of Security Administration* 16, no. 2 (1993), pp. 35–43.
6. Eugene Ferraro, "End Game," *Security Management* 44 (August 2000), p. 70.
7. U.S. Department of Justice, *Report of the Task Force on Private Security*, p. 244.
8. George Caldwell, "Do It Yourself or Outsource It?" *Security Technology & Design* 12 (March 2001), pp. 18–20.
9. Richard Maurer, "Outsourcing: An Option or a Threat?" *Security Technology & Design* 10 (August 2000), pp. 14–18.
10. Richard Maurer, "Remote Site Access Control vs. Cost Return on Investment," *Security Technology & Design* 10 (February 2000), pp. 18–22.
11. Edmund DeJesus, "Managing Managed Security," *Information Security* 4 (January 2001), pp. 34–49.
12. John McCumber, "Outsourcing Security," *Security Technology & Design* 10 (August 2000), pp. 108–109.

10

Investigations

OBJECTIVES

After studying this chapter the reader will be able to:

1. List and discuss the six basic investigative questions.
2. Describe at least five types of investigations in the private sector.
3. Differentiate among proprietary and contract investigations, private and public investigations, and overt and undercover private investigations.
4. Explain the relationship between an investigator and an auditor.
5. List and explain at least five aids to the investigative process.

An investigation is a search for information. Information usually is obtained from people, such as victims, witnesses, suspects, and informants, and from physical evidence, such as fingerprints, DNA, shoe prints, and tool marks.

There are six basic questions to ask in an investigation:

1. *Who?* Who are the individuals involved in the particular incident being investigated? Names, addresses, and telephone numbers are important.
2. *What happened?* What is the story of the incident? For instance, what happened before, during, and after a theft incident at a manufacturing plant?
3. *Where?* The location of the incident and the movement of people and objects are important. For example, where exactly were witnesses and the suspect when the theft occurred?
4. *When?* A notation of the times of particular activities during an incident is necessary for a thorough investigation. If a particular theft occurred between 7 and 8 P.M. on April 9, and Joe Doe is a suspect, he later can be exonerated because he really was at another location at that time.
5. *How?* The focus of this question is on how the incident was able to take place in the face of (or absence of) loss prevention measures. After a theft, investigators often attempt to find out how the thief was able to

circumvent alarms. In the case of an industrial accident, investigators attempt to find out how the accident occurred while safety equipment was supposedly in use.

6. *Why?* This question can be difficult to answer. However, the answer can lead to the discovery of a pressing problem that may not be obvious. An example is seen with numerous losses in a manufacturing plant brought about by low employee morale. In this case, theft and destruction of company property can be reduced by, for example, increasing management's concern for employees through praise, a sports program, contests, and high-quality meals in the cafeteria.

The answer to the "why" question helps to establish the motive for the loss activity. Once the motive is established, suspects can be eliminated. A recently fired employee would have a motive of retribution for setting fire to his or her former place of employment.

Investigations are not always criminal in nature, and not every investigation requires answering all six investigative questions. Once an investigator gathers sufficient information, a report is written and submitted to a supervisor. After that, the information in the report causes action or inaction by supervisors and management. Typically, investigative reports lead to either punitive or nonpunitive action. Punitive action can include firing or prosecution or both. Nonpunitive action can include exonerating a suspect, hiring an applicant, promoting an employee, or insurance reimbursement. Investigations can also result in corrective action such as the creation of a better loss prevention program.

Investigations are unique to each type of business, institution, or organization served. The varieties and depths of investigations vary; they reflect management's needs, objectives, and budget. The personnel involved also vary and may include company investigators, auditors, managers, contract investigators, public police, and attorneys.

TYPES OF INVESTIGATIONS

There are several types of investigations in the private sector. The following list illustrates some of the more common ones, categorized according to the target of the investigation.

The ground rules or laws for each type of investigation vary. An *applicant background* investigation requires adherence to the laws discussed in Chapter 6. A private investigation of a *criminal* offense requires knowledge of criminal law and evidence. In a private-sector criminal investigation, the notification of public police will depend on such factors as whether the suspect was arrested by company investigators and whether management wants to prosecute. *Computer crime* investigations focus on a variety of illegal acts involving computers and information systems. The Internet has expanded the scope and complexity of these investigations. In an *accident* investigation, the investigator usually is knowledgeable about safety, the Occupational Safety and Health Act, workers' compensation insurance, and applicable laws. One major objective of a *fire and arson* investigation is to determine the probable cause of a fire. Sophisticated equipment may be used to identify what substance was employed to accelerate a fire. A *civil or negligence and liability* investigation involves, among other things, gathering evidence to show that failure to exercise reasonable care in a situation caused harm to someone or something. For example, a retail store has poor housekeeping, which caused customer injury. Both the plaintiff initiating the suit (the customer) and the defendant (the retail store) may conduct investigations and present evidence in court.

A civil court decides on both liability (who is responsible) for a negligent act and any obligation (money award to the plaintiff) enforceable by the court. *Insurance* investigations, which at times result in litigation, are conducted to determine losses and their causes, and to assist in deciding on indemnification. Both an insurance company and the insured may conduct separate investigations before an insurance claim is settled. Investigations of *labor* matters (e.g., workers' activities during a strike) are often sensitive. Legal counsel is necessary to guide the investigator because of associated federal and state laws. *Due diligence*, as defined in Chapter 4, is the attention and care legally expected in checking the accuracy of information and omissions. It can range from determining a customer's financial status to assessing the desirability of acquisition targets.

Proprietary and Contract Investigations

Proprietary investigations are undertaken by in-house company employees who perform investigative work. A *contract investigation* requires the contracting of an outside company (agency) to supply investigative services for a fee.

There are inadequate and varied laws regulating contract investigative employees and firms. But several jurisdictions have effective regulation (e.g., requirements of license, residency, training, experience, no felony convictions, examination, and insurance) that protect clients.

For the most part, proprietary investigators are not subject to government regulation. Many businesses, institutions, and organizations maintain their own investigators. Large corporations, utilities, insurance companies, and banks are some of the many concerns that rely on a large staff of proprietary investigators.

Numerous firms utilize both contract and proprietary investigators. If a large corporation has a particular season when the investigative workload is heavy, some of the extra workload can be assigned to a contract investigation company. This approach frees proprietary investigators for more pressing and specialized problems.

Citizens frequently obtain a distorted picture of private investigations via television, which produces misconceptions that falsify the various kinds of investigative work—work that is interesting, exciting, and also often boring. Another misconception is that many investigators in the private sector are armed. Few are armed, and those who are rarely use their weapons.

Private and Public Investigations

Private investigations serve the private sector (e.g., businesses). Public investigations feature public police agencies, for the most part serving the public. Both investigative efforts often are entwined. This can be seen, for example, when an office building is burglarized and company investigators call local police in a joint effort to solve the crime. But how much time and effort can the public police devote to the office building burglary in comparison to the company investigators? Public police can devote only limited resources to such a crime. Typically, a uniformed public police officer will arrive for a preliminary investigation, and an incident report will be completed. Next, the incident report is transferred to a detective unit. Within a day or two, a detective arrives at the scene of the crime and conducts a follow-up investigation that involves gathering additional information and perhaps some placation, a public relations effort that assures the citizens that the police are doing everything possible to solve the crime.

The inability of the criminal justice system to assist adequately in private loss prevention efforts can also be illustrated by clearance rates, which are the proportion of cases solved by an arrest. Clearance rates are higher for crimes against people (e.g., murder, 69 percent; rape, 50 percent; robbery, 28 percent) and lower for crimes against property (e.g., burglary, 14 percent; larceny, 19 percent).[1] The success of private-sector investigations is difficult to gauge since many firms do not prosecute and the outcome of investigations is usually confidential and unpublished.

Overt and Undercover Private Investigations

An *overt investigation* is an obvious investigation. People coming into contact with the overt investigator know that an investigation is taking place. A common scenario would be a company investigator, dressed in a conservative suit, arriving at the scene of a loss to interview employees and collect evidence. An *undercover investigation* (UI), on the other hand, is a secret investigation. A typical approach is when an undercover investigator is hired as a regular employee, a truck driver, for example, and collects information by associating with employees who are not knowledgeable about the undercover investigation. Law prohibits such investigators from collecting information on union activities.

Each type of investigation serves many useful purposes. An overt investigation that begins immediately after a loss shows that the loss prevention staff is on the job. This in itself acts as a deterrent. An overt investigation does not have to be in response to a loss; for example, pre-employment investigations prevent losses.

Accident at Hardy Furniture Plant

The Hardy Furniture Plant provided more than 700 jobs to Clarkston residents as sales boomed. Most workers at the plant were satisfied with their jobs. Unfortunately, a group of young forklift drivers were becoming increasingly bored while transporting furniture throughout the plant. One day two forklifts collided and both drivers were hospitalized with broken arms and legs. The forklifts were slightly damaged; furniture on the forks was a total loss. Immediately, the company loss prevention staff began an investigation. The forklift drivers and witnesses were interviewed. All interviewees reported that neither forklift operator saw the other because excessive furniture on the forks obstructed the views. Investigators and a forklift mechanic inspected the forklifts and found no irregularities.

The investigators became suspicious when all of the interviewees produced identical stories during questioning. Later, another round of questioning included nonwitnesses. Finally, after two weeks of persistent interviewing, the case broke when an older employee, loyal to the company, informed investigators that several bored employees bet on forklift drivers who were "playing chicken" while racing toward each other. It was learned that five previous contests had taken place involving hundreds of dollars in cash. Also, one minor accident had occurred that resulted in damaged furniture. Two supervisors were involved in covering up the loss of the damaged furniture.

When the investigation was complete, loss prevention investigators filled out appropriate reports and presented their findings to management. The two forklift drivers and the two supervisors were fired.

An example can illustrate the usefulness of a UI. The XYZ warehouse is losing thousands of dollars of merchandise every week. Management believes that employees are stealing the merchandise. In an effort to reduce losses, management decides to hire a private investigator. The investigator interviews numerous employees over a two-week period, but the case remains unsolved. An executive of the company argues to management that the private investigator idea is a waste. The executive points out that the private investigator is unfamiliar with the warehouse operations, cannot penetrate the employee informal organizations, has no informers, is wasting time during surveillance from another building, and has no substantial leads. After three weeks, the private investigator is terminated. The vocal executive argues for a UI. A loss prevention service company is contacted, and an undercover investigator is placed in the warehouse. After three weeks, the new investigator penetrates the informal employee organization. Four key employees are implicated and fired. Losses are reduced. The company decides to conduct a yearly UI as a loss prevention strategy.

Undercover Investigation of Missing Shirts

The Chester Garment Company, headquartered in New York City, experienced a loss of hundreds of men's shirts at its plant in North Carolina. Company executives were concerned and worried because they had no experience with losses and no loss prevention program.

The plant manager in North Carolina had notified the New York office that 900 shirts were missing. Because of their limited knowledge of loss prevention strategies, company executives decided to contact Harmon Lorman Associates, a company specializing in loss prevention and investigation. A meeting between managers of the investigative company and the garment company decided that an undercover investigator, assigned to the North Carolina plant, would be a wise strategy. The UI would cost $1,500 per week for an unspecified time period.

One week later, the investigator, Gary Stewart, arrived at the Chester Garment Plant in North Carolina to seek employment. The plant manager, who was the only plant employee who knew about the UI, hired Gary and assigned him to shipping and receiving.

Gary was from New York and educated at a college in North Carolina. The investigative company felt that his experience, a college degree in criminal justice, and his living experience in the South would add up to a good background for this assignment. Anyway, he was the only company investigator who had lived in the South.

Harmon Lorman executives told Chester executives that Gary had been working with them for a year and a half. Also, they told them that Gary had extensive experience and loss prevention training. The truth was that Gary had been recently hired with six months of previous investigative experience. Gary had no previous loss prevention training; he had a criminal justice degree with no loss prevention or business courses.

After two weeks in the plant, Gary had established numerous contacts. His fictitious background ("cover") pointed out that he grew up in Maryland. He arrived at the Chester Garment plant because a friend said that he could get a job there while taking a semester off from college. Gary obtained North Carolina license plates as soon as he entered North Carolina from New York.

Gary mailed three to five reports per week to his supervisor at Harmon Lorman Associates. The first few reports contained background information on the plant, such as the plant layout and the names, addresses, telephone numbers, description of autos, and plate numbers of select employees. Thereafter, the reports contained information pertaining to loss prevention features and loss vulnerabilities. Janitorial service, employee overtime, Saturday activities, and any unusual events were also reported.

Within three months of undercover investigation, Gary had made close contacts with employees and had worked in numerous assignments throughout the plant. His findings showed numerous instances of pilferage by many employees. Women sewing-machine operators were hiding several manufactured shirts under their outer clothes immediately before the work day ended.

Gray's reports were "edited" by his superiors and then sent to the home of one of Chester Garment's executives. After three months, Chester Garment executives became impatient. They wanted better quality results and threatened to terminate the investigation.

Harmon Lorman executives assured Chester Garment executives that "a break in the case was imminent." Increased pressure was put on investigator Gary Stewart, who realized that the investigation was being prolonged for profit. He responded by withholding information from reports for dry spells when good information was unavailable. As the investigation went on, the report quality went down.

Finally, after two more weeks, Chester Garment executives ordered an inventory at the plant. Surprisingly, half of the missing shirts were accounted for and a previous inventory was criticized as inaccurate. The undercover investigation was terminated. Gary returned to New York.

Investigator and Auditor

An auditor examines accounting records to check on irregularities. These irregularities usually include (1) deviations from the particular firm's accounting methods, (2) mistakes, and (3) criminal activity. Auditors also are referred to as *internal auditors* or *investigative auditors*.

Public (e.g., federal, state, municipal) and private investigation practitioners have expanded their competency in accounting. A major reason for this is a response to increased investigations into the white-collar crime arena.

Cross-training can be used to reduce the knowledge gap between auditor and criminal investigator. Cross-training involves the auditor being trained in criminal investigation and the criminal investigator being trained in auditing. An auditor's training could include criminal law, evidence, interviewing, and interrogation. A criminal investigator's training could include accounting principles and procedures and auditing. Both should have training in information systems and related investigative methods. The Association of Certified Fraud Examiners promotes professionalism, training, and certification (CFE). The Web address is http://www.cfenet.com/.

What type of investigative work do you think you would prefer as a career?

Important Considerations

The following considerations relate to investigations in general:

1. The supervision of investigators must be adequate enough to produce tangible results. Rarely will a supervisor/investigator ratio of 1 to 20 prove adequate. Investigators may require close supervision by attorneys and other specialists.
2. Sensitive and confidential information must be safeguarded.
3. Information resulting from investigations can be used to improve loss prevention efforts and reduce vulnerabilities. For example, if machine shop workers are constantly stealing company tools, then it may be a good idea to have all workers provide their own tools.
4. Investigations can support the loss prevention budget by documenting vulnerabilities and losses.
5. Investigations should be cost effective. If an investigation costs more than the loss, the expense of the investigation may not be worthwhile. For example, the loss of a box of pencils is not worth an investigator's time when more serious losses are occurring.
6. Although computer crimes can be committed remotely, modern technology also permits investigations to be conducted remotely. For example, instead of an investigator visiting stores to check out CCTV videos of cashier–customer transactions, a system can link CCTV with register data to be viewed together online.
7. The investigator's job is to collect information and facts. Supervisors and managers decide what to do with the investigative results.
8. An investigation may be required of senior management because of criminal, civil, or regulatory misconduct. Authorization and direction for such a sensitive investigation may come from the corporate board of directors.

LAW

A knowledge of law is indispensable to the investigative process. For example, the Fair Credit Reporting Act (FCRA) and how it controls background investigations is covered in Chapter 6. Additionally, the FCRA prohibits employers from retaining the services of an outside firm to investigate suspected employee misconduct without first notifying the employee that an inquiry will be conducted. The employee must then be notified of the results, including the names and comments of witnesses. Because the FCRA treats private investigators as credit reporting agencies and employees as consumers, this law is far-reaching, and it hinders corporate inquires concerning workplace security and safety. Strong opposition to this law will likely result in modifications to it.

Another important area of law pertains to electronic surveillance (electronic devices used to listen to conversations) and wiretapping (listening to telephone communications). The U.S. Supreme Court has called these techniques a *dirty business*. Generally, both are prohibited unless under court authority. However, because of the difficulty of detection and the advantages in information gathering, some private (and public) sector investigators violate the law. Federal law imposes a $10,000 fine and up to five years in prison for these offenses.

Conflict of interest is another concern. An example of conflict of interest can be seen when a full-time public police officer works part-time for a private firm. The *Report of the Task Force on Private Security* states that "a citizen might file a defamation-of-character suit against a city, law enforcement agency, or officer by claiming that surveillance conducted by an off-duty law enforcement officer working as a private investigator gave others the impression he was the target of a law enforcement criminal investigation."[2] Other problems can evolve, such as a suspect's rights during private-sector questioning by a public police officer working part-time in private security. States have prohibited public police from obtaining private investigator licenses. The task force recommended that public police officers should be "strictly forbidden" from performing private-sector investigative work.

Investigations can protect an organization from legal liability. One example is background investigations to prevent negligent hiring charges. At the same time, poorly executed investigations can result in liability. In one case a bank investigator believed that a loan manager had mob connections and an investigation was conducted, resulting in termination. Police brought charges, but the judge dismissed the case on groundless charges, and the manager sued and was awarded damages. In another case an oil company terminated an agent who was manipulating prices, but the prosecutor declined to bring charges because of insufficient evidence. When a truck driver stated to someone that the agent was a "thief," the agent sued for slander. Investigators can protect themselves from slander and libel by the use of privilege when issuing reports. *Qualified privilege* permits defamatory statements if made in the discharge of duty and without malice. At one company an employee was fired for a security violation and sued by claiming defamation from a security report, but the court held that the investigator was responsible for reporting security breaches, that she acted within her authority, and that her report was privileged. *Attorney/client privilege* is another form of protection—ensure that reports are issued directly to counsel. However, the best defense is accurate reports.[3]

International Perspective: Overseas Investigations[4]

Global business has resulted in increasing demand for overseas investigations. Such investigations are conducted for a variety of reasons, including potential locations for investment. The following information provides tips and guidelines for overseas investigations.

Carefully plan and check with the following U.S. agencies:

- *U.S. Department of State* ensures that passports are current and valid for all countries not off limits to U.S. citizens. Some countries require a special visa. Fact sheets are provided on many countries and include information on such topics as political stability and crime.
- *U.S. Department of Health and Human Services* determines whether travel to particular countries requires immunization.
- *U.S. Department of Commerce* publishes information to alert U.S. citizens to countries that may be dangerous to U.S. travelers.
- Because legal systems vary among countries, a major rule in conducting a foreign investigation is to study the legal and policing system of the respective country.
- Investigations are fundamentally about personal interaction, so another major rule is to study and understand the host culture and try to speak some of the language.
- The international investigator who travels to many countries and freely investigates is actually Hollywood fantasy. Foreign countries do not permit such activities and neither does the U.S. State Department. Without careful research, an investigator can find himself or herself in jail in a foreign country.
- An option is to work with an official of the foreign country, such as a police official or attorney, or contract the investigation to an investigator in that country. The key is to select someone who has experience in the country, has reliable contacts, and speaks the language.
- Avoid bringing a firearm to a foreign country. Illegal possession of a firearm aboard any U.S. airline is a felony.

INTERVIEWING AND INTERROGATION

Interviewing and interrogation are methods of gathering information from people. During an *interview*, the suspect supplies information willingly; but during an *interrogation*, the suspect is often unwilling. The investigator needs to know the techniques associated with each type of situation. There is no one correct method of conducting an interview or interrogation. The circumstances of each particular situation dictate the characteristics of these investigative functions. Members of private security are more likely to interview, whereas public police are more likely to interview and interrogate.

Why are interviews or interrogations conducted? A primary reason is to learn the truth. Other possible reasons are to obtain evidence or a confession to aid in prosecution, eliminate suspects, recover property, and obtain information that results in corrective action. This chapter emphasizes investigations in the private sector, although many of the ideas presented are used in public-sector investigations.

The preliminaries include:

1. Maintaining records
2. Planning the questioning
3. Making an appointment, if necessary
4. If a procedure or law question arises, consulting with a superior or an attorney
5. Questioning in privacy, if possible
6. Making sure someone of the same sex as the interviewee is present
7. Identifying yourself to the interviewee
8. Openly recording the questioning, if possible, on audio or videotape

Regarding the interviewee:

1. Consider the interviewee's background, intelligence, education, biases, and emotional state.
2. Communicate on the same level.
3. Watch for nervousness, perspiration, and fidgeting.
4. Reluctance to talk can indicate that the interviewee feels the need to protect himself or herself or others.
5. Responding freely can indicate that the interviewee may need to relieve guilt or may want to cause problems for an enemy not involved in the loss.

The objectives of the investigator include:

1. Establishing good rapport (e.g., asking, "How are you?")
2. Maintaining good public relations
3. Maintaining eye contact
4. Not jumping to conclusions
5. Maintaining an open mind
6. Listening attentively
7. Being perceptive to every comment and any slips of the tongue
8. Maintaining perseverance
9. Controlling the interview
10. Carefully analyzing hearsay (what one person says another person told him or her; unverified information)

Strategies by the investigator include the following:

1. Asking *open-ended questions*, those questions that require lengthy answers—for example, "What happened at the plant before the accident?" *Close-ended questions* require short yes or no answers that limit responses—for example, "Were you close to the accident?"

2. Maintaining *silence* makes many interviewees feel uncomfortable. Silence by an investigator, after an interviewee answers an open-ended question, may cause the interviewee to begin talking again.
3. Building up interviewee memory by having the interviewee relate the story of an incident from its very beginning.
4. To test honesty, asking questions to which you know the answers.

The reader probably is familiar with movies and television programs that portray the interrogation process as a "third degree," in which one bright light hangs over the seated suspect in a dark room and investigators stand around constantly asking questions and using violence when they try to "break" the suspect. Court action against police has curbed this abuse. However, because of the unpleasant connotations associated with interrogations, for the private sector, to prevent litigation, a less threatening term such as "intensive interview" is more appropriate.

During interrogation or "intensive interview" (an extension of the interview):

1. Discuss the seriousness of the incident.
2. Request the story several times. Some investigators request the story backward to catch inconsistencies.
3. Appeal to emotions; for example, "Everybody makes mistakes. You are not the first person who has been in trouble. Don't you want to clear your conscience?"
4. Point out inconsistencies in statements.
5. Confront the interviewee with some of the evidence.

Why would a private security investigator choose to "interview" rather than "interrogate"?

Polygraph: Proper Testing Procedures under the EPPA

In the course of a workplace investigation, an employer cannot suggest to employees the possible use of a polygraph instrument until these ten conditions are satisfied:

1. *Economic loss or injury.* The employer must administer the test as part of an investigation of a *specific incident* involving economic loss or injury to the business, such as theft or sabotage.
2. *Access.* The employee who is to be tested must have had access to the property that is the subject of the investigation.

3. *Reasonable suspicion*. The employer must have a reasonable suspicion of the worker's involvement in the incident under investigation.

4. *Before the test*, an employer's failure to adhere to guidelines can void a test, and subject the employer to fines and liability. The employee who is to be tested must be notified in writing at least 48 hours, not counting weekends and holidays, prior to the test:

   - Where and when the examination will take place
   - The specific matter under investigation
   - The basis for concluding that the employee had access to the property being investigated
   - The reason the employer suspects the employee of involvement
   - The employee's right to consult with legal counsel or an employee representative before each phase of the test

Also before the test, the employee must be provided with the following:

   - Oral and written notice explaining the nature of the polygraph, its physical operation, and the test procedure
   - Copies of all questions that will be asked during the test
   - Oral and written notice, in language understood by the employee and bearing the employee's signature, advising the worker of his or her rights under the EPPA

5. *Procedural requirements for polygraph examinations* include the following:

   - The test must last at least 90 minutes unless the examinee terminates the test.
   - Either party, employer or employee, can record the test with the other's knowledge.
   - Questions cannot pertain to religious, political, or racial matters; sexual behavior; or beliefs, affiliations, or lawful activities related to unions or labor organizations; and they cannot be asked in a degrading or needlessly intrusive manner.
   - A worker can be excused from a test with a physician's written advisement that the subject suffers from a medical or psychological condition or is undergoing treatment that might cause abnormal responses during the examination.
   - An employee has the right to consult with counsel before, during, and after the examination but not to have counsel present during the actual examination.
   - An employee must be advised that his or her confessions may be grounds for firing or demotion and that the employer may share admissions of criminal conduct with law enforcement officials.
   - A worker can terminate or refuse to take a test and cannot be demoted or fired for doing so. But, the employer can demote or fire the worker if he or she has enough separate supporting evidence to justify taking that action.

6. *After the test*, the employee has a right to a written copy of the tester's opinion, copies of the questions and corresponding replies, and an opportunity to discuss the results with the employer before an employer can take action against a worker based on the test results. An employee may be disciplined, fired, or demoted on the basis of the test results if the employer has supporting evidence, which can include the evidence gathered to support the decision to administer the test, to justify such action. Test results cannot be released to the public, only to the employee or his or her designate; the employer; a court, government agency, arbitrator, or mediator (by court order); or appropriate government agency if disclosure is admission of criminal conduct (without court order). The examiner may show test results, without identifying information, to other examiners in order to obtain second opinions.

7. *Qualifications of examiners.* An employer can be liable for an examiner's failure to meet requirements, which cover licensing, bonding, or professional liability coverage; testing guidelines; and formation of opinions.

8. *Waiving employee rights.* A worker cannot be tested—even at his or her insistence—if the employer cannot meet procedural requirements and prove reasonable suspicion and access. Employees may not waive their rights under the EPPA except in connection with written settlement of a lawsuit or pending legal action.

9. *State law and collective bargaining agreements.* The EPPA does not preempt any state or local law or collective bargaining agreement that is more restrictive than the act.

10. *Record keeping requirement.* Records of polygraph exams should be kept for at least three years by the employer and the examiner, who must make them available—within 72 hours upon request—to the Department of Labor.

Source: U.S. Chamber of Commerce. See Chapter 6 for the Employee Polygraph Protection Act of 1988.

INFORMATION SOURCES

Traditional information sources include interviewing people in person; traveling to a government agency, library, or other location to comb through records and information; obtaining information over the telephone; and conducting surveillance. Additionally, the Internet has made it easier than ever to investigate personal and business information.[5] For a nominal fee, a variety of information can be obtained with a computer from the comfort of one's office or home as illustrated here:

> http://www.pimall.com/ An excellent site offering a wealth of information and links to information brokers, private investigators (PIs), a PI store, PI associations, training, and magazines.

http://www.ussearch.com/ This site can be used to locate someone, conduct a background check, and seek the following records: criminal, department of corrections, court, real estate, bankruptcies, divorce, and death. Business searches include due diligence and verification of professional licenses.

http://www.datahawk.com/ Similar to the above sites; costs are readily available.

http://www.teldir.com/ To check for people outside the United States, this site has links to Yellow Pages, White Pages, business directories, e-mail listings, and more from more than 150 countries.

One problem with these databases is selecting the most appropriate information broker. Another problem is that data may not be verified. Also, the scope of the search must be considered. What geographic area and what months or years were searched? Information brokers must adhere to legal restrictions and should provide such guidelines to clients.

Despite the problems with databases, such information sources are used in a variety of ways by security practitioners. One airport security director uses such databases to locate owners of vehicles abandoned in the airport's parking lots. Another security practitioner conducts asset searches of employees suspected of fraud; a database may show that an employee earning $45,000 per year has purchased a $600,000 house.

Legal Restrictions When Collecting Information

Investigator ability to obtain usable information in today's privacy-protected environment has been reduced. In earlier years, the "old boy" network was in greater use. It consists of employees in both the public and private sectors who informally assist each other with information. An example is when a retired police officer joins an investigative firm and contacts friends from the police agency where he or she was previously employed to obtain criminal history information on individuals subject to a private-sector investigation. There have been indictments against people involved in acquiring nonpublic information.

The reality of information acquisition must be explained. No information is totally secure from unauthorized acquisition. Although difficult to measure, information often is obtained in an unethical or illegal manner; that is the reality of information acquisition. An example can be seen when a private-sector investigator pays money to an employee of a bank to secure nonpublic information about an individual. This activity should be condemned because it violates individual rights and laws.

The following list presents some sources of information for the investigator. A case-by-case approach to each source of information is advised because availability varies and laws can be restrictive.

Less Restrictive/Public	*More Restrictive/Private*
Libraries	Hospitals
Government agencies containing public records (e.g., criminal and civil court records, real estate)	Credit bureaus
	Financial institutions
Telephone toll records	Credit card statements
Depositions	Employment wages

Another problem for the investigator results when he or she mistakenly collects information that is not usable in court. In litigation, information improperly obtained and not authenticated or certified by the respective agency could subject a litigation team to civil or criminal action, unless the records are subpoenaed or are part of a court action (civil or criminal). Another challenge is waiting for a Freedom of Information Law request to obtain documents, which can take as long as a year. The *Freedom of Information Law* (FOIL) grants citizens access to public documents because an informed electorate is essential to safeguard democracy and because publicity is a protection against official misconduct. This law requires all federal agency documents to be publicly disclosed, unless exempted. This law also recognizes the need to restrict intrusions into a private individual's affairs.

The Internet as a Liability and an Asset

Here we illustrate how the Internet can harm and help businesses. First we see how a manager was scammed, then we see how corporations can protect themselves against extremist groups.

Care should be exercised with the Internet because it contains a variety of fraudulent information. Internet fraud is rising rapidly and the Securities and Exchange Commission (SEC), a federal regulatory agency that enforces laws to reduce financial fraud, has reported many cases of individuals and companies attempting to deceive investors and others through the Internet. In one case a credit manager tried the Internet to investigate the creditworthiness of a customer seeking a large order of computer components. The manager checked the Web site of the customer and found impressive graphics, solid financial data, multiple corporate locations across the country, impressive biographies of corporate executives, and testimonials (with links) to customers and vendors. Following this research, the manager knew that his days of spending hours on the telephone checking credit references were over, and he approved the large order. When the bill was past due, he called the customer, but the telephone had been disconnected, and he checked the Web site, but it was gone. He was victimized by a scam that set up the Web site on an Internet service provider (ISP) host rather than obtaining a domain name. They paid for their ISP account with a stolen credit card number. The testimonials were e-mail links to confederates. The "ship to" address was leased space paid for by a check from a shell corporation with a bank account established with fraudulent identification. All the merchandise was gone. To prevent such victimization, obtain business credit reports, use the SEC's database (http://www.sec.gov/edgarhp.htm), enter PR Newswire (http://www.prnewswire.com/), type the company name into your favorite search engines, use the telephone to check credit and other references, and consider a thorough investigation by a specialist.[6]

On the other hand, the Internet is a useful source of information to protect personnel and businesses against extremist groups. Activists, for example, are known to place their plans (e.g., demonstrations) online. Security practitioners should conduct online searches by entering key words such as "anti-capitalism" and "socialism." Research "sucks.com" sites such as "walmart-sucks.com" which have been created to vent at companies. Through these searches, corporations will be better prepared to protect people and assets.[7]

IDENTITY THEFT

Identity theft is the illegal acquisition of another individual's personal identifying information to be used fraudulently for illegal gain. There are many ways in which an offender can steal personal information and there are many types of crimes committed by using another person's identity.

Traditional methods of obtaining personal information include looking over another's shoulder at a bank or ATM, searching trash (i.e., "Dumpster diving"), impersonation over the telephone, stealing a wallet or mail, fraudulently ordering a copy of a victim's credit record, or going to a cemetery to locate a deceased person whose age, if living, would approximate the offender's age and securing documents to develop the identity. The Internet has expanded the opportunities to steal identities. As we know from previous pages, various Web sites offer a wealth of personal information. Also, hackers penetrate corporate databases and e-commerce Web sites and download credit card numbers. Another method is "skimming," which is the electronic lifting of data from the magnetic stripe of a credit card to be transferred to a counterfeit card. A retail clerk, for example, can swipe a customer card for the sale and then swipe it again through the skimmer.[8]

An offender can use a victim's identity to secure credit cards, open bank and checking accounts, apply for a loan, purchase and sell a home or car, establish cellular service, file for bankruptcy, obtain a job, seek workers' compensation, file a lawsuit, and commit a crime in the victim's name. The possible offenses are endless and victims often learn about the identity theft months after it occurred.

This crime affects half a million new victims annually, and it has been labeled as the fastest growing crime in America.[9] Congress passed the Identity Theft and Assumption Deterrence Act of 1998 to make identity theft a federal crime. This crime is investigated by the FBI, the U.S. Postal Service, and the U.S. Secret Service.

Personal protection strategies include the following:

- Protect personal information in public, over the telephone, and online. Carry only necessary ID.
- Closely study bills and completely destroy unneeded papers containing personal information.
- When making online transactions, be sure they are made over secure, encrypted connections and verify the address and telephone numbers on Web sites.
- If you have been victimized, contact: creditors, the three major credit reporting agencies (Equifax, 800-685-1111; Experian, 888-397-3742; and TransUnion, 800-680-7293), and file a report (and obtain a copy) with police.[10]

The problem of identity theft is further illustrated by research by the California Public Interest Research Group and the Privacy Rights Clearinghouse, which found the following: victims learned of their identity theft 14 months after it occurred, 55 percent of the cases were unsolved, victims spent an average of 175 hours seeking to clear their names, bogus charges averaged $18,000, dissatisfaction was expressed toward police and credit bureaus, and the need for reform was noted.[11]

INVESTIGATIVE LEADS

Investigative work requires patience and perseverance, and difficult cases often tax the abilities of investigators as they search for answers. Investigative leads are aids to the investigator.

Scene of the Loss

A search of the scene of the loss can provide answers to investigative questions. *Offenders at a crime scene often leave something (e.g., fingerprints) or take something with them (e.g., stolen item), either of which ties them to the crime.*

The loss scene needs to be protected from unauthorized people. Photographs, video, and sketches should be made without disturbing the characteristics of the scene and before evidence is removed.

Evidence

Evidence is used to prove a fact. It usually consists of testimony by a victim or witness and physical evidence. Good evidence answers questions. In addition to interviewing, physical evidence at the loss scene can aid investigators. Physical evidence is varied and can include fingerprints, documents, clothing, fibers, chemicals, explosives, weapons, or almost anything visible or even invisible. When a person was at the scene of a loss, it is possible that he or she left something that is unique to that individual.

If physical evidence is removed from the scene of the loss, careful documentation and preservation are necessary. Documentation includes statements about the evidence such as the investigator's name, date, and exact location where found.

Victim

Good leads can be obtained by checking the background of the victim. The victim can be a business or organization or a person. A person owning a failing business may have perpetrated an accident, arson, or other crime to collect on an insurance policy. A male employee may falsely claim that he was attacked at work by his wife's lover. Sometimes employees are hurt off the job but are able to go to work, claim injury on the job, and hope for improved compensation. In most instances, the victim is not an offender; however, the investigator must maintain an open mind.

Motive

The motive behind the loss is an important consideration. Questions of concern include these: Who will gain from the loss? Are there any ulterior motives? What types of persons would create such a loss? Why? The investigator also must recognize that the human factor may not be involved in the loss. Equipment malfunction or weather may be the cause.

Witnesses

Investigative leads frequently are acquired from witnesses. Good interviewing is important and can turn up valuable leads.

Informants

Why do informants divulge information? Sometimes, it is to seek favors or money, or because they see it as their duty, or because they want to get someone in trouble (e.g., competitor, unfaithful lover). Informants often supply misinformation to investigators. An investigator can test the informant by asking questions to which he or she knows the answers. The investigator must never become too involved with informants or perform any unethical or criminal activity to acquire information. Obviously, the informant's identity must be protected, unless a court requires otherwise. Many investigators (private and public) have money in their budgets specifically designed to pay informants for information. A common practice of investigators is to catch an individual in violation of a rule or law but not seek punishment (e.g., prosecute) if that individual supplies the investigator with useful information.

Modus Operandi

MO stands for modus operandi, or method of operation. An investigator may ask, "What method was used by the burglar?" Because people differ, they commit crimes in different ways. Many police departments have MO files on offenders. When a crime takes place, investigators may check the MO files for suspects who are known to commit crimes in a certain way. A particular offender may use a specific tool during a burglary. A robber may wear a unique style of clothing during robberies. A saboteur at a manufacturing plant may be using a particular type of wire cutter. Sometimes, an uncommon MO is discovered: for example, a burglar who defecates at the crime scene.

Software

Various types of software are available that assist investigators. *Artificial intelligence* uses software and databases containing a variety of stored investigative information to analyze data to link crime scene evidence to a suspect. The *Identi-Kit*, which has been used by police for years, consists of hundreds of overlays of facial features (e.g., eyes, noses, chins) that are selected by a victim or witness to create a drawing of the suspect. Computer-aided identification software uses the same principle and stores more than 100,000 facial features.[12] Another product is *link analysis software*, which is especially helpful with complex investigations involving large amounts of information. It requires data entry of such topics as people, places, events, vehicles, telephone calls, bank accounts, and businesses to produce countless scenarios and combinations in the form of charts and graphs for analysis. This software helps to produce thorough and effective investigations that are easy to display.[13]

> Offenders at a crime scene often leave something or take something with them, either of which ties them to the crime.

SURVEILLANCE

Surveillance, watching or observing, is an investigative aid used widely to acquire information. Among the kinds of cases in which surveillance is helpful are these examples: assembly line workers are suspected of stealing merchandise; an employee is suspected by company investigators of passing trade secrets to another company; truck drivers while on their routes experience unexplainable losses between company facilities; and an employee claiming to be unable to work because of an on-the-job accident is observed building an extension on his home.

Two major kinds of surveillance are stationary and moving. *Stationary surveillance* requires the investigator to remain in one spot while observing; for example, an investigator sitting in an auto watching a suspect's house. This type can be tedious and frustrating. In *moving surveillance*, investigators follow a suspect—for example, tailing a truck driver whose cargo was "lost."

During surveillance, an investigator must be careful not to attract attention. The person being watched usually has the advantage and can attempt to lose the investigator by a variety of quick moves (e.g., going out a back door, jumping on a bus, driving through a red light). Therefore, the investigator must blend into the environment to prevent detection.

Another type of surveillance is audio surveillance. This includes wiretapping and eavesdropping, which are restricted by law.

Equipment used during surveillance can include binoculars, a telescope, communication equipment, cameras, listening devices, video and audio recorders, and auto tracking devices. *One of the most successful methods of surveillance is the use of a concealed pinhole lens camera.* If a video motion sensor is used, time will not have to be spent on reviewing many hours of tape. The loss prevention investigator must keep informed about these devices and related legal restrictions on usage.

> Concealed pinhole lens cameras are a popular method of surveillance. What is your view of this technique?

INFORMATION ACCURACY

An investigation is essentially an information-gathering process. The accuracy of the information not only reflects on the investigator but also has a direct bearing on the consequences of the investigation. The following guidelines are helpful in obtaining accurate information:

1. Double-check information whenever possible.
2. Ask the same questions of several people. Compare the results.
3. To check on the reliability of a source, ask questions for which you know the answers.
4. Cross-check information; for example, if you have a copy of a person's employment application and college transcript, cross-check name, date of birth, social security number, and so on.
5. Read information back to a source to check for accuracy.
6. If possible, check the background of a person providing information or check the accuracy of a records system.
7. Maintain accurate notes, records, photographs, and sketches; do not depend on memory for details.

8. If you are unable to write notes or a report, for instance while driving an auto, record the information on a tape recorder.
9. Provide adequate security for information and records to prevent tampering or loss.

REPORT WRITING

Report writing usually begins after the investigator has invested time and energy in collecting sufficient information on the basic investigative questions. How well these reports are prepared will have a definite impact on the investigator's career. Many supervisors get to know their subordinates more through reports than from any other means of communication. Furthermore, many supervisors consider report writing a major skill when promoting investigators.

Reports have a variety of uses aside from punitive results. They are used by management to analyze critical problems (e.g., excessive thefts or accidents). Summations of many reports can assist planning and budgetary efforts. Reports also may be used in litigation.

Investigators usually record information in a small notebook before formulating a report. An investigator has many thoughts in mind during an investigation that prevent the report from being written as the investigation proceeds. Also, after appropriate information is collected, the investigator has a bird's-eye view of the incident; this assists in the development of an outline that will improve the structure of the report.

Standard reports are used by many investigators. These reports are formulated by management to guide investigators in answering important questions. A typical standard report begins with a heading that includes the type of incident, date, time, and location. Next is a list of persons involved in the incident along with their addresses, telephone numbers, ages, and occupations. Another section can include a list of evidence. The narrative, sometimes called the *story*, follows, usually written in chronological order. The end of the report contains a variety of information such as the investigator's name and the status of the investigation. Diagrams and photographs may be attached. Report characteristics vary depending on need.

During report writing, the investigator should get to the point in easily understood language. An impressive vocabulary is not an asset to a report. Neatness and good grammar are important. Supervisors often complain about poor narratives by subordinates. Let's look at some blunders that have reflected on the investigator.

*   "When the employee was approached by loss prevention staff he had a switchblade he had bought in his lunch box."

- "A telephone pole of manufacturing plants within our corporation showed that 15 percent of employees were ignoring loss prevention rules."
- "The woman caused the loss because her newborn son was branded as illiterate."
- "The sick employee was honestly in bed with the doctor for two weeks even though he did not give her any relief."

TESTIMONY

Security practitioners periodically testify in depositions or in court. A *deposition* is a pretrial discovery method whereby the opposing party in a case asks questions of the other party (e.g., victim, witness, expert) under oath, usually in an attorney's office, and while a word-for-word transcript is recorded. Depositions help to present the evidence of each side of a case and assist the justice system in settling cases before the expensive trial stage. Most civil and criminal cases never make it to trial.

Well-prepared testimony in both criminal and civil cases can be assured most readily by the following suggestions. (See Table 10-1 for additional advice.)

1. Prepare and review notes and reports. Recheck evidence that has been properly labeled and identified. Confer with an attorney.
2. Dress in a conservative manner, if not in uniform. Appear well groomed.
3. Maintain good demeanor (conduct, behavior). Do not slouch or fidget. Do not argue with anyone. Remain calm (take some deep breaths without being obvious).
4. Pause and think before speaking. Do not volunteer information beyond what is requested. Never guess. If you do not know an answer, say so.
5. If you bring notes, remember that the opposing attorney can request that the notes become part of the evidence. Recheck notes to prevent any unwanted information from entering the case.
6. Request feedback from associates to improve future performance.

Search the Web

Refer to the Web sites in this chapter to check the variety of personal information offered. What can you find out about yourself?

Check "sucks.com" sites and search on "anti-capitalism" to view sites that are in contention with corporate America.

Table 10-1 Brief Review of Common Tactics of Cross-Examination

Counsel's Tactic	Example	Purpose	Officer's Response
Rapid-fire questions	One question after another with little time to answer.	To confuse you; attempt to force inconsistent answers.	Take time to consider the question; be deliberate in answering; ask to have the question repeated, remain calm.
Condescending counsel	Benevolent in approach, over-sympathetic in questions to the point of ridicule.	To give the impression that you are inept, lack confidence, or may not be a reliable witness.	Firm, decisive answers, asking for the questions to be repeated if improperly phrased.
Friendly counsel	Very courteous, polite; questions tend to take you into his confidence.	To lull you into a false sense of security, where you will give answers in favor of the defense.	Stay alert; bear in mind that the purpose of defense is to discredit or diminish the effect of your testimony.
Badgering, belligerent	Counsel staring you right in the face, shouts "That is so, isn't it, officer?"	To make you angry so that you lose the sense of logic and calmness. Generally, rapid questions will also be included in this approach.	Stay calm, speak in a deliberate voice, giving prosecutor time to make appropriate objections.
Mispronouncing officer's name; using wrong rank	Your name is Jansen, counsel calls you Johnson.	To draw your attention to the error in pronunciation rather than enabling you to concentrate on the question asked, so that you will make inadvertent errors in testimony.	Ignore the mispronunciation and concentrate on the question counsel is asking.
Suggestive question (tends to be a leading question allowable on cross-examination)	"Was the color of the car blue?"	To suggest an answer to his or her question in an attempt to confuse or to lead you.	Concentrate carefully on the facts, disregard the suggestion. Answer the question.

Counsel's Tactic	Example	Purpose	Officer's Response
Demanding a yes or no answer to a question that needs explanation	"Did you strike the defendant with your club?"	To prevent all pertinent and mitigating details from being considered by the jury.	Explain the answer to the question; if stopped by counsel demanding a yes or no answer, pause until the court instructs you to answer in your own words.
Reversing witness's words	You answer, "The accident occurred 27 feet from the intersection." Counsel says, "You say the accident occurred 72 feet from the intersection?"	To confuse you and demonstrate a lack of confidence in you.	Listen intently whenever counsel repeats back something you have said. If counsel makes an error, correct him or her.
Repetitious questions	The same question asked several times slightly rephrased.	To obtain inconsistent or conflicting answers from you.	Listen carefully to the question and state, "I have just answered that question."
Conflicting answers	"But Officer Smith, Detective Brown just said . . ."	To show inconsistency in the investigation. This tactic is normally used on measurements, times, and so forth.	Remain calm. Conflicting statements have a tendency to make a witness extremely nervous. Be guarded in your answers on measurements, times, and so forth. Unless you have exact knowledge, use the term "approximately." Refer to your notes.
Staring	After you have answered, counsel stares as though there were more to come.	To have a long pause that one normally feels must be filled, thus saying more than necessary. To provoke you into offering more than the question called for.	Wait for the next question.

Source: Reproduced from *The Training Keys* with permission of the International Association of Chiefs of Police, Gaithersburg, MD.

CASE PROBLEMS

10A. The Loreton Company, a California manufacturer of televisions, continuously increased profits because of high output at six company-owned plants. A recent inventory at the largest plant located outside of Los Angeles showed that more than 200 televisions were missing. The management of the Loreton Company became desperate about the losses. You are a partner at Klein and Smith Loss Prevention Associates, a consulting firm specializing in loss problems. Loreton Company executives contact you for assistance. A meeting is arranged. After competition with two other security and loss prevention firms, Loreton executives decide on a two-month contract for your firm's services. You are in charge. What are your specific plans and actions?

10B. You are senior investigator for the Bolt Corporation, which is a top 100 corporation with large holdings in electrical supplies, oil and gas exploration, and drugs. Because you have an excellent record and 11 years of varied investigative experience with Bolt, you are selected by the director of loss prevention to train five newly hired college educated investigators. The director stresses that you will design a 105-hour training program to span three weeks. Practical investigative aids will be the essence of the program. After three weeks, the investigators will be assigned to various divisions within Bolt, where they will receive specialized training while working with experienced investigators. The director states that your typed curriculum design is due tomorrow for a 4 P.M. loss prevention meeting. She requires that you list the topics, hours for each topic, and why the particular topics and hours were chosen.

NOTES

1. Federal Bureau of Investigation, *Uniform Crime Report, 1998* (Washington, D.C.: U.S. Government Printing Office, 1999).
2. U.S. Department of Justice, *Report of the Task Force on Private Security* (Washington, D.C.: U.S. Government Printing Office, 1976), p. 238.
3. David L. Ray, "When Bad Things Happen to Good Businesses," *Security Management* 44 (October 2000), p. 94.
4. George Van Nostrand and Anthony J. Luizzo, "Investigating in a New Environment," *Security Management* (June 1995), pp. 33–35.
5. Michael Blotzer, "Privacy in the Digital Age," *Occupational Hazards* 62 (July 2000), pp. 29–31.
6. Ronald Mendell, "Is the Internet Just a Web of Misinformation?" *Security Management* 43 (June 1999), p. 130.
7. Elmer Snow, "Adapting Technologies to the Task," *Security Management* 44 (June 2000), pp. 60–64.

8. National Crime Prevention Council, "Identity Theft on the Rise," *Catalyst* 19 (November 2000), pp. 2–3. And, Sandy Jaeger, "Who Am I?" *Security Technology & Design* 10 (June 2000), p. 6.

9. Ibid., p. 2.

10. "Do You Know Where Your Identity Is?" *Security Watch* 3002 (January 15, 2001), p. 7.

11. "Victims Describe Identity Theft," *Security Management* 44 (August 2000), p. 16.

12. James Gilbert, *Criminal Investigation*, 5th ed. (Upper Saddle River, NJ: Prentice-Hall, 2001), p. 543.

13. Michael F. Brown, *Criminal Investigation: Law and Practice*, 2nd ed. (Boston: Butterworth–Heinemann, 2001), p. 67. And, Rita Premo, "Case Closed," *Security Management* 44 (September 2001), p. 24.

11

Accounting, Accountability, and Auditing: Keys to Survival

OBJECTIVES

After studying this chapter the reader will be able to:

1. Define and explain the importance of accounting, accountability, and auditing.
2. Explain why the loss prevention function should work closely with accounting operations.
3. Describe how accountability is applied to the areas of evidence collection, cashier operations, and purchasing.
4. Explain why loss prevention professionals should work with auditors to uncover fraud and the misappropriation of assets.

Accounting, often referred to as the language of business, is concerned with recording, sorting, summarizing, reporting, and interpreting data related to business transactions. Accounting information aids managers in decision making. Virtually every type of concern requires accounting records. For the most part, the day-to-day recording of business data is performed by bookkeepers; accountants design the accounting systems and prepare and interpret reports. For example, a bookkeeper in a business, after counting cash and checking cash sales receipts, records the amount in the cash receipts journal. Or, based on accounting data—specifically, inventory reports—an accountant decides that shrinkage is too high in a particular business; the loss prevention department is notified.

> Accounting is the language of business.

Accountability defines a responsibility for and a description of something. For example, John Smith is responsible (i.e., is held accountable) for all finished products in a plant, and he maintains accurate records (i.e., a description) of what is in stock. Another example would be a loss prevention officer keeping a log of people entering and leaving a restricted area. Or, while a truck is being loaded for shipment, a clerk records on a tally the number of items being shipped. In both examples, employees sign their names to the documents (log, tally, or inventory); they are responsible, and accountability is maintained.

Auditing is the examination or check of something; the major purpose of an audit is to uncover deviations. An audit can be simple or intricate. For example, a loss prevention officer audits (checks) a CCTV system to ensure that it is working properly. Or, an auditor audits the financial records of a company and reports that they are fair, reliable, and conform to company policies and procedures.

ACCOUNTING

Within a business, for example, the accounting department has control over financial matters that are vital to business operations. Common components of an accounting department are cashiering operations, accounts receivable, accounts payable, payroll, and company bank accounts. Each component of an accounting department has the responsibility for maintaining accounting records that are scrutinized by management to ascertain the financial position of the business. Without adequate loss prevention strategies or controls in these important areas, businesses, institutions, or organizations could not survive.

Potential losses are possible throughout the accounting department. A cashiering operation must be protected not only from burglary and robbery but also from employee theft. Accounts receivable must be protected from opportunities that allow employees to destroy bills and pocket cash. Accounts payable also needs protection; employees in collusion with supply company employees have been known to alter invoices to embezzle money. A frequent scheme by some payroll clerks is to maintain fictitious employees on the payroll and cash their paychecks.

Accounting also is a system of principles and procedures that enable clerks and bookkeepers to record financial data in a logical manner. A record of an individual transaction does not have as much impact as the summation of transactions in a financial statement or business report (see Table 11-1). The accounting statements assist management in decision making.

Accounting statements assist management in answering many questions:

What is the financial condition of the concern?

What is the financial value?

Was there a profit or loss?

Which part of a firm is doing well (or poorly)?

How serious are losses attributed to crime, fire, or poor safety?

This book concentrates on concerns related to the last question, although the losses affect all the questions that preceded it. Those who plan a career in loss prevention and may have to investigate a crime associated with accounting records are well advised to study accounting at the college level to prepare for investigative tasks that involve interpretation of accounting procedures and records.

Table 11-1   Financial Statements of Two Separate Companies

Trico Corporation
*Balance Sheet June 30, 20_*

Assets		Liabilities		
Cash	4,000	Accounts payable	44,000	
Accounts receivable	100,300	Notes payable	100,000	
Inventory	100,000			144,000
Equipment	34,000			
Land	80,000	Capital		
Buildings	300,400			
	618,700	Preferred stock	74,700	
		Common stock	400,000	
				474,700
		Total liabilities		
Total assets	618,700	and capital		618,700

Simple examples of an income statement and a capital statement follow. Note that "expenses" and "net income" are two additional major categories of accounting besides assets, liabilities, and capital.

Quality Loss Prevention Service
Income Statement
*for month ended October 31, 20_*

Sales and service		11,800
Operating expenses:		
Salary expenses	6,000	
Supplies expense	1,100	
Rent expense	1,400	
Miscellaneous expense	1,300	
		-9,800
Net income		2,000

Quality Loss Prevention Service
Capital Statement
*for month ended October 31, 20_*

Capital, October 2, 20_		10,000
Net income for the month	2,000	
Less withdrawals	-1,000	
Increase in capital		1,000
Capital, October 31, 20_		11,000

ACCOUNTABILITY

The definition of formal accountability points to the documentation or description of something. Informal accountability usually is verbal and results in no documentation; for example, a loss prevention manager asks a subordinate if a fire extinguisher was checked (audited). The subordinate states that it was audited. Thus, a basic audit of a loss prevention device is accomplished. What if two weeks pass, a fire takes place near the particular fire extinguisher, and it is found to be inoperable? An employee who tries to extinguish the fire with the inoperable extinguisher complains to management. The loss prevention manager is asked by superiors if the extinguisher was checked. The manager states that it was audited. The superiors ask for documentation to support the statements. Because of the verbal accountability, no record exists. From that point on, the loss prevention manager realizes the value of formal accountability and develops an excellent system of records.

The importance of accountability must not be underestimated. It is a key survival strategy. The documentation can be the result of many types of loss prevention activities. Examples are a variety of investigative reports (e.g., crimes, accidents); security system maintenance; alarm activations; visitor logs; crime prevention, fire protection and life safety plans; meetings; policies and procedures; and training. As well as aiding a loss prevention practitioner when supporting a contention, documentation can assist in planning, budgeting, preparing major reports, and general reference.

> Accountability is a key survival strategy.

Evidence Collection and Presentation

The accountability for physical evidence, especially before it reaches a court of law, can have a definite impact on a case. The "chain of possession" of evidence must be controlled. A loss scene should be protected, photographed, videotaped, and sketched before evidence is touched.

The proper labeling, packaging, and storage of evidence is equally important. The accountability for evidence often is brought forth in court. Attorneys are sure to scrutinize the paperwork and procedures associated with the evidence. The following questions are among the many frequently asked in court. Who saw the evidence first? Who touched it first? Where was it taken? By whom? How was it stored? Was the storage area locked? Who had the keys? How many keys were there?

Cashier Operations

A detailed procedure for accountability in retailing is illustrated next:

> The key to front end control is accountability. Each cashier must have his or her own cash register drawer. Relief cashiers should bring their own drawer, and the cashier going on relief should lock up her cash or remove her drawer during relief periods. The relief person should also sign the register tape when taking over, and the regular cashier should sign when leaving the register.
>
> The head cashier should periodically review register detail tapes, watching for continuity of transaction numbers. If the last transaction on the register Monday night was number 112334, then the first transaction on Tuesday morning must be 112335. If it is not, the missing chronological numbers may indicate theft of several sales by the cashier and destruction of the tape containing the missing transaction numbers.[1]

Retail cashier operations have been enhanced by computers. More on retail accountability and point-of-sale accounting systems in Chapter 15.

Purchasing

Because procedures vary and various types of computer software are available to enhance purchasing systems, a generalized approach to purchasing is presented here. Four forms are discussed in the subsequent purchasing system: purchase requisition, purchase order, invoice, and receiving report.

When a company orders merchandise, equipment, or supplies, for example, the order should be in writing to avoid any misunderstanding. Suppose a maintenance department head at a plant is ordering something. Generally, the documentation process begins when the order is written on a standard form known as a *purchase requisition*. This form lists, among other things, the originator (who placed the order), the date, the item, a description, justification for need, and cost. Once the originator completes the purchase requisition and makes a copy for filing, superiors approve or disapprove the purchase and sign the original order. If approved, the purchasing department reviews the purchase requisition and selects the best vendor. A pre-numbered *purchase order* is completed by the purchasing staff. Copies of the purchase order are sent to the originator, the receiving department, and the accounts payable department; the original purchase order is retained by the purchasing department. The purchase order contains, among other things, the originator, the item, quantity, possibly an item code number from a vendor catalog, and the cost. The purchase order is sent to the vendor. Upon fulfillment of the order, the vendor sends an *invoice* to the buyer's accounts payable department. An invoice contains the names and addresses of both the buyer and the vendor, cost, item, quantity, date, and method of shipment.

When the accounts payable department receives the invoice, it checks it for accuracy by comparing it with a copy of the purchase order. Cost, type of item, proper quantity, and address of buyer are checked.

The receiving and purchasing departments of the buyer receive copies of the invoice to be able to check them for accuracy. To decrease the possibility of mistakes (or collusion), the purchase order and invoice sent to the receiving department may have the number of items deleted. When the merchandise arrives, the receiving person records the number of items, type, and also checks for irregularities (e.g., damage). This form often becomes a *receiving report*. Copies are made and then sent to the purchasing and accounts payable departments. The purchasing department compares the receiving report with the invoice. The accounts payable department makes payment after examining the purchase order, invoice, and the receiving report. These three documents and a copy of the check constitute the inactive file for this purchase (see Figure 11-1).

The system may appear complicated; however, without such accountability, losses can increase. For example, in one company, accounting employees in collusion with outside supply company employees altered records so items paid for were never delivered, but sold on the black market for illegal gain. In another case, a mid-level accountant for a utility company submitted bogus check requests for payments to vendors. The accountant had set up accounts at a bank for phony companies, and when the utility paid the "vendors," the accountant simply transferred the money to his personal account at the same bank.[2]

Another widespread loss-provoking activity in purchasing results from *kickbacks*, when the purchaser receives favors or cash from the seller for buying the seller's product or service. Losses occur, especially if the product or service is inferior and overpriced in comparison to the competition. For example, in a secret deal, John Doe Forklift Company agrees to pay Richard Ring, purchaser for Fence Manufacturing, $1000 cash for each forklift purchased. After the forklifts are delivered, it is discovered that the forklift tires are too smooth for the outside gravel and dirt grounds of the manufacturing company. With limited traction, the forklifts frequently get stuck and employees are unable to work until delivery trucks return and pull the forklifts free. The losses include both cash and lost time.

Loss prevention strategies in purchasing include the following suggestions:

1. Centralize all purchasing through a purchasing department.
2. Maintain accountability through documents (standard forms), signatures, and carefully designed computer software.

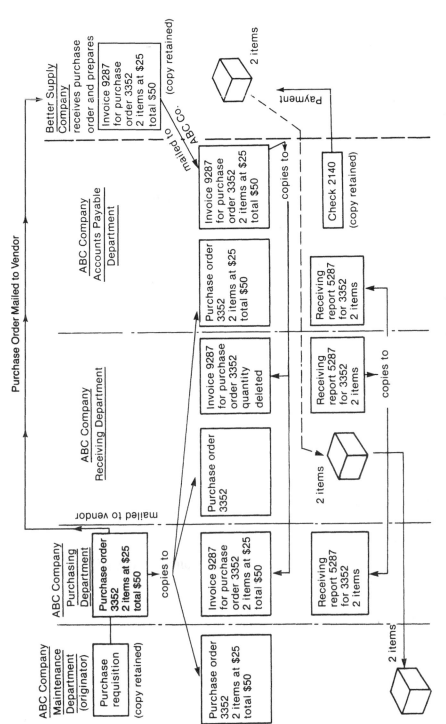

Figure 11-1 Accountability and paper trail for purchase of two items by ABC Company.

273

3. Separate duties and responsibilities so that each person and department can check on the others' work.
4. Test by deliberate error.
5. Use unalterable paper to prevent alterations or erasures.
6. Pre-number purchase order forms (and other forms when needed).
7. Conduct loss prevention checks without notice.
8. Conduct periodic audits.
9. Scrutinize the purchasing department to prevent favoritism and kickbacks.
10. Prohibit gifts or favors from vendors (sellers).
11. Screen applicants for employment.
12. Develop clear policies and procedures.

Inventory

In a wholesale or retail business, merchandise is continuously purchased and sold. This sale of merchandise is the primary source of revenue. A substantial amount of a business's resources is invested in saleable merchandise, and this merchandise is the largest asset. Therefore, this asset must be protected. The term *inventory* includes merchandise for sale, raw materials, and unfinished goods. Inventory is reported on the balance sheet as an asset.

Shrinkage is the amount of merchandise that has disappeared through theft, or has become useless because of breakage or spoilage, or is unaccounted for because of sloppy recording. This often is expressed as a percentage. Levy and Weitz define shrinkage as "the difference between the recorded value of inventory (at retail prices) based on merchandise bought and received and the value of the *actual* inventory (at retail prices) in stores and distribution centers divided by retail sales during the period."[3] For example, if accounting records indicate the inventory should be $1,500,000, the *actual* count of the inventory reveals $1,236,000, and sales were $4,225,000, the shrinkage is 6.2 percent, or ($1,500,000 – $1,236,000)/$4,225,000.

In many businesses, shrinkage of 3 percent or more is a serious loss problem. Loss prevention managers frequently express the objective of their job as lowering shrinkage. An accurate measurement of shrinkage depends on the quality of the inventory system; both have a definite impact on the loss prevention program and its manager.

Two primary inventory systems are the periodic and the perpetual systems. The *periodic inventory system* results in a physical count of merchandise only at specific intervals, usually once per year. When this system is used, daily revenue from sales is recorded in accounting records but no transaction is recorded to adjust the inventory account to reflect the fact that a sale was made. The periodic system makes it difficult to measure shrinkage accurately. To make matters worse, when a monthly or quarterly financial statement is necessary for a particular business using the periodic inventory system, managers sometimes estimate the inventory without taking a physical count.

The *perpetual inventory system* uses accounting records that maintain an up-to-date inventory count. These systems typically are computerized. Handheld microcomputer technology and point-of-sale (POS) computers capture data through bar-code scanning. In addition to recording daily revenue from sales, an individual inventory record is maintained for each type of merchandise sold, which enables a continuous count. Thus, the accounting records reflect cost of goods sold and the inventory quantity. This information provides a better opportunity to measure shrinkage than that available with the periodic system.

To increase the accuracy of an inventory and the shrinkage statistic, these strategies are recommended:

1. Maintain a careful inventory system.
2. Establish accountability.
3. Standardize forms and procedures for the count.
4. Make sure employees can count accurately.
5. If possible, do not subject employees to extensive inventory counts at any one time.
6. Automate the process by using handheld microcomputer technology that captures data through bar codes on merchandise.
7. Conduct surprise counts of a sample of the merchandise at erratic time intervals. Compare manual counts with computer data.
8. If possible, require pre-numbered requisition forms for merchandise taken out of inventory.
9. Prohibit unnecessary people (e.g., truck drivers, service people, other employees) from entering merchandise storage areas.
10. Use an undercover investigator to participate in the inventory count.
11. The loss prevention manager should have an opportunity to examine the methods used to formulate the shrinkage statistic, especially because it will reflect on him or her and on the loss prevention program.

Another type of inventory focuses on assets such as equipment, tools, supplies, and information. Knowing what a company or institution owns and where assets are at all times is an important aspect of protection programs. This task is made easier by applying innovations such as bar-code technology. With this method, a number is assigned to each asset to be tracked. Software generates a bar-code tag (to be attached to each item) encoded with the respective item's asset identification number. The number links each item to its electronic file, which may contain information on the person assigned to the item, its location, restrictions on movement, monetary value, vendor, and warranty. Such a system can generate reports on assets and assist with investigations.[4] Furthermore, electronic article surveillance tags, as used in retail stores, can be embedded into assets to signal an alarm and direct CCTV to the asset when it is moved out of its assigned area.

AUDITING

A popular and convenient way to conduct an audit is through an audit questionnaire. A typical audit questionnaire has a list of questions to remind the person conducting the audit to focus attention on specific areas of concern. Questionnaire results provide feedback that helps to pinpoint and correct deviations and deficiencies. Here are some sample questions from *The Journal of Accountancy* for a small business, but many of the questions are relevant to other organizations.

- Are accounting records kept up-to-date and balanced monthly?
- Are monthly or quarterly financial reports available to the owner?
- Are the personal funds of the owner and his or her personal income and expenses completely segregated from the business?
- Does the company practice "separation of functions" (e.g., separate check preparation from check authorization) so accountability is assigned and each employee can check on the other?
- Are employees rotated periodically among financial jobs and are they required to take vacations?
- Are over-the-counter receipts controlled by cash register tapes, counter receipts, and so on?
- Are employees who handle funds bonded?
- Do two different people reconcile the bank records and make out the deposit slip?
- Are pre-numbered checks used?
- Is the owner's signature required on checks?
- Does the owner review the bank reconciliation?
- Does the owner never sign blank checks?
- Do different people reconcile the bank records and write the checks?
- Are work orders or sales invoices pre-numbered and controlled?
- Is credit granted only by the owner?
- Is the person responsible for inventory someone other than the bookkeeper?
- Are periodic physical inventories taken?
- Are perpetual inventory records maintained?
- Are there detailed records available of property assets and allowances for depreciation?
- Does someone other than the bookkeeper always do the purchasing?
- Are suppliers' monthly statements compared with recorded liabilities regularly?
- Does the owner approve, sign, and distribute payroll checks?[5]

Certified Public Accountants

The qualifications for a certified public accountant (CPA) certificate generally require a college degree with an accounting emphasis, plus a passing grade on an examination prepared by the *American Institute of Certified Public Accountants* (AICPA). Most states require a few years of experience before successful candidates can practice as independent CPAs. The Board of Accountancy in each state can supply specific information about qualifications.

During an audit by an independent auditor (i.e., CPA), guidance is provided by state and federal statutes, court decisions, the contract with the client, and professional standards as established by Generally Accepted Auditing Standards and Generally Accepted Accounting Practices. Because it is impossible to check every financial record and transaction, the CPA narrows the audit to certain records such as financial reports and areas where problems are common to the particular concern. How accounting data are recorded and summarized is frequently studied.

At times, the CPA may encounter misleading financial information that attempts to make a business look better than its true financial position. The misleading information often is an attempt by management to attract investors. To counter this problem, cautious investors are more likely to favor a business that has had an audit by an outside independent CPA, as opposed to no audit or one performed by an internal auditor.

When the independent CPA has completed the audit, a report is prepared. If the business's financial records are dependable and credible, then the CPA expresses this favorable opinion in the audit report. This is known as the *attest function*.

CPAs, like other skilled professionals, are liable for damages proximately caused by their negligence. A CPA is liable to a client when he/she negligently fails to detect or fraudulently conceals signs that an employee of the client is embezzling. Also, the CPA is liable for not detecting and reporting to the client that internal audit controls are lax.[6]

Many firms maintain internal auditors. These internal auditors audit various internal activities that independent auditors may or may not audit. For instance, in addition to studying specific accounting records, internal auditors may examine whether management's policies and procedures are being followed. An internal auditor also can conduct surprise audits.

Fraud

Fraud is a broad term that includes a variety of offenses that share the elements of deceit or intentional misrepresentation of fact, with the intent of unlawfully depriving a person of property or legal rights. Here are some estimates on fraud and embezzlement losses: The average organization loses 6 percent of its annual revenues to employee fraud. The Association of Certified Fraud Examiners puts annual losses at $400 billion, with the average cost of embezzlement by nonmanagerial employees at $60,000, and the average by managers at $250,000. The accounting firm Ernst & Young revealed that over a five-year period, two in five businesses suffered more than five fraud-related losses. The reasons for this huge problem are varied, including greed and ethical problems; profit margins that have squeezed out nonrevenue-generating departments such as internal audit and security; mergers and acquisitions that have increased exposure; and sweeping incidents "under the rug" (e.g., quietly firing offenders) to avoid an impact on stockholder value, regulatory attention, and being sued for improper controls.[7]

Why do you think fraud is such a huge problem?

A survey of 322 internal auditors conducted by the Institute of Management and Administration, publishers of *Preventing Business Fraud*, and the Institute of Internal Auditors found:

- Half of respondents characterized their fraud-risk analysis process as "reactive"
- Respondents called for more ethics training and internal controls
- A fifth cited the need for realistic production and sales goals as a way to prevent fraud
- A third claimed that the CPAs who visit to audit are inept at fraud detection
- A third claimed pressure from others in their organization to compromise ethical conduct to achieve business objectives
- More than a third favored informing the corporate board of directors about fraud[8]

Do you think there is too much pressure on executives to reach business goals? Explain your answer.

Until 1995, pressure on auditors to uncover fraud was only moderately strong. However, in 1995 Congress passed the *Private Securities Litigation Reform Act*, which requires CPAs who audit publicly held companies to take steps to detect fraud. Following this legislation, the AICPA, the national body that sets standards for the accounting profession, revised its auditing standard, specifically replacing the word *irregularity* with the word *fraud* and formally holding accounting professionals responsible for detecting fraud. The standard, entitled Consideration of Fraud in a Financial Statement Audit, identifies two areas that auditors should diligently work to detect: *financial reporting fraud* and *misappropriation (theft) of assets.* The second area, especially, is likely to bring auditors to rely on the expertise of loss prevention professionals who can provide documentation that the company has controls in place to prevent losses.[9] This also is *a ripe opportunity for loss prevention professionals to show the value of security and to strengthen the protection budget.*

Reg Hayton, in *Security Management*, presents sound recommendations to reduce fraud in businesses which may involve the theft of money, goods, and information. He argues that fraud is a bigger threat than conventional theft and that fraud prevention programs in businesses are typically fractured among departments and reactive. Hayton states that the most effective and least expensive strategies are an ethical climate, clear policies, and discipline. He also recommends thorough screening of applicants, more involvement by the IT director in programming controls, and a coordinated approach through a multidisciplinary fraud team composed of the directors of audit and security, legal counsel, and top executives.[10]

IT Staffers Influenced to Go Bad[11]

In what may be a trend, the U.S. Securities and Exchange Commission (SEC), which enforces laws to reduce fraudulent financial reporting, is increasingly charging IT directors with securities fraud. Sensormatic Electronics Corp., for example, is in trouble because its home security systems firm had its IT personnel roll back computer clocks so sales could be booked sooner to inflate revenue figures. In another company, Bio Clinic Corp., more than 400 invoices with a value of $6 million, which had already been paid, were added into the ledger a second time (to falsify revenue) by reprogramming the accounting software. The SEC notes that IT directors are responsible for the accuracy and integrity of the documents and data generated by a company computer system. And, they should know if unauthorized changes have been made in general ledger, accounts receivable, and other accounting software.

Loss Prevention Auditing

A loss prevention audit may focus on only loss prevention services, systems, policies, and procedures; or instead, the focus may extend to all aspects of a business. This could include all policies and procedures and operating activities (e.g., cash handling, shipping and receiving, warehousing, production, and purchasing).

Management can prepare an audit form to remind loss prevention employees what to audit. Questions can emphasize the conditions of locks, alarms, doors, windows, fire extinguishers, and the like and ask for reports of unusual incidents. When audit forms are returned, supervisors can review and provide feedback to subordinates, which is helpful as a training technique.

Loss prevention officers commonly are assigned to fixed posts or they are mobile. Many "fall asleep mentally" while on the job. By performing an audit, these officers can obtain increased satisfaction from their jobs while performing a useful activity.

Computerization

Management has become dependent on computers because of cost savings, efficiency, and speed. Computers can perform an array of activities such as monitor inventories, issue purchase orders, and bill customers. As with manual accounting systems, computerized accounting systems need controls and audits.

Computerized accounting systems are not totally exempt from manual activities. Raw data (e.g., cash receipts and receiving reports) must be entered into the computer. Consequently, the human factor is involved in computerized accounting systems; and error, manipulation, and losses are possible. For instance, instructions can be entered into a computer to overpay an invoice or to favor a high-priced vendor.

Controls and auditing are necessary for computerized accounting systems. Controls are numerous and can include permitting no changes in the system without authorization, requiring that accountability be maintained when changes are allowed, making sure no one person is responsible for the complete processing of any transaction, and periodic rotation of personnel. Many of the controls applicable to manual accounting systems are applicable to computerized accounting systems.

Auditing for computerized accounting systems is varied. One technique to audit a computerized inventory system, for example, is to have employees count the physical inventory and compare this count to the computer count. A variety of software programs are available that perform controls and auditing of computerized accounting systems.

Search the Web

To learn more about preventing and detecting fraud, embezzlement, and other white-collar crime, check these Web sites:

National Coalition for the Prevention of Economic Crime at http://www.ncpec.org/
National White Collar Crime Center at http://www.nw3c.org/
Association of Certified Fraud Examiners at http://www.cfenet.com/
Institute of Management & Administration at http://www.ioma.com/

CASE PROBLEMS

11A. With reference to the purchasing accountability section of this chapter and Figure 11-1, design an accountability system to strengthen control and prevent losses when merchandise travels from the receiving department to the originator. Look for any other weaknesses and suggest controls.

11B. You are a director of loss prevention for a medium-sized corporation that manufactures computer components. Your boss asks you to prepare a plan of anti-fraud strategies. Prepare a list of what you think are the top five strategies that will be the heart of your plan.

11C. As a corporate IT director you have been asked by a top executive to program software so revenue will appear greater than it actually is because of a slowing economy. What are your choices in the matter, and how do you respond to the executive?

11D. As director of loss prevention for a corporation, you learn that the company president and the head of IT have conspired to fraudulently alter financial records to show revenue higher than what is expected. What do you do?

NOTES

1. Bob Curtis, "Executive Insights," *Security World* 17, No. 2 (February 1980), p. 14.
2. Richard Mann and Barry Roberts, *Essentials of Business Law*, 7th ed. (Cincinnati: West Pub., 2001), p. 470.
3. Michael Levy and Barton Weitz, *Retailing Management*, 4th ed. (New York: McGraw-Hill Irwin, 2001), p. 548.
4. Frederick C. Herdeen, et al., "Get a Lock on Inventory," *Security Management* (October 1996), pp. 71–76.
5. "A Small Business Internal Control Questionnaire," *The Journal of Accountancy* (July 1978), p. 54. Copyright © 1978 by the American Institute of Certified Public Accountants.
6. David Twomey, Marianne Jennings, and Ivan Fox, *Anderson's Business Law & the Regulatory Environment*, 14th ed. (Cincinnati: West Pub., 2001), p. 926.
7. John Conley, "Knocking the Starch Out of White Collar Crime," *Risk Management* 47 (November 2000), pp. 14–22.
8. "PBF/IIA Survey," *Preventing Business Fraud*, Issues 99-10, -11, -12 (October, November, December 1999).
9. "Soon, Auditors Will Demand More from Security Managers," *Security Management Bulletin* (January 25, 1997), pp. 1–3.
10. Reg Hayton, "Why Are Companies Losing the Fraud Fight?" *Security Management* 43 (September 1999), pp. 222–224.
11. Kim Nash, "IT Staffers Charged in Accounting Frauds," *Computerworld* (December 1999), p. 20. http://www.infotrac-college.com/.

12

Fires and Other Disasters

OBJECTIVES

After studying this chapter the reader will be able to:

1. Discuss the problem posed by fire.
2. Explain the roles of private organizations and public fire departments.
3. List and explain five fire prevention strategies.
4. Discuss HAZMAT.
5. List and explain five fire suppression strategies.
6. List three suggestions for improving planning and decisions for integrated fire and security systems.
7. List three human-made disasters and three natural disasters.
8. List ten strategies for emergency planning and disaster recovery.

THE PROBLEM POSED BY FIRE

As written in Chapter 2, the United States has one of the highest fire death rates in the industrialized world. Data from the Web in 2001, from the National Fire Data Center, showed that in 1999, 3,570 Americans lost their lives and another 21,875 were injured as a result of fire; more Americans were killed by fire than by all natural disasters combined; and about 1.8 million fires were reported, causing direct property loss of $10 billion.[1]

Private Organizations Involved in Fire Safety

A number of private organizations assist public and private sector efforts in minimizing the problem of fire. The *National Fire Protection Association* (NFPA), established in 1896, is a potent voice in fire prevention and suppression. The NFPA publishes fire standards and codes that often are incorporated into state and local fire laws. Two popular codes are the National Electric Code and the Life Safety Code. Property owners, insurance companies, and associations, among other groups, have input into the formulation and revision of NFPA standards. The *Fire Protection Handbook*, first published in 1896 by the NFPA, is "presented in the tradition of fulfilling the needs of the fire protection community for a single-source reference book on good contemporary fire protection practices."[2] Topics within this lengthy publication include the characteristics and behavior of fire, fire hazards, building design and construction, water supplies, alarm systems, extinguishing agents, and fire protection systems. (See Chapter 3 for additional information and Web addresses for the NFPA and UL.)

Underwriters Laboratories, Inc., is a nonprofit corporation interested in public safety through the investigation and testing of materials and products. It is supported by fees from manufacturers who request that their products be tested. Each year UL publishes lists of manufacturers whose products have met UL standards for safety. Some specific departments of UL show its relationship to loss prevention: the burglary protection and signaling department, the casualty and chemical hazards department, and the fire protection department. UL representatives make periodic examinations of products at factory sites. From time to time, factory product samples are selected to determine compliance with UL requirements. Manufacturers of products that are not in compliance must correct the deviation or remove the UL label (see Figure 12-1) from the product.

Another private organization involved in fire safety is the *Factory Mutual System* (http://www.factorymutual.com/; 1151 Boston-Providence Turnpike, Norwood, MA 02062; Tel.: 781-762-4300). This group works on

Figure 12–1   One of UL's registered marks, which can be found on products that meet safety standards of Underwriters Laboratories, Inc.

improving the effectiveness of fire protection systems and new fire suppression chemicals, as well as cost evaluation of fire protection systems. The Approval Group tests materials and equipment submitted by manufacturers, to see if they can withstand fire tests. An approval guide is published each year. Like UL, it issues labels to indicate that specific products have passed its tests.

The *American Insurance Association*, or AIA (http://www.aiadc.org/; 1130 Connecticut Ave., Suite 1000, Washington, D.C. 20036; Tel.: 202-828-7100) studied contributing causes of major fires in the United States during the late 1800s and early 1900s. With this information as a foundation and with NFPA standards, AIA developed codes for fire prevention in urban areas. The National Building Code evolved, which has been adopted by many local governments. A Fire Prevention Code for cities also was published by the AIA. The AIA continues to serve the insurance industry by providing safety services, publications, and database services covering hundreds of topics.

Fire Department Prevention Efforts

Because this book is primarily prevention oriented, it stresses public fire prevention tasks that often involve private-sector loss prevention practitioners. These tasks include facility planning, prefire planning, public education, codes, inspections, and legal implications.

Facility Planning

In many locales, it is legally mandatory that public fire personnel review construction plans for new facilities. This may entail consultation with architects, engineers, and loss prevention practitioners on a number of subjects ranging from fire codes to water supplies for sprinkler systems. On-site inspections by fire personnel ensure compliance with plans. Fire and water department officials often prepare recommendations to local government bodies concerning improvements in water supply systems for new industrial plants to ensure an adequate water supply in the event of a fire. Cooperation and planning with interested parties can create an improved atmosphere for preventing and suppressing fires.

Prefire Planning

Preparatory plans assist fire personnel in case of fire. An on-site survey is made of a particular building with the aid of a checklist. Then the actual prefire plans are formulated for that structure. Drawings are used to identify the location of exits, stairs, firefighting equipment, hazards, and anything else of importance. Additional information is helpful: construction characteristics and that of adjacent buildings, type of roofs, number of employees, and the best response route to the building. Prefire plans also serve as an aid to training. Naturally, firefighting personnel do not have the time to prepare prefire plans for all structures in their jurisdiction. One- and two-family residential structures are omitted in favor of more complex structures where greater losses can occur, such as schools, hospitals, theaters, hotels, and manufacturing plants.

Public Education

This fire prevention strategy involves educating the public about the fire problem and how to prevent it. The public can become a great aid in reducing fires if people are properly recruited through education campaigns. Public education programs utilize mass media, contests, lectures, and tours of firehouses. Building inspections also educate the public by pointing out fire hazards.

Codes

Years ago, as the United States was evolving into an industrial giant, buildings were constructed without proper concern for fire prevention. Building codes in urban areas either did not exist or were inadequate to ensure construction designed to prevent fire-related losses. In fact, a year before the great Chicago fire in 1871, Lloyd's Insurance Company of London halted the writing of policies in that city because of fire-prone construction practices.

Prompted by the difficulty in selling insurance because of higher rates for hazardous buildings and the losses incurred by some spectacular fires, insurance companies became increasingly interested in fire prevention strategies. Improvements in building construction and fire departments slowly followed.

Although insurance associations played an important role in establishing fire standards, government support was necessary to enforce fire codes. Today, local governments enforce state regulations and local ordinances that support fire codes. Fire department personnel inspect structures to ensure conformance to standards and codes that are specified in regulations and ordinances. To strengthen compliance by owners of buildings, penalties are meted out for violations so that fire hazards are reduced. Penalties usually are in the form of fines.

Codes can be in the form of fire codes and building codes. Frequently, there is disagreement about what should be contained in each and what responsibility and authority should be given to fire inspectors as opposed to building inspectors.

Generally, construction requirements go into building codes, and these codes are enforced by building inspectors. Model building codes are from the Building Officials Code Administrators, Southern Building Code Congress International and the International Conference of Building Officials, the new International Building Code, and the Life Safety Code (NFPA 101). The building codes contain fire resistance ratings of floors, walls, ceilings and other construction features that affect code requirements for electrical installations, sprinkler systems, exits, vents, and the like.[3]

Fire codes, enforced by firefighting personnel, deal with the maintenance and condition of various fire prevention and suppression features of buildings (e.g., sprinkler systems). Also, fire codes cover hazardous substances, hazardous occupancies, and general precautions against fire.

A code that has been adopted in whole by many federal, state, and local jurisdictions is the *Life Safety Code* (NFPA 101). Its objective is to establish minimum requirements for safety from fire in buildings and other structures. Examples of requirements include an ample number of exits for evacuation and the avoidance of locks that prevent escape during an emergency. Codes often are used in litigation when there is a claim of negligence.

Local fire codes have afforded buildings greater fire protection, especially when compared to earlier days. But there are numerous localities where codes are of poor quality. A prime factor is construction costs. Interest-group (e.g., the construction industry) pressure on government officials who stipulate codes has been known to weaken fire codes. A typical sad case is when a high-rise building catches fire and people perish because no sprinklers were installed on upper floors, and the fire department was ill equipped to suppress a fire so high up. Later, the media broadcasts the tragedy and government officials meet to satisfy the public outcry. Stronger fire codes often emerge.

Inspections

The primary purpose of building inspections by firefighting personnel is to uncover deviations from the fire code. The frequency and intensity of these inspections vary. Because of budget constraints and a shortage of personnel, many fire departments are not able to conduct enough inspections to equal national standards of several inspections per year for hazardous buildings. The *NFPA Inspection Manual* outlines methods for conducting inspections.

Legal Implications

Fire marshals are provided with broad powers to ensure public safety. This is especially evident in fire inspections and investigations, in rights to subpoena records, and in fire marshal's hearings. Most courts have upheld these powers.

In almost all local jurisdictions, the state has delegated police powers so that local officials regulate safety conditions through ordinances. Fire ordinances stipulate inspection procedures, number of inspections, violations, and penalties. When differences of opinion develop over individual rights (e.g., of a building owner) versus fire department police powers (e.g., building inspection), the issue is often resolved by the courts. Courts have stated that administrative searches are significant intrusions on individual liberties protected by the Fourth Amendment. *Probable cause* is required for a warrant as stipulated in the Fourth Amendment. To establish probable cause, the courts have pointed to whether a logical sequence of inspections is occurring in the area, the time span since the last inspection, the type of building, and associated hazards. These inspection warrants or administrative warrants permit the investigation of any possible fire code violation.[4]

FIRE PREVENTION AND FIRE SUPPRESSION STRATEGIES

Fire prevention focuses on strategies that help to avoid the inception of fires. *Fire suppression* applies personnel, equipment, and other resources to suppress fires.

The following practical strategies are emphasized for loss prevention programs:

Fire Prevention	Fire Suppression
Inspections	Technology and computers
Planning	Detection of smoke and fire
Safety	Contact the fire department
Good housekeeping	Extinguishers
Storage and transportation of hazardous	Sprinklers
substances and materials	Standpipes and hose systems
Prevention of injuries and deaths	Fire walls and doors
Training	Fire-resistive buildings
	Training and fire brigades

The fire triangle (see Figure 12-2) symbolizes the elements necessary for a fire. Fire requires heat, fuel, oxygen, and then a chemical chain reaction. When all three characteristics, plus a chemical chain reaction, are present, there will be fire. If any one is missing, either through prevention strategies (e.g., good housekeeping, safety) or suppression (i.e., extinguishment), fire will not exist. Heat often is considered the ignition source. A smoldering cigarette, sparks from a welder's torch, or friction from a machine can produce enough heat to begin a fire.

Almost every working environment has fuels, heat, and oxygen. Loss prevention practitioners, and all employees in general, must take steps to reduce the chances for fire by isolating fuels and controlling heat. Not much can be done about pervasive oxygen, but fuels such as gasoline and kerosene should be stored properly away from sources of heat.

Fire Prevention Strategies

Inspections

Inspections or audits to check on fire hazards are the mainstay of any organization's strategy against fires.[5] Checklist questions include the following. Are new facility designs and manufacturing processes being submitted to appropriate personnel for fire protection review? Do employees receive periodic training on fire prevention and suppression systems, polices, and procedures (see Figure 12-3)? What is the condition of fire suppression equipment? Are plant wastes, oily rags, and other combustibles properly disposed of? The basic purpose of

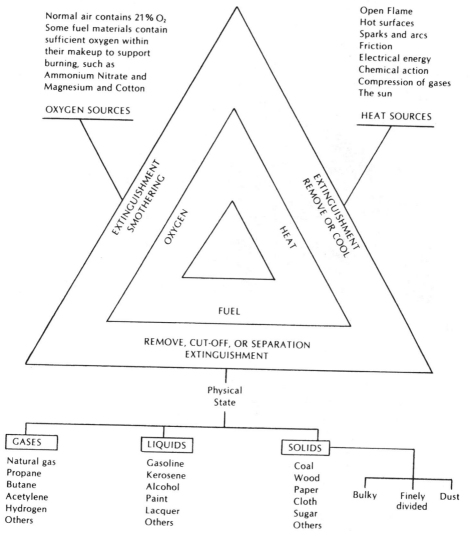

Normal air contains 21% O₂
Some fuel materials contain
sufficient oxygen within
their makeup to support
burning, such as
Ammonium Nitrate and
Magnesium and Cotton

OXYGEN SOURCES

Open Flame
Hot surfaces
Sparks and arcs
Friction
Electrical energy
Chemical action
Compression of gases
The sun

HEAT SOURCES

EXTINGUISHMENT
SMOTHERING

EXTINGUISHMENT
REMOVE OR COOL

OXYGEN

HEAT

FUEL

REMOVE, CUT-OFF, OR SEPARATION
EXTINGUISHMENT

Physical
State

GASES	LIQUIDS	SOLIDS			
Natural gas	Gasoline	Coal			
Propane	Kerosene	Wood			
Butane	Alcohol	Paper	Bulky	Finely divided	Dust
Acetylene	Paint	Cloth			
Hydrogen	Lacquer	Sugar			
Others	Others	Others			

Figure 12–2 Fire triangle.

inspections is to uncover deficiencies. Then, corrective action becomes the heart of the inspection prevention strategy.

Planning

Feedback from inspections helps in planning for strategies against fire losses. An interdisciplinary planning group often is an excellent source for plans. Fire department personnel, architects, engineers, insurance specialists, loss

Figure 12–3   Training and inspections improve fire protection.

prevention practitioners, and others can provide a multitude of ideas. Management support is an important ingredient in the planning process. By supplying adequate personnel, money, and policies and procedures, management can strengthen the fire protection program.

Besides local codes, OSHA Standard 1910.38, *Employee Emergency Plans and Fire Prevention Plans*, requires employers to prepare fire prevention plans to protect workers. The plans are required to include a list of major fire hazards, proper handling and storage of hazardous materials, potential ignition sources and control, fire protection equipment, maintenance, and the names and titles of employees responsible for fire protection.[6]

The following questions serve as additional points to reinforce planning:

1. Are plans carefully analyzed, detailed in writing, adequately implemented, and revised to conform to changes?
2. Do employees know what to do in case of fire?
3. Is there adequate training for fire prevention and suppression?
4. Is there a continuing liaison with public service agencies and public utilities?
5. Are first aid and emergency medical services available?
6. Does the entity have adequate insurance coverage?
7. In the event of fire-related losses, are contingency plans available? Can production be maintained or restored quickly through establishing alternative sources of equipment and resources?
8. Are high-value items separated to avoid large losses?

Safety

Some safety strategies for a fire prevention program follow:

1. Set up smoking and no smoking areas that are supervised, safe, and clearly marked with signs.
2. In smoking areas, provide cigarette butt and match receptacles or sand urns.
3. When equipment or devices are selected, select those that have been approved by a reputable testing organization (e.g., Underwriters Laboratories, Inc.).
4. In the use of heating systems, such as boilers, maintain safety when lighting up, during usage, and when shutting down.
5. Examine motors frequently to ensure safe operation and to prevent overheating.
6. Never overload electrical circuits.
7. Maintain lightning protective devices (e.g., lightning rods).
8. Employ an electrician who is safety conscious.
9. Prohibit the use of welding equipment near flammable substances or hazardous materials.
10. Watch sparks during and after welding.
11. Train employees to create an atmosphere of safety.
12. Conduct inspections and correct deficiencies.
13. Ensure fire protection standby for hazardous operations.

Good Housekeeping

Good housekeeping is another fire prevention strategy. It consists of building care, maintenance, cleanliness, proper placement of materials, careful waste and garbage disposal, and other general housekeeping activities.

Hazardous Materials (HAZMAT) Incidents

The prevention of disasters from hazardous substances and materials is extremely important. Such materials are used in every community and transported by trucks, railcars, ships, barges, and planes. All communities are subject to possible losses. Examples of hazardous substances and materials are plastics, fuels, corrosive chemicals (e.g., acids), and radioactive materials. A tremendous amount of information exists concerning their physical and chemical properties, methods for storage and transportation, and the most appropriate strategies in the event of fire or accident. Weapons of mass destruction (e.g., nuclear, chemical, biological) present additional problems requiring planning and preparation.

Federal legislation known as the Superfund Amendments and Reauthorization Act (SARA) of 1986 directs employers and employees to follow OSHA Standard 1910.20, which requires training for HAZMAT incidents. HAZMAT responses require *caution* because the effects can be deadly. Approaches, with proper protective clothing, should be made from upwind, uphill, and upstream, and vehicles should be parked facing out for quick escape. Initially, objectives are to isolate the area, identify the substance for subsequent action, and deny entry to reduce exposure.[7]

> Why is it essential that thorough training be conducted for HAZMAT incidents?

Prevention of Injuries and Deaths

Whatever fire prevention strategies are planned, a key factor must be to prevent injuries and deaths. Two vital considerations are *evacuation* and *medical services*. Evacuation plans and drills help people prepare for a possible fire. Smoke and fire alarms often provide warning for escape. Emergency exit maps and properly identified emergency doors also prevent injuries and deaths. Employees should turn off all equipment, utilize designated escape routes and fire escapes, avoid elevators, and report to a predetermined point on the outside to be counted. While employees are evacuating, firefighters may be entering the premises. Here is where a coordinated traffic flow is crucial. Firefighting equipment and personnel need to be directed to the fire location. Personnel should also be assigned to crowd control.

If injuries do take place, the quickness and quality of emergency medical services can save lives and unnecessary suffering. Preplanning will improve services. Specific employees should be trained to administer first aid.

Training

Through training, fire prevention becomes everybody's responsibility. Employees must first understand the disastrous effects of serious fire losses. This includes not only harm to humans, but also lost productivity and jobs. Topics within training can include safety, good housekeeping, hazardous substances and materials, evacuation, and first aid. Knowledge is transmitted via lectures, videos, demonstrations, drills, visits by public fire prevention personnel, pamphlets, and posted fire prevention signs. Actually starting a small outside fire in a controlled area, with the assistance of the local fire department, allows employees to practice using fire suppression equipment. Incentive programs, whereby employees compete for prizes (e.g., the best fire prevention poster) also can increase fire prevention awareness.

> What do you think can improve fire prevention in the United States?

Fire Suppression Strategies

The success of fire suppression strategies depends primarily on preplanning, preparation, equipment quality, and the readiness of personnel.

Integrated Systems

Integrated fire suppression systems perform a variety of functions. Detectors can measure smoke and the rate of temperature rise. If danger is evident, an alarm is sounded at the earliest stages of a fire. The fire can be extinguished automatically by water from sprinklers. Other functions include displaying written text and CCTV pictures on a computer screen to pinpoint the fire, notifying the fire department, activating a public address (PA) system to provide life and safety messages to occupants, starting up emergency generators for emergency lights and other equipment, detecting changes in sprinkler system water pressure, turning off certain electrical devices and equipment (e.g., shutting down fans that spread fire and smoke), venting specific areas, closing doors, creating safe zones for occupants, and returning elevators to ground level to encourage the use of emergency stairways. If a human being were to analyze the fire threat and make these decisions, the time factor would obviously be greater than the split second needed by a computer.

Haphazard Fire Protection at Bestbuy Service Company

The Bestbuy Service Company was a unique and rapidly growing business that sold numerous consumer items similar to those in department stores. Bestbuy's success was due to a no-frills store design and customer self-service. Each store essentially was a warehouse located away from main roads. Loss prevention was of minimal concern to management. Strategies against crime, fire, and accidents were haphazard.

One store, which also served as a distribution center, had an unfortunate experience. Late one afternoon, before closing, a salesperson threw a lighted cigarette butt into a trash container. The trash and then some boxes nearby caught fire. When store personnel were surprised by the spreading fire, they panicked. The first thing they all did was to run out of the warehouse with the customers. While the employees watched the burning warehouse in amazement, the manager asked if anybody had called the fire department. Nobody responded, so he told a young salesperson to run to a nearby gas station to call the fire department. The manager continued to watch the fire and remembered that the automatic sprinklers were turned off because of freezing temperatures. Also in his thoughts were the thousands of dollars worth of merchandise burning up.

For the Bestbuy Company, the store and its contents were a tremendous loss. Insurance covered only a small part of the losses, especially because many insurance company recommendations went unheeded: the local fire department was never contacted for prefire plans, and employees were never trained for simple fire procedures. Senior management was clearly at fault.

Detection of Smoke and Fire

Many businesses utilize a combination of the following detectors for increased protection:

- *Smoke detectors* are widely used, especially since most human casualties in fires result from smoke and the toxic fumes or gases within smoke. These detectors operate with photoelectric light beams and react when smoke either blocks the beam of light or enters a refraction chamber where the smoke reflects the light into the photo cell.
- *Ionization detectors* are sensitive to invisible products of combustion created during the early stages of a fire. These detectors are noted for their early warning capabilities.
- *Thermal detectors* respond to heat either when the temperature reaches a certain degree or when the temperature rises too quickly. The latter is known as a *rate-of-rise detector.* Thermal detectors are made with either feature or a combination of both.
- *Flame detectors* detect flame and glowing embers. These detectors are sensitive to flames not visible to the human eye. The infrared kind is responsive to radiant energy that human beings cannot see.
- *Sprinkler water flow detectors* contain a seal that melts when heat rises to a specific temperature. Then, water flows from the sprinkler system. An alarm is activated when the water flow closes pressure switches.
- *Carbon monoxide detectors* protect against what is often called the *silent killer,* because carbon monoxide is difficult to detect. In fact victims, in their drowsy state, may be wrongly diagnosed as being substance abusers.
- *Gas detectors* monitor flammable gases or vapors. These devices are especially valuable in petroleum, chemical, and other industries where dangerous gases or vapors are generated.
- *Combination detectors* respond to more than one fire-producing cause or employ multiple operating principles. Examples include smoke/heat detector or rate-of-rise/fixed temperature heat detector.

Contact the fire department. Sometimes simple things can be overlooked. When a serious fire begins, the local fire department must be contacted as soon as possible to reduce losses. The best strategy to prevent a situation in which everybody thought somebody else had contacted the fire department is to ask: "Who called the fire department?" Another problem develops when *people think that they can extinguish a fire without outside assistance.* It is not until precious time has elapsed and serious danger exists that the fire department is contacted.

Alarm signaling systems are automatic or manual. With *automatic systems,* the attachment of a siren or a bell to a smoke or fire detection device or sprinkler system will notify people in the immediate area about a smoke or fire problem. This kind of alarm is called a *local alarm.* Unless incorporated into this system, the local alarm will not notify the fire department. Automatic systems also consist of a local alarm and an alarm that notifies a central station or the fire department. Many large industries have a central, proprietary monitoring station that monitors smoke, fire, burglar, and other alarms. *Manual fire alarm signaling systems* use a pull station fixed to a wall. This is a local alarm unless an alarm signal is transmitted to a central station or fire department.

Portable Extinguishers

The following classes of fires provide a foundation for firefighting and use of portable extinguishers.

- *Class A* fires consist of ordinary combustible materials such as trash, paper, fibers, wood, drapes, and furniture.
- *Class B* fires are fueled by a flammable liquid, such as gasoline, oil, alcohol, or cleaning solvents.
- *Class C* fires occur in live electrical circuits or equipment such as generators, motors, fuse boxes, computers, or copying machines.
- *Class D* fires, the rarest of the four types of fires, are fueled by combustible metals such as sodium, magnesium, and potassium.

Portable fire extinguishers are used to put out a small fire by directing onto it a substance that cools the burning material, deprives the flame of oxygen, or interferes with the chemical reactions occurring in the flame. Ratings and effectiveness of these extinguishers are in NFPA 10, Standard for Portable Fire Extinguishers.[8]

Employees and loss prevention practitioners must be knowledgeable about the proper use of extinguishers. If the wrong extinguisher is used, a fire may become more serious. Water must not be used on a flammable liquid such as gasoline (Class B fire) because the gasoline may float on the water and spread the fire. Neither should one spray water on electrical fires (Class C fires) because water conducts electricity, and electrocution may result. Many locations use multipurpose dry chemical extinguishers that can be applied to A, B, or C fires. This approach reduces confusion during a fire. Class D fires are extinguished with dry powder extinguishers. Employee training can provide the appropriate response to fires.

Fire extinguishers should be checked at least every week during a loss prevention officer's patrol. Service companies recharge extinguishers when necessary. A seal is attached to the extinguisher that certifies its readiness.

Sprinklers

A sprinkler system consists of pipes along a ceiling that contain water under pressure, with an additional source of water for a constant flow. Attached to the pipes, automatic sprinklers are placed at select locations. When a fire occurs, a seal in the sprinkler head ruptures at a pre-established temperature and a steady stream of water flows.

An Angry Ex-Employee's Revenge

Albert Drucker had been warned numerous times about pilfering small tools from the maintenance department at Bearing Industries. When he was caught for the third time, via a strict inventory system, management decided to fire him. When Drucker was informed, he went into a rage and stormed out of the plant. While leaving, he vowed, "I'm gonna get you back for this." Management maintained that it made the right decision and forgot about the matter.

Two weeks later, Drucker was ready with his vindictive plan. At 2:00 one morning, he entered the Bearing plant by using a previously stolen master key. No loss prevention devices or services hindered his entrance. It took him 15 minutes to collect three strategically located fire extinguishers. When Drucker arrived home, he quickly emptied the contents of the extinguishers and then filled each one with gasoline. By 5:30 A.M., the three extinguishers were replaced and Drucker was home sleeping.

At 2:00 P.M., two days later, when the Bearing plant was in full production, Drucker sneaked into the plant unnoticed and placed, on a pile of old rags, a book of matches with a lighted cigarette underneath the matchheads. By the time Drucker was a few miles away, the old rags and some cardboard boxes were on fire. When employees discovered the fire, they were confident that they could extinguish it. They reached for the nearest extinguishers and approached the fire. To their surprise, the fire grew as they supplied it with gasoline. Their first reaction was to drop the extinguishers and run; one extinguisher exploded while the fire intensified. The fire caused extensive damage but no injuries or deaths. The police and management suspected arson. When police investigators asked management if there was anybody who held a grudge against the company, Albert Drucker was mentioned. He was arrested a week later and charged with arson.

Sprinklers are an effective fire suppression strategy. Statistics from the National Fire Data Center reveal that "the average loss is significantly less where automatic sprinklers are installed and operating properly than where there are no sprinklers."[9] The NFPA has kept records of automatic sprinkler performance for more than 80 years; that organization reports: "These remarkably comprehensive records show that in 95 percent of the some 117,770 fires in sprinklered buildings (where the Association has reliable data), the sprinklers have performed satisfactorily."[10] The failure of a sprinkler system most often is due to human error—the water supply was turned off at the time of the fire.

A sprinkler system is a worthwhile investment for reducing fire losses. Lower insurance premiums actually can pay for the system over time.

There are several kinds of automatic sprinkler systems. Two popular ones are the wet-pipe and dry-pipe systems. With the *wet-pipe system* (see Figure 12-4), water is in the pipes at all times and is released when heat ruptures the seal in the sprinkler head. This is the most common system and is

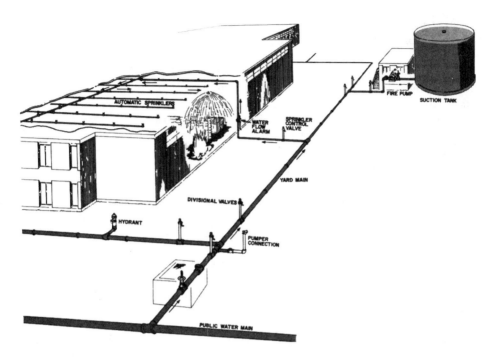

Figure 12–4 Total concept of the wet-pipe automatic sprinkler system.

applicable where freezing is no threat to its operation. Where freezing temperatures and broken pipes are a problem, the *dry-pipe system* is useful. Air pressure is maintained in the pipes until a sprinkler head ruptures. Then, the air escapes, and water enters the pipes and exits through the opened sprinklers.

Older buildings may have pipes that apply fire-suppressant chemicals such as *carbon dioxide* or *Halon*. Fire codes now prohibit these chemicals. The former absorbs oxygen, creating a danger to humans, whereas the latter depletes the earth's ozone layer.

Standpipes and Hose Systems

Standpipes and hose systems enable people to manually apply water to fires in buildings. *Standpipes* are vertical pipes that let a water supply reach an outlet on each floor of a building. In multiple-story structures, standpipes often are constructed within fire-resistant fire stairs as an added defense for the standpipe, hoses, and firefighting personnel. The typical setup is a folded or rolled 2-1/2-inch hose enclosed in a wall cabinet and identified with fire emergency information. A control valve, which looks like a small spoked wheel, enables water to flow. Automatic extinguishing systems (e.g., sprinklers) often are the preferred system; however, the standpipes and hose systems are advantageous when the automatic system fails or is not present, when sections of a building are not accessible to outside hose lines and hydrants, and when properly trained employees are capable of fire suppression.

Training is needed for employees if they are to have the responsibility for fighting a fire. With hoses, two people are needed: one to stretch the hose to its full length, and another to turn the water flow valve. Without training, employees may be injured if they do not understand the danger of turning the valve before the hose is stretched. This could cause the coiled section of the hose to react to the water pressure by acting like a whip and possibly striking someone.

Fire Walls and Doors

Fire walls are constructed in buildings to prevent the spread of fire. These walls are made of materials that resist fire. They are designed to withstand fire for several hours. Fire walls are weakened by openings such as doorways. Therefore, fire doors at openings help to strengthen the fire wall when resisting fire. Fire doors often are designed to close automatically in case of fire. Nationally recognized testing laboratories study the reliability of these doors.

Stairwells

During evacuation, stairwells (made of masonry construction) provide a fire-resistant path for escape. Fire codes often require stairwells to withstand a fire for at least two hours. Stairwells may be equipped with fans to reduce smoke during evacuation.

Access Control

During an emergency, electronically controlled doors should be connected to the life and safety system to permit escape. From the security perspective, this presents a problem because an alarm condition may provide an opportunity for an offender to enter or exit with ease. To deal with such a vulnerability, CCTV and security officers can be applied to select locations.

Building codes mandate the use of exit devices that enable quick escape during emergencies. A door locked from the outside may be easily unlocked from the inside to allow theft or unauthorized passage. Therefore, the door needs to be secured from both sides while permitting quick escape in case of an emergency. Often, the solution is a controlled exit device (see Figure 12-5). One type of controlled exit device stays locked for a fixed time, usually 15 seconds, after being pushed, while sounding an alarm. Signage and Braille are required to alert people of the delay, but it provides time for security to respond. In a true emergency, such a device is unlocked immediately through a tie-in with the building's fire protection system as specified in the Life Safety Code (NFPA 101).[11]

The Las Vegas MGM Grand Hotel fire in 1985 provides a graphic example of security (locked exit doors) being one of the major reasons for a large

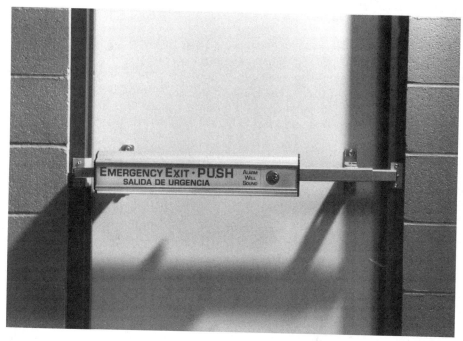

Figure 12–5   Emergency exit. Courtesy: Sargent & Greenleaf, Inc.

loss of life. All the exit doors to the stairwell had a controlled exit device (panic hardware). However, once the occupants were in the stairwell, they encountered smoke. Unfortunately, the doors were locked on the stairwell side to ensure security for each floor. A person had to exit the building on the first floor to regain access. With heavy smoke rising in the stairwell, and no access to any of the upper floors, the occupants were trapped and died.[12]

Fire-Resistive Buildings

The report by the National Commission on Fire Prevention and Control, "America Burning," pointed to a major weakness in building design and construction. That weakness is the architects and builders. Frequently, these professionals think in terms of dollars without seriously considering fire protection. Quite often, after a building has been constructed and insurance practitioners have decided on a premium, fire hazards are exposed. If a person stops to think about the tons of combustible materials transported into a building during construction and as it becomes operational, he or she may be hesitant to enter. Wood in construction and furnishings, cloth and fibers in curtains and carpets, paper, cleaning fluids, and other combustibles are hazardous. But reinforced concrete or protected steel construction and fire-resistive roofs, floors, ceilings, walls, doors, windows, carpets, furniture, and so on, all help to produce greater fire protection.

Training and Fire Brigades

With the threat of fire, employee training is of tremendous importance (see Figure 12-6). Of top priority during a fire should be to safeguard lives, and then to secure valuable assets during orderly evacuation. If specific employees are responsible for fire suppression, thorough training is required. This is especially true when local public firefighting capabilities are incompatible with the type of fire that may develop at a site. In this case, a private fire

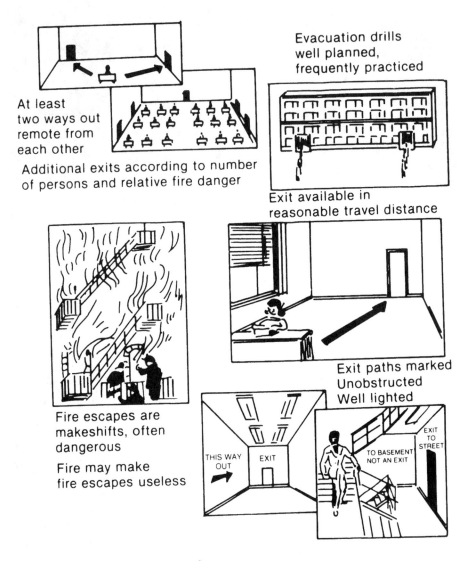

Figure 12–6 Principles of exit safety.

department at the site is appropriate. Fire brigades are expensive, and to meet OSHA's standard (1910.156), a company must ensure that all brigade members are outfitted and trained to think and act like professional firefighters.[13]

Integrating Fire and Security Systems

There are many horror stories of state-of-the-art, integrated fire and security systems that do not operate as originally touted. As confusion and disappointment mounts, each manufacturer may blame the other. And, fire authorities may refuse to issue an acceptance of the fire alarm portion of the system. Unfortunately for the loss prevention manager, he or she must explain why the corporation is spending so much money for a system that does not operate properly. Besides referring to integration guidelines stated earlier in this book, here are additional suggestions:

1. Hire engineers with verified skills in security and fire alarm systems. Have them prepare specifications and a budget.
2. Contact the local fire department for their input.
3. Develop the fire alarm system as the first priority because of the need to deal with the fire authority's jurisdiction and codes and standards. This approach is in light of the limited codes and standards in the security industry, which leads to abuses in systems application, design, and installation.
4. The *National Fire Alarm Code*, adopted by the NFPA, describes the minimum acceptable requirements for all fire alarm systems.[14]

Performance-Based Design

A *performance-based fire protection* approach is an alternative to following a rigid set of guidelines by evaluating hazards and planning the most appropriate protection in innovative ways to meet performance goals. Supported by codes, this approach is also driven by computer software that run reliable fire models, technical analysis that is less subjective than traditional planning, and performance-based design that offers comparisons of products. The trend is in the direction of an International Building Code and an International Fire Code with a mandate to develop both a prescriptive code and a performance-based code to allow a parallel fire safety design process.[15]

Inspection, Testing, and Maintenance

NFPA 25 establishes minimum inspecting, testing, and maintenance for fire protection systems. Local, state, and federal regulatory agencies are Authorities Having Jurisdiction (AHJ) and all may require compliance. Many questions should be answered during inspecting, testing, and maintenance. Examples are: Has the occupancy classification changed? What building alterations have occurred and what is the impact on fire protection and codes? Documentation of the process is essential to reinforce corrective action and for the AHJ.[16]

> What do you think can improve fire suppression in the United States?

OTHER DISASTERS

Planning and training are two key strategies to reduce losses when disasters strike. Employees need to know what to do to protect lives and assets.

Constructed Disasters

Accidents

An accident at, for example, a manufacturing plant has the potential for serious injury, death, and production slowdown. Thousands of lives, hundreds of thousands of injuries, and billions of dollars of losses are sustained each year because of accidents. Prevention is a key strategy. The seriousness of this problem is pointed out in Chapter 13.

Bomb Threats and Explosions

Because of past bombings and terrorism (see Chapter 18), bomb threats and the possibility of bombings are taken very seriously today. Even the commonly circulated statistic that 98 percent of bomb threats are hoaxes makes decision makers more concerned than ever about the other 2 percent. According to the Bureau of Alcohol, Tobacco and Firearms (ATF) and the Federal Bureau of Investigation (FBI) databases, there were 38,362 reported explosives incidents from 1988 through 1997 in the United States. Motives were known for about 8,000 of these incidents, with vandalism and revenge cited most frequently. Pipe bombs and Molotov cocktails were most often encountered.[17] Accurate statistics are difficult to gather on bomb threats, attempts, and actual bombings. Organizations may not report threats. Police agencies may "play down incidents" to prevent copycat threats and bombings.[18]

Here are basic strategies for protection against bomb threats and explosions:

1. Seek management support and prepare a plan and procedures.
2. Ensure that employees know what to ask if a bomb threat is made over the telephone (see Figure 12-7).

3. Establish criteria and procedures for evacuation. Post routes. The evacuation decision can be especially difficult for management because of safety concerns versus the thousands of dollars in productivity lost due to evacuation of large numbers of employees.
4. Recruit and train *all* employees to observe and report suspicious behavior, items, or vehicles. And, something suspicious should never be approached or touched.
5. Control parking and access according to the unique characteristics and requirements of the facility.
6. Control and verify outsiders (e.g., service personnel) prior to access.

Date of Threat: _____

Time: _____ Number of minutes on telephone: ___

Exact words of caller: _____

_____

_____

_____

_____

_____

Ask the caller these questions: _____
When will the bomb explode? _____
Where is bomb? _____
What type of bomb? _____
What does it look like? _____
Why did you place bomb? _____

_____

Description of caller's voice: Age: _____ Accent: _____
Sex: _____ Background noise: _____
Tone of voice: _____
Additional comments: _____

_____

Employee receiving call: _____ Telephone number: _____

Figure 12–7 Smith Corporation bomb threat form.

7. Screen mail. Route deliveries to a specific location for screening, rather than permitting direct access to employees (see Figure 12-8). More on mail protection in Chapter 18 in the information on terrorism.
8. Maintain unpredictable patrols to avoid patterns that can be studied by offenders.
9. Inspect the exterior and interior of buildings.
10. Ensure that emergency plans, response teams (e.g., fire brigades), and public safety agencies are coordinated for action. What are the qualifications, experience, and response time of the nearest bomb squad?

Strikes

The direct and indirect costs of a strike are astronomical. Major losses include productivity, profits, employees and customers who never return, vandalism, additional loss prevention services, and legal fees. *The best defense for a strike is early preparation.* If possible, a company that antici-pates a strike should build up inventory and oversupply customers. When a labor contract is almost ready to run out, trouble can be expected. Manage-

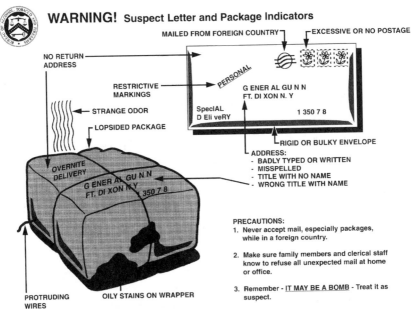

WARNING! Suspect Letter and Package Indicators

MAILED FROM FOREIGN COUNTRY — EXCESSIVE OR NO POSTAGE

NO RETURN ADDRESS

RESTRICTIVE MARKINGS

STRANGE ODOR

LOPSIDED PACKAGE

PERSONAL

G ENER AL GU N N
FT. DI XON N. Y

SpecIAL
D Eli veRY   1 350 7 8

RIGID OR BULKY ENVELOPE

ADDRESS:
- BADLY TYPED OR WRITTEN
- MISSPELLED
- TITLE WITH NO NAME
- WRONG TITLE WITH NAME

OVERNITE DELIVERY

G ENER AL GU N N
FT. DI XON N Y   350 7 8

PRECAUTIONS:
1. Never accept mail, especially packages, while in a foreign country.

2. Make sure family members and clerical staff know to refuse all unexpected mail at home or office.

3. Remember - IT MAY BE A BOMB - Treat it as suspect.

PROTRUDING WIRES   OILY STAINS ON WRAPPER

FOR MORE INFORMATION ON BOMB SECURITY OR BOMB THREATS, CONTACT YOUR LOCAL ATF OFFICE.
ATF I 3324.1 (6/95)

Figure 12–8 Suspect letter and package indicators.

ment should contact local law enforcement agencies to ensure that peace is maintained and property protected. Security is likely to focus on perimeter protection for the facility, the protection of key executives and their families, and evidence gathering. Both public and private police will be working together in most instances.

Both striking workers and a company have certain legal rights. The *National Labor Relations Board* (NLRB) controls relations between management and labor.

It is essential that management and loss prevention personnel be familiar with labor laws to avert charges of unfair labor practices. Surveillance and investigation of union activities is a violation of the National Labor Relations Act, which makes it an unfair labor practice to interfere with, restrain, or coerce employees in the exercise of the rights to self-organize, to assist labor organizations, and to bargain collectively through representatives. One type of surveillance, photographing activities of striking workers, is unlawful unless there is a legitimate purpose, such as gathering evidence for the prosecution of criminal acts (e.g., assault or destruction of property). In one case, a security service company took 60,000 pictures and collected thousands of hours of videotape that were used in court against strikers, who ended up owing $64 million in fines.[19]

Care must be exercised when instituting loss prevention strategies during management–labor tension. Precautions (e.g., additional officers, CCTV) to protect company property may be construed as interference with union activities. For example, courts have declared illegal the observance by officers of who is going in and out of union meetings. Also, it has been held that even "creating the impression" of surveillance (e.g., management implying that surveillance is taking place) is illegal. The NLRB found that aiming CCTV on a company building in which a union meeting was held created the impression of surveillance. Undercover investigations that conduct labor surveillance are illegal.

Civil Disturbances

Demonstrations and precipitating incidents have evolved into destructive riots. Demonstrations are common as groups display their views. A typical precipitating incident is a public police arrest of a minority group member for a minor charge. Sometimes, all it takes for a crowd to go into a contagious frenzy is a rock thrown into the crowd. Whatever the cause of civil disturbances, deaths, injuries, and extensive property damage can result. The public police may not be able to contain rioters, and the private sector must be prepared for the worst. Summer months and high temperatures, when people gather out of doors, may precede a civil disturbance. Rumors also are dangerous. The social and political climate can be analyzed for possible predicting indicators.

Sabotage

Production can be deliberately hindered by a destructive act such as cutting electrical wires. The threat of sabotage can come from both internal and external sources.

Utility Failure

Electrical breakdowns are known to produce not only production obstacles but serious threats to loss prevention measures. Without a source of electric power, alarms, CCTV, access control, electrically activated extinguishing systems, electric fire pumps, and other systems are useless. Secondary power sources such as generators should be in place.

Natural Disasters

Windstorms

Tornadoes (called *cyclones* in some regions) are extremely violent and destructive, often occurring without warning. Hurricanes (called *typhoons* in the eastern Pacific Ocean) usually afford more warning time than tornadoes. The Atlantic and Gulf coasts are more susceptible to hurricanes, whereas tornadoes occur in many parts of the United States. Loss prevention efforts should concentrate on studying local climate conditions and then preparing contingency plans. The following measures are useful:

1. Design buildings for maximum wind velocity expected.
2. Closely follow weather reports.
3. Close down production when necessary.
4. Establish a safe, low-level area for employees.
5. Instruct employees to stay away from windows.
6. Open doors and windows on the side of the building away from the storm. This will help to equalize pressure and prevent building collapse.
7. Acquire emergency power sources.
8. Set up a communications system.
9. Anchor and protect company property from being damaged or blown away.
10. Cooperate with local officials.
11. Take steps to hinder looting.

Floods

Lowlands along bodies of water are subject to flooding. Dams and dikes have reduced this problem, but it is still a threat to many locales. Some practical remedies are these:

1. Work with the U.S. Army Corps of Engineers, which provides assistance to those areas subject to frequent flooding.
2. Work with local officials for employee safety and to hinder looting.
3. Provide a safe place for valuable assets.
4. Exit from the flood area in time to avoid being marooned. Secure adequate gasoline for vehicles.
5. If a team remains at the plant site, ensure adequate supplies, such as food, blankets, a boat, life preservers, rope, communications equipment, first-aid kit, sandbags, and pumps.
6. Store valuable records, equipment, tools, and chemicals above the expected flood level. Shut off utilities.

Blizzards

Blizzards are snowstorms accompanied by high winds and very cold temperatures. Sufficient warning usually is obtained from weather forecasts. Injuries and deaths occur because people do not reach proper shelter. If a blizzard is forecast, employees should be sent home. Preplanning is essential if employees have a chance of being stranded at work. Food, bedding, a heat supply, radios, communications equipment, and televisions will aid those stranded.

Earthquakes

Stringent building codes and adequate building design in suspect areas (e.g., California) are vital for reduced losses. Building collapse, damage to bridges, and falling debris are major causes of injuries and deaths. If indoors, one should take cover in a basement or under reinforced floors or doorways. If outdoors, one should watch out for falling objects and electrical wires.

> What do you think is the most serious potential disaster facing your community or organization? What protection methods do you recommend?

Emergency Planning and Disaster Recovery

Emergency planning focuses on preparation that increases the chances that people and an organization will survive a disaster. *Disaster recovery* aims to place an organization in the position it held prior to a disaster.

No one plan can be applied to all organizations to prepare and recover from a disaster. Unique needs must be met. A high-rise building, for example, should select and train individuals and teams from each floor to assist

International Perspective: The U.S. View of Hazards: Thoughts from Europe[20]

Here is a critical thinking perspective of the U.S.-driven paradigm that social and technological approaches to mitigation can act, overall, to reduce the incidence or severity of disastrous events. Rockett counters the U.S. paradigm by arguing that disasters are not the result of external forces, but rather the way we live our lives. Social, political, and economic forces are as much the cause of disasters as the natural environment. We already know where earthquakes, hurricanes, and flooding are likely to occur. Furthermore, we also know that many technologies (e.g., automobiles, which cause pollution) carry with them the power of mass disruption. Consequently, disaster reduction will only result from fundamental changes in political and social mores.

Rockett's viewpoint is illustrated when people, businesses, and organizations insist on congregating on a well-known tectonic fault when predictable earthquakes cause multibillion-dollar losses. Yes, we are speaking of Los Angeles as one example. But this is a global problem. Other types of predictable disasters occur when, for example, a Yangtze or Bangladesh flood kills tens of thousands of people. Such hazards of the environment are impossible to eliminate, and continuing to have children and building in these areas loads the costs of disasters.

What is suggested by Rockett is to change social structure and not social reaction. "Progress in disaster reduction will occur when we accept that we are the creators of disaster rather than its victims." Rockett argues that as we build stronger structures and invent more efficient mitigation systems, we run the risk of engendering a false sense of safety and security that will, when the bigger event arrives, lead to an even greater catastrophe.

What is your opinion of Rockett's contentions?

with emergencies and evacuation. Similar planning is required for a hospital, plus staff sleeping and food arrangements are needed so patient care is not interrupted. A retail chain with stores in the path of a hurricane would establish a command post, track the hurricane, and render aid so affected stores can be operational as soon as possible.

The list that follows provides a foundation for emergency planning and disaster recovery:

1. As with other threats requiring attention, seek management support from the top and competent leaders.
2. Prepare policies and procedures, a command structure, and lines of authority.
3. Rely on checklists during planning and recovery.
4. Focus on the prevention of injury and death, the protection of assets, and the continuation of business.

5. Store vital records at two locations.
6. Plan for disasters that are likely to occur, but also consider the unexpected. Study similar businesses, climate, geography, insurance and risk management reports, among other sources. Rate the likelihood of risks.
7. Consider the impact of each potential disaster on the company's financial condition, sales, and legal and regulatory requirements.
8. Identify all the organizations that might be involved in a disaster: police, fire service, emergency medical service, utilities, and so forth. Hold a meeting and develop a master plan.
9. Plan a command post with a common communication channel.
10. Plan for disruption of essential services: electricity, telephone, computer, water, and sanitation.
11. Plan for shortages of food, water, and medical services.
12. Consider that there may be denial of access to the building by government agencies because of unsafe conditions.
13. Conduct annual training and unannounced drills. Note weaknesses and improve performance.
14. Ensure that employees know how to operate equipment such as fire extinguishers.
15. Compile a list of employee skills (e.g., first aid) that may be useful.
16. Consider employee problems such as injury, family and home needs, and transportation.
17. Ensure that emergency procedures and equipment are in compliance with the Americans with Disabilities Act of 1990.
18. Work with insurers to help the business manage risks and survive.
19. Research the possibility of moving the business to an alternative site during recovery.
20. Locate recovery service companies.
21. List critical tasks that must be performed for business recovery and consider personnel and equipment requirements.
22. Prepare a directory of people and organizations that can be helpful during emergencies and recovery.
23. Put in writing the emergency and disaster recovery plans and review it annually for improvements.

Federal Emergency Management Agency

The central point of contact within the federal government for a wide range of emergency management activities is the *Federal Emergency Management Agency*, or FEMA (National Emergency Training Center, Emmitsburg, MD 21727-8998; Tel.: 301-447-1000; FEMA, DC; Tel.: 202-566-1600). This agency is involved in planning and preparedness activities while providing financial and technical support for a full range of emergencies from local disasters to nuclear war. FEMA extends through all levels of government and the private sector. Among FEMA's activities are:

- Coordinating civil emergency preparedness for nuclear accidents or attack
- Ensuring continuity of government and coordinating mobilization of resources during national security emergencies
- Supporting state and local governments before, during, and after disasters
- Reducing the nation's losses from fire through the U.S. Fire Administration
- Coordinating federal aid for presidentially declared disasters and emergencies
- Providing training and education at all levels of government
- Administering national flood insurance
- Operating the National Defense Executive Reserve program for recruiting and training a group of senior executives from the private sector to enter government service in the event of a national emergency

---

Search the Web

Visit the Web site for FEMA at http://www.fema.gov/.
    Use your favorite search engines to see the wealth of helpful information on topics of this chapter, such as fire protection, HAZMAT, and natural disasters.

CASE PROBLEMS

12A. As a loss prevention manager at company headquarters, your superior tells you to design a fire protection program for a new window and door manufacturing plant. A lot of wood cutting with electric circular saws will take place at this plant. Workers then will assemble the windows and doors using electric drills. A large stock of wood products will be stored in the plant. What will you recommend to the architects who will design the building? What are your fire prevention plans? What are your fire suppression plans?

12B. As a loss prevention manager at an office building containing 800 employees, your boss requests that you prepare criteria for evacuation of the building in case of a bomb threat. List criteria for management to consider and estimate the cost of a two-hour evacuation if the average employee earns $40,000 annually.

12C. As a corporate loss prevention manager, you have been assigned the task of designing a protection plan against windstorms for manufacturing plants located along the coast of Florida and those located in Kansas. What general plans do you have in mind?

NOTES

1. National Fire Data Center (2000), *The Overall Fire Picture—1999*. http://www.usfa.fema.gov/ (February 16, 2001).
2. Gordon P. McKinnon, ed., *Fire Protection Handbook*, 14th ed. (Boston: National Fire Protection Association, 1976), p. ix.
3. Traci Bangor and Joseph Faust, "Basic Fire Protection Strategies," *Security Technology & Design* 11 (April 2001), pp. 68–71.
4. Robert Klinoff, *Introduction to Fire Protection* (Albany, NY: Delmar Pub., 1997), p. 298.
5. See Sandra L. Breisch, "Is Your Workplace Fireproof?" *Safety and Health* (July 1989), pp. 40–44.
6. "Enhancing Your Fire Prevention Plan: A Three Part Approach," *Security Watch* 2907 (April 1, 2000), p. 6.
7. Klinoff, pp. 416–419.
8. Dennis Nolan, *Encyclopedia of Fire Prevention* (Albany, NY: Delmar Pub., 2001), pp. 83–85.
9. U.S. Department of Commerce, U.S. Fire Administration, *Fire in the United States* (Washington, D.C.: U.S. Government Printing Office, 1978), p. 54.
10. James Angle, et al., *Firefighting Strategies and Tactics* (Albany, NY: Delmar Pub., 2001), p. 199. And, Percy Bugbee, *Principles of Fire Protection* (Boston: National Fire Protection Association, 1978), p. 170.
11. Dick Zunkel, "Delayed Egress Magnetic Locks Are a Technology Standard," *Security Technology & Design* 10 (February 2000), pp. 34–38.
12. Wayne D. Moore, "Balancing Life Safety and Security Needs," *Security Technology and Design* (January-February 1997), pp. 69–70.
13. "Does Your Company Need a Fire Brigade?" *Security Watch* 2910 (May 15, 2000), p. 6.
14. Wayne D. Moore, "The Art of Integrating Fire and Security Systems," *Security Technology and Design* (March 1994), pp. 61–62.
15. Daniel Gemeny, "Performance-Based Design: An Overview," *Security Technology & Design* 10 (August 2000), pp. 64–68.
16. Douglas Danenberger, "Setting Up a Fire Protection Program," *Security Technology & Design* 10 (January 2000), pp. 70–73.
17. Office of Justice Programs, *A Guide for Explosion and Bombing Scene Investigation* (Washington, D.C.: U.S. Department of Justice, June 2000), pp. 2–3.
18. David H. Estenson, "Should Bomb Blasts Be Kept Quiet?" *Security Management* (November 1995), p. 120.
19. Brenda P. Sunoo, "Managing Strikes, Minimizing Loss," *Personnel Journal* (January 1995), p. 58.
20. Jan Rockett, "The US View of Hazards and Sustainable Development: A Few Thoughts from Europe," *Risk Management: An International Journal* 3 (1) (2001), pp. 71–74.

13

Safety

OBJECTIVES

After studying this chapter the reader will be able to:

1. Explain why safety is important.
2. Discuss the history of safety legislation and workers' compensation.
3. Explain OSHA's development, objectives, jurisdiction, standards, record keeping requirements, and inspections.
4. Describe at least four strategies for improving safety in the workplace.

What is meant by *safety, accident,* and *injury*? Safety is a major loss prevention measure to reduce the likelihood of accidents and injuries. When accidents and injuries occur, both losses and a drain on profits inevitably result. Webster's *New Collegiate Dictionary* defines *safety* as "the condition of being safe from undergoing or causing hurt, injury, or loss" and "to protect against failure, breakage, or accident." *Accident* is "an unfortunate event resulting from carelessness, unawareness, ignorance, or a combination of causes." *Injury* is "hurt, damage, or loss sustained."

ACCIDENT STATISTICS AND COSTS

Since the earlier part of this century, great strides have been made to increase safety in the workplace. Safer machines, improved supervision, and training all have helped to prevent accidents. If one were to apply the industrial fatality rate that existed in 1910 to the present workforce in the United States, more than 1.3 million workers would lose their lives each year from industrial accidents. In the past, a manual worker's welfare was of minimal concern to management; the loss of life or limb was "part of the job" and "a normal business risk." In the construction of tall buildings, it was expected that one life would be lost for each floor. A 20-story building would yield 20 lost lives. During tunnel construction, two worker deaths per mile was the norm. Coal mining experienced exceedingly high death rates.[1]

Today, annual losses for American workers are 6,000 deaths from injuries, 50,000 deaths from illnesses caused by workplace exposures, and 6 million nonfatal workplace injuries. Injuries alone cost U.S. businesses more than $110 billion annually.[2]

Confined Area Entry

Hazards that are not easily seen, smelled, or felt can be deadly risks to people who work in confined areas. For instance, storage tanks may reduce oxygen or leak combustible or toxic gases. The cardinal rule for entry into a confined area is, "Never trust your senses." A harmless-looking situation may indeed be a potential threat. Some of the deadliest gases and vapors have no odor. *Before entry, the following safety strategies are recommended: proper training, equipment to identify hazards, and an entry permit issued by a safety specialist.* OSHA's standard for confined spaces, Title 29 Code of Federal Regulations (CFR), Part 1910.146, contains the requirements for practices and procedures to protect employees from the hazards of entry into permit-required confined spaces.

In the petroleum industry, for example, a storage tank had been rinsed and vented for several days. When it was checked with gas detection equipment, no flammable gases were measured. But, after workers removed loose rust, scale, and sediment, the percentage of flammable gas rose, and the gas ignited.

As another example, two employees of a fertilizer company descended into an old 35-foot well to repair a pump. The well was covered with a concrete slab and entry was made through a covered manhole. About 6 feet below the opening was a plank platform. When the first worker dropped to the platform, he was immediately overcome and fell unconscious into the water below. His partner sought help quickly. When two helpers entered the well, they, too, fell unconscious to the water below. A passerby, in an attempt to save the drowning men, jumped into the water and drowned also. By this time the fire department had arrived. The fire chief, wearing a self-contained breathing apparatus, went to rescue the victims. On the platform he removed his face mask to give instructions to those above and was overcome. Subsequent tests revealed that the well atmosphere contained a lethal concentration of hydrogen sulfide. Five men died from pulmonary paralysis.[3]

Direct and indirect losses are costly; for example, the death of a worker in a manufacturing plant immediately creates a tremendous direct loss to family and friends. Direct losses also involve an immediate loss of productivity, medical costs (e.g., first aid, hospitalization), and insurance administration. Indirect costs include continued grief by family and friends, continued loss of productivity, profit loss, selection and training of a new employee, overtime for lost production, and possible litigation. In addition, internal and external relations may suffer. The lowering of employee morale can result from the belief that management is incompetent or does not care. Rumors frequently follow. In the eyes of the community, the company may appear to have failed.

Hazards

A *hazard* can be defined as a dangerous condition, behavior, or object that can cause an accident, injury, or death. A list of common hazards follows:

Failure to use safety devices on machinery
Noncompliance with safety policies and procedures
Electrical malfunctions
Poorly supported ladders and scaffolding
Blocked aisles, exits, and stairways
Overloaded inventory storage bins
Inadequate training
Excessive noise
Poor supervision
Dangerous storage of toxic or flammable substances
Fire
Inadequate firefighting equipment
Inadequate fire prevention measures
Insufficient lighting
Poor ventilation
Horseplay; running

HISTORY OF SAFETY LEGISLATION

In eighteenth-century England, as the Industrial Revolution progressed, a number of statutes governing working conditions were passed. One of the first statutes for safety resulted from a serious outbreak of fever at cotton mills near Manchester in 1784. Because child labor was involved, widespread attention added to public concern and government pressure to improve the dangerous and unsanitary conditions in factories. A few years later, additional legislation dealt with hours, conditions of labor, prevention of injury, and government inspectors. In 1842, the *Mines Act* provided for punitive compensation for preventable injuries caused by unguarded mining machinery. Subsequent to this law, a series of mining accidents caused more laws to be passed for miner safety. During this time "strong evidence" pointed to incompetent management and the neglect of safety rules. Laws relating to factory safety also were expanded. More and more trades were brought under the scope of the law.

In the United States, textile factories increased in number between 1820 and 1840. Massachusetts, first of the United States to follow England's example, passed laws in 1876 and 1877 that related to working children and inspection of factories. Important features pertained to dangerous machinery and necessary safety guards. As years went on, some industries increasingly realized that hazards were potentially harmful to workers, production, and profits. Consequently, more and more industrialists became safety conscious. However, serious hazards still existed in the workplace through the twentieth century.[4]

Workers' Compensation

Increasing concern for workers led to *workers' compensation laws*. In essence, these laws require employers to compensate injured employees. England passed such laws in 1897, and the United States followed in 1902, when Maryland passed this country's first workers' compensation law—although, essentially, the Maryland law was so restrictive that it was almost useless. In 1911, Wisconsin passed the first effective workers' compensation law. Seven other states passed similar legislation during that year. Amid controversy between businesspeople and groups interested in the welfare of laborers, the Supreme Court upheld the constitutionality of these laws in 1916. Businesspeople argued that they could never bear such compensation costs nor could they control accidents; they predicted that the cost of goods would rise considerably. Those who favored workers' compensation laws believed that these laws would provide the impetus for greater safety, because business owners and managers would want to control losses.

Workers' compensation laws provided insurance companies with a new opportunity. As states enacted these laws, business owners became concerned about their ability to pay for workers' compensation. Therefore, insurance companies sold casualty insurance policies to businesses that needed the security from a possible workers' compensation burden. *A concurrent benefit of such insurance was that insurance companies were willing to reduce premiums if a company instituted accident prevention measures.* To remain competitive, insurance companies provided safety specialists who would survey a business and recommend prevention strategies (e.g., safeguards on machines). Businesspeople became increasingly interested in safety; insurance companies developed safety expertise.

Today, all states have workers' compensation laws. These laws vary from state to state, but each requires the reporting of injures that are compensable. Most employers are insured for workers' compensation judgments by private insurance companies. Other employers are self-insured (insurance provided by the employer and not purchased through a private insurance company; it is regulated by a state insurance commissioner) or place this insurance with state insurance funds. When an employee is injured, medical benefits usually are granted, and benefits for wages lost are granted when an employee is incapacitated and cannot work.

The workers' compensation system of today has its problems. Because dealings with the insurance industry are frequently adversarial, injured employees often believe that the system helps them only when they obtain the services of an attorney. Insurers, on the other hand, claim that they must protect their interests and that fraud (i.e., worker malingering) is a very serious problem.

Are workers' compensation laws necessary today? Support your viewpoint.

The Development of OSHA

With the advent of improved safety conditions, accidents and injuries declined until the 1950s. In the late 1950s, rates leveled off until the late 1960s, when accidents and injuries began to increase. This upward turn caused the federal government to become increasingly concerned about safety. Several safety-related laws were passed during the 1960s, but none was as monumental as OSHA. OSHA stands for the *Occupational Safety and Health Administration*, a federal agency, under the U.S. Department of Labor, established to administer the law on safety and health resulting from the William Steiger Occupational Safety and Health Act of 1970. This federal legislation was signed into law by the then president, Richard Nixon, and became effective on April 28, 1971. The basic purpose of the OSHA legislation was to provide a safe working environment for employees engaged in a variety of occupations (U.S. Department of Labor, OSHA, P.O. Box 37535, Washington, DC 20013; Tel.: 202-219-4667; Web site: http://www.osha.gov/).

The OSHA act was significant because it was the first national safety legislation applying to every business connected with interstate commerce. "The need for such legislation was clear. Between 1969 and 1973 [in the United States] more persons were killed at work than in the Vietnam war."[5]

OSHA is administered by the Secretary of Labor via ten regional offices. The secretary has the authority and responsibility to establish occupational safety and health standards. Workplace inspections can result in citations issued to employers who violate standards.

The National Institute for Occupational Safety and Health (NIOSH) performs numerous functions that aid OSHA and those striving for worker safety. These functions relate to research, the development of criteria and standards for occupational safety and health, training OSHA personnel and others (e.g., employers and employees), and providing publications dealing with both toxic substances and strategies on how to prevent occupational injuries and illnesses. NIOSH (http://www.cdc.gov/niosh) is under the U.S. Department of Health and Human Services.

Objectives of OSHA

The OSHA act of 1970 states that it is "to assure so far as possible every working man and woman in the Nation safe and healthful working conditions and to preserve our human resources." At the beginning of the twenty-first century OSHA is focusing on three strategic goals:

- Improve workplace safety and health for all workers, as evidenced by fewer hazards, reduced exposures, and fewer injuries, illnesses, and fatalities
- Change workplace culture to increase employer and worker awareness of, commitment to, and involvement in safety and health
- Secure public confidence through excellence in the development and delivery of OSHA's programs and services.[6]

The Act's Jurisdiction

OSHA rules extend to all employers and their employees in the fifty states, the District of Columbia, Puerto Rico, and other U.S. possessions. An employer is anyone who maintains employees and engages in a business affecting commerce. This broad coverage involves a multitude of fields: manufacturing, construction, agriculture, warehousing, retailing, longshoring, education, and so on. The act does not cover self-employed persons, family-owned and operated farms, and workplaces protected by other federal agencies. Although federal agencies are not covered by OSHA, agencies are required to maintain a safe working environment equal to those groups under OSHA's jurisdiction. State and local government employees are impacted by OSHA.

OSHA Standards

OSHA promulgates legally enforceable standards to protect employees in the workplace. *Since OSHA standards are constantly being updated and reviewed, it is the employer's responsibility to keep up-to-date.* Two of the best sources for standards and changes are the Web site of OSHA found at http://www.osha.gov/ and the *Federal Register* at http://fr.cos.com/.

There are actually thousands of OSHA standards. Some pertain to specific industries and workers, whereas others are general and practiced by most industries. Examples include safety requirements for machines, equipment, and employees, such as requiring face shields or safety glasses during the use of certain machines; unobstructed aisles and exits in the workplace; prevention of electrical hazards; adequate fire protection; adequate lunchrooms, lavatories, and drinking water; and monitoring of employee exposure to chemical or toxic hazards.

The following standards demonstrate OSHA's concern for worker safety and health.

Subpart 1—Personal Protective Equipment

1910.132 General requirements.

(a) Application. Protective equipment, including personal protective equipment for eyes, face, head, and extremities, protective clothing, respiratory devices, and protective shields and barriers, shall be provided, used, and maintained in a sanitary and reliable condition wherever it is necessary by reason of hazards of processes or environment, chemical hazards, radiological hazards, or mechanical irritants encountered in a manner capable of causing injury or impairment in the function of any part of the body through absorption, inhalation or physical contact.

Subpart K—Medical and First Aid

1910.151 Medical services and first aid.

(a) The employer shall ensure the ready availability of medical personnel for advice and consultation of matters of plant health.

(b) In the absence of an infirmary, clinic, or hospital in near proximity to the workplace which is used for the treatment of all injured employees, a person or persons shall be adequately trained to render first aid. First aid supplies approved by the consulting physician shall be readily available.

(c) Where the eyes or body of any person may be exposed to injurious corrosive materials, suitable facilities for quick drenching or flushing of the eyes and body shall be provided within the work area for immediate emergency use.

OSHA Hazard Communication Standard

This standard was established because more than 32 million workers could be exposed to one or more chemical hazards; and more than 650,000 hazardous chemical products exist, with hundreds of new ones being introduced annually. Also known as a *right-to-know law*, this standard requires all employers who have employees that may be exposed to hazardous substances on the job to inform them about such substances and how to deal with them. Employers are required to write and implement a hazard communication program, conduct a chemical inventory, ensure that a *Material Safety Data Sheet* (MSDS) is available for each chemical, label chemical containers, and train employees on the safe use of chemicals (e.g., protective equipment, procedures).[7]

OSHA Bloodborne Pathogens Standard

This standard limits exposure to blood and other potentially infectious materials, which could lead to disease or death. The standard covers all employees facing potential exposure. Employers are required to establish an exposure control plan covering safety procedures, protective equipment, and the control of waste. The hepatitis B vaccination is to be made available to all employees who have occupational exposure to blood. Postexposure evaluation and follow-up is to be made available to all employees who have had an exposure incident, including laboratory tests at no cost to the employee. Exposure records must be confidential and kept for the duration of employment plus 30 years. Training is required on all aspects of this standard, and the training records must be maintained for three years.[8]

Lockout/ Tagout

OSHA standard 1910.147 is designed to control hazardous energy. Better known as lockout/tagout, the aim is to prevent the accidental startup of machines or other equipment during maintenance and servicing. The rule requires that hazardous energy sources must be isolated and rendered inoperative before work can begin. Elements of a lockout/tagout program are written procedures, training, and audits. Examples of OSHA citations involving this standard include Lifetime Doors, for 37 alleged violations after employees suffered finger amputations at the door manufacturing plant. OSHA proposed penalties of $1.1 million. In another case, an employee of Hanna Paper Recycling entered a baler to dislodge a jammed cardboard bale and was crushed to death between the bale and the gathering ram. OSHA cited Hanna for 19 alleged violations and proposed penalties for $59,200.[9]

OSHA Record Keeping and Reporting

Before the development of OSHA's centralized record keeping system, workplace statistics on injuries and illnesses were kept by some states and private organizations. No uniform, standardized system existed. Today, with the help of OSHA's comprehensive statistics, it is easier to pinpoint serious hazards and work toward improvements.

Although OSHA record keeping by an employer may appear burdensome, the task does not require much time or energy. In fact, the records actually can help employers reduce losses by revealing hazards. The employer is responsible for keeping the records up-to-date and available to OSHA inspectors. These records are not to be sent to OSHA, but remain at the workplace for five years beyond the year of recording. Workplaces in low-hazard industries such as retail, finance, and insurance are exempt from record-keeping requirements.

The records for employers are described as follows:

OSHA No. 200, Log and Summary of Occupational Injuries and Illnesses: Each recordable occupational injury and illness must be logged on this form within six working days from the time the employer learns of it. If the log is prepared at a central location by automatic data processing equipment, a copy current to within 45 calendar days must be present at all times in the establishment. A substitute for the OSHA No. 200 is acceptable if it is as detailed, easily readable and understandable as the OSHA No. 200.

OSHA No. 101, Supplementary Record of Occupational Injuries and Illnesses. The form OSHA No. 101 contains much more detail about each injury or illness. It also must be completed within six working days from the time the employer learns of the work-related injury or illness. A substitute for the OSHA No. 101 (such as insurance or workers' compensation forms) may be used if it contains all required information.

Annual Survey. Employers selected to participate in the annual statistical survey use form No. 200 as the source of information.

How does OSHA define occupational injury and illness?

An *occupational injury* is any injury such as a cut, fracture, sprain, or amputation which results from a work-related accident or from exposure involving a single incident in the work environment. An *occupational illness* is any abnormal condition or disorder, other than one resulting from an occupational injury, caused by exposure to environmental factors associated with employment.

When does OSHA require occupational injuries and illnesses to be recorded? Death must be recorded regardless of the length of time between injury and death and regardless of the length of the illness. One or more lost workdays for an employee, restriction of work or motion, loss of consciousness, transfer to another job, or medical treatment other than first aid must be recorded. If an on-the-job accident occurs that results in the death of an employee or the hospitalization of three or more employees, *all* employers must (by law) report the accident, in detail, to the nearest OSHA office within 8 hours.[10]

Additional OSHA Employer Responsibilities

An employer is required to post specific OSHA-related material for employee review. The OSHA poster Job Safety and Health Protection informs employees about their rights and responsibilities and must be displayed in an appropriate location for employees. Copies of the OSHA act and relevant rules and regulations must be available if requested by employees. A summary of petitions for variances also must be posted—an employer is allowed to petition OSHA for a *variance*, that is, an opportunity to do something contrary to the usual method of a standard or regulation, if the employer cannot comply right away or if the employer can show that his or her method is equal to the OSHA method. The employer also is required to display copies of citations for violations of standards and the summary of injuries and illnesses (see OSHA Form 200).[11]

OSHA Inspections

An important priority of OSHA compliance inspectors was to view the workplace as it functions on a typical day. To attain this goal and to prevent an employer from altering typical workplace characteristics by concealing unsafe conditions, inspections frequently were made unannounced. However, only a few years after this practice began, it was challenged in the courts. In 1975, the president of a utility installation company, who posted a copy of the Bill of Rights on his office wall, sued while claiming that the Fourth Amendment restricts warrantless searches. The federal appellate court upheld the employer's contention. The case was appealed, and in May 1978 the Supreme Court, in *Marshall v. Barlow*, ruled that the Fourth Amendment protection against unreasonable searches protects commercial establishments as well as private homes. Therefore, OSHA inspectors must obtain a warrant before making an inspection, unless employers consent. Such a warrant is to be based on administrative probable cause: the inspector is required to show a judicial officer that the inspection is part of OSHA's general administrative plan to enforce safety and health laws, or upon evidence of a violation.[12]

When an inspection takes place, the employer and even employee representatives may join the inspector. The inspector is obligated to show credentials that contain a photograph and serial number. The number can be verified via the nearest OSHA office. Typically, machinery, equipment, and other workplace characteristics are examined. The inspector can interview the employer and employees in public or in private. Any interference with the inspector's duties can result in stiff penalties. The employer is wise to document the inspection and comments by the inspector through note taking. This information may become useful if a disagreement or a dispute of a citation or penalty evolves.

Because millions of workplaces are subject to inspections, OSHA has established priorities. Obviously, workplaces with serious accidents and injuries will be subject to inspections. A high-priority inspection will result from a report of an accident that causes the death of an employee or the hospitalization of three or more employees. Other inspections might result from employee complaints, belonging to a hazardous industry, or merely routine inspections.

In fiscal year 2001, OSHA had a staff of 2,370 including 1,170 inspectors and a budget of $426 million. Twenty-six states run their own OSHA programs with 2,948 employees including 1,275 inspectors. In fiscal year 2000, 36,350 Federal and 54,510 state inspections were conducted. Penalties range to $70,000 per violation.[13]

The National Federation of Independent Businesses' (NFIB) publication *Mandate* recommends the following strategies "when the OSHA inspector shows up at your door":

1. The method for dealing with an OSHA inspector should be worked out with an attorney as soon as possible.
2. Find out if the inspector is from the state or federal OSHA. Get name and credentials.
3. Ask the inspector why he is at your business. Was there an employee complaint? Is he responding to a workplace injury? Is this a random search?
4. In the event the inspector has a warrant, find out what judge issued it and when. Note the specific workplace areas mentioned on the warrant.
5. Contact your attorney.[14]

A violation of an OSHA standard may cause the issuance of a citation and then a penalty. Severe violations can result in civil and criminal penalties. Citations inform both the employer and employees about characteristics of the violation and the time span for correction. Citations must be posted for employees.

OSHA: Criticism and Controversy

Through the years since its inception, OSHA has been the target of considerable criticism and controversy. Most of the OSHA battles have taken place on Capitol Hill, when different interest groups pressure legislators either to maintain and expand OSHA or to reduce or eliminate it. The forces in favor of OSHA are primarily OSHA itself, the AFL-CIO labor organization, and select legislators. Those opposed to OSHA consist mainly of businesspeople, business organizations, and select legislators. Some say the controversy essentially is between "big labor" and "big business."

The main arguments against OSHA are the following:

1. "Regulatory overkill" is a major theme of those against OSHA. Many business organizations believe that OSHA has gone beyond what is necessary for fostering a safe and healthy workplace. Businesspeople and employers often rate OSHA as the prime example of excessive government regulation; they state that the agency's overzealous inspectors afflict employers with rules.
2. OSHA is not cost effective. It provides limited benefits.
3. The costs of OSHA, reduced productivity, lost jobs, and higher prices for goods add to inflation and are a threat to companies' competitive position.
4. OSHA and other government bureaucrats, who are appointed rather than elected and thus are not accountable to the people, are making decisions that businesspeople should be making for themselves.

5. OSHA has had an impact on the labor–management process that has compounded labor troubles. Many unions have become involved in worker safety and employees' rights under OSHA to the point where productivity is hindered.
6. Numerous employers have become paranoid due to adverse publicity and labor disputes arising from unnecessary OSHA citations.

The major arguments in favor of OSHA are these:

1. OSHA is essential to reinforce a safe and healthy workplace for employees.
2. Many deaths and injuries have been prevented because of OSHA.
3. In today's technologically complex business world, employees need protection that only government regulation can provide.
4. Employers who oppose OSHA are too interested in the costs of safety and health, and in productivity and profits, and they are not concerned enough about employees.
5. There are employers who have a favorable attitude toward OSHA and benefit from its existence. These employers actively work with OSHA in a joint effort to prevent and reduce safety and health problems. To these businesspeople, OSHA compliance is cost effective.

Ergonomics

The issue of ergonomics illustrates the controversy discussed above. *Ergonomics* is the application of biology and engineering knowledge to improve the interaction of humans and technology. The OSHA ergonomics rule required companies to provide information about reducing musculoskeletal disorders (MSDs), also referred to as repetitive stress injuries, such as carpal tunnel syndrome. If an employee reports symptoms of a disorder, and it is determined to be work-related, then the employee is entitled to medical care and work restriction protection (WRP) or time off with pay. If other employees are exposed to possible injuries, then the employer must reduce the problem. Whereas OSHA and organized labor favor WRP because they believe employers will intimidate workers to hide MSDs, industry groups oppose WRP because they fear malingerers will abuse it. The controversy was settled by Congress, which appealed OSHA's ergonomics rule in early 2001 under the 1996 Congressional Review Act. This act permits Congress to nullify laws imposed by federal agencies and prevents any new regulations from being issued that are similar to the old one.[15]

What are your viewpoints on the ergonomics controversy?
Are you for or against OSHA? Support your viewpoint.

Assistance with Problems

There are many sources of assistance for employers concerned about workplace safety or health problems:

1. Many insurance companies provide personnel who visit, inspect, and recommend strategies for preventing and eliminating hazards at client workplaces.
2. Trade associations and employer groups have become more conscious about safety and health.
3. Trade unions and employee groups are often interested in coordinated activities for preventing and eliminating hazards.
4. The National Safety Council has an extensive information service (Address: 1121 Spring Lake Dr., Itasca, IL 60143; Tel.: 1-800-621-7615; Web site: http://www.nsc.org/).
5. Local doctors may be willing to provide information on a consulting basis about workplace medical matters. The Red Cross is a source of first-aid training. An employer who is not able to locate a local chapter should contact the American National Red Cross, National Headquarters, Safety Programs, 8111 Gatehouse Rd., Falls Church, VA 22042; Tel.: 703-206-7090; Web site: http://www.redcross.org/.
6. The Web and libraries contain a wealth of information on safety and health matters.
7. Local colleges and universities may have educational programs in the field of occupational safety and health. If an employer contacts the relevant departments, educators may provide useful information.
8. Free on-site consultation is offered in many states through agreements between OSHA and either a state or private contractor. These consultants do not write citations but expect cooperation or OSHA will be contacted. Enforcement action is rare, especially because the employer requested the consultant and showed a concern for safety and health.

SAFETY STRATEGIES

The *OSHA Handbook for Small Businesses* states four basic elements for "Developing a Profitable Strategy for Handling Occupational Safety and Health":

1. The manager or management team leads the way in setting policy, assigning responsibility, setting an example, and involving employees.
2. The worksite is continually analyzed to identify all hazards.
3. Methods for preventing or controlling existing or potential hazards are put in place and maintained.
4. Managers, supervisors, and employees are trained to understand and deal with worksite hazards.[16]

Safety and Health Committee

A safety and health committee can be an important part of an effective loss prevention program. When employees jointly communicate about and work toward increased safety and health, consciousness raising is a result, and employees develop a greater awareness of associated problems and solutions. At meetings, topics to discuss can include past accidents and illnesses, OSHA standards and inspections, and cases of accidents, illnesses, and remedies that occurred at similar facilities.

Socialization

Training is a prime strategy for accident prevention. The objective of training is to change the behavior of the employee. He or she should think and act in a safe manner. Safety videos and lectures by specialists are useless unless employees are motivated to continually act in a safe manner. Even if familiar with safety procedures and other relevant information, an employee will not necessarily "practice what is preached." A method for stimulating the employee to act safely and to use safety knowledge is necessary. This objective is accomplished through incentive programs.

Incentive Programs

Incentive programs motivate employees to work safely. Articles in *Occupational Hazards* exemplify several kinds of safety incentive programs:

1. When a particular company has no accidents for a specific time period (e.g., a week or so) the coffee vending machines are open to all employees.
2. Every time a manufacturing plant reaches a million hours in its ascent to 7,500,000 worker hours without a lost-time accident, every employee receives a gift. The gifts have included blankets, picnic sets, and umbrellas. This company spent $100,000 on the incentive program during one year.
3. Safety bingo was initiated at a plant. Numbers are drawn every workday for a week and posted on a sign in the employee parking lot. If an employee completes a row, $25 is awarded. If the whole card is filled, $1,000 is won. When lost-time accidents occur, the game is halted until a month later.
4. Companies often set safety goals for individual departments, which facilitate a competitive spirit to win prizes.
5. Safety, rewarded by merit pay increases for employees, will also reduce accidents. Employees who perform unsafe acts or resist safety equipment or other features of the safety program lose eligibility to participate in incentive programs for specific periods.[17]

What are the results of such incentive programs? Safety incentives provide a powerful, cost-effective management tool to prevent accidents.

Enthusiasm and safety awareness increase. Employees are more vigilant about other workers' safety. Incentive programs provide fun in the workplace, which results in higher morale. As accidents decline, so do insurance premiums for workers' compensation. Money is saved. Fewer accidents mean fewer production interruptions and greater profits. It is feasible to use incentives for a comprehensive loss prevention effort involving not only safety but also crime and fire prevention.

The Dangers of Safety Incentive Programs[18]

There are three basic types of safety incentive/reward programs as described here, along with concerns.

Traditional programs offer rewards to employees for going a certain period of time without a recordable injury. The focus is on results. OSHA, labor unions, and some employers argue that these programs may be used by employers to take the place of formal programs. Also, employees may feel pressured not to report injuries because coworkers would be upset about not winning incentives, and so a serious workplace hazard might go undetected by management.

Behavior-based programs offer rewards to employees for behaviors (e.g., wearing personal protective equipment) that promote safety. Labor groups say that this approach places safety on the shoulders of employees and then management blames them when accidents occur. Furthermore, employers watch actions and may ignore hazards that can be corrected.

Safety activities offer rewards to employees for suggestions to improve safety, identifying and correcting hazards, participating in inspections, and serving on a committee, among other activities.

Whereas the first two programs often involve a greater level of participation, safety activities are frequently voluntary; however, everyone should be involved in safety. Since each type of program can create concern, the employer and employees should seek to understand each one and capitalize on the beneficial aspects of each.

Investigations

After an accident, an investigation is vital to prevent future accidents; the cause of an accident can be pinpointed so that corrections can follow. Established procedures important for well-planned accident investigations include the following:

1. Respond quickly to reinforce that loss prevention personnel are "on the job." This will also show employees that management cares.
2. Find out the following: who was involved, where did it occur, when did it happen, who was injured, and what was damaged?

3. Try to pinpoint the cause. Investigate possible direct and indirect causes. Study equipment, work procedures, the environment, and the employees involved. Is a drug test required?
4. Estimate injuries and direct and indirect costs.
5. Use a standard accident report that fits management's requirements and aids the investigative inquiry.
6. Maintain an open mind, remaining aware that some employees attempt fraudulent workers' compensation claims by staging an accident or by providing false information.
7. If necessary, complete appropriate forms (e.g., workers' compensation, OSHA).
8. Prepare a presentation for the safety and health committee concerning the accident. Solicit feedback from the committee to solve problems.
9. Follow up on corrective action to ensure safety.

One of the most difficult questions to answer during an accident investigation is the *cause*; often considerable controversy is generated. Opinions vary, but facts are necessary.

Harry Nash, Machinist, Is Injured Again

As Harry Nash was cutting a piece of metal on a band saw, he accidentally cut off his thumb. Workers in the surrounding area rushed to his aid. The foreman and the loss prevention manager coordinated efforts to get him and his thumb to the hospital as quickly as possible. After Harry was in the care of doctors, the foreman and the loss prevention manager began an investigation. A look at Harry's record showed that he had been working for the company for eight years. During the first year he slipped on some oil on the workplace floor and was hospitalized for three weeks with a sprained back. The third year showed that he accidentally drilled into his finger with a drill press. The report stated that Harry did not receive any training from a now-retired foreman, who should have instructed Harry on drill-press safety techniques. By the fifth year Harry had had another accident. While carrying some metal rods, he fell and broke his ankle because he forgot about climbing one step to enter a newly constructed adjoining building.

Even though Harry had had no training in operating the band saw, the loss prevention manager and the foreman believed that Harry was accident prone. The foreman, angry about Harry spoiling the department's safety record and incentive gifts, wanted Harry fired. The loss prevention manager was undecided about the matter.

Later, management, and the foreman and the loss prevention manager, decided to assign Harry to a clerical position in the shipping department. Harry eventually collected workers' compensation for his lost thumb.

There are two primary causes of accidents: unsafe conditions and unsafe acts by people. Frequently, unsafe conditions (e.g., unguarded moving parts, poor lighting) are known, but corrections are not made because of inaction or costs. Unsafe acts by people can result from ignorance, poor training, negligence, drugs, fatigue, emotional upset, poor attitude, and high production demands. Other circumstances also can cause accidents. One of the oldest and most controversial theories of accident causation is the *accident-proneness theory.* This theory suggests that people who repeatedly have accidents are accident prone. Many experts agree that about 20 percent of the people have most of the accidents, whereas the remaining 80 percent have virtually no accidents. However, because susceptibility to accidents varies from person to person, there is no profile of characteristics that can positively identify accident-prone employees.

Additional Safety Measures

Other safety measures are to display safety posters, create a safety-by-objectives program, and recognize employees with excessive accident records and reassign or retrain those workers. Safety posters or signs are effective if certain guidelines are used. Research indicates that if the safety message is in negative terms (e.g., "Don't let this happen to you," followed by a picture of a person with a physical injury), it causes fear, resentment, and sometimes anger. Posters with positive messages (e.g., "Let's all pitch in for safety") produce better results. Posters and signs (see Figure 13-1) are more potent when they reflect the diversity of employees (e.g., multiple languages), are located in appropriate places, are not too numerous, and have attractive colors. A safety-by-objectives program is a derivative of management by objectives. In a manufacturing plant, department heads formulate safety objectives for their departments. Management makes sure that objectives are neither too high nor too low. Incentives are used to motivate employees. After a year, the objectives are studied to see if the objectives were reached. Future objectives are modified or increased.

Search the Web

For a wealth of information on safety, check out OSHA on the Web at http://www.osha.gov/.

Another source is *Best's Safety & Security Directory* (http://www.amb-est.com/safety), which contains information on products and services, company profiles, training articles, self-inspection checklists, and OSHA standards.

Figure 13–1 Safety signs.

CASE PROBLEMS

13A. As a loss prevention practitioner for a large corporation, you are asked by a local college professor to lecture on the pros and cons of OSHA. What will your comments be to a class of safety management students?

13B. If you were a company loss prevention manager, how would you react to an OSHA inspection? What conditions in your company do you think would influence your reaction?

13C. In reference to the case describing Harry Nash, do you feel that the loss prevention manager and the foreman were justified in labeling Harry as accident prone? Support your answer.

NOTES

1. C. Richard Anderson, *OSHA and Accident Control Through Training* (New York: Industrial Press, 1975), pp. 5–6.
2. U.S. Department of Labor, OSHA, *OSHA Strategic Plan* http://www.osha.gov/ (May 3, 2001).

3. *A Primer on Confined Area Entry*, Bio Marine, Inc., 456 Creamery Way, Exton, PA 19341. Also, Michael Chacanaca, "Specialty-Confined-Space Rescues," *Emergency* (February 1996), pp. 61–65.

4. John V. Grimaldi and Rollin H. Simmonds, *Safety Management* (Homewood, IL: Richard D. Irwin, 1975), pp. 33–43.

5. Joseph B. Mason, "OSHA: Problems and Prospects," *California Management Review* 19, no. 1 (Fall 1976), p. 21.

6. U.S. Department of Labor, OSHA, *OSHA Revised Strategic Plan, FY 1997–FY 2002* http://www.osha.gov/ (May 2, 2001).

7. U.S. Department of Labor, OSHA, *Chemical Hazard Communication* (Washington, D.C.: USGPO, 1998), pp. 1–24.

8. U.S. Department of Labor, OSHA, *Occupational Exposure to Bloodborne Pathogens* (Washington, D.C.: USGPO, 1996), pp. 1–27.

9. "Lockout/Tagout," *Occupational Hazards* 63 (January 2001), p. 17.

10. U.S. Department of Labor, OSHA, *All About OSHA 2000 (Revised)* http://www.osha-slc.gov/Publications/8sha2056.pdf (May 2, 2001), pp. 1–65.

11. U.S. Department of Labor, OSHA, *Employer Rights and Responsibilities Following an OSHA Inspection* (Washington, D.C.: USGPO, 1999), pp. 1–34.

12. U.S. Department of Labor, OSHA, *All About OSHA 2000 (Revised)*, pp. 1–65. Also, Mark S. Dreux, "When OSHA Knocks, Should an Employer Demand a Warrant?" *Occupational Hazards* (April 1995), p. 53.

13. U.S. Department of Labor, OSHA, *OSHA Statistics* http://www.osha.gov/ (May 2, 2001).

14. National Federation of Independent Business, "Standing up to OSHA," *NFIB Mandate* (150 West 20th Avenue, San Mateo, CA 94403), no date, p. 5.

15. Jeffrey Teolis, "Is There Life After Death for OSHA's Ergo Rule?" *Safety Compliance Letter* 2375 (April 1, 2001), pp. 1–2. And, James L. Nash, "The Ergonomics Rule: A Tale of Two Provisions" *Occupational Hazards* 63 (January 2001), pp. 31–35.

16. U.S. Department of Labor, OSHA, *OSHA Handbook for Small Businesses, 1996 (Revised)* http://www.osha.gov/ (May 3, 2001).

17. John C. Bruening, "Incentives Strengthen Safety Awareness," *Occupational Hazards* (November 1989), pp. 49–52. Also, S. L. Smith, "Reaping the Rewards of Safety Incentives," *Occupational Hazards* (January 1996), pp. 99–102.

18. William Atkinson, "The Dangers of Safety Incentive Programs," *Risk Management* 47 (August 2000), pp. 32–38.

14

Risk Management and Insurance

OBJECTIVES

After studying this chapter the reader will be able to:

1. Define risk management.
2. Explain the role of the risk manager and the tools of risk management.
3. Describe the insurance industry.
4. Discuss types of insurance.
5. Elaborate on insurance claims.

Risk is exposure to possible loss. Crime, fire, and accident are by no means the only kinds of risk that confront businesses. The wise businessperson is knowledgeable about all possible risks. Business interruption, for example, results from crime, fire, accident, flood, tornado, and the like. Another risk is liability. A customer might become injured on the premises after falling or be harmed in some way when using a product manufactured by a business.

RISK MANAGEMENT

The most productive way of handling unavoidable risks is to manage them as well as possible. Hence, the term risk management has evolved. *Risk management* makes the most efficient before-the-loss arrangement for an after-the-loss continuation of a business. Insurance is a major risk management tool.

Risk management and loss prevention are naturally intertwined. Loss prevention is another tool for risk managers to make their job easier. Insurance is made more affordable through loss prevention methods. Additional risk management tools are described in succeeding pages.

Both loss prevention and risk management originated in the insurance industry. Fire insurance companies, soon after the Civil War, formed the National Board of Fire Underwriters, which was instrumental in reducing loss of life and property through prevention measures. Today, loss prevention has spread throughout the insurance industry and into the business community. Risk management is also an old practice. The modern history of risk management is said by many insurance experts to have begun in 1931, with the establishment of the insurance section of the American Management Association. The insurance section holds conferences and workshops for those in the insurance and risk management field.

The Role of the Risk Manager

Traditionally, businesses purchased insurance through outside insurance brokers. Generally, a broker brings together a buyer and a seller. Insurance brokers are especially helpful when a company seeking insurance has no proprietary risk manager to analyze risks and plan insurance coverage. Not all businesses can afford the services of a broker or a proprietary risk manager; however, risk management tools are applicable to all businesspeople.

The risk manager's job varies with the company served. He or she may be responsible for insurance only; or for security, safety, and insurance; or for fire protection, safety, and insurance. *One important consideration in the implementation of a risk management (or loss prevention) program is that the program must be explained in financial terms to top executives.* Is the program cost effective? Financial benefits and financial protection are primary expectations of top executives that the risk manager must consider during decision making.

Research in England of the activities of risk managers in thirty different organizations showed five major factors influenced risk managers' roles. *Top management* had a major influence on the risk manager in the form of direct instruction on primary tasks. *External influences* included recommendations from outside groups to increase attention to risk management within businesses and requirements for risk reporting. The *nature of the business, corporate developments* (e.g., expansion and exposures), and *characteristics of the risk management department* (e.g., resources available) also influenced the role of the risk manager.[1]

Among the many activities of the risk manager are to develop specifications for insurance coverage wanted, meet with insurance company representatives, study various policies, and decide on the most appropriate coverage at the best possible price. Coverage may be required by law or contract such as workers' compensation insurance and vehicle liability insurance. Plant and equipment should be reappraised periodically to maintain adequate insurance coverage. Also, the changing value of buildings and other assets, as well as replacement costs, must be considered in the face of depreciation and inflation.[2]

It is of tremendous importance that the expectations of insurance coverage be clearly understood. The risk manager's job could be in jeopardy if false impressions are communicated to top executives, who believe a loss is covered when it is not. Certain things may be excluded from a specific policy that might require special policies or endorsements. Insurance policies state what incidents are covered and to what degree. Incidents not covered are also stated. An understanding of stipulations concerning insurance claims, when to report a loss, to whom, and supporting documentation is essential in order not to invalidate a claim.

During this planning process, loss prevention measures are appraised in an effort to reduce insurance costs. Because premium reductions through loss prevention are a strong motivating force, risk managers may view strategies, such as security officers, as a necessary annoyance.

Deductibles are another risk management tool to cut insurance expenses. There are several forms of deductibles, but generally the policyholder pays for small losses up to a specified amount (e.g., $100, $1,000), while the insurance carrier pays for losses above the specified amount, less the deductible.

A major concern for the risk manager in the planning process is *what amount of risk is to be assumed by the business beyond that covered by insurance and loss prevention strategies.* A delicate balance should be maintained between excessive protection and excessive exposure.[3]

Within the planning process and before a final decision is made on risk countermeasures, the practitioner should consider five additional tools for dealing with risk:

- *Risk avoidance.* This approach asks whether or not to avoid the risk. For example, the production of a proposed product is canceled because the danger inherent in the manufacturing process creates a risk that outweighs potential profits. Or, a bank avoids opening a branch in a locality that is subject to yearly flooding.
- *Risk transfer.* Risk can be transferred to insurance. The risk manager works with an insurance company to tailor a coverage program for the risk. This approach should not be used in lieu of loss prevention measures but rather to support them. *Insurance should be last in a series of defenses.* Another method of transferring risk is to lease equipment rather than owning it. This would transfer the risk of obsolescence.
- *Risk abatement.* In abatement, essentially a risk is decreased through a loss prevention measure. Risks are not eliminated, but the severity of loss is reduced. Losses from fire, for example, are reduced by alarms and sprinklers.
- *Risk spreading.* Potential losses are reduced by spreading the risk among multiple locations. A large retail store can scatter cash register locations to minimize risks associated with operation. In another example, vital records can be duplicated and stored at a remote, secure location.

- *Risk assumption.* In the assumption approach, a company makes itself liable for losses. One path is when no action is taken and no insurance is obtained. This may result because the chance for loss is minute. Another path, self-insurance, provides for periodic payments to a reserve fund in case of loss. Risk assumption may be the only choice for a company if insurance cannot be obtained. With risk assumption, prevention strategies become essential.

A trend today in the risk management field is known as *enterprise risk management*. It refers to a comprehensive risk management program that addresses a variety of business risks. Examples are: risk of profit or loss; uncertainty regarding the organization's goals as it faces its strengths, weaknesses, opportunities, and threats; and risk of accident, fire, and crime. By packaging all of these risks into one program, planning is improved and overall risk can be reduced. Because risks frequently are uncorrelated (i.e., all of them causing loss in the same year), insurance costs are lower. For example, the following risks are unlikely to occur in the same year: fire, adverse movement in a foreign currency, and homicide in the workplace.[4] Since enterprise risk management is interdisciplinary in nature, corporations are forming committees for planning. At Hallmark Cards, Inc., the enterprise risk management oversight committee consists of personnel from finance, risk management, legal, human resources, IT, and internal audit.[5]

Should a security and loss prevention manager be part of an enterprise risk management committee? Why or why not?

International Perspective: Risk Management in a Multinational Business[6]

Overseas business operations require specific information about each country in which business will be conducted. A host of questions require research: How is business conducted in comparison to the United States? How strong is the currency? How vulnerable is the area to natural disasters, fire, and crime? What are the potential employment practices liability issues? What is the track record of shipments to and from the area?

Political risks are especially challenging in overseas operations. Are terrorist groups or the government hostile to foreign companies and their employees? Does the host government have a record of: instability and war; seizing foreign assets; capping increases in the price of products or adding taxes to undermine foreign investments; and imposing barriers to control the movement of capital out of the country?

Eighty percent of the terrorist acts committed against U.S. interests abroad target U.S. businesses, rather than governmental or military posts. These threats include kidnapping, extortion, product contamination, workplace violence, and IT sabotage.

The concept of enterprise risk management can be especially helpful with multinational businesses because of a multitude of threats. A key challenge for the risk manager is to bring together a full range of resources and network in the United States and overseas prior to potential losses so, if a loss occurs, a speedy and aggressive response helps the business to successfully rebound.

Options for insurance include buying it in the home country and arranging coverage for overseas operations; however, this may be illegal in some countries that require admitted insurance. Another approach is to let the firm's management in each country make the insurance decision, but this means that corporate headquarters has less control of risk management. A third avenue is to work with a global insurer who has subsidiaries or partner insurers in each country; this approach offers uniform coverage globally. A key question in these approaches: *Is the insurer financially solvent to pay the insured following a covered loss?*

INSURANCE

Insurance is the transfer of risk (exposure to possible loss) from one party (the insured) to another party (the insurer), in which the insurer is obligated to indemnify (compensate) the insured for economic loss caused from an unexpected event during a period of time for which the insured makes a premium payment to the insurer. The essence of insurance is the sharing of risks; insurance permits the insured to substitute a small cost (the premium) for a large loss under an arrangement whereby the fortunate many who escape loss will indirectly assist in the compensation of the unfortunate few who experience loss. For an insurance company to function properly, a large number of policyholders is required. This creates a "shared risk."

The technical aspects of the insurance industry involve the skills of statisticians, economists, financial analysts, engineers, attorneys, physicians, and of course, risk managers and loss prevention specialists, among others. Insurance companies must carefully set rates, meticulously draft contracts, establish underwriting guidelines (i.e., accepting or rejecting risks for an insurance company), and invest funds prudently.

Insurance rates are dependent on two primary variables: the frequency of claims and the cost of each claim. When insurance companies periodically review rates, the "loss experience" of the immediate past is studied.

The insurance industry is subject to two forms of control: competition among insurance companies and government regulation. Competition enables the consumer to compare rates and coverage for the best possible buy. Government regulatory authorities in each state or jurisdiction have a responsibility to the public to assure the solvency of each insurance company so policyholders will be indemnified when appropriate. Furthermore, rates should be neither excessive nor unfairly discriminatory. Problems with the state system of regulation came to light following the case of Martin Frankel, who looted $200 million from insurance companies he owned during the 1990s. Since the case affected insurers in five states, Congress asked the U.S. General Accounting Office (GAO) to investigate. A Fall 2000 report by the GAO blamed the states for inadequate regulatory policies, procedures, practices, and investigations, and a lack of information sharing. There are calls for a federal regulatory system, but the states will fight for the revenue—$10.2 billion in insurer premium taxes and fees while spending $839 million to regulate the industry. Insurance industry executives argue that "fifty monkeys are better than one gorilla."[7]

To check on the financial health of an insurer, contact an insurance company rating service and look for a rating of A+ or better. Examples of these firms are A.M. Best and Standard & Poors.

Types of Insurance

Insurance can be divided into two broad categories: government and private. Government insurance programs include social security, Medicare, unemployment insurance, workers' compensation, retirement, insurance on checking and savings accounts in banks, flood insurance, and numerous other programs on the federal and state levels.

Private insurance is divided into property and liability (casualty) insurance and life and health insurance.

The private insurance industry provides 2.3 million jobs among 3,366 property and liability insurers and 1,563 life and health insurers administering trillions of dollars of assets. The premiums written in 1998 for property and liability insurance totaled $269 billion, and for life insurance the figure was $120 billion.[8]

Property and liability insurance covers fire, ocean marine, inland marine (i.e., goods shipped on land), and liability insurance, which is a broad field such as general liability (e.g., from sales of products, professional services), automobile, crime, workers' compensation, boiler and machinery, glass, and nuclear, among other types. The property and liability field also includes multiple-line insurance (i.e., two or more perils covered under one policy) and fidelity and surety bonds.

Advisory organizations have been established in the property and liability field to offer a variety of research services to insurance companies; develop policy forms; and pool loss statistics among insurance companies to increase the accuracy of rates. Two major advisory organizations are the

Insurance Services Office (ISO) and the American Association of Insurance Services (AAIS).[9]

Because types of insurance are numerous, varied and confusing, groups such as the ISO develop insurance contracts and forms and seek standardization. This group's effort is illustrated through the commercial package policy (CPP) that contains multiple coverage in a single policy, fewer gaps in coverage, lower premiums because individual policies are not purchased, and convenience. The CPP is used by retail stores, office buildings, manufacturers, motels, hotels, apartments, schools, churches, and many other organizations. CPP coverage commonly contains two or more coverage parts. A business may select, for example, coverage focusing on commercial property, general liability, auto, and crime.[10]

Crime Insurance and Bonds

Two basic kinds of protection against crime losses are fidelity and surety bonds and burglary, robbery, and theft insurance. The first covers losses caused by dishonesty or incapacitation from persons entrusted with money or other property who violate this trust. The second type of protection covers theft by persons who are not in a position of trust.

Various crime coverage forms, which describe what is covered, are currently in use.[11] These forms can be issued as a monoline policy or as part of a CPP.

The Surety Association of America has developed forms pertaining to employee dishonesty and loss from forgery. Examples include Form A, Employee Dishonesty; Form B, Forgery or Alteration; and Forms O and P, Public Employee Dishonesty. The coverage of Form A, a bond, includes embezzlement of funds by a company's treasurer or stealing by a cashier.

What are the differences between insurance and a bond? A *bond* is a legal instrument whereby one party (the surety) agrees to indemnify another party (the obligee) if the obligee incurs a loss from the person bonded (the principal or obligor). Although a bond may seem like insurance, there are differences between them. Generally, a bonding contract involves three parties, whereas an insurance contract involves two. With a bond, the surety has the legal right to attempt collection from the principal after indemnifying the obligee; collection would be absurd by an insurer against an insured party unless fraud was evident. Another difference is that insurance is easier to cancel than a bond. The insured can cancel insurance by simply notifying the insurer or by nonpayment of premium. Breach of the insurance contract by the insured, or nonpayment of premium, is the insurer's frequent reason for cancellation and also a legal defense by the insurer to avoid liability. On the other hand, with a bond, the surety is liable to the beneficiary even though breach of contract or fraud occurred by the principal.

Fidelity Bonds

Generally, a fidelity bond requires that an employee(s) be investigated by the bonding company to limit the risk of dishonesty for the insured. If the bonded employee violates the trust, the insurer (bonding company) indemnifies the employer for the amount of the policy.

Fidelity bonds may be of two kinds: (1) those in which an individual is specifically bonded, by name or by position, and (2) "blanket bonds," which cover a whole category of employees.

Surety Bonds

A surety bond essentially is an agreement providing for compensation if there is a failure to perform specified acts within a certain period of time. One of the more common surety bonds is called a contract construction bond. It guarantees that the contractor(s) involved in construction will complete the work that is stipulated in the construction contract, free from debts or encumbrances.

Several types of surety bonds are used in the judiciary system. A fiduciary bond ensures that persons appointed by the court to supervise the property of others will be trustworthy. A litigation bond ensures specific conduct by defendants and plaintiffs. A bail bond ensures that a person will appear in court, otherwise the entire bond is forfeited.

Burglary, Robbery, and Theft Insurance

Understanding the definitions for *burglary, robbery,* and *theft* is important when studying insurance contracts. In reference to businesses, a valid burglary insurance claim requires the unlawful taking of property from a closed business that was entered by force. In the absence of visible marks showing forced entry, a burglary policy is inapplicable. Robbery is the unlawful taking of property from another by force or threat of force. Without force or threat of force, robbery has not occurred. Theft is a broad, catchall term that includes all crimes of stealing, plus burglary and robbery.

The following is a sample of ISO forms:

Form C, Theft, Disappearance, and Destruction. This form covers the theft, disappearance, or destruction of money and securities inside the premises. Examples of this coverage are: a robbery or burglary, damaged containers (e.g., safe, cash register), money destroyed in a fire, and property in the care of a messenger.

Form D, Robbery and Safe Burglary (property other than money and securities). Examples of coverage under form D are: a store owner who is robbed of valuable paintings; the loss of property other than money and securities from a safe burglary inside the premises; and an employee who is robbed of store merchandise outside the premises.

Form F, Computer Fraud. This form covers the theft of money, securities, and property by computer fraud.

Despite the availability of insurance, crime against property is one of the most underinsured perils. Estimates are that less than 10 percent of loss to property from ordinary crime is insured. Risk assumption remains the often-used tool to handle the crime peril.

Federal Crime Insurance

The *Federal Crime Insurance Program*, established by Congress, began operation in 1971 to counter the difficulty of obtaining adequate burglary and robbery insurance, particularly in urban areas. The program was discontinued in 1995. Private insurers and their agents administered the coverage, and the federal government, through the *Federal Insurance Administration*, was the bearer of the risk.

Kidnapping and Extortion Insurance

Another form of crime insurance covers losses from a ransom paid in a kidnapping or through extortion. During the 1970s, an upsurge in domestic and international kidnappings and terrorism created a need for this form of insurance. U.S. banks and corporations with overseas executives are especially interested in this coverage. These policies cover executives, their families, ransom money during delivery to extortionists, and corporate negligence during negotiations, among other areas of coverage.

Internet Insurance

More and more insurers are offering businesses Internet insurance against risks such as viruses, denial of service attacks, and theft of information. Because this insurance field is complicated and evolving quickly, the insured must be careful in selecting an insurer and understanding the definitions, terms, and limitations of these policies. Some technology insurers offer the added benefit of a security audit so the insured can reach a certain insurable standard.[12]

You Be the Judge #1[*]

Cliff Hawkins, the newest member of Conway Excavation's repair crew, pulled his rolling tool chest to a stop and extended his hand to his new supervisor.

"Well," said Dave Greco, smiling and shaking Hawkins's hand, "it looks like you brought everything but the kitchen sink."

"A good mechanic can't do much without a good set of tools," replied Hawkins, patting the chest gently. "It took me five years and almost $3000 to build up this set. Which reminds me"—he glanced around the garage—"if you expect me to leave these tools here, you'd better have some kind of security."

"You've got nothing to worry about," replied Greco. "We lock up at night, and nothing has ever been stolen yet."

But there's a first time for everything. A short time after Hawkins started working for Conway Excavation, the garage was broken into. Hawkins's tools were stolen.

"I thought you said my tools would be safe here," Hawkins fumed when he faced Greco.

"I never said that," Greco corrected him. "I said this garage had never been broken into. And it hadn't."

"Yeah, well I hope this company is prepared to reimburse me," Hawkins said.

Greco sat up in his chair, surprised. "Reimburse you?" he echoed. "No way! You knew our security wasn't very extensive, but you chose to leave your tools here anyway."

"I had to leave may tools here," Hawkins said angrily.

Greco shrugged. "Still, they were your tools and their loss isn't this company's responsibility."

"We'll see about that," Hawkins said as he stormed out of the office.

Hawkins went to court to try to force Conway Excavation to reimburse him for his stolen tools. Did Hawkins get his money?

Make your decision; then turn to the end of the chapter for the court's decision.

*Reprinted with permission from *Security Management—Plant and Property Protection*, a publication of Bureau of Business Practice, Inc., 24 Rope Ferry Road, Waterford, CT 06386.

Fire Insurance

Historically, the fire policy was one of the first kinds of insurance developed. For many years, it has played a significant role in assisting society against the fire peril. Prior to 1873, fire insurance contracts were not standardized. Each insurer developed its own contract. Omissions in coverage, misinterpretations, and conflicts between insurer and insured resulted in considerable problems. These individualized contracts and resultant ambiguities caused the state of Massachusetts, in 1873, to establish a standard contract. Seven years later, the standard contract became mandatory for all insurance companies in the state. Today, except for minor variations in certain states, the wording of fire insurance contracts is very similar. But, in recent years, these standard fire policies have diminished in importance as broad coverage policies have increased in number.

An understanding of insurance rating procedures provides risk managers and loss prevention managers with the knowledge to propose investments in fire protection that can show a return. Factors that influence fire insurance rates include the ability of the community's fire alarm, fire department, and water system to minimize property damage once a fire begins. Class 1 communities have the greatest suppression ability, whereas Class 10 have the least. Strategies such as convincing the community to take steps to improve its grade and installing sprinkler systems can produce a return on investment.[13]

Property and Liability Insurance

Business Property Insurance

The building and personal property coverage form is one of several property forms developed by the ISO program. It covers physical damage loss to commercial buildings, business personal property (e.g., furniture, machinery, inventory), and personal property of others in the control of the insured. Additional coverage includes debris removal, pollutant removal, and fire department service charge. A cause-of-loss form is added to the policy to have a complete contract. A basic cause-of-loss form covers fire, lightning, explosion, windstorm or hail, smoke, aircraft or vehicles, riot, vandalism, sprinkler leakage, and other perils. A broader form can be selected to expand coverage to, for example, glass breakage and earthquake.[14]

Another important kind of insurance is business income insurance (formerly called business interruption insurance). It indemnifies the insured for profits and expenses lost because of damage to property from an insured peril.

Liability Insurance

Legal liability for harm caused to others is one of the most serious risks. Negligence can result in a substantial court judgment against the responsible party. There are several kinds of exposures in the liability area for businesses. Relevant factors are the functions performed, relationships involved, and care for others required, such as the employee–employer relationship, a contract situation, consumers of manufactured products, and professional acts. Examples of liability exposures are bodily injury or death of customers, product liability, completed operations (i.e., faulty work away from the premises), environmental pollution, personal injury (e.g., false arrest, violation of right of privacy), sexual harassment, and employment discrimination.

In many jurisdictions the law views the failure to obtain liability insurance against the consequences of negligence as irresponsible financial behavior. Mandatory liability insurance for automobile operators in all states is a familiar example.

Several kinds of business liability insurance are available. The commercial general liability (CGL) policy, developed by ISO, is widely used and can be written alone or as part of a CPP.

Workers' Compensation Insurance

Coverage includes loss of income and medical and rehabilitation expenses that result from work-related accidents and occupational diseases. An employer can obtain the coverage required by law through three possible avenues: (1) commercial insurance companies, (2) a state fund or a federal agency, and (3) self-insurance (risk assumption).

Claims

When an insured party incurs a loss, a claim is made to the insurer to cover the loss as stipulated in the insurance contract. For an insurance company, the settling of losses and adjusting differences between itself and the policy-holder is known as *claims management*. Care is necessary by the insurer because underpayments can lead to lost customers, yet overpayments can lead to bankruptcy.

An insurance company investigation of a claim commonly includes (1) a determination that there has been a loss, (2) a determination that the insured has not invalidated the insurance contract, (3) an evaluation of the proof of loss, and (4) an estimate of the amount of loss. An example of item 2 occurs when the insured has not fulfilled obligations under the insurance contract, such as not protecting property from further damage after a fire or not adequately maintaining loss prevention measures.

Furthermore, most insurance contracts specify that the insured party must give immediate notice of loss. The purpose of that is to give the insurer an opportunity to study the loss before evidence to support the claim has been damaged. Failure to provide immediate notice may render the insurance invalid. The insured usually has 60 to 90 days to produce proof of loss. Accounting records, bills, and so on that might help in establishing the loss are expected to be provided by the insured.

Before a settlement is reached, the insurer checks the coverage, the claim is investigated, and loss reports and claim papers are prepared. Then, the insurance company claims department studies the loss, the policy is interpreted and applied to the loss, and a payment is approved or disapproved.

RIMS Benchmark Survey[15] and Repricing Risk After the September 11, 2001 Terrorist Attack[16]

The Risk and Insurance Management Society (RIMS) and Ernst & Young publish an annual *Benchmark Survey* (formerly called *Cost of Risk Survey*). The purpose of this survey is to provide an opportunity for risk managers to measure their organization's risk management performance against that of other similar organizations. The survey shows that risk is a manageable and controllable expense and that risk managers can contribute to the bottom line. The survey applies to businesses, public entities, and nonprofits.

A major gauge in the survey is the cost of risk (COR) per $1000 of revenue. Two industries are compared here as a sample from the 2000 survey, which resulted in 779 usable responses.

In the health care industry the COR was $18.30 as compared to an average of $5.20 for all respondents. (The COR in 1995 for this industry was $19.27.) This group's liability costs were more than six times higher than the average, workers' compensation costs were more than double the average, and it had one of the highest numbers of risk management employees.

In the retail industry the COR was $4.64. (The COR in 1995 for this industry was $6.07.) This group's property and liability costs were both lower than the survey average, while its workers' compensation costs were above average.

Overall the survey found that the cost of risk declined in the United States, but rose in Canada; the insurance market continues to be competitive; workers' compensation cost-control methods are being widely applied; and employment practices liability coverage is being purchased by a majority of respondents.

High-consequence events raise the cost of risk. Following the September 11, 2001, terrorist attack, the economy has repriced risk, which is embedded in every product and service. Extra security costs and higher insurance premiums (because insurers cannot predict terrorist acts and assume the worst) represent a drag on a company's competitiveness and profitability.

You Be the Judge #2[*]

A vice president had been embezzling money from the Michigan Mining Corporation for several years, but Security Director Steve Douglas had finally caught him. It was something of a Pyrrhic victory, however—the culprit was nabbed, but the company was out $135,000. Luckily, MMC had comprehensive business insurance that Douglas was sure would cover most of the loss.

The security director looked over the two policies, but they were poorly written and very confusing, so he called Lester Blank, the agent who handled the policies.

"I limped through the policies," Douglas explained, "and I think I get the gist of them. MMC's covered for $100,000, right?"

"Wrong," Blank said. "The second policy replaced the first. You're only covered for $50,000."

Douglas was stunned, but he recovered quickly. "Now, wait a minute," he said. "I may not have caught every mixed-up word in these policies, but the second one says we can collect on the first one for up to a year after its expiration date, provided the loss occurred during the time the first policy was in effect."

"But the total limit is still $50,000," insisted the insurance agent. "You'll find a clause to that effect in the second policy, if you read carefully."

"If I read carefully!" Douglas cried. "This second policy is so full of spelling and clerical errors that it's anybody's guess what it means. One look at this piece of slipshod writing and any court will side with us."

> So MMC went to court, claiming that because the policy was so complicated and poorly written, it should be interpreted in the company's favor.
> Did the court agree with MMC?
> Make your decision; then turn to the end of the chapter for the court's decision.

*Reprinted with permission from *Security Management—Plant and Property Protection*, a publication of Bureau of Business Practice, Inc., 24 Rope Ferry Road, Waterford, CT 06386.

Insurance companies employ different classifications of adjusters to settle claims. An insurance agent (i.e., salesperson) may serve as an adjuster for small claims up to a certain amount. A company adjuster is more experienced about claims and handles larger losses. Independent adjusters offer services to insurance companies for a fee. Public adjusters represent the insured party for a fee.

From the insurance industry's perspective, the work of an adjuster is demanding. A high priority is to satisfy claimants in order to retain customers. At the same time the interests and assets of the insurance company must be protected. Some claimants make honest mistakes in estimating losses. They may place a value on destroyed property that is above the market value. Exaggerations are common. Confusion may arise when claimants have not carefully read their insurance policy. Consequently, a process of education and negotiation often takes place between the adjuster and the claimant. Once the claimant signs the proof of loss papers or cashes the settlement check, this signifies that the claimant is satisfied and that further rights to pursue the claim are waived. In a certain number of claims, an agreement is not reached initially. The policy states the terms for settling claims. Typically, arbitration results. Each party appoints a disinterested party to act as arbitrator. The two arbitrators then select a third disinterested party. Agreements between two of the three arbitrators are binding. In liability cases, the court takes the place of arbitrators.

Dishonest claimants are a serious problem for the insurance industry, and for society. Insurance fraud is pervasive and costly. Policyholders are the ultimate group that pays for these crimes through increased premiums.

Arson is unfortunately a popular way of defrauding insurance companies. Generally, a property owner sets a fire to collect on an insurance policy. A professional arsonist may be recruited. Arson is difficult to prove because the fire destroys evidence. However, law enforcement agencies and the insurance industry have increased efforts to combat arson through additional arson investigators, improved training, better detection equipment, and computers that search data for patterns of those who defraud insurance companies.

Claims for Crime Losses

A loss prevention practitioner may be confronted with important decisions in a claim in an attempt to minimize losses for his or her employer. Although crime claims are emphasized here, several points are applicable to other types of claims.

When a person or business takes out an insurance policy to cover valuables, the insurance agent frequently does not require proof that the valuables exist. But when a claim is filed, the insurer becomes very interested in not only evidence to prove that the valuables were stolen, but also evidence that the valuables in fact existed. Without proof, indemnification may become difficult. To avoid this problem, several steps are useful. First, the insured should prepare an inventory of all valuables. Accounting records and receipts are good sources for the inventory list. The list includes the item name, serial number, date it was purchased, price, and a receipt. Photographs and video of valuables are also useful. Copies should be located in two separate safe places.

After a burglary the policyholder contacts the insurer immediately and also the local police. An insurance representative asks for the policy number, the policyholder's name, and business name and location. A police report ordinarily is required by the insurer; documentation requirements depend on the circumstances and the insurer. Signs of forced entry are usually a burglary policy stipulation.

Bonding Claims

Numerous insurance companies have found the fidelity bond business to be generally unprofitable. To compound the situation, businesspeople have attempted to used fidelity bond claims to cover losses from mysterious disappearance and general inventory shortages, rather than for their intended purpose—coverage for internal theft. For these reasons, when a claim takes place, the insurer and insured have a tendency to enter negotiations as adversaries. The strength of the loss prevention practitioner's case will definitely affect the settlement. Care must be exercised throughout the interaction with the insurer so as not to in any way invalidate the contract. Furthermore, the burden of proof for losses rests entirely on the insured.

Depending on the type of bond, the employee ordinarily completes an application for bonding and undergoes an investigation prior to bonding. Before 1970, the insurer investigated applicants and notified the insured of any criminal history of the applicant that would bar coverage. Because of economy measures and the difficulty of checking into a person's background, a shift has been made by many insurers to the insured for verifying the applicant's past. Bonds stipulate that past dishonesty by the employee justifies an exclusion from bonding from the day the information is discovered. If a loss occurs and the insurer can prove that this information was known to the insured company but not reported to the insurer, the bond is likely to be invalid.

Another way to invalidate a bond is through restitution by the employee to the employer without notifying the insurer. In many cases, the employee is eager to pay back what was stolen initially, but only makes a few payments before absconding. Thereafter, if a claim is made, the bond is useless.

In reference to the burden of proof, the loss prevention practitioner should have considerable expertise when dealing with the insurer on behalf of his or her employer. Confusion often arises from the "exclusionary clause" of the fidelity bond policy. This clause essentially states that the bond does not cover losses that are dependent on proof from inventory records or a profit and loss computation. Prior to 1970, these records were not even allowed to establish the extent of losses even though employees had confessed. But, in the early 1970s, courts began to be more flexible in limiting the exclusionary clause and thus allowing inventory records and associated computations to establish the amount of the loss when independent proof also has been introduced to establish that there has been loss due to employee theft.

A confession is of prime importance to bonding claims. A guilty verdict by a criminal court or a favorable labor arbitration ruling are additional assets for the claimant.

What do you think are the most difficult aspects of a risk manager's job?

Search the Web

Check out the Insurance Services Office (ISO), Inc. (http://www.iso.com/) for a wealth of insurance-related information. This site's *Links for Insurance Research* contains many helpful resources.

The American Risk and Insurance Association is a professional association of insurance and risk management scholars and professionals on the Web at http://www.aria.org/.

The Risk and Insurance Management Society (RIMS) is a professional association for risk managers and corporate buyers of insurance: http://www.rims.org/.

The American Insurance Association (AIA) is a major trade organization of the property and casualty insurance industry: http://www.aiadc.org/.

The International Risk Management Institute is a research and publishing company: http://www.irmi.com/.

FREEADVICE.com is a leading legal site for consumers and businesses. Check out "Insurance Law" and "Accident Law."

The following are some groups that confront insurance fraud issues:

Coalition Against Insurance Fraud: http://www.insurancefraud.org/
International Association of Special Investigation Units: http://www.iasiu.com/
Insurance Committee for Arson Control: http://www.arsoncontrol.org/

CASE PROBLEM

14A. As a loss prevention manager, you will soon explain to top management why they should provide support and funds to initiate a risk management program by hiring a risk manager. You have formulated four areas to answer for top management:

(a) How a risk manager can help to perpetuate the business

(b) Why the hiring of a risk manager would be cost effective

(c) How five risk management tools are applied

(d) How the risk manager and loss prevention manager will work together, and what each will do for the company

THE DECISION FOR "YOU BE THE JUDGE #1"

Hawkins got reimbursed for the stolen tools. The court held that, when Hawkins left his tools in the work area overnight with the knowledge and consent of his employer, his employer accepted temporary custody of the property. This situation is known as a *bailment*, and in such a situation the party accepting custody of the property usually is responsible for its care and safekeeping. Under the laws of the state in which this case was tried, Conway Excavation might have escaped liability for the theft of Hawkins's tools if it had taken more extensive steps to make the garage secure. Instead, it had to pay him some $3,000.

This case is based on *Harper v. Brown & Root* 398 Sa2d 94. The names in this case have been changed to protect the privacy of those involved.

THE DECISION FOR "YOU BE THE JUDGE #2"

The court disagreed with MMC, concluding that, although the policy was complicated and full of errors, it was not ambiguous in spelling out the limits of its liability—$50,000. MMC would have to absorb the rest of the loss itself. Security Director Douglas *could have saved his company a lot of money if he had taken the time to read the insurance policy when it was first issued.* That's the time to ask questions and demand clarification. If you can't understand the policy, find someone who can—the insurance agent or your company's attorney are two of the best people to ask. After the company puts in a claim, it may be too late to clear up the ambiguities.

This case is based on *Davenport Peters v. Royal Globe Ins.*, 490 FSupp 286. The names in this case have been changed to protect the privacy of those involved.

NOTES

1. Stephen Ward, "Exploring the Role of the Corporate Risk Manager," *Risk Management: An International Journal* 3 (2001), pp. 7–25.
2. Robert M. Bieber, "The Making of a Risk Manager-Part One," *Risk Management* (September 1987), pp. 23–30.
3. Luther T. Griffith, "10 Survival Skills for Managing Corporate Risks in the Future," *Risk Management* (January 1989), pp. 16–20.
4. George Rejda, *Principles of Risk Management and Insurance*, 7th ed. (Boston: Addison Wesley, 2001), pp. 64–66.
5. John Conley, "Leaders of the Evolution," *Risk Management* 47 (December 2000), pp. 43–50.
6. Barbara A. Morris, "Risk Takes on the World," *Risk & Insurance* 12 (April 16, 2001), pp. 22–30.
7. Rob Gurwitt, "The Riskiest Business," *Governing* 14 (March 2001), pp. 18–24.
8. *The Fact Book 2000*, "Property/Casualty, Insurance Facts" (New York: Insurance Information Institute, 1999), p. 1.9. Also, *Life Insurance Fact Book 1999* (Washington, D.C.: American Council of Life Insurance, 1999), p. 78.
9. Emmette Vaughan and Therese Vaughan, *Essentials of Risk Management and Insurance*, 2nd ed. (New York: John Wiley & Sons, Inc., 2001), pp. 112–113.
10. Rejda, pp. 266–268.
11. Ibid., pp. 320–325.
12. David Gersh, "Untouchable Value," *iSecurity* (November 2000), p. 20.
13. C. Arthur Williams, Jr., et al. *Risk Management and Insurance*, 7th ed. (New York: McGraw-Hill, 1995), pp. 341–345.
14. Rejda, pp. 268–274.
15. Risk and Insurance Management Society, *2000 RIMS Benchmark Survey* (New York: RIMS, 2000). http://www.rims.org/.
16. Steven Pealstein, "Repricing Risk after Attacks Takes Long-Term Toll," *The Washington Post* (October 7, 2001), p. F1. And, correspondence with Mike Moberly, Southern Illinois University (October 11, 2001).

SPECIALIZED PROBLEMS IN LOSS PREVENTION

15

Retail Loss Prevention

OBJECTIVES

After studying this chapter the reader will be able to:

1. Discuss the problem of shrinkage.
2. List human resources problems in retailing and countermeasures.
3. List and explain at least four internal loss prevention strategies for retailers.
4. List the types of losses at checkout counters and countermeasures.
5. Explain the credit card fraud confronting e-businesses and countermeasures.
6. Discuss the shoplifting problem and countermeasures.
7. Elaborate on robbery and burglary countermeasures.

Numerous factors can be attributed to an unsuccessful retail business. Poor management, unwise store location, noncompetitive marketing (selling) techniques, and consumer dissatisfaction with merchandise can all hinder profits.

Another important factor that can make or break a retail business is the quality of the loss prevention program. With a very small profit margin in many retail businesses, loss prevention is a necessity for survival. Vulnerability to employee theft, shoplifting, burglary, robbery, fire, and poor safety can cause extensive losses.

SHRINKAGE

The term *shrinkage* is used by retailers to mean inventory losses from internal theft, shoplifting, damage, and paperwork errors. In retail businesses, guidelines are often in place to hold managers of stores, departments, and loss prevention responsible for shrinkage. When shrinkage becomes a measurable objective in annual reviews and bonus programs, an increased commitment to loss prevention can be expected.[1] And, the reality of retailing is that those who fail to meet shrinkage goals are likely to be dismissed.[2]

Consequently, shrinkage must be kept as low as possible; it is gauged after an inventory and an accurate inventory is vital.[3]

The University of Florida, noted for its *National Retail Security Survey,* found that in 1999 loss prevention executives attributed shrinkage to the following sources: 48 percent to employee theft, 34 percent to shoplifting, 18 percent to paperwork errors, and 6 percent to vendor fraud. This research also showed that the level of employee theft was the highest ever reported in the seven years this survey has been conducted. The top five categories of items stolen were (1) books and magazines; (2) cards, gifts, and novelties; (3) toys and hobbies; (4) jewelry; and (5) recorded music and videos. Average costs per incident were $212 per shoplifting incident; $1,058 per employee theft; $8,020 per armed robbery; and $8,340 per burglary.[4]

Human Resources Problems in Retailing

Because retail loss prevention is highly dependent on the efforts of all employees, it is important to discuss the realities of human resources problems in retailing:

1. Many part-time or temporary employees
2. Inexperienced workers (e.g., usually young people at their first jobs)
3. Employees dissatisfied with working conditions (e.g., low wages and long hours)
4. High rate of turnover

Loss can become a by-product of each of these personnel factors. For instance, some part-time employees may be working during holiday seasons to make extra money and also may be stealing to support gift expenses. An inexperienced worker may unknowingly undercharge customers for merchandise. A dissatisfied employee may perform a variety of vindictive activities. A high rate of turnover creates additional training expenses and, moreover, many inexperienced employees. These problems, coupled with poor performance, are especially troublesome to retailers because such employees are in direct contact with customers and this can have a negative impact on sales and customer loyalty.[5]

Losses caused by part-time or temporary workers can be reduced by cost-effective screening, adequate socialization, and good methods for accountability of inventory. Another possible measure would be to assign part-time and temporary workers to be supervised by and work with regular employees. Additionally, these types of workers could be barred from performing certain tasks and entering specific areas.

Although the potential exists for losses from part-time and temporary employees, potential losses from full-time regular employees must not be underestimated.

Screening

The quality of job applicant screening is dependent on numerous factors. In a small store, the owner may interview the applicant; record pertinent information, such as the address, telephone number, and social security number; and ask for a few references. In large multistore organizations, however, employment procedures commonly are more structured and controlled.

The *National Retail Security Survey* found that more than half of respondents verify past employment, check for criminal records, contact personal references, look into credit histories, and conduct multiple interviews of applicants. Over a third verify education, check driving history, screen for drugs, and give honesty tests.[6]

Socialization

Various training programs can be instituted to assist in adequately socializing an employee toward business objectives. Training can reduce employee mistakes, raise productivity, create customer satisfaction, and reduce turnover. A loss prevention training program can reinforce attitudes that result in decreased losses.

The *National Retail Security Survey* showed that an average of 6.8 different loss prevention awareness programs were being used by each retailer. These programs included discussions during orientation, bulletin boards and posters, anonymous telephone hotlines, codes of conduct, videos, newsletters, and honesty incentives.[7]

Some retail businesses require employees to sign a statement that they understand the loss prevention program. This procedure reinforces loss prevention programming. Furthermore, as models of appropriate work attitudes and behavior, executives should *set a good example* and *practice what is preached.*

INTERNAL LOSS PREVENTION STRATEGIES

Theft is a major factor in internal losses. There are numerous targets for internal theft: merchandise, damaged items, cash, repair service, office supplies and tools, parts, time, samples for customers, food and beverages, and personal property.

Although internal theft is a major part of the internal loss problem, there are other categories of internal losses:

1. Accidents
2. Fire
3. Unproductive employees
4. Unintentional and intentional mistakes
5. Excessive absenteeism and lateness

Here are strategies used by companies to address the problem of internal loss:

- *Motivation, morale, and rewards.* Attempts must be made by management to help employees feel as if they are an integral part of the business organization. Praise for an employee's accomplishment can go a long way in improving morale. Other methods of increasing morale and motivation are clean working conditions, participative management, and a company sports team. Contest and reward programs also reinforce improved morale and motivation. The employee with the best loss prevention idea of the month could be rewarded with $50 and recognition in a company newspaper.
- *Employee discounts.* Employee discounts usually range between 15 and 25 percent. An identification card is often issued so employees can shop at various branches of a large retail chain. These discounts are an obvious benefit to employee morale even though the discount is sometimes abused by purchases for relatives and friends.
- *Shopping service.* A *shopping service* is a business that assists retail loss prevention efforts by supplying investigators who pose as customers to test cashiers and other retail employees for honesty, accuracy, and demeanor. One common test of salesclerks involves two shoppers who enter a store separately, acting as customers. One buys an item, pays for it with the exact amount of money needed, and leaves, while the second shopper, pretending to be a customer, observes whether the salesclerk rings up the sale or pockets the money. Theft of cash is not the only source of loss; revenues are lost because of the curt or even abrasive behavior of some sales personnel.
- *Undercover investigations.* Investigations can be used as a last resort when other controls fail. By penetrating employee informal organizations, investigators are able to obtain considerable information that may expose collusion and weaknesses in controls.
- *Insurance.* Some retailers rely solely on insurance as a bulwark against losses. This is a mistake. Insurance should be an integral part of a comprehensive loss prevention program. Loss prevention procedures, policies, services, and devices are primary measures that are backed up by insurance on failure.

How can e-mail and the Internet be applied to retail loss prevention challenges?

Preventing Losses at the Checkout Counter

Checkout counters are also called point-of-sale (POS) areas and point-of-purchase (POP) areas. These locations in a retail business accommodate customer payments, refunds, and service. Although most cashiers are honest and bar codes and scanning technology prevent losses, the following activities hinder profits:

1. Stealing money from the register
2. Failing to punch in the sale and then stealing the money (this is especially tempting when no customer change is required)
3. Failing to punch in the sale, leaving the cash register drawer open for the customer's change, and then stealing the money
4. Overcharging customers, keeping a mental record, and stealing the money at a later time
5. Presenting the customer with the wrong change
6. Accepting bad checks, bad charge cards, and counterfeit money
7. Making pricing mistakes
8. Undercharging for relatives and friends
9. Failing to notice an altered price tag
10. Failing to notice shoplifted items secreted in legitimate purchases

Cashier Socialization of Procedures

The quality of training will have a direct bearing on accountability at cash registers. Procedural training can include, but is not limited to, the following:

1. Assign each cashier to a particular register.
2. Have each transaction recorded separately and the cash drawer closed afterward.
3. Establish a system for giving receipts to customers.
4. Train cashiers to meticulously count change.
5. Show cashiers how to spot irregularities (e.g., altered price tags).
6. Encourage cashiers to seek supervision when appropriate (e.g., to check price of item, question about customer credit).

Accountability of Voids

Voids are used to eradicate and record mistakes by cashiers at cash registers. Theft occurs when, for instance, a cashier voids a legitimate no-mistake sale and pockets the money. Fraudulent voids can be prevented by limiting void keys to supervisors who must sign and complete a short void form. Appropriate records can provide feedback to cashiers with excessive voids. Technological changes have altered methods of completing voids and auditing them.

Point-of-Sale Accounting Systems

Retailers are increasingly making use of point-of-sale (POS) accounting systems and bar-code technology to produce vital business information. Merchandise contains a bar code that is read by a scanner during inventory or at the checkout counters. This stored information provides a perpetual inventory, helpful in ascertaining what is in stock and in assisting with recorders of merchandise. In addition to shrinkage figures, POS systems can also be designed to produce a variety of loss prevention reports, exposing cashiers who repeatedly have cash shortages, voids, bad checks, and so forth. Ratios are also helpful to spot losses. Examples include cash to charge sales and sales to refunds.[8]

CCTV

CCTV can be integrated with POS systems to give a loss prevention practitioner an opportunity to view a cash register total and compare it with the merchandise sold. System capabilities enable the register total to appear on the TV monitor with the date and time. Furthermore, "exceptions" (e.g., voids) noted by the POS system can also trigger CCTV and a recording for later reference. Certain retailers are recording every transaction on every register.[9] Figure 15-1 shows a remote monitoring system.

The Internet is enhancing the capabilities of CCTV systems. At one retail store chain, the plan is to keep an eye on widely dispersed stores, avoid the expense of a central station, and reduce time and travel costs of loss prevention personnel. The installed system permits real-time video through the Internet from a PC or laptop. Video is accessed through a secure, password-protected Web site. The digital video is archived on a secure server at a remote location without the need for loss prevention personnel to maintain files or backup tapes. Optional features helped to sell the system to senior executives. Examples are customer traffic counting, time and attendance of employees, and the transmission of in-house commercials to store TV screens. CCTV cameras are placed at front and back doors, the POS, and the back hallway. The cameras at the doors are linked to contact alarms so that each time a door is opened, loss prevention personnel receive an e-mail. In one case a manager was caught improperly opening a back door by not following strict procedures. The manager was called on the telephone immediately for corrective action. Eventually, this retail chain will have one central data gathering system for security and administrative information.[10]

Refunds and Repair Service

Losses may be sustained by the retailer during refund and repair service activities. Such losses can be attributed to activities of employees, customers, or both.

Figure 15–1   Remote monitoring system. Courtesy: TeleSite USA, Inc.

In loosely controlled businesses, employees have an opportunity to retain a customer receipt (or hope that the customer leaves one) and use it to substantiate a fraudulent customer refund (merchandise supposedly returned for money). With the receipt used to support the phony refund slip, the employee is "covered" and can pocket the cash.

Especially bold offenders might enter a store, pick up an item, and then go directly to the refund desk and demand a cash refund without a receipt. Another ploy is to use a stolen credit card to purchase merchandise and then obtain a refund at another branch store. In other instances, collusion may take place between employees and customers. Employees simply issue refunds to family and friends.

Refund fraud is minimized through well-controlled supervision and accountability. A supervisor should account for returned merchandise before it is returned to the sales floor and sign and date the sales receipt after writing *refund*. Some retailers guarantee money (e.g., $5) to customers if the customer does not receive a receipt.

Losses involving repair services for customers can also drain profits. Employees sometimes fix their own items using company time and parts.

Repair employees have been known to steal all the parts necessary to construct an entire product.

Loss from repair operations is prevented via supervision of repair work orders. Close accountability for parts is also essential.

International Perspective: Refund Fraud in Australia[11]

The refund fraud problem in Australia provides an illustration of how a few universally applied preventive procedures can reduce this growing multi-million-dollar problem in that country. "Unfortunately, most retail outlets are their own worst enemy; their refund policies are so weak, outdated and customer friendly that they cater [to] the criminal." This crime is easy money and such a soft target that it brings a wide range of types of offenders: major and minor criminals, drug addicts, the unemployed, and first offenders. Basically, the offender lies about the origin of the property to obtain cash or other property. The majority of the items result from shoplifting or other forms of theft. Bold offenders are confident enough to walk out of a retail store with an exposed item as if they just paid for it. Teams of offenders rely on busy, overworked staff members to distract during their crimes. More sophisticated offenders use copiers, computers, and printers to create receipts or duplicate bar codes to purchase items at a lower price. To deal with this problem, and other retail crimes, almost every large police department in Australia has a retail crime unit. The refund fraud problem will not be eliminated, but, as in the United States, a few simple procedures will reduce it: proof of purchase, identification of the customer, and a refund form to record information.

Bad Checks and Credit Card Losses

Because of technological innovation and an aim toward expediency, *debit card* transactions are gaining momentum. This system operates with the assistance of a centralized computer, which contains individual financial records. When a customer purchases merchandise, the cost is fed into a computer (via a terminal at the store) and payment is transferred from the customer's account (savings) to the store's account. *Chip cards* are also being introduced, which is a migration from magnetic stripe credit cards. Chip cards contain a tiny computer enabling several features, such as being loaded with money in advance. Because these systems will require additional years before dominating retail transactions, millions of customers will continue to make purchases with personal checks. Therefore, personal checks and a variety of other types of checks will continue to be a source of losses for retailers.

Checks: Types and Irregularities

Checks are categorized by the Small Business Administration as follows:[12]

1. *Personal check.* Issued as a blank form by banks, the personal check is written and signed by the person offering it. Most of the time, a bad personal check happens when the check is not backed up by sufficient funds. Usually, customer negligence in personal bookkeeping causes this problem; the situation is often quickly rectified. Some customers knowingly write bad personal checks. At other times, lost or stolen personal checks are used, or bad checks are written on accounts that are either closed or never existed.

2. *Two-party check.* A two-party check is issued by one person to a second person, who endorses it so that it may be cashed by a third person. This kind is most susceptible to fraud because the maker (the first party) can stop payment at the bank.

3. *Payroll check.* An employer issues a check to an employee for services performed. Sometimes offenders pick a business at random or establish a phony company and print bogus payroll checks. An attempt is made to cash them with merchants who, if they called the "company" for verification, would be reassured that the person presenting the check is an employee.

4. *Government check.* Issued by many agencies of the government, these checks cover salaries, tax refunds, benefits, and so on. Government checks frequently are stolen from mailboxes and signatures forged for endorsement.

5. *Traveler's check.* Traveler's checks are sold with a preprinted amount to travelers who do not want to carry large amounts of cash. The traveler signs the checks at the time of purchase and should countersign them only in the presence of the person who cashes them. Offenders often forge the countersignature on stolen or lost traveler's checks.

6. *Money order.* A money order, usually bought to send in the mail, can be passed as a check. Most stores should not accept money orders in face-to-face transactions.

A check is nothing more than a piece of paper until the money is collected. It may be worthless. Characteristics of bad checks include an inappropriate date, written figures that differ from numeric figures on the same check, and smeared ink. Of about 61 billion checks written each year, about 1.3 million are fraudulent. The FBI estimates losses at $12 to $15 billion to businesses each year.[13] The problem is growing worse because of computers, desktop publishing, check-writing software, newer color copier machines, scanners, and laser printers.

Prevention of Bad Checks

Among the kinds of checks just described, personal checks create the greatest problem for retailers. Several methods can be used to reduce the problem. One method is for the retailer to refrain from accepting checks. This approach would eliminate the problem, but customer convenience will suffer and sales will be lost. More practical alternatives, which are prevention oriented, follow.

- *Policies, procedures, and training.* When employees know what is expected of them, they can act to cut losses. Guidelines include carefully examining checks, not accepting checks over a certain amount, seeking supervisory approval for checks written over a certain amount, prohibiting checks from out of state, and never providing cash for a check.
- *Proper identification.* Proper identification is a key factor in reducing the bad check problem. Retail employees should scrutinize customer identification for irregularities. Many employees look at identification cards but do not see irregularities. *Concentration is necessary to match (or not to match) the customer with the identification presented.* Many retailers require two types of identification before a check is accepted. A driver's license, vehicle registration, or credit card is usually acceptable. Many other types of identification (e.g., social security cards, birth certificates, insurance cards) are easier to obtain, forge, and hold for a period of time without detection.
- *Malfunctions in the identification system.* No identification system is totally foolproof. For instance, an offender may steal a person's identity by searching through a victim's trash or by obtaining information from the Web.
- *Records.* Careful record keeping is a practical measure to reduce bad checks. A system of recording the names of customers who have passed bad checks and a record of employees who accept many bad checks is advisable. Retailers often have systems listing customers who regularly cash checks. When a customer cashes the first check, appropriate information is entered into the system. Thereafter, customer convenience is facilitated. Referrals are made to this system when needed.
- *Check clearing service.* Online check clearing services maintain a database of customers who pass bad checks. Retailers subscribe to such a service to make decisions on whether to accept checks from customers. These services also cover checks that bounce even though the service cleared the customer, provided the retailer followed guidelines established by the service.
- *Photo identification and fingerprint systems.* A photo ID system records a picture of the check passer, the check, and the identification presented. The customer simply stands in front of the camera at the checkout. These pictures have been used to prosecute persons passing bad checks. The photo identification system primarily is a deterrent. A retailer should analyze the cost versus benefits of such a system in light of losses due to bad checks. The system can be costly and ineffective. One retail store had a wall in the loss prevention office that was

completely covered with photos of bad-check passers. The number of photos was in the hundreds, which made identification difficult. Another strategy requires the customer's fingerprint. Shoppers who cash checks are asked to leave an inkless fingerprint on a sticker attached to the check. If a check for a large amount bounces because it was stolen or forged, police can use the fingerprint to catch the offender by running it through the FBI's computer system.

- *CCTV.* This is a deterrent and source of evidence. Customers should be made aware of recordings via exposed cameras or signs.

Recovery from Bad Checks

A retailer's recovery from a bad check depends on the circumstances. Many times a customer with bad record-keeping practices will quickly cover the bad check after being notified. If difficulties arise for the retailer, alternative action may be necessary with the assistance of the justice system. Procedures depend on the state. Usually, a retailer must send the check writer a registered letter requiring payment within 5 to 15 days. If the letter is not effective, the retailer can sign a warrant against the person who wrote the bad check.

In one jurisdiction, a "bad-check brigade" was formed. A magistrate coordinates the warrants, which are distributed to constables (part-time law enforcers) who are paid for each warrant served. Each week the brigade takes numerous offenders to jail. Retailers should check with public police about local practices. Some jurisdictions require collection through civil procedures. Another strategy, especially for large retailers, is to contract collection work to specialized firms.

If a retailer receives a check returned from a bank stating that there is "no account" or "account closed," then fraud may have been perpetuated. The police should be notified. An altered or forged U.S. government check should be reported to the U.S. Secret Service.

Credit

Credit is basically a method used to increase sales volume. This strategy may fail, however, and a loss will be sustained on customer nonpayment.

Several kinds of credit are used by retailers. *Open account credit* allows a customer to receive items and pay at a later date. *Installment credit* permits customers to spread payments over a long period of time. *Revolving credit* allows a customer to purchase items up to a specified limit. This line of credit remains open as long as the limit is not exceeded. Monthly payments depend on the unpaid balance. Many large retailers issue their own credit cards to customers.

Because of the popularity of Visa and MasterCard, few retailers are refraining from participating in this type of bank-issued credit. Retailers may choose to use their own credit program and credit cards in addition to bank credit cards.

Three major groups are involved in credit card usage: *card issuers* (banks, oil companies, retail businesses, travel, and entertainment groups), *acceptors* (merchants), and *users*. All of these groups are susceptible to losses due to fraud. Lost or stolen cards can cause monetary loss to users. Acceptors who are careless may become financially responsible for fraud under certain circumstances and could even be placed at a competitive disadvantage if no longer authorized to accept the issuer's card.

Crime involving credit cards is varied. The theft of credit cards from the postal system, for example, creates enormous losses. Bank card fraud includes illegal counterfeiting of Visas and MasterCards. New technology has aided offenders in producing, from scratch, exact replicas of existing cards with security features. The next generation of cards, "smart cards," will contain computer chips to store more information on the holder, and a PIN will be required. Naturally, as today and throughout history, offenders will follow technological changes in an effort to defeat security.[14]

Techniques to counter a multitude of criminal methods against issuers, acceptors, and users of credit cards involve lengthy training. The following information emphasizes acceptor (retailer) preventive measures.

Acceptors are wise to check credit cards for the following characteristics:

1. The card has expired or is not yet valid.
2. Alteration of the card is obvious.
3. Signatures on the card and charge slip are significantly different.

Of particular importance for the retailer is to ensure that credit cards are subject to electronic authorization (swiped through the magnetic reader). This helps to ensure that accounts are valid and purchases are within credit limits.

E-Business

Mail-order, phone-order, and e-businesses (using Internet-based technologies) are particularly vulnerable to fraud because the customer and the credit card are not present for the transaction. Offenders obtain card numbers from many sources (e.g., discarded credit card receipts, stealing customer information in the workplace, and hacking into a business), establish a mail drop, and then place fraudulent orders.

E-businesses use the Internet to sell globally; this great opportunity also attracts offenders. In one case the owner of a computer parts company in New Jersey became concerned when he received a $15,000 order from Bucharest, Romania. The owner tried to contact the credit card authorization company and the bank that works with the processing company to verify the credit cards. However, they were not able to assist, so the owner telephoned the customer and had him fax his Romanian driver's license and other documents to the owner. The owner then shipped the parts via UPS at about the same time the bank became suspicious and called the owner to say that all the cards used in the order were fraudulent. The owner was lucky when the shipment was intercepted in Bucharest.

Other complaints abound of such fraud and the inability of card issuers to assist. E-business owners argue that "there is no financial incentive for the banks and credit card companies to do anything about the problem because it is the merchant who, in virtually all cases, ultimately bears the cost of fraudulent Internet purchases." Disinterest by law enforcement is another concern because personnel and resources are limited.

In another case, an e-business owner in the United States telephoned Canadian police and told them about an individual, living a few miles from the police station, who was attempting to commit credit card fraud against the e-business owner. The police response was that nothing could be done until the e-business owner flew to Canada and posted a $10,000 bond to guarantee a court appearance to testify.[15] Loss prevention and investigation are obviously major necessities to survive in the world of e-business. Many businesses contract fraud screening to outside firms as seen on the Internet. (Conduct a search by typing "credit card fraud.")

Counterfeiting

Counterfeiting is the unlawful duplication of something valuable to deceive. Counterfeit items can include money, coupons, credit cards, clothes, and jewelry. Here, the emphasis is counterfeit money. This federal offense is investigated by the U.S. Secret Service, a branch of the U.S. Treasury Department.

Persons who recognize that they have counterfeit money will not be reimbursed when they give it to the Secret Service. Because of this potential loss, many people knowingly pass the bogus money to others. The extended chain of custody from the counterfeiter to authorities causes great difficulty during investigations.

Counterfeiting is a growing problem because of the newer color copier machines, scanners, computers, and laser printers that are in widespread use. The U.S. government has countered the problem through a security thread embedded in the paper running vertically to the left of the Federal Reserve seal on all notes above $1. Microprinting also appears on the rim of the portrait.

The best method to reduce this type of loss is through the ability to recognize counterfeit money, and an excellent way to do this is by comparing a suspect bill with a genuine bill. One should look for the red and blue fibers that are scattered throughout a genuine bill. These fibers are curved, about

1/4 inch long, hair thin, and difficult to produce on bogus bills. Also, look for the security thread and microprinting. Another technique is to watch for $1 bills that have counterfeit higher denomination numbers glued over the lower denomination numbers. Also, compare suspect coins with genuine coins.

> What do you think is the most serious vulnerability at the checkout counters? Support your answer and include countermeasures.

SHOPLIFTING

Shoplifting is a multibillion-dollar problem. To deal with this serious problem, loss prevention practitioners should have an understanding of the kinds of shoplifters, motivational factors, shoplifting techniques, and countermeasures.

Kinds of Shoplifters: Understanding Motivational Factors

Amateur

The amateur shoplifter, also referred to as a *snitch*, represents the majority of shoplifters. This person generally steals on impulse while often possessing the money to pay for the item. Individuals in this category represent numerous demographic variables (e.g., sex, age, social class, ethnicity, and race). The distinguishing difference between the amateur and the professional thief is that the former shoplifts for personal use, whereas the latter shoplifts to sell the goods for a profit.

Juvenile or Student

Generally, juveniles take merchandise that they can use, such as clothing and recreational items. Frequently working in groups, their action is often motivated by peer pressure or a search for excitement.

Easy-Access Shoplifter

The easy-access shoplifter is neither a retail company employee nor a customer. Because of their work, they have easy access to retail merchandise and are familiar with basic retail operations and loss prevention programs. Delivery personnel, salespeople, repair personnel, and public inspectors make up this category. Even public police and fire personnel have been known to represent this group, especially during emergency situations. The motivation is obvious: to get something for nothing. The extent of this problem is difficult to ascertain, but it does contribute to the shoplifting problem.

Drunk or Vagrant

Fairly easy to detect, the drunk or vagrant shoplifter usually shoplifts liquor, food, and clothing for personal use or shoplifts other merchandise to sell for cash. These persons often are under the influence of alcohol and have a previous alcohol-related arrest record.

Addict

The addict shoplifter is extremely dangerous because of the illegal drug dependence problem and accompanying desperation. This person generally peddles stolen loot to a "fence," who pays less than one-third the value of the merchandise. The addict may also "grab and run."

Professional

The professional or "booster" accounts for a small percentage of those caught shoplifting. (This low figure could be the result of the professional's skill in avoiding apprehension.) The motive is profit or resale through the shoplifting of watches, rings, cameras, electronic gear, clothing, and other expensive items. The professional may utilize a *booster box* (a box that looks wrapped and tied, but really contains a secret entrance), hooks on inside clothing, or extra long pockets. A criminal record is typical, as are ties to the underworld organization (e.g., fences) that will supply bail money and attorney assistance.

Kleptomaniac

Kleptomania is a rare, persistent, neurotic impulse to steal. The kleptomaniac usually shoplifts without considering the value or personal use of the item, and seemingly wants to get caught. This type of shoplifter usually has a criminal record from previous apprehensions and may have been caught several times at the same retail store. According to one observer, "The criminal prosecution of a kleptomaniac may present the district attorney with a problem when it becomes necessary to rebut the defense of insanity. Moreover, it appears that kleptomaniacs as a group are the least likely to be deterred by criminal prosecution."[16] Another relates, "One man, whose wife had such a compulsion, made an arrangement with the stores frequented by his wife, whereby they would send him the bills for the things that his wife took."[17]

Shoplifting Techniques

The following list presents only a few of the many shoplifting techniques:

1. Shoplifters may work alone or in a group.
2. A person may simply shoplift an item and conceal it in his or her clothing.
3. A person may "palm" a small item and conceal it in a glove.
4. Shoplifters often go into a fitting room with several garments and either conceal an item or wear it and leave the store.
5. An offender may ask to see more items than a clerk can control or send the clerk to the stockroom for other items; while the counter is unattended, items are stolen.
6. A self-service counter can provide an opportunity for a shoplifter to pull out and examine several items while returning only half of them.
7. Merchandise often is taken to a deserted location (e.g., restroom, elevator, stockroom, janitor's supply room, and so on) and then concealed.
8. A shoplifter may simply grab an item and quickly leave the store.
9. A shoplifter may drop an expensive piece of jewelry into a drink or food.
10. Shoplifters arrive at a store early or late to take advantage of any lax situation.
11. Offenders have been known to pick up an item and walk directly to a salesperson to try to get a refund without a receipt.
12. Disguised as a priest (or other professional), the shoplifter may have an advantage when stealing.
13. Some bold offenders have been known to impersonate salespeople while shoplifting and even to collect money from customers.
14. Price tags are often switched to allow merchandise to be bought at a lower price; sometimes the desired price will be written on the price tag.
15. Shoplifters are aided by large shopping bags, lunch boxes, knitting bags, suitcases, flight bags, camera cases, musical instrument cases, and newspapers.
16. Dummy packages, bags, or boxes ("booster box") are used, which appear to be sealed and tied but contain false bottoms and openings to conceal items.
17. Hollowed-out books are used by shoplifters.
18. Stolen merchandise is often concealed within legitimate purchases.
19. Expensive items are placed in inexpensive containers.
20. Shoplifters sometimes slide items off counters and into some type of container or clothing.
21. Sometimes shoplifters wear fake bandages or false plastic casts.
22. Professional shoplifters are known to carry store supplies (e.g., bag, box, stapler, price tickets, or colored tape) to assist in stealing.
23. A shoplifter may remove a staple and receipt from the bag of a recent purchase, open the bag, deposit stolen items, and then reseal the bag with the receipt.
24. Baby carriages and wheelchairs have been utilized in various ways to steal.

25. Shoplifters sometimes wear oversized clothing, clothing with hooks or special belts on the inside, large pockets, socks with pockets, or slit pockets that permit access to inner clothing.
26. Sometimes items are hidden in a store for subsequent pickup by an accomplice.
27. Various contrived diversions (e.g., appearing to be drunk, dropping and breaking an item, faking a heart attack, fainting, choking, pretending to have an epileptic seizure or labor pains, setting a fire or smoke bomb, breaking a glass, or having someone call in a bomb threat) have been used to give an accomplice a chance to shoplift.
28. Teenagers sometimes converge on a particular retail department, cause a disturbance, and then shoplift.
29. Adult shoplifters have been known to use children to aid them.
30. Sometimes "blind" accomplices with "guide" dogs are used to distract and confuse sales personnel eager to assist the disadvantaged.
31. "Crotchwalking" is a method whereby a woman wearing a dress conceals an item between her legs and then departs.

Prevention and Reduction of Shoplifting through People

People are the first and primary asset for reducing shoplifting opportunities. The proper utilization of people is the test of success or failure in preventing shoplifting. Management, salespeople, store detectives, uniformed officers, and fitting-room personnel can all provide assistance. *Good training is very important.*

- *Management.* Management has the responsibility for planning, implementing, and monitoring anti-shoplifting programs. The quality of leadership and the ability to motivate people are of paramount importance. The loss prevention manager and other retail executives must cooperate when formulating policies and procedures that do not hamper sales.
- *Salespeople.* An anti-shoplifting program increases a shoplifter's anxiety. One method to accomplish this is by having salespeople approach all customers and say, for instance, "May I help you?" This approach informs the potential shoplifter that he or she has been noticed by salespeople and possibly by loss prevention personnel. Obviously, the anxiety level will be raised. Sometimes salespeople annoy honest customers by hounding them with persistent offers of assistance. This can hinder sales. A moderate approach is appropriate. For those who have been store detectives, there are few activities as annoying as a salesperson who unknowingly interferes with a potential apprehension of a shoplifter. To avoid this problem, policies and procedures must be formulated and communicated to appropriate employees. One solution

may be to have the store detective signal salespeople, for example, by carrying a certain colored bag. The colored bag would signify to salespeople that they should ignore the potential shoplifter.

- *Store detectives. A good store detective must have the ability to observe without being observed, remember precisely what happened during the offense, know criminal law and self-defense, effectively interview, testify in court, and recover stolen items.* Store detectives must blend in with the shopping crowd and look like shoppers. This can be done by dressing like the average shopper, carrying a package or two and even a bag of popcorn. The detective can also wear a pair of special glasses with small mirrors on the sides the facilitate seeing behind. The antiquated term "floor walker" for *store detective* should be limited to historical discussions. This will help to professionalize the image of this important role in loss prevention.

- *Uniformed officers.* The differences between a uniformed officer and a store detective are obvious. Store detectives usually covertly watch and finally apprehend shoplifters. Officers, on the other hand, watch shoppers in an overt manner, and only a foolish shoplifter would steal in the presence of an officer. The physical presence of an officer, for example, at a doorway to a store, will remind shoppers of the presence of a loss prevention program, increase the anxiety of a potential shoplifter, and thus deter shoplifting. A well-planned anti-shoplifting program must not lose sight of the systems approach to loss prevention. As one writer reports:

> The store had four security guards or personnel. These people were also looked upon as "jokes." The security personnel were primarily concerned with catching shoplifting customers. Most of their time was spent behind two-way mirrors with binoculars observing shoppers. So in reality while the security personnel caught a customer concealing a pair of pants in her purse, an employee was smuggling four pairs of Levi's out the front door. Security was concerned with shoppers on the floor while all employee thefts usually occurred in stockrooms.[18]

- *Fitting-room personnel.* Employees who supervise merchandise passing in and out of fitting rooms play a vital role in reducing the shoplifting problem. Many stores place a limit on the number of items that can be brought into a fitting room.

Training

Employees must realize the economic impact of shoplifting and other crimes. They must understand that, if crime is not prevented, the retail store may go out of business and jobs will be lost. Thus, everyone should play a role in reducing the crime problem.

At frequent training sessions, employees should become familiar with various crimes such as shoplifting and associated techniques. A knowledge of basic criminal law may help to avert lawsuits. Training sessions can include discussions of company policies and procedures. Simulated shoplifting incidents can give employees an opportunity to make mistakes and learn. Shoplifting equipment (e.g., booster box, specially designed clothing with hooks) can be demonstrated. A store newsletter can be used as an additional educational tool.

Allocation of Personnel

Research results have produced a mixture of times and locations when there appeared to be a high incidence of shoplifting in retail stores. Holiday seasons show an increase in shoplifting. Each retail store is unique, so loss prevention managers should determine the times and locations when shoplifting is most prevalent. With such research results, a more efficient allocation of personnel is possible. Because the research results probably will be based on analyzing apprehensions, these statistics must be used cautiously. There is the possibility that another time and location may represent the true extent of shoplifting, but this information may not be attainable because of the absence of apprehensions.

Reward Program

A reward program can effectively motivate employees into assisting retail stores in countering shoplifting. Research results have shown that many customers are heavily absorbed in their shopping activities and do not notice many shoplifting incidents. Customers who do witness shoplifters stealing may not report the offense to retail employees because of fear of a counter suit and court appearance. The cost benefit is minimal for customer reporting of shoplifting.

Retail personnel, especially salespeople, must receive increased cost benefits for reporting shoplifters. Reward programs could include, for instance, a gift certificate worth 50 percent of the item shoplifted. (These programs can also be used to reduce employee theft.)

Managers must carefully plan a reward program to minimize adverse consequences such as excessive complaints, false charges, and conflicts with public police agencies. A multistore retail company can institute an experimental reward program at one store to study the advantages and disadvantages of various plans.

Community Education Programs

Community education programs include media campaigns and discussions at educational institutions. These programs are especially important because many students have underestimated the economic consequences (e.g., higher prices) and seriousness of shoplifting.

Prevention and Reduction of Shoplifting through Devices

Devices are the second major asset of an effective anti-shoplifting program. However, *devices are only as good as the people operating them.* A retail company can spend millions of dollars on anti-shoplifting devices, but if personnel are not knowledgeable about the maintenance, operation, limitations, and advantages of these devices, then their usefulness will be stymied.

Physical Design

Physical design includes architectural design and store layout (e.g., merchandise displays). Three objectives of physical design are to create an environment that stimulates sales, and for the purposes of this text, to comply with the ADA and to create crime prevention through environmental design (CPTED), as covered earlier in the text. The ADA requires the removal of barriers that hinder the disabled. An example of CPTED is increased visibility of customers by retail personnel by designing an employee lounge that is raised above the sales floor and has a large glass window. Also, POS locations that are raised a few inches increase visibility.

A balance between attractiveness and loss prevention is essential. Counters containing merchandise should be set up to let employees at the POS observe activities down the aisles. Adequate lighting is essential. Merchandise or other store features that obstruct the view of employees will aid shoplifters. Eight-foot paneling, for example, would be more appropriate along the store's perimeter walls.

The proper utilization of turnstiles, corrals, and other barriers can limit the circulation of shoplifters and funnel customer traffic to select locations (e.g., toward the POS). Usable exits can be limited, and restrooms locked so that customers need to ask for the restroom key.

Other methods to hinder theft include locking display cabinets, displaying only one of a pair, using dummy displays (e.g., empty cosmetic boxes), arranging displays neatly and in a particular pattern to allow for quick recognition of a disruption in their order, having hangers pointing in alternate directions on racks to prevent "grab and run" tactics, and placing small items closer to cash registers.

Electronic Article Surveillance

The electronic article surveillance (EAS) system is an innovative and effective method of thwarting shoplifting and employee theft. This device watches merchandise instead of people. Generally, electronic tags are placed on merchandise and removed by a salesperson when appropriate. If a person leaves a designated area with the tagged merchandise, a sensor at an exit activates an alarm.

This device has been on the market since the late 1960s. Because these plastic tags tended to be large (about 3 or 4 inches) and difficult to attach to many goods, they were used on high-priced merchandise such as coats.

However, improved technology has permitted manufacturers to develop devices the size of price tags, at a lower cost. The newer device is small, with an adhesive back to allow it to stick to merchandise. Several new types include low-cost (pennies) disposable labels and higher-cost ($1 to $2) reusable tags.

Two major kinds of EAS are covered next. The *radio frequency* type contains a tiny circuit that can be hidden virtually anywhere on a product or in packaging. If the cashier does not remove or deactivate it (which can be done automatically as items are scanned for prices at the POS) and the customer walks between a radio transmitter and a sensor, then the circuit picks up the signal and an alarm is triggered. Its weaknesses are that shoplifters can cover the labels with aluminum foil and that the tags cannot be used on metal objects. At the refund desk a verifier can be used to check for "live" tags that may indicate that an item was not purchased legitimately. A second kind, *electromagnetic*, employs a metal strip (called an EM strip) that interferes with a magnetic field at an exit. A unique feature of the EM strip is that it can be reactivated, which makes this system especially suitable for libraries.[19]

Each company contends that its system is best. None is without problems nor is any foolproof. False alarms or failure of the cashier to deactivate or remove the tag has led to retailers being sued for false arrest. Another problem results from employees who carry an EAS tag on their person and activate the system as a pretext to stop and search suspicious customers. High-quality training and caution and politeness when approaching customers will prevent litigation. Many state that the bigger problem of employee theft is not alleviated by EAS. Others view the tags and labels as too expensive to be justified as both price tags and EAS for low-cost merchandise. Many tag only high-shrinkage items. Despite these disadvantages plus initial costs and maintenance, this device can be cost effective and is popular. In fact, such systems are being used in certain industries to watch inventories. Prisoners and patients also are being monitored with such technology.

Innovations have further enhanced EAS technology. Integrated systems use programmable CCTV technology to target an alarm location or "walk a beat" (see Figure 15-2). Inktags attached to items leak an indelible dye when forcibly removed and, thus, ruin merchandise for the shoplifter (see Figure 15-3). Another type of tag sends out an audible alarm when tampering occurs. *Source tagging* is growing in popularity and involves the manufacturer placing a hidden EAS tag into the product during manufacturing, to be deactivated at the POS. This saves the retailer the labor of tagging and untagging merchandise.[20]

Alarms

In addition to EAS, a variety of alarms protect merchandise from theft. *Loop alarms* consist of a cable that forms a closed electrical circuit that begins and ends at a battery-operated alarm device. This cable usually is attached through appliance handles and openings. When the electrical circuit is

Figure 15–2 CCTV, camera domes, and EAS (white portals at exit) work as an integrated system. Courtesy: Sensormatic, Inc.

disrupted by someone cutting or breaking it, the alarm sounds. *Cable alarms* also use a cable that runs from the merchandise to an alarm unit. This alarm differs in that a pad attached to the end of the cable is placed on the merchandise. Each item has its own cable pad setup, which is connected to an alarm unit. Cable alarms are useful when merchandise does not have openings or handles. Retailers also use heavy nonalarmed cables that are also woven through expensive items such as leather coats. This cable usually has a locking device.

Wafer alarms are sensing devices that react to negative pressure. This device, about the size of a large coin, is placed under the protected item; if a thief removes the item, an alarm sounds.

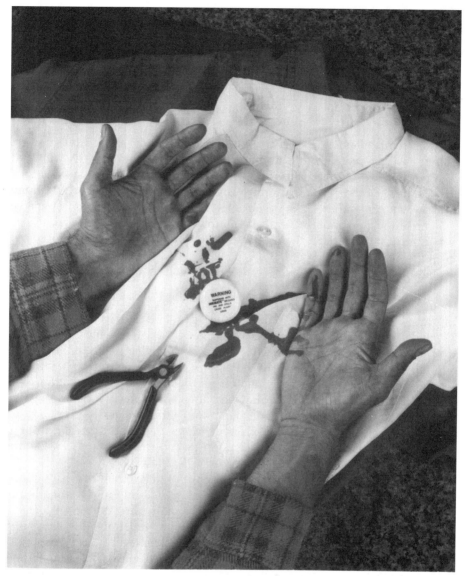

Figure 15–3   Inktag. Courtesy: Sensormatic, Inc.

Oil paintings on canvas can be protected by a *seismic geophone* that detects the vibrations of touch. *Ribbon alarms* can be placed on or under the cushions of antique furniture. They react to the pressure of a person sitting.

Display cases are often locked and sometimes alarmed. Depending on the expense of the items on display, some display cases are equipped with sophisticated alarms that sound if a salesperson leaves the display area.

Plug alarms allow expensive appliances to be plugged into alarmed outlets. When a thief removes the plug, the alarm is activated. Hotels and motels use this device for television sets.

Closed-Circuit Television

Closed-circuit television has become a popular anti-shoplifting device. Cameras with remote control and zoom lenses can be strategically located within a store and moved automatically at preset patterns. Sometimes, systems contain both real and dummy cameras, although too many dummy cameras can cause these fake deterrents to become a farce. Comprehensive systems allow personnel actually to follow people through a store. Close communications between the monitoring station and personnel throughout the store are necessary. Since CCTV primarily is a deterrent, people should be made aware of it through signs and by displaying the system.

Mirrors

The primary mirrors used to curb the shoplifting problem are see-through mirrors and wide-angle convex mirrors. These mirrors are relatively inexpensive and provide personnel with advantages that aid in the surveillance of shoplifters.

Observation booths usually are equipped with see-through mirrors; their location is above the sales floor at various places within a store. Personnel often use binoculars while watching customers (and employees) from these vantage points. A good communication system is necessary to summon aid because, when the observer leaves the booth, the shoplifter's actions are not being watched. If the shoplifter returns the item before being apprehended, the retail store may be faced with a lawsuit.

Wide-angle convex mirrors have been placed extensively throughout small and large retail stores to facilitate greater visibility and reduce blind spots around corners. Convex mirrors and regular mirrors can be located along walls, ceilings, at support columns, above merchandise displays, and at any point to create greater visibility and thus deter theft.

In one case, a juvenile was shoplifting recorded music items by sliding them into the bottom of a bag that had been stapled closed with a receipt attached. The incident occurred while the store was closing, and more than 20 retail personnel attentively watched the shoplifter in action from the other side of a 7-foot-high partition that had a convex mirror placed above it. The situation was interesting because the music department had been cleared of retail employees and the juvenile rushed around the department selecting items while nervously watching for people he did not know were watching him via the mirror.

Additional Devices and Measures

Fake deterrents are debatable loss prevention methods. A dummy camera or a periodic, fake loudspeaker statement (e.g., "dispatch security to main floor") may prevent shoplifting, but the level of effectiveness is difficult to measure. Many stores combine fake and real methods.

The acquisition of store supplies can be an aid to shoplifters. Salespersons must carefully control the store's shopping bags, boxes, string, colored tape, and price tags.

Shopping bags that are folded at the top and stapled closed, with the receipt attached, will hinder shoplifters. Colored tape is used on large items that cannot fit into bags. A receipt is placed under the tape to verify payment. Self-destructing price tags that tear when removed create difficulty when attempts are made to switch price tags.

International Perspective: What Deters Shoplifters?[21]

Gill, Bilby, and Turbin interviewed 38 experienced shoplifters in England to assess the effectiveness of anti-shoplifting strategies. Their research is summarized here:

- *Retail staff.* While 9 out of 38 respondents suggested that retail staff would sometimes deter them, 24 answered "never." They argued that salespeople were too busy or uninterested in shoplifting.
- *Security personnel.* Three-fourths of respondents said that they were able to spot plain-clothed store detectives. Only three claimed to be deterred always. The majority said that they would be deterred if a store detective actively observed them. Respondents claimed that one advantage of being followed by a store detective was that it would help an accomplice.
- *Signs.* Most of the sample claimed that signs stating "shoplifters will be prosecuted" would not deter them, especially because certain retailers do not follow what the sign states.
- *EAS and inktags.* Twenty respondents stated that EAS tags would never deter them and 14 claimed that they would remove the tags in the store, some with pliers and one with a bottle opener to pop it off. Some respondents avoided EAS tags, which illustrates some deterrent value. Respondents were evenly split on the deterrent effect of inktags. Claims were made that by putting a condom over it or freezing it before removal the merchandise would not be ruined. Manufacturers should study shoplifting methods more closely to design more effective systems.
- *CCTV.* Thirty-three out of 38 respondents claimed that CCTV would never deter them. Picture quality was perceived to be too poor for prosecution. They claimed that CCTV helped them if they could see where cameras were aimed so they could steal away from the camera's view. Blind spots were also helpful. These research results show the value of dark camera domes so the offender cannot see the camera's direction.

This research demonstrated that offenders make rational choices and that situational crime prevention (i.e., measures that increase risk for the offender) deters crime, but with the respondents in this study who are experienced shoplifters, a minority were deterred. A combination of security methods appear to have more of an impact than any one method. More research is needed to see how security methods impact amateurs. Also, research can focus on how security methods are classified within the three models of security and maxims of security (see Chapter 3).

Confronting the Shoplifter

Detection and Apprehension

Most shoplifters exhibit the following activities and characteristics before, during, and after a theft: extreme sensitivity to those around them, surveillance of the sales floor, nervousness and anxiety, and walking repeatedly to certain areas. Other characteristics that invite suspicion are a group of juveniles or a person wearing excessive clothing on a warm day.

Two *prerequisites to an apprehension* are *make sure to have seen the shoplifter conceal the store's merchandise*, and *never lose sight of the shoplifter*. The observer must be positive that he or she saw the item removed from a rack, because the customer could have brought the item into the store. If a customer wears a store item out of the store or alters or switches a price tag, one must make sure an eyewitness account is available. Some shoplifters panic on being observed and "ditch" the concealed merchandise or give it to an accomplice. Some people conceal merchandise, return it to the counter unnoticed, and hope to be apprehended in order to sue to collect damages. To help prove intent, the offender should be permitted to pass the last cash register and exit the store.

Juveniles are handled differently from adults. Police and parents usually are called. A loss prevention practitioner should be familiar with local procedures regarding juveniles.

Many security personnel who work alone prefer to work on the sales floor instead of from an observation booth. A disruption of eye contact occurs if a store detective witnesses a shoplifting incident and must travel from the booth to the floor. A team approach with a communications system is vital.

If a retail employee is not certain about a shoplifting incident, no apprehension should take place. In this situation, some practitioners recommend the "ghosting technique," which involves a salesperson carrying a duplicate of the shoplifted item as he or she walks close to the suspect. No words are spoken, but the message is obvious, if a theft has taken place. This technique has advantages for prevention, but it may permanently frighten customers from the store.

When retail personnel positively witness a shoplifting incident, loss prevention personnel must be notified for apprehension purposes. The detector (e.g., salesperson) should assist as an eyewitness. Additional personnel can stand by in case the subject becomes violent. Only a reasonable degree of force can be used to control the subject. *It is best to avoid a physical confrontation because the subject may be armed and the liability potential is significant. If the suspect flees, obtain a description and call police.* Immediately on approaching the subject, loss prevention personnel identify themselves by displaying identification or a badge. Personnel must never threaten the subject. *To reduce the problems associated with error, it is wise not to accuse the subject of stealing; the subject can be asked, "Would you mind answering a few questions about an item?"* The next step is to quickly ask the subject to accompany personnel to the loss prevention office. This perhaps is the most crucial point of the confrontation. At all times, careful observation of the subject is important because the merchandise may be "ditched" or escape may be attempted. If the subject escapes, again, avoid a physical confrontation and call police.

Detention and Arrest

After entering the loss prevention office, the subject usually is asked to produce some type of identification as well as the concealed merchandise. If the subject does not comply with these requests, the loss prevention officer should call the public police.

After the merchandise is received, a receipt should be requested to reduce the possibility of error. Usually, a shoplifter will state some type of excuse in an attempt to cover up not having a receipt.

Many jurisdictions have adopted the retailer's privilege of detaining shoplifters. *The difference between an arrest and detention is that the former requires the arrester to turn the suspect over to the public police, whereas the latter does not. Conditions for detention involve probable cause (reasonable grounds to justify legal action, such as an eyewitness account) and a reasonable time span, for detention, to accomplish questioning and documentation.* Many shoplifting statutes protect the retailer's right to detain, provided legal action was conducted in a reasonable manner. If an arrest is made, the crime charged by the retailer should be shoplifting (not larceny) to retain the right to detain under the shoplifting statute. For both detention and arrest, probable cause is necessary, and the suspect's freedom is restricted. The detention of a person can evolve into an arrest. Many attorneys argue that any type of restricted movement placed on the suspect is equal to an arrest. The ultimate decision may rest with a jury in a lawsuit.

Loss prevention personnel—or any store personnel—should refrain from touching the subject. If force is used to exercise legal action, it must be reasonable. When a shoplifter is controlled after a struggle, it would be unreasonable to strike the offender. Deadly force is restricted to life-threatening situations. *Unreasonable force can lead to prosecution difficulties, as well as criminal and civil action.*

Subsequent to proper detention or arrest, shoplifting statutes generally do not stipulate how merchandise is to be located and recovered from the shoplifter. Some states permit a search, whereas others forbid it. A shoplifter can be requested to empty his or her pockets and belongings to produce the stolen items. The public police should be called for obstinate shoplifters, and the police should conduct the search.

If the subject complies voluntarily, an arrest has not been made unless specified. *The loss prevention officer should ask the offender to sign a civil release form, which is vital before releasing the subject. It provides some protection against civil liability and also becomes a record of the incident.* The form contains, in addition to basic information (e.g., name, date), a voluntary confession of the store's items stolen, the value, and a statement that retail personnel did not use force or coercion and that the cooperation is voluntary. Although a release may state that the subject agrees not to sue, the retail personnel still can be sued. The release has psychological value in that the subject may believe that a suit is impossible and not seek legal advice, although a claim possibly can be made that the subject signed while under duress. If the shoplifter is obstinate or violent, an arrest is appropriate; handcuffing may be necessary. With this situation, the public police must be summoned; they usually will act in an advisory capacity and transport the prisoner to jail. A decision to call the police and prosecute makes obtaining a signature on the form less important. A criminal conviction perhaps is the best protection against civil liability. If the retailer intends to release the shoplifter without calling public police, then the civil release form is vital for some protection against litigation.

The courts have yet to require private security personnel to state to a suspect the *Miranda* rights (civil liberties) prior to questioning, as public police are required to do. Courts have held that any involuntary confession, gained by public or private police, is inadmissible in court. To strengthen their case, many loss prevention practitioners recite the *Miranda* rights and request that subjects sign a waiver-of-rights form if willing to confess.

When apprehended shoplifters are uncooperative and an arrest is appropriate, the stolen merchandise and the eyewitness to the shoplifting incident will be the primary evidence that will aid in the prosecution. The interviewer must not coerce the shoplifter into a confession by prolonged questioning or tricky tactics. This forceful approach can easily destroy a case.

Throughout the confrontation, at least two retail employees should be present. One employee must be of the same sex as the shoplifter. Problems inevitably develop if no witnesses are present or if two male employees forcibly retrieve an item from within the clothing of a woman. A witness and video recording can prevent charges related to brutality, coercion, a bribe, or sexual assault. *Racial profiling* is another potential problem that can result in a lawsuit by a customer or suspected shoplifter who claims that they were targeted for surveillance because of their racial background. Since recordings of surveillance activities can be taken out of context by a plaintiff's attorney, security personnel should explain to the defense side how surveillance is conducted. Examples include monitoring any customer who continuously looks around to see who is watching or walks into a high-risk area. Also, it may be an employee who is under surveillance rather than the customer.[22] Insurance companies write coverage protecting retailers against liability for false arrest, malicious prosecution, willful detention or imprisonment, libel, slander, and defamation of character.

Prosecution

The deterrent effect of prosecution is debatable. However, many retailers favor the prosecution of all shoplifters, believing that *shoplifters will avoid a "tough" store that has a reputation for prosecutions.*

Retailers should institute policies that are cost effective. Prevention appears to be less costly than a strict apprehension program.

When a shoplifter is arrested and about to be prosecuted, the witness or loss prevention practitioner probably will be asked to sign a complaint or warrant, the legal document containing the facts making up the essential elements of the crime. The loss prevention practitioner should read it before signing and maintain and safeguard all relevant records and forms. Public police, prosecutors, judges, and juries will be interested in facts. In most cases, especially minor cases, the defendant pleads guilty in a lower court, pays a fine, and a trial is avoided. For serious cases, a preliminary hearing may be necessary to give the judge an opportunity to review evidence and to decide on the necessity for a trial. Most defendants waive their rights to a hearing and a trial in exchange for a plea-bargaining opportunity. Some defendants choose to go to trial and retain an attorney. Security personnel facing a criminal trial must have an excellent case, or else an acquittal is likely to lead to a lawsuit.

The testimony of the eyewitness as to the shoplifting incident often is the main evidence in a shoplifting case. CCTV systems provide visual evidence to strengthen cases.

The responsibility for preserving physical evidence for a court appearance is part of the loss prevention practitioner's job. Accurate records are necessary. The evidence should be properly labeled and secured in a box or plastic bag. Two problems exist related to the preservation of physical evidence. First, millions of dollars of confiscated merchandise are not returned to the sales floor at hundreds of retail stores. Court congestion and delays can extend to months and years until the merchandise is out of date. Second, perishable items can deteriorate. A package of eight-month-old chicken breasts would present obvious resale problems when released after it was no longer needed as court evidence.

A solution to these problems involves photographing the stolen and recovered merchandise. Local requirements will vary concerning this procedure. A witness to the photographs can assist in strengthening the case. Color photos that contain a ruler marked with measurements will also aid in the effectiveness of this evidence.

If the prosecution of shoplifters becomes expensive and time consuming, if repeat offenders are not deterred, if the justice system becomes a "revolving door" (i.e., in for prosecution, out to commit another crime), and if cases are not successful, then anti-shoplifting strategies must be changed.

Civil Recovery

Almost every state has a civil recovery law that holds shoplifters liable for paying damages to businesses. Some states even extend these laws to employee theft. Civil recovery laws vary and may allow retailers, for example, to request three times the actual damages. These civil demand statutes aim to recover attorney's fees, court costs, and even the cost of security. Essentially, the expense of theft is passed on to thieves.

To recover damages a retailer sends a shoplifter a demand letter and a copy of the state's civil recovery law. Guidance can be obtained from a state retail association or an attorney. If there is no response, a second letter is sent stating that nonpayment may result in civil court action. With no response after a second letter, a retailer will have to decide whether to pursue the case in small claims court and whether a favorable judgment for damages can be collected.

Loss prevention personnel at some businesses may attempt civil recovery while the accused shoplifter is still in custody because the chance for recovery diminishes once the suspect leaves the store. The problem with this approach is that the shoplifting case may be based on faulty evidence. And, in some states, a guilty verdict may be necessary before civil action is sought. Other states permit simultaneous criminal and civil actions. In addition to the possibility of having a weak case against a suspected shoplifter, civil demand following an apprehension may result in legal action against the retailer for false imprisonment, extortion, and intentional or negligent infliction of emotion distress. The law of the respective state should be carefully studied as a foundation for store policies.[23]

A retailer may want to establish an in-house recovery program or contract with a service firm (this is the trend) that usually charges 30 percent of any money collected. Outside firms save the retailer the time and expense of operating a civil recovery program.

> If you were a retailer, what steps would you take to deal with the shoplifting problem?

ROBBERY AND BURGLARY

Robbery is the taking of something from an individual by force or threat of force. *Burglary* is unlawful entry into a structure to commit a felony or theft.

Loss prevention specialists repeatedly call for retailers to prevent *burglary* by (1) *hardening the target*, (2) *creating a time delay*, and (3) *reducing the loot*. Hardening the target pertains to security devices such as locks and alarms. The reasoning behind creation of a time delay is to increase the time necessary to commit the crime and, thereby, frustrate the offender. The offender may abort the offense or the delay may provide additional time for police apprehension. When the loot is reduced, losses are minimized. Some people may mistakenly favor all three of these measures for *robbery*. In Table 15-1, a robbery/burglary matrix illustrates some problems when all three strategies are incorrectly applied to robbery.

Table 15-1 Robbery/Burglary Matrix

	Robbery	Burglary
Harden the target	Yes[a]	Yes
Create time delay	No[b]	Yes
Reduce loot	Yes	Yes

[a] For instance, a retail business hardened for robbery may include an alarm and hidden cameras; however, if the robber becomes trapped because of a metal gate that has blocked the only exit (for example), then violence and a hostage situation may develop.

[b] Once a robbery is in progress, for safety's sake a time delay can be dangerous. The exception would be if there were no threatening situation (unlikely in a robbery); then a time delay might aid in immediate apprehension. Police agencies favor robber–police confrontation outside of the crime scene, away from innocent bystanders.

Robbery Countermeasures

According to the FBI, in 1999, there were 409,676 robberies, the lowest number since 1973. Losses totaled $463 million, with an average loss ranging from $620 at convenience stores to $4,552 at banks. Forty-eight percent of robberies occurred on streets and highways, 24 percent at commercial and financial businesses, and 12 percent at residences. Most robberies occurred in December and the fewest in February.[24]

Employee Socialization of Procedures

- *Opening.* The daily opening of a store is often referred to as the "opening routine." This can be a dangerous time because a "routine" can aid a robber who carefully studies a target. Therefore, a varied opening procedure reduces the chances for robbery. A typical procedure is for one employee to go inside the store while another waits outside; the person returns within 5 minutes and signals that the "coast is clear." If the employee does not signal correctly or fails to appear, the police are called. The signal should be changed periodically to limit routine. Retailers in urban areas frequently open stores in the presence of security people or with a group of three to five employees. Many have permits for handguns.
- *Closing.* Closing procedures should include positioning a trusted store employee either inside or outside of the store with easy access to a telephone. Various signaling procedures also are advisable.
- *Cash handling and transportation.* The POS should be located at the front of the store to enhance visibility by those passing by. A self-locking gate or Dutch door prevents access to the register by nonemployees. The cash drawer should require a key or code for access. Reducing the "loot" available will reduce the loss. When cash and other valuables (e.g., checks and credit receipts) accumulate, a pickup system is

necessary. Usually retail managers walk to each cash register for collections while performing associated accountability procedures. Then, the money is taken to the store money room. Two retail employees often participate in this operation. After the money is accounted for in the money room, a retail employee (or two) takes the money to a bank or an armored car pickup takes place. Procedures vary. Persons handling and transporting cash must be known by employees. If an employee transports money to a bank, use of a money bag is not advisable. It is better to use an innocuous paper bag. Local police sometimes are available as escorts to banks.

Whatever procedures are employed to protect people and money, there is always the possibility that a present or former employee has provided such information to offenders. In the restaurant business, most robberies have a connection to current or former employees.[25] Therefore, *periodically change procedures and signals.*

Security Manager Looks Bad

A retail executive from headquarters came to a chain store, displayed a company badge on his impressive suit, and systematically collected, with the usual moneybox, more than $2,000 from eight cash registers before leaving the store after the unauthorized collection. The purpose was to test security.

In the event of robbery, employees should have been trained to act in the following ways:

1. Concentrate on *safety*; don't try to be a hero; accommodate the robber's requests as well as possible.
2. If safety permits, activate alarm and camera; give the robber bait money.
3. Concentrate on details: description of the robber(s), license tag, type of vehicle, if any, and direction of travel.
4. After the robber leaves, telephone the police immediately.

Devices and Services

- *Alarms.* The retail employee activates robbery alarms. A button or foot device signals a silent alarm to authorities. Another type of alarm is activated when money is removed from a money clip within the cash register drawer. The employee must try to prevent the robber from noticing the silent alarm activation by hand or foot movement.

- *CCTV.* A recording of a robbery is helpful in identifying and prosecuting robbers.
- *Safes.* A *drop safe* permits a deposit into the safe without opening it; only management can open the safe. Certain sections of a *time-delay safe* cannot be entered until preset times. *Dual-key locks* on safes require a key from two people, such as a retail employee and an armored car officer. Care must be exercised when designing safe access because a robber may become impatient and resort to violence; warning signs to deter robbers provide some protection.
- *Bait money.* Bait money, also known as *marked money,* has had the banks of issue, denominations, series years, and serial letters and numbers recorded by the retailer. This record should be kept in a safe place. Prosecution of the robber is strengthened if he or she is found with this money. Retail employees should carefully include the bait money with the loot.
- *Security officers.* Armed, rather than unarmed, officers should be used to prevent robbery at high-risk locations. Another method is to hire off-duty police officers.
- *Armored car service.* An armored car service can increase safety for retail employees while providing security for the transportation of money.

Burglary Countermeasures

According to the FBI, in 1999, there were 2,099,739 burglaries, the lowest number since 1969. Losses totaled $3.1 billion, with the average loss at about $1,400 for residential and nonresidential locations. Two-thirds of burglaries occurred at residences and 60 percent of these occurred during the day. For nonresidential burglaries, 61 percent occurred at night. Most burglaries occurred in August and the fewest in February.[26]

Employee Socialization

Employee socialization can involve the following:

1. Surveying possible burglar entry points
2. Leaving lights on (inside and outside)
3. Overturning cash register money trays on top of opened cash register drawers, at closing
4. Rechecking doors, windows, and alarms at closing
5. Preserving the crime scene to protect any evidence upon discovering a burglary

Physical Defense

The burglar's most frequent method of intrusion is by forcing open a door or window. Thus, good construction is vital. This is associated with hardening the target.

If you were a retailer, which problem do you think would be more serious, robbery or burglary? Why?

SHOPPING MALL STRATEGIES

The size of a retail operation has a direct bearing on the extent of its loss prevention program. A small, one-owner retail store obviously will require a different program than a shopping mall. A mall's loss prevention program would include not only countermeasures for crime, fire, and accident, but also methods for numerous merchant needs, crowd control, parking lot problems (e.g., traffic, dead batteries, keys locked in autos), and lost people and merchandise. The size and complexity of malls compound loss problems. Market research at malls indicates that the customers' number one concern is personal safety.[27]

Career: Retail Security

Retailers are plagued by shoplifting, internal theft, bad checks, and credit card fraud. Retail security positions generally do not pay as highly as security positions in other industries. However, this field offers valuable work experience. Part-time work is available and many college students begin their careers in retail security.

Duties: Surveillance and investigating suspected shoplifting and employee theft incidents. Retail security managers are responsible for a single store or multiple locations requiring travel. Management duties include training, analyzing trends, planning and budgeting, and performing security and safety inspections.

Prerequisites: For management, associate or undergraduate degree, 5 years of experience, knowledge of retail operations.

Demographics of typical practitioner: Undergraduate degree; 10–15 years in security; 8–10 years in specialty; CPP preferred; salary of $35,000–60,000 yr.; titles: Loss Prevention Manager; Director of Security, Vice President of Security.

Source: American Society for Industrial Security, *Career Opportunities in Security* (Alexandria, VA: ASIS, 1998), p. 14.

A shopping mall's loss prevention program should be centralized and headed by an executive who responds to overall needs. Monthly meetings with merchants will facilitate cooperation and the sharing of problems, ideas, and resources. These meetings can provide an opportunity for a short training program. Special sales and events require further preparation. For malls experiencing many crime incidents, the establishment of a police sub-station is helpful.

Search the Web

For further information on retail security and loss prevention check these sites:

International Mass Retail Association http://www.imra.org/.

America's Network specializes in the bad check problem. http://www.badcheckcollector.com/.

U.S. Secret Service, "Know Your Money" http://www.treas.gov/usss/.

Use your favorite search engines to research "retail security," "retail internal theft," "shoplifting," and "credit card fraud."

CASE PROBLEMS

15A. A group of eight merchants who own retail stores at a small shopping center have hired you as a loss prevention consultant. These people are interested in reduced losses and increased profits. Their loss problems are employee theft, losses at the POS, shoplifting, robbery, and burglary. As a loss prevention consultant, what is your plan? Don't forget, you must earn your fee, satisfy the merchants to develop a good reputation, and produce effective loss prevention measures that will reduce losses and increase profits.

15B. As a regional loss prevention manager for a retail chain, you are growing increasingly suspicious of one of the stores in your region. The store manager and employees constantly state that the high shrinkage of 4 percent at the store is due to shoplifters. The manager argues that very little shrinkage results from damaged merchandise or employee theft. EAS and CCTV systems are functioning at the store, but no security personnel are employed; a variety of nonsecurity employees maintain and operate these systems. What questions would you ask the store manager on an upcoming visit? What action would you take?

NOTES

1. Michael J. Kelly, "Essentials of Retail Loss Prevention," *Security Technology & Design* 10 (June 2000), pp. 37–38.
2. Philip Purpura, *Retail Security & Shrinkage Protection* (Boston: Butterworth–Heinemann, 1993), p. ix.

3. See Chapter 11 for a discussion of inventory and shrinkage. Also, Michael Levy and Barton Weitz, *Retailing Management*, 4th ed. (New York: McGraw-Hill Irwin, 2001), p. 548. And, Purpura, pp. 103–109.
4. "How Stores Fight Theft," *Security Watch* 2902 (January 15, 2000), p. 5.
5. Levy and Weitz, pp. 304–305.
6. "How Stores Fight Theft," p. 5.
7. Ibid., p. 5.
8. Philip Purpura, *Modern Security and Loss Prevention Management* (Boston: Butterworth–Heinemann, 1989), p. 240.
9. "Retail Security Roundtable," *Access Control & Security Systems Integration* 42 (November 1999), p. 11.
10. Teresa Anderson, "Up and Running," *Security Management* 45 (January 2001), pp. 22–23.
11. Michael A. Freauf, "Refund Fraud: Australian Police Unit Cracks Down," *Law and Order* (February 1996), pp. 92–95.
12. Leonard Kolodny, Small Business Administration, *Outwitting Bad Check Passers* (Washington, D.C.: U.S. Government Printing Office, June 1976), p. 3.
13. Thomas Holland, "Checks and Balances," *Security Management* 43 (August 1999), pp. 76–82. And, Michelle Vachon, "Check Fraud Booming, Thanks to Technology," *Scripps Howard News Service* (March 30, 1997).
14. Keith Slotter, "Plastic Payments, Trends in Credit Card Fraud," *FBI Law Enforcement Bulletin* (June 1997), pp. 1–7.
15. Mike Brunker, "Internet Merchants Fight Back," *MSNBC* (May 16, 2001; http://www.msnbc.com/news/377221.asp).
16. A. James Fisher, *Security for Business and Industry* (Englewood Cliffs, NJ: Prentice-Hall, 1979), p. 175.
17. Loren E. Edwards, *Shoplifting and Shrinkage Protection* (Springfield, IL: Charles C Thomas Publishing Co., 1958), p. 52.
18. David L. Altheide, et al., "The Social Meanings of Employee Theft," *Crime at the Top* (New York: J. B. Lippincott Co., 1978), p. 115.
19. "EAS Systems Technical Overview," Tag Point Ltd. (May 16, 2001) http://www.tagpoint.co.il/tagtech.htm. Also, Emily Harwood, "Source Tagging Without Limits," *Security Technology & Design* 10 (September 2000), p. 102. And, Robert DiLonardo, "Electronic Article Surveillance: What's Up?" *Security Technology and Design* (October 1996), pp. 50–57.
20. Harwood, pp. 100–108.
21. Martin Gill, Charlotte Bilby, and Vicky Turbin, "Retail Security: Understanding What Deters Shop Thieves," *Journal of Security Administration* 22(1) (1999), pp. 29–39.
22. Roger Schmedlen, "A Picture of Profiling," *Security Management* 44 (May 2000), pp. 70–73.
23. Michael Gips, "Shoplifter Shakedown?" *Security* (January 1997), p. 10.
24. U.S. Department of Justice, *Crime in the United States, 1999 Uniform Crime Reports* (Washington, D.C.: U.S. Government Printing Office, 2000), p. 28. http://www.fbi.gov/ucr.
25. "Retail Security Roundtable," p. 6.
26. U.S. Department of Justice, *Crime in the United States, 1999, Uniform Crime Reports*, p. 40.
27. "Retail Security Roundtable," p. 4.

16

Loss Prevention
at Select Facilities

OBJECTIVES

After studying this chapter the reader will be able to discuss loss problems and countermeasures for:

1.   Computer facilities.
2.   Nuclear facilities.
3.   Businesses under a Department of Defense contract.

COMPUTER FACILITIES

High-profile media stories of information technology (IT) under attack from cybercrime can distort the picture of threats facing computer facilities. Here, we seek to "cut through the hype," begin with "the basics," and provide a broad picture of losses and countermeasures. We begin with cybercrime, but later cover losses from misuse, errors, fires, and disasters.

Cybercrime

Cybercrime can be grouped into two categories: crimes in which computers are used as *instruments* of the offense and crimes in which computers are the *object* of the offense. The former includes embezzlement, fraud, and larceny. The problem of credit card fraud via the Internet, as covered in the previous chapter, serves as another example of computers used as instruments of crimes. Computers can be the object of a crime when an offender intends to cause damage to hardware or software (programs). Examples are data destruction or alteration and vandalism of a computer system. The media contains a wealth of stories on both categories of cybercrime.[1]

Research by the Computer Security Institute (CSI) in cooperation with the FBI found that computer crime is on the rise. Eighty-five percent of 538 computer security practitioners in U.S. businesses and institutions surveyed detected computer security breaches causing losses of nearly $378 million in 2000. In 1999, 249 respondents reported losses of $266 million. Both years showed the most serious financial losses from theft of proprietary information and financial fraud. Forty percent reported penetration from outside in 2000 compared to 25 percent in 1999. Thirty-eight percent reported denial-of-service attacks in 2000 with 27 percent reporting such attacks in 1999. Only 36 percent reported intrusions to police, up from 16 percent five years earlier.[2]

A study by Datamonitor showed that computer security breaches cost global businesses more than $15 billion annually. If e-businesses can solve security problems, the firm estimates that business-to-business sales (called B2B) can climb to $5.9 trillion by 2005. However, Datamonitor estimates that more than 50 percent of global businesses spend 5 percent or less of their IT budgets on security.[3]

Because hacker attacks can be so devastating to businesses and organizations, the FBI and its National Infrastructure Protection Center (NIPC), found on the Web at http://www.nipc.gov/, have formed an alliance with businesses and educational entities to share information anonymously. A goal is to have one chapter in each state focusing on information about attacks and security. The FBI is seeking to alert businesses under attack to avoid taking their networks off-line because evidence is destroyed and the opportunity to track a hacker is reduced. Also, the Economic Espionage Act of 1996 allows the FBI to investigate cyber-attacks anonymously; this reduces the problem of unwanted publicity.[4] Despite FBI efforts, the NIPC has been criticized for being inadequately staffed and slow to respond to "911" calls. Another source of assistance is the Computer Emergency Response Team (CERT) http://www.cert.org/ at Carnegie Mellon University. It is a clearinghouse of computer security information and technical advisor on incident response for businesses and government agencies.

Cyberwarfare[5]

The military of many countries have expanded operations to cyberspace. Conflict in the Middle East serves as an example. Israeli and Palestinian hackers attacked each other's Internet infrastructures, seeking to disrupt economic and information systems. During 2000, the Israeli government reported numerous attacks that crashed computers in the government, in the military, and at e-commerce companies. At the same time, Israeli hackers were also busy working to disrupt Palestinian Web sites. The United States has faced similar problems, and cyberwarfare and cyberterrorism are signs of how future conflicts will be fought.

Techniques of Cybercriminals

Here is a sample list of techniques used by cybercriminals. Such lists are constantly being updated and expanded. As new defenses block cybercriminals, they seek new techniques to access and harm systems.

- *Distributed denial-of-service (DDoS).* This networking prank, also called a "flood attack," initiates many requests for information to clog the system, slow performance, and crash the site. It may be used to cover up another cybercrime.
- *Scans.* Probes of the Internet to determine types of computers, services, and connections to take advantage of weaknesses in a particular make of computer or software.
- *Sniffer.* Software that covertly searches individual packets of data as they pass through the Internet and capturing items such as passwords.
- *War dialing.* Programs that automatically dial thousands of telephone numbers in search of an access through a modem.
- *Password crackers.* Software that can guess passwords. A blacklisting feature that locks out an account if too many invalid passwords are entered can possibly block this technique.
- *Spoofing.* Faking an e-mail address or Web page to dupe users into divulging critical information such as passwords or credit card numbers.
- *Trojan horse.* A program, unknown to the user, that contains instructions that exploit a known vulnerability in software.
- *Viruses and worms.* The purpose is to cause damage to an application or network and delete files. A worm is similar to a virus except it can self-replicate (i.e., spread itself across networks and the Internet). Defenses include behavior blockers that stop suspicious code based on behavior patterns, not signatures, and applications that quarantine viruses in shielded areas. The LoveLetter virus, which infected millions of computers within hours of its release in 2000, showed the speed with which new scripts could spread as well as the limitations of conventional anti-virus defenses.
- *Time bomb.* Also called a logic bomb, it contains instructions in a program that creates a malicious act at a predetermined time. Programs are available that monitor applications seeking to change other applications or files when a time bomb goes off.
- *Social engineering.* Tricking an employee into revealing information helpful to gain unauthorized access to a computer system. This could occur through a telephone call from an "employee," or the offender may send an e-mail posing as a network administrator who requests a password for a system upgrade.
- *Dumpster diving.* Searching garbage for information, sometimes used to support social engineering.[6]

> **What are your ideas on strategies against cybercriminals?**

IT Security

Planning

Maxims that apply to physical security also apply to IT security:

1. Security is never foolproof.
2. Even state-of-the-art security has its vulnerabilities.
3. Security often is as good as the time it takes to get through it (see Chapter 3).

The three models of security also apply to IT security. Every security strategy either protects people and/or assets, accomplishes nothing, or helps offenders (see Chapter 3).

Using IT terminology, an *integrated information security architecture* (IISA) is a well-reasoned and thoroughly researched plan for developing and implementing an effective security program to serve an enterprise's goals and needs. (The term "enterprise" means a business organization, and in the IT literature the term "enterprise security" refers to the protection of an organization's information systems.) An IISA is an avenue to build a security infrastructure from the ground up. It consists of these steps: (1) evaluation of an organization's internal and external risks; (2) determining what defensive tools and protocols are needed; and (3) planning for the implementation of a defense of new and legacy systems for today's "virtual perimeter" environment. The IISA provides a base for policies, procedures, and contingency plans. Furthermore, by adopting security standards, an organization can monitor its performance. Standards provide a baseline for measuring effectiveness that can result in improvements.[7]

Strategies[8]

1. Establish an IT security committee to plan and lead.
2. Because IT security changes rapidly, invest in quality training.
3. Monitor and track alert bulletins and best practices.
4. Consider efforts to establish generally accepted benchmarks for securing computer networks. Such standards define levels of security that an organization can measure itself against. However, standards must be dynamic to keep up with "Internet time."[9]
5. Use a layered approach to security. This creates multiple "roadblocks" for offenders.

6. Provide physical security for computer facilities and include desktops, laptops, and servers.

7. When designing a computer facility, avoid glass walls or doors, single paths for power to communications lines, uncontrolled parking, underground locations (because of flooding), multitenant buildings, signs describing the facility, information about the facility on the Web or a video, and off-site tape storage that does not meet high security criteria.[10]

8. Automatic access control systems for a computer facility are popular in combination with limited entrances, the double-door entry concept, visual verification, badge identification systems, and access control according to time, place, and specific personnel. Access controls are required not only for the computer facility but also for the computer itself. This includes protection against unauthorized remote access. Biometric access control systems (see Chapter 7) enable identification by fingerprints and so forth. Access to sensitive data must be safeguarded on the premises and from remote locations, even by legitimate computer users.

9. *Passwords* or *codes* are identification procedures that permit access only after the proper code is entered into the computer. The code should be changed periodically. Alarms to signal attempts at unauthorized access should be incorporated into computer software.

10. *Firewalls* are software and hardware controls that permit system access only to users who are registered with a computer. Attempts to gain access are challenged by the use of passwords. These challenges are "layers" that data must go through before reaching its destination. A firewall sits between a company's internal computer network and outside communications. Firewall products offer a range of features such as file or virus checking, log and activity reports, encryption, security and authentication schemes, and monitoring and alarm mechanisms for suspicious events or network intruders. Putting up a firewall is similar in certain respects to implementing physical security—assess the vulnerability, determine need, and after understanding the technology, decide on a proper level of protection.[11]

11. Use intrusion detection software which is like a physical intrusion detection system, only for the network.

12. Be proactive and conduct searches for hacker programs that may be used in an attack. Hackers tend to brag about their successes to the hacker community, so check out sites that attract hackers.

13. Carefully evaluate new techniques, such as those that purport to filter and trace malicious software sent over the Web.

14. Disable unused services. Most software programs include services that are installed by default. These unused services can be a path for hackers.

15. Update software for improved security. Quickly install security patches. Software firms develop "patches" for protection when hackers

attack their programs. Thus, when a patch is offered to a client it should be installed as quickly as possible.

16. Use decoy programs that trick hackers into attacking certain sites where they can be observed and tracked while the important sites remain secure.

17. Audit IT security through frequent, rigorous vulnerability testing. Such tools are available from many commercial sources.

18. Because of the trend of companies concentrating on their core business and outsourcing everything else, "managed security services" is a growing option (as covered in Chapter 9). Essentially, the work contracted to an outside firm can be as broad as surrendering "enterprise security" to the contractor. This includes security technologies, infrastructure, services, and management. Many questions evolve from this concept. Examples: What is to be retained and what is to be outsourced? Who is to be responsible for losses?

Encryption

Many practitioners in the computer field consider encryption the best protection measure for data within a computer or while it is being transmitted. Once the domain of government, encryption has traditionally been used to protect military or diplomatic secrets. During the 1970s the private sector began marketing encryption products, and with the growth of computers and the Internet, encryption likewise grew.

Encryption consists of hardware or software that scrambles (encrypts) data, rendering it unintelligible to an unauthorized person intercepting it. The coding procedure involves rules or mathematical steps, called an *algorithm*, that converts plain data into coded data. This transformation of data is accomplished through what is called a *key*, which is a sequence of numbers or characters or both. The key is used in both transmitting and receiving equipment. Key security is vital because it is loaded into both ends of the data link. Furthermore, encryption tools should be changed periodically because breaches have become something of a game. Developers of encryption systems are finding that their estimates of how long it would take to crack the codes are too long. Rapidly evolving technology has shortened the life of promising encryption systems. Another point is noted by computer expert John M. Carroll, who adds that, when you become mesmerized by the wonder of some promising crypto device, ask yourself one question: "How much do I trust the person who sold me this gadget?" He extends this question to the international level by claiming that it would be unlikely for any country, even an ally, to provide an encryption system to another without retaining the keys.[12]

Controversy has developed over whether the U.S. government should have the power to tap into every telephone, fax, and computer transmission by controlling keys. From the law enforcement perspective, such control is necessary to investigate criminals and spies. Opponents claim violations of privacy and damage to the ability of American businesses to compete internationally. Without tight controls over encryption systems, the U.S. government also fears that criminals will use such systems to send and receive secret communications, making investigations very difficult. Although the issues remain, organizations need encryption systems for sensitive information, which, without encryption, is like sending a postcard. One computer security expert quipped that no legislation can stop the spread of encryption systems and there are hundreds of foreign encryption products.[13]

The explosive growth of the Internet and business on the Internet has created the need for strong algorithms and their all-important key lengths to secure electronic interactions. Internet users are seeking privacy, confidentiality, and verification of individuals and businesses they are dealing with.[14]

One major answer to the challenges cited above is the public key infrastructure (PKI) and its authentication and encryption capabilities. Whereas the handshake or handwritten agreement have been tradition for centuries, a modern trend is the digital handshake and signature through the PKI. The PKI addresses three primary security needs: authentication, nonrepudiation, and encryption. The first need verifies an individual's identity. The second need means that an individual cannot deny they have provided a digital signature for a document or transaction. The workhorse behind PKI is cryptography that encrypts and decrypts information.[15]

As an IT security specialist, would you enter Web sites on hacking? Why or why not?

Research on IT Security

The 2000 *Information Security* reader survey, resulting in 1,897 respondents, showed that destructive viruses are the number one concern of security professionals, insiders pose a more serious threat than outsiders, and layered security increases protection and increases the chances of detecting breaches.[16]

A *Security Management* reader survey of nearly 200 respondents found that the following security strategies were in use (with percentage): virus detection systems (71), firewalls (59), encryption (34), intrusion detection systems (32), physical security for hardware (30), content monitoring or filtering software (21), penetration testing (12), tracing services for laptops (5), network/hacking insurance (5), and biometrics for computer access (2).[17]

Research by the CSI/FBI (cited earlier) offers compelling evidence that neither technologies nor policies alone offer effective defense. Intrusions take place despite firewalls. Trade secrets are stolen despite encryption. Net abuse flourishes despite management edicts against it. Survival depends on a comprehensive approach to IT security, embracing both human and technical measurers. Also, there is the need to properly fund, train, and staff IT security.[18]

Inside the Mind of an IT Security Professional[19]

Critical thinking skills are essential to "think securely" while exposing IT security hype. Jay Heiser, an IT security specialist, notes that the ability to make intuitive, quick, and useful decisions about IT security is a learned skill that improves with practice and time. This does not mean that the security specialist is a good guesser; it means that the specialist has enough experience, judgment, and "sense" to make intelligent guesstimates based on relatively small amounts of information. Heiser adds that "to determine the relevance of a vulnerability to your systems, evaluate the source of the warning, and then analyze its historical context and exploitability within your computing environment. If you can't do that, you'll be constantly blown by the wind, and you'll have no credibility with your employer."

Heiser recommends the following:

1. Don't accept a security warning at face value. Vendors want your money and are notorious for exaggerating risks.
2. Know where to go for proven analysis, but remember that the experts are often wrong. Find multiple sources.
3. Recognize that no attack is ever completely new. Each attack is a variation of something old. Understand what happened before to develop present solutions.
4. Most vulnerabilities are never exploited because most don't offer attackers something useful. Attackers have consistent goals and methods. Vulnerabilities that are inconsistent with the needs of cybercriminals are rarely a problem.

What similarities and differences do you see between IT security and security and loss prevention?

Misuse and Errors

Crime is not the only way in which organizations sustain losses from IT systems. Losses are sustained when employees misuse computer resources. According to a survey by *Security Management*, 27 percent of nearly 200 organizations disciplined or terminated employees for violating computer policy. The causes of sanctions were: viewing inappropriate Web sites (21 percent), sending inappropriate e-mails (15 percent), and excessive personal use of the organization's computer (10 percent). Five percent of those disciplined had been operating another business using an internal computer and 3 percent were caught committing a crime, such as hacking. Only 16 percent of respondents answered that they monitor the content of e-mail messages.[20]

Personnel errors involving computer operations are another cause of losses. One common error is to feed incorrect data into a computer. Other errors result when an overenthusiastic employee devises a faster way to obtain specific data from a computer that differs from standard procedures; during the shortcut, precise computer programs are altered, and inaccurate data is produced during subsequent computer operations. If vital business decisions are based on inaccurate data, the damage can be enormous. Other examples are seen when inexperienced employees accidentally delete files, update the wrong records, or unknowingly supply outsiders with sensitive information.

Methods to hinder errors and other losses include recruiting and employing appropriately qualified individuals, good training, establishing and communicating policies that are enforced, requiring accountability of those active with computer operations, and designing computer programs that cross-check and notify management of errors and irregularities.

Fire Protection

Fires at computer facilities usually are caused by fires in adjacent facilities and electrical problems. Numerous wires and electrical components and accumulations of paper provide combustibles for fire. Because important records are maintained at computer centers, one fire can create financial ruin for a business. In addition, expensive equipment can be destroyed. But, with adequate fire prevention and fire suppression measures, losses can be minimized.

Fire prevention entails the enforcement of no smoking rules, the proper disposal of trash, preventive maintenance, good employee socialization, and audits of prevention measures. Furnishings that are flammable should be removed or treated with sprays to hinder flammability. Underfloor areas, where many electrical wires are located, need to be cleaned and checked periodically.

Fire suppression is aided by smoke sensors. Ionization detectors are most efficient because they detect the earliest stages of smoke or flame. Carbon monoxide (CO) gas detectors can also save lives. Detectors normally are placed on ceilings, under raised floors, in air ducts, and within equipment. The detectors should be connected to separate power supplies since electricity and air-conditioning units are often turned off during a fire. This will prevent electrocution of an employee if water is sprayed on burning equipment, reduce damage to the computer, and keep air-conditioning units from blowing fire and smoke to other parts of a building. Emergency lighting is important in conjunction with these strategies.

A primary method of fire suppression for computer facilities is a sprinkler system, which may be required by local codes. However, sprinklers are controversial because of the potential danger to people due to electrocution and likely equipment damage. Such systems may be activated by accident or by a small fire that could have been extinguished with a portable extinguisher. To reduce the impact of a sprinkler system, consider a dry pipe system with a shutoff valve nearby, noncombustible construction materials, a one-hour fire resistance rating surrounding the computer room, and noncombustible water-resistant covers for computer equipment.

Halon 1301 (Freon) was popular as an extinguishing agent for computer rooms; however, it is no longer being manufactured because it harms the ozone layer. Existing halon systems are not required to be removed.[21] Carbon dioxide extinguishing systems were another earlier alternative to water, but these systems should be avoided because they smother a fire by cutting off oxygen, an obvious danger to humans.

Portable fire extinguishers are helpful to suppress small fires. If portable carbon dioxide extinguishers are used, careful planning (e.g., evacuation) and caution are important because of the danger to humans.

Prevention of Disasters

Human-made or natural disasters have the potential for producing considerable disruption and damage to computer centers. Through careful site location, construction, and design, the impact of disasters can be reduced. *Contingency plans are a key loss prevention measure.*[22] An auxiliary power supply (i.e., a generator) will provide power in case the main source of electricity fails. A backup air-conditioning/heating unit will ensure that the proper temperature is maintained so that valuable equipment is not harmed. Backup computers and the protection of records are essential considerations for the continuation of both computer operations and the organization. Mutual assistance agreements enable two or more separate computer centers to rely on each other in case of an emergency. Associated problems may entail system incompatibility, program differences, and computer time requirements. To ensure reliability, a computer specialist should conduct an initial study and then periodic evaluations. Special computer safes protect computer media from fire, theft, and adverse environmental conditions. A second copy of data stored at another secure location also will avert losses. Off-site data need to be updated repeatedly.

Business on the Internet has added new risks that have the potential for disaster. In fact, a debate is occurring as to whether we are discussing an IT security issue or a business continuity issue.[23] Whatever camp wins on this issue, the primary concern should be to minimize losses and ensure business survival. The risk management perspective adds further input to the potential for disaster. This camp refers to a "lack of preparedness" by companies doing business on the Internet. One technology underwriter noted that "it takes about three years from when a risk is first identified for managing it to become commonplace."[24]

NUCLEAR FACILITIES

Supporters of nuclear energy favor it as a safe way to reduce America's dependence on imported oil. Detractors frantically testify about dangers from unsafe conditions and radiation. The debate will continue for years.

Public utilities and government have developed guidelines for maintaining a safe and secure environment. The American nuclear industry and its 103 commercial reactors are responsible for fully implementing the requirements for protecting the public health and safety as prescribed by the U.S. Nuclear Regulatory Commission (NRC). But the NRC has been criticized over the years for not fulfilling its mandate and overlooking serious safety problems to keep plants on-line. Also, whistle blowers have come forward.[25] A nuclear power plant contains more than a thousand times the radiation that would be released by an atomic bomb. Losses could reach hundreds of thousands of deaths and billions of dollars in property damage.[26] The threat of terrorism, especially following the September 11, 2001 attack, has caused increased concern and an outcry for improved protection of reactors. Despite the criticism, an enormous amount of effort in terms of money, personnel, and equipment is expended to reduce the chances of accidents, attacks, and losses. The nuclear industry has a responsibility to the community, stockholders, and customers.

Nuclear Security

The NRC, in conjunction with other federal agencies, develops physical security criteria or standards for nuclear operations. These standards involve defenses against both internal and external threats. A possible internal threat is someone on the inside, with or without cooperation from others, who commits sabotage or theft of special nuclear materials (SNM). SNM can be used to manufacture a nuclear weapon. An external threat could be posed by several people who are dedicated to their objectives, well trained in military skills, and possess weaponry and explosives. An insider may be part of this threat. Nuclear security programs typically are designed to protect against radiological sabotage and the theft or diversion of SNM. Radiological sabotage of nuclear materials, during shipment or at the plant site, can endanger the public by exposure to radiation. Theft or diversion of SNM could be used for extortion, terrorism, publicity, or financial gain.

The NRC regulates the nuclear industry by licensing companies to build and operate nuclear reactors and to use nuclear materials. Rules and standards must be followed by licensees to ensure safety and security. A proposed program must be technically adequate before legal permission is granted to the licensee to operate. NRC inspections are conducted periodically to ensure compliance; corrective action often results. NRC security regulations stipulate which security levels must be maintained at nuclear plants. Physical security criteria assist licensees prior to submitting, for approval, a physical security plan (PSP). The PSP guards against two key threats—sabotage and theft—among others. NRC criteria stress *redundancy* (i.e., duplication) and *in-depth protection*. Examples are two barriers and two intrusion alarm systems. A backup is required for every sensor, transmitter, processor, and alarm so terrorists cannot simply cut a line and catch a facility off-guard.[27] Through a combination of defenses, an adversary probably would be detected and reported as quickly as possible; a strong response would follow.

Separate monitoring systems operate at nuclear plants. Three specific monitoring systems are security, fire, and safety. The trend in other industries to integrate these systems into one computer-controlled system has not caught on in nuclear facilities. The security system is similar to a proprietary central station. Sophisticated and redundant equipment features (e.g., additional communications paths) provide safeguards against malfunctions. A modern, well-designed computer system can be connected to perimeter intrusion alarms, access controls, CCTV, duress alarms, and communications equipment. A record-keeping function is essential, especially to comply with stringent NRC record keeping regulations.

Title 10, Code of Federal Regulations, Part 73, explains elements of an acceptable nuclear security program.[28] It includes physical security organization, supervision, training, physical barriers, intrusion detection, access requirements, communications, testing and maintenance, and armed response requirements. Following the 1993 World Trade Center bombing, the NRC ordered all nuclear power plants to install barriers against vehicle bombs. The September 11, 2001 attack heightened security even more.

A double fence frequently is constructed along nuclear plant perimeters. Both microwave and e-field intrusion detection systems are common at the same site. Sophisticated and expensive CCTV cameras enable viewing during adverse weather conditions. NRC regulations necessitate minimum lighting levels, which usually are exceeded. Access controls can be very complex and effective. Special-purpose detection devices (e.g., X-ray, weapons, explosive), strategically placed, are integrated with other systems.

SNM need protection as an integral part of the security program. Accountability and frequent inventories will reduce the possibility of losses while increasing the chances of recovery in the event of a loss.

Portal of the Future[29]

Because the U.S. Department of Energy (DOE) maintains sites that support nuclear weapons production, it plays a lead role in designing security portals that search incoming and outgoing vehicles. Searching trucks and cars is labor intensive and time consuming, and when technology makes the task easier, the ideas spread to such locations as nuclear plants. DOE ideas include the following. A *fiber optic weight-in-motion system* enables operators to weigh vehicles as they are moving up to 5 mph. Security personnel can weigh a vehicle before and after it enters a site to note discrepancies. An *under-vehicle scanning system* provides video of the bottom of vehicles and photographs the license plate. An *enclosed space detection system* detects vibrations from a heartbeat from a person hiding in an enclosed space. This system uses seismic geophones or microwaves to detect the shock waves created by a beating heart. Other systems detect explosives and small radiation levels. Such technology can be applied to tighten security not only at sites containing nuclear materials but also at prisons, borders, military posts, and other high-security locations.

Protection Force

NRC regulations require an armed response force present at a nuclear facility at all times (see Figure 16-1). Criteria established by NRC reinforce adequate selection, training, weapons, and equipment. Sufficient power is expected from the response force to counter an adversary. This entails the use of deadly force in self-defense or in the defense of others. Local law enforcement assistance is to be called in the event of an attack. However, because of a response time delay from local authorities, the primary armed defense is expected from the on-site nuclear security force. The licensee has an obligation to convince the NRC licensing staff that the security measures are capable of detecting and delaying an attack until the response force intervenes.

Nuclear security officers spend most of their time ensuring plant protection. Certain areas need to be regularly inspected, CCTV monitors and alarms require attention, and employees and visitors are scrutinized and searched at access points.

DEPARTMENT OF DEFENSE REQUIRED SECURITY [30]

U.S. technology and industry are vital to our nation's defense. Businesses under contract with the Department of Defense (DOD) must protect government classified information. Here we present a summary of the Defense Security Service (DSS), which provides security services to the DOD. Then,

Figure 16–1 Security officers at a nuclear generating plant. Courtesy of Wackenhut Corporation. Photo by Ed Burns.

we will emphasize the Industrial Security Program (ISP), under DSS, which impacts private industry.

The DSS is under the Assistant Secretary of Defense. Formerly known as the Defense Investigative Service (DIS), DOD redesignated DIS as the Defense Security Service in November 1997 in recognition of its broader mission. DSS has three primary missions: the Personnel Security Investigations Program (PSI), the Industrial Security Program (ISP), and Security Education and Training.

PSIs are used by DOD facilities to determine an individual's suitability to enter the armed forces, access classified information, or hold a sensitive position within the DOD. The ISP includes the Defense portion of the National Industrial Security Program (NISP), the Arms, Ammunition and Explosives Program, and the Critical Assets Assurance Program. The NISP was established to ensure that private industry and colleges and universities, while performing government contracts or research and development, safeguard classified information. The DSS provides security advice and assistance, counterintelligence support, and industrial security oversight to cleared civilian contractor facilities performing on classified contracts. The DSS Academy provides security education and training programs to support DOD agencies and DOD Military Departments and Contractors.

The DSS clears approximately 800,000 industry personnel under the NISP. The DSS has Industrial Security oversight and assistance responsibility for more than 11,000 cleared facilities participating in the NISP. Additionally, it is estimated that there are 11 million classified documents in the hands of U.S. industry. A compromise of classified information, particularly if it relates to a system's susceptibility to counterattack, can have disastrous consequences, including loss of life and reduced warfighter capability. Appropriate security safeguards must be developed and integrated throughout the life cycle of major classified procurements, from inception through final delivery and performance. The time to think about security is not when a weapon system is put onboard an aircraft but during the earliest stages of its development.

The DSS works with contractors to ensure that they implement and maintain sound security programs in accordance with the National Industrial Security Operating Manual (NISPOM) and safeguard classified information.

The following DSS report shows how the Internet is affecting national security. Based on reports of suspicious foreign contacts submitted to the DSS, the Internet is the fastest growing modus operandi of unsolicited correspondence using computer elicitation between foreign entities and cleared U.S. companies and their employees. Reports continue to arrive at the DSS about foreign entities using the Internet to contact a wide variety of knowledgeable persons, with the intention of collecting various pieces of information from each based upon their area of expertise. This information is then put together in an amazingly clear mosaic, revealing a level of detail that no one individual would have been able to provide. Use of the Internet offers a variety of advantages to a foreign collector. It is simple, low cost, nonthreatening, and relatively risk free for the foreign entity attempting to collect classified information. These foreign entities can remain safe within their own borders while sending hundreds of requests for assistance to targeted U.S. companies and their employees. The DSS offers a variety of strategies to prevent the loss of information.[31]

Do you think national security is a serious issue, or do you think the issue has been exaggerated? Explain your answer.

Search the Web

Use your favorite search engines to type: computer security associations.

For computer security and a variety of related information go to http://www.sans.org/. Also, the Internet Fraud Complaint Center is located on the Web at http://www.ifccfbi.gov/.

CASE PROBLEMS

16A. Select two types of facilities explained in this chapter, and describe why the ones you chose are unique in terms of loss problems and prevention strategies.

16B. Choose two types of facilities from this chapter. For each, establish a priority list of the five most important measures to counter losses. Explain the reasoning behind each ranked list.

16C. Select two facilities mentioned in this chapter. (1) Refer to additional sources to gather further information, and (2) explain why you would prefer to work in one rather than the other. Maintain a bibliography.

16D. Of the locations discussed in this chapter, which do you think is the most demanding for a security manager? Justify your answer.

NOTES

1. Jay Albanese, *Criminal Justice* (Boston: Allyn & Bacon, 2001), pp. 81–82.
2. "Computer Crime Increases," *Risk & Insurance* 12 (May 2001), p. 8.
3. "Insecurity Costs," *Security Management* 45 (March 2001), p. 35.
4. Carey Adams, "A Partnership to Expose Cybercrime," *iSecurity* 44 (February 2001), p. 1.
5. M. E. Kabay and Lawrence Walsh, "The Year in Computer Crime," *Information Security* 3 (December 2000), p. 34.
6. Ken Brandt, et al., "Battle Plans," *Information Security* 4 (March 2001), pp. 86–94. And, Ira Sager, et al., "Cybercrime," *Business Week* (February 21, 2000), p. 40.
7. Stan Kiyota, "Planning Makes Perfect," *Information Security* 3 (November 2000), p. 104.
8. Sager, et al., pp. 37–42. And, "10 Tips That Help Security and IT Stop Hackers," *Security Watch* 2912 (June 15, 2000), pp. 1–3.
9. "Internet Companies Set Security Benchmarks," *Security Management* 45 (January 2001), p. 36.
10. Lloyd Reese, "Designing a Safe House for Data," *Security Management* 45 (February 2001), pp. 56–60.
11. Amy Thompson, "Smoking Out the Facts on Firewalls," *Security Management* (January 1997), pp. 25–30.
12. John M. Carroll, *Computer Security*, 3rd ed. (Boston: Butterworth–Heinemann, 1996), p. 249.
13. Vic Sussman, "Policing Cyberspace," *U.S. News and World Report* (January 23, 1995), pp. 55–60.
14. Illena Armstrong, "Encryption, Where Next?" *SC Magazine* 11 (June 2000).
15. Joachim Vance, "Public Key Infrastructure: Addressing Corporate Deployment," *Security Technology & Design* 10 (October 2000), pp. 46–51.
16. Andy Briney and Kirk Fretwell, "Security Focused," *Information Security* 3 (September 2000), p. 41.

17. Dequendre Neeley, "Protection Progress Report," *Security Management* 44 (May 2000), p. 34.
18. "Cybercrimes Are Soaring," *Security Watch* 3010 (May 15, 2001), p. 4.
19. Jay Heiser, "Think Securely," *Information Security* 4 (February 2001), p. 106.
20. "Polling Corporate Practices," *Security Management* (June 2000), p. 39.
21. Craig Hofmeister, "Halon Replacement Options Update," *Security Technology & Design* 10 (March 2000), pp. 100–103.
22. Bill Zalud, "Here's How to Survive a Disaster," *Security* (May 1989), pp. 48–50.
23. Jan Rothstein, "BCP Comes of Age," *Information Security* 3 (July 2000), pp. 86–91.
24. Michael Capozzi, "Businesses Unprepared for High-Tech Risks," *Risk & Insurance* 12 (April 1, 2001), p. 9.
25. Brian Morrison, "Fiber Optic Technology for Nuclear Plants," *Security Technology & Design* 10 (June 2000), p. 62. And, Eric Pooley, "Nuclear Warriors," *Time* (March 4, 1996), pp. 46–54.
26. "Protecting against Nuclear Threats," *Access Control & Security Systems Integration* 43 (March 2000), pp. 24–26.
27. Morrison, p. 66.
28. Code of Federal Regulations, "Part 73-Physical Protection of Plants and Materials" (USGPO, January 1, 2000) http://www.access.gpo.gov/nara/cfr (May 17, 2001).
29. "Oak Ridge's Portal of Future Putting Emphasis on Security," *Security Concepts* (October 1996), p. 7.
30. U.S. Department of Defense, "About DSS," http://www.dss.mil/aboutdss/index.htm (May 21, 2001).
31. U.S. Department of Defense, "DSS Counterintelligence," http://www.dss.mil/cithreats/internet.htm (May 21, 2001).

17

Loss Prevention
at Select Institutions

OBJECTIVES

After studying this chapter the reader will be able to discuss loss problems and countermeasures for:

1. Educational institutions.
2. Healthcare institutions.
3. Banks and financial institutions.
4. Government institutions.

EDUCATIONAL INSTITUTIONS

Two major kinds of educational systems are emphasized here: school districts and higher education campuses. A big difference between school districts and college and university campuses is that, in the former, students normally go home at night and buildings often are empty. On campuses, students often live on the premises in dormitories. Exceptions are community and technical colleges whose students often commute. School districts and campuses both schedule evening and weekend activities such as classes, sports events, and meetings. A major factor for those who plan and implement loss prevention programs for these institutions is that the protection measures must cater to the needs and characteristics of the particular institution (see Figure 17-1).

Problems and Losses at Educational Institutions

Today, many educational institutions are faced with financial crises. And, losses from crimes, fires, and accidents make matters worse. Therefore, cost-effective loss prevention measures are especially vital.

Figure 17–1 Protection must cater to the unique needs of institutions. Courtesy: Talk-A-Phone.

Crimes against people are among the most serious offenses. Theft of educational property is a recurring problem. Burglary, larceny, and internal theft cause the disappearance of computers, books, and laboratory, audiovisual, and sports equipment. Drug abuse and distribution are common at educational institutions. *Vandalism*, the deliberate destruction of property, is a particularly annoying expense to school districts, more so than at colleges and universities. Damage includes broken windows, destroyed educational equipment, graffiti, and ruining of entire buildings.

There has been a long-held belief that campuses of higher education are a sanctuary immune to crime. However, this is not so. Large wooded campuses create criminal opportunities, as do colleges with public streets going through their campuses. Well-publicized crimes and security-negligence lawsuits, drug abuse, and "date rape" awareness all have brought campus security and safety issues into the open.[1] As with the rest of society in the United States and elsewhere, vulnerability also exists on campuses. Registration, when students pay tuition, presents robbery temptations. Numerous property crimes occur in dormitories. Sports events require traffic, parking, and crowd control. When controversial speakers or VIPs appear on the premises, extra security is required. Student activism is another potential threat. The 1960s and 1970s were decades of major student unrest, when riots and building "takeovers" occurred, and these courses of action are not going to disappear. IT needs protection against manipulation and attack. Bomb threats, fires, and arson are also troublesome.

Countermeasures

Several strategies are useful for school districts and colleges and universities. Typical measures are identification cards, access controls, emergency telephones, intrusion alarms, patrols, lighting, and CCTV.

The following list describes additional measures for the protection of school districts and institutions of higher education:

1. Lock doors and windows.
2. Consider an automatic access control system.
3. Provide secure locations for valuables. If possible, bolt portable equipment to stationary surfaces.
4. Mark expensive items to deter theft and fencing and to aid in criminal apprehension and return of stolen property.
5. Maintain accountability, and conduct inventories of equipment and valuables.
6. Install electronic article surveillance systems in libraries to reduce book thefts.
7. Stagger custodial shifts to ensure round-the-clock presence in buildings.

8. Use unarmed students to supplement security forces, especially for special events; provide good training.
9. Conduct drug abuse education and prevention programs. Contact local alcohol and drug abuse agencies for aid.

If it is possible to contribute loss prevention advice before the construction of a new building, the following suggestions are cost effective:

1. Design buildings with "defensible space" in mind (e.g., surveillance opportunities through windows and unobscured walkways to promote safety).
2. Avoid planting high shrubbery that provides hiding places and hinders visibility.
3. Do not plant trees close to buildings.
4. Avoid unnecessary exterior fixtures.
5. Limit roof access by eliminating low overhanging roofs.
6. Lock roof doors and hatches.
7. Install flexible internal gates in halls to impede access to specific areas.
8. Avoid suspended ceilings in restrooms and locker rooms.
9. Use self-closing faucets; ensure proper drainage in case of flooding.
10. Use vandal-resistant construction materials, especially glass made of unbreakable substances.

School Districts

Although multiple homicide events at schools have captured headlines in recent years, the chance of suffering a school-associated violent death is still less than one in a million. The *1999 Annual Report on School Safety* points out that less than 1 percent of the more than 2,500 children nationwide who were murdered or committed suicide were at school.[2] Research shows that students are about twice as likely to be victims of serious violent crime away from school as at school. The publication *Indicators of School Crime and Safety, 2000* reports that, in 1998, students ages 12 to 18 were victims of more than 2.7 million total crimes at school, including 253,000 serious violent crimes, such as sexual assault, robbery, and aggravated assault. At the same time, this report shows indicators of greater safety: a decline in the percentage of students carrying weapons and fewer gangs at schools.[3]

A comprehensive school district loss prevention program must involve the community: students, teachers and administrators, parents, public safety agencies, civic groups, and businesses.[4] The program can be divided into three components: special programs, personnel, and physical security.

Special programs include character education to help students distinguish right from wrong, conflict resolution, diversity, prevention of bullying, and programs that involve parents. One popular program is the Gang

Resistance Education and Training (GREAT) program that provides students with tools to resist the lure and trap of gangs. Modeled after the Drug Abuse Resistance Education (DARE) program, the GREAT program introduces students to conflict resolution skills, cultural sensitivity, and negative aspects of gang life. This program has spread to all fifty states and several other countries.[5]

Research of school administrators by Sheley showed the following measures taken to reduce violence (with the percent applying the measure): automatic suspension for weapons (96), revised disciplinary codes (81), "drug-free" zone (74), conflict resolution and mediation programs (71), "gun-free" zone (66), dress codes (63), sensitivity training (60), and locker searches (55).[6]

All employees at schools should be trained on early warning signs of inappropriate behavior or violence. These signs include feelings of isolation, rejection, and being persecuted, plus behaviors indicating anger or violence. Intervention and counseling are vital in response to such signs. However, caution is advised because there is no way to predict violence. As one principal said: "I don't think I could [predict violence] because teenagers are in such a roller-coaster time of their lives that at any one moment they could be very angry and depressed. They have these highs and lows, and on any given day I think I have a hundred kids who feel suicidal. The next day it might be a different hundred kids."[7]

A combined counseling and education approach might reduce student hostility and funnel student time into constructive activities. Traditional suspension from school often sends troublesome students to the streets where more trouble is likely. On the other hand, if students remain at school in an appropriate program, improved results are probable.

Personnel consist of teachers, teacher aids, administrators, counselors, security officers, and School Resource Officers. SROs are police officers on duty at schools who provide visibility, create rapport with students, and respond to incidents. Parents and volunteers play an important role in supplementing employees. All those who perform job duties at schools should undergo constant training and clearly understand policies and procedures for day-to-day events, such as student discipline problems and how to care for people during emergencies. Crisis plans should be in place to respond to violence, weapons, hostage situations, bombs/explosions, abused students, aggressive parents who are on the premises, and incidents involving parental rights. Many school districts distribute their crisis plans to public safety agencies who have a ready reference containing maps and building plans, utility shutoffs, staff and parent telephone numbers, a yearbook to identify people, and a set of keys.

In earlier years, *physical security* stressed keeping strangers out because they were the greatest threat. Now the major concern is students (see Figure 17-2). CCTV, handheld and walk-through metal detectors, and

Figure 17–2   In the past, physical security at schools stressed keeping strangers out. Today, the concern is students. Courtesy: Garrett Metal Detectors.

duress alarms are in widespread use. Physical security is a challenge because students must be safe without feeling as if they are in a prison.

According to the National Center for Injury Prevention and Control, Centers for Disease Control and Prevention, CCTV, metal detectors, and locker searches have little effect beyond the immediate environment of the school building; school officials should work closely with other agencies in their communities to develop a comprehensive approach to prevent violence and crime.[8] *If school security planners argue for more security personnel and hardware to curb school crime, they may be faced with others who see broader solutions to the problem.* And, whatever strategies are implemented, they should be subject to research and evaluation to produce the best possible solutions and utilization of resources.

Colleges and Universities

In response to increasing crime on college campuses and the need for more accurate statistics, Congress passed the *Student-Right-to-Know and Campus Security Act of 1990.* This legislation requires crime awareness and prevention measures at colleges and reporting campus crime to the FBI *Uniform Crime Reports* program, while making these statistics available to students and the general public. Such data enables comparisons among colleges and universities. However, there is conjecture that some schools omit reporting acts of violence to protect recruiting efforts and their reputations.[9] FBI crime data has been criticized over the years because it represents crimes *reported* to police, and many crimes are never reported or recorded, as shown by victimization studies.[10]

In 1992, the Campus Sexual Assault Victim's Bill of Rights amended the above act, requiring schools to develop policies to deal with sexual assault on campus. This is an important issue requiring prompt action by schools, especially in light of a Bureau of Justice Statistics estimate of 35 incidents of rape per academic year on a campus with 1,000 women.[11] Further amendments in 1998 added two crimes to reporting, arson and negligent manslaughter, and required schools to report on crime at property owned by a school but not at the main campus. Schools not reporting crime data are subject to a $25,000 fine. In nearly every category of crime, college campuses showed lower incidence of crime than comparable data for the nation as a whole.[12]

Research by Bonnie S. Fisher and John J. Sloan produced guidelines that should be considered when evaluating programs designed to reduce campus crime. Some of their major points follow:

- A comprehensive evaluation requires identifying the individual departments or groups on campus that will be involved and assigning safety and security responsibilities to them.
- A comprehensive approach includes security, faculty members, staff members, students, and public law enforcement personnel.
- Campus administrators should conduct surveys of the campus community to understand the nature and extent of crime and fear, perceptions of the effectiveness of security, and participation in crime

prevention programs and whether participants adopted any of the preventive measures. Until evaluations become an integral part of responding to campus crime, administrators will continue to make poor decisions on security strategies.

- Research has confirmed that crime on campuses is influenced by poor lighting, excessive foliage, blocked views, and difficulty of escape by victims. (As we can see, crime prevention through environmental design, or CPTED, as discussed earlier in the text, has universal application.)
- Location measures (e.g., proximity to urban areas with high unemployment) are predictors of high campus crime rates.[13]

Numerous campuses have implemented the strategy of many public police agencies, namely, community policing. *Community policing* aims to control crime through a partnership of police and citizens, and it strives to become a dominant philosophy throughout a police department. This partnership strives to develop a higher level of trust and cooperation (see Figure 17-3). And, rather than police reacting to the same problem over and over again, a unique, proactive approach is employed for problem solving. For a campus, preventive strategies are designed in cooperation with various campus departments, community service agencies, and other groups.[14]

What do you view as the top three strategies to prevent violence at school districts? How would you answer this same question for colleges and universities?

One particular group that has advanced the professionalism of campus safety and security is the International Association of Campus Law Enforcement Administrators (IACLEA; http://www.iaclea.org/). This group began in 1958 with eleven schools and today it represents 1,000 colleges and universities worldwide with membership of over 1,500. The group holds an annual conference, offers training and position statements, and publishes *Campus Law Enforcement Journal*.

Fire Protection at Educational Institutions

The *National Fire Protection Association Code for Safety to Life from Fire in Buildings and Structures*, concisely referred to as the *NFPA Life Safety Code*, defines *educational occupancies* as "including all buildings used for gatherings of groups of six or more persons for purposes of instruction, such as schools, universities, colleges, and academies."[15] The principal fire haz-

University of Nebraska at Omaha-Campus Security   Page 1 of 1

Policies and Crime Statistics
Emergency Procedures
Safety Hints & Tips
Location & Hours
Main Campus Map
Other Services
Parking Information
South Campus Map
Visitor Information

Campus Security

University of Nebraska at Omaha

6001 Dodge St. EAB 100

Omaha, NE 68182-0057

Phone: (402) 554-2648

Fax: (402) 554-3675

Campus Emergency's dial 4-2911 or 4-2648

E-Mail security@unomaha.edu

`003726`

This page and subsequent pages, were created and are maintained by the UNO Campus Security Department. We'd appreciate FEEDBACK on this page, (hints, tips, or gripes). Last updated on 9-15-2000.

UNO HOME PAGE

Figure 17–3 Community policing seeks to partner with citizens to control crime. A Web page links campus security to its customers. Courtesy: University of Nebraska at Omaha.

ards endangering life in places of public assembly are (1) overcrowding; (2) blocking, impairing, or locking exits; (3) storing combustibles in dangerous locations; (4) using an open flame without proper precautions; and (5) using combustible decorations.[16] Furthermore, hazards of educational buildings vary with construction characteristics and with the age group of students.

Younger students, for example, require protection different from that for older students. The NFPA Life Safety Code specifies that kindergarten and first grade rooms should be on the floor of exit discharge so that stairs do not endanger these students. Building codes also specify similar guidelines. Because junior and senior high schools contain laboratories, shops, and home economics rooms, these facilities should have construction with a fire-resistance rating of one hour. School kitchens require similar protection. Distance to exits must not exceed 150 feet unless the building has an

---

Loss Prevention at Virginia Tech[17]

Virginia Tech is the home of 25,000 students and it is the state's largest university. The school is situated on 2,600 acres and includes 100 buildings. Located in a rural area, the school enjoys a relatively low crime rate. The most troublesome crime problem is petty theft—students steal from each other. Bomb threats are a recurring problem, usually around exam time. The school takes a *broad based approach to loss prevention* through the efforts of risk management, insurance, safety and health, and campus police. Staff is always seeking to prevent losses. As examples, if an engineering department is using hoists, or if the ROTC unit will be rappelling, training becomes a top priority. For emergencies, such as a violent crime or a major snowstorm, Virginia Tech is prepared through a Core Crisis Team and a plan of action.

---

automatic extinguishing system specified by the Life Safety Code; with the system, the distance may be increased to 200 feet. A fire alarm system is required for all educational buildings. Most schools conduct fire drills for pupils. The Life Safety Code and many good building codes provide numerous standards for increasing fire safety.

For colleges and universities, the Life Safety Code is applied depending on building characteristics and use. If buildings are windowless, the Life Safety Code requirements for special structures are applicable. This would include automatic extinguishing systems, venting systems for smoke, and emergency lighting and power. Because many campus buildings are multistory, specific safeguards are necessary. Fire drills and training are important for residence halls and academic buildings.[18]

HEALTHCARE INSTITUTIONS

Hospitals, nursing homes, and other healthcare institutions possess specific crime, fire, and safety weaknesses that require countermeasures. Violence is a recurring problem. A large inventory of consumable items are located within healthcare buildings: food, medical supplies, linens, drugs, and wheelchairs. Thousands of meals and prescriptions are served each day in many of these locations. Assorted crimes are possible (e.g., theft, kickbacks to purchasers, fraud). Drugs are susceptible not only to internal theft but also to robbery. Expensive medical and office equipment and patient and employee belongings are other tempting targets for offenders. Moreover, the safety of people must be a high priority. There is a never-ending flow of employees (doctors, nurses, assorted specialists, nonprofessional support personnel, volunteers), patients, visitors, salespeople, and repair technicians. A large number of female employees need protection, especially during night-time shift changes. Patients are particularly vulnerable at all times because of their limited physical capabilities. What makes protection difficult is that these institutions remain open 24 hours a day.

Emergency plans and special equipment are necessary in case of fire, explosion, accidents, bomb threats, and strikes. Flammable medical gases and oxygen support combustion, which necessitates safety precautions. Accumulations of trash as well as safety in the operating rooms are additional considerations.

Strategies for Healthcare Institutions

Accountability and Inventory Control

Because much of the inventory in healthcare institutions can be used by employees at home or sold to others, accountability and inventory control can minimize shrinkage. Imaginative preventive techniques should be applied where possible. For example, Russell L. Colling, in *Hospital and Healthcare Security*, explains that the loss of hospital scrub suits, which are a popular garment worn by a variety of people, can be reduced by issuing them to individuals and a soiled suit can be exchanged for a clean one through either an issue window or an automatic uniform dispenser. The dispenser, similar to an ATM, credits a returned suit and issues a clean one; this is another use of an automated access card.[19] Linen and other property permanently imprinted with the name of the institution will also aid shrinkage control efforts. Disposable items (e.g., paper towels) are less expensive but also subject to pilferage. Soiled-linen chutes are convenient hiding places for stolen goods. Offenders often wrap stolen merchandise in dirty linen for later recovery. Daily inspection of soiled linens and trash collection and disposal systems ensure that these theft techniques are impeded.

Auditing

When accounting and other safeguards are checked for deviations, loss prevention programs are strengthened. Do accounting records conform to management expectations? Are patients being properly billed? How accurate are accounts receivable and accounts payable records? In the food service operation, how careful are the controls over the ordering of foods and food preparation and distribution? The food service area is a prime location for theft. Every loss prevention measure should be audited to make sure it is functioning as designed.

Applicant Screening

Losses are caused by both professional and nonprofessional staff members. Equipment and supplies may accompany doctors from a hospital to his or her private practice. Likewise, nurses have access to a broad spectrum of items. Low-skilled healthcare workers create additional problems.

Several measures can be instituted to obtain quality employees. A good employment application and background investigation are wise choices. The time and effort expended on applicant screening will help to avert the hiring of quacks as well as drug and sex offenders who are attracted to healthcare facilities.

Access Controls

When entrances are limited, unauthorized entry is hindered. Uniformed officers should be stationed at each entrance. Of course, emergency exits are a necessity for safety; but alarms on these doors will deter usage. Identification badges worn by employees assist in recognition by other employees. Outside individuals on the premises for any extended period of time (e.g., contractors or technicians) should be issued ID badges.

The control of visitors must be handled with compassion and empathy. Visitors wanting to see an ill family member are often emotionally upset. Furthermore, recovery of the patient can be aided by visits from loved ones. These factors must be stressed in healthcare training programs. Many locations issue visitor passes to avoid overcrowding in patients' rooms and to inhibit a variety of problems such as the deviant man who dresses like a doctor to "examine" female patients.

Patrols, CCTV

Surveillance of interior and exterior areas, through the use of patrols and CCTV, deters crime. Good lighting is an integral aspect of this effort. Large medical centers have a command center for communications and CCTV observation. More intense vigilance usually is needed at night, but assorted crimes are possible at any time—to name a few, surreptitious entry, theft, vandalism, and disorderly conduct. Automobiles may be broken into in parking lots to obtain valuables. Doctors' automobiles are particularly vulnerable, especially if medical bags are left behind. Aggressive patrolling and surveillance are required during shift changes; women are escorted to their vehicles to foil attempts at purse snatching, assault, or rape. During slow periods when traffic is limited, uniformed officers should resume patrolling while checking for safety hazards.

Some locations have chosen sports jackets or blazers for loss prevention personnel to create a "nonpolice image." But most facilities seem to favor uniforms to provide a "police image" to reinforce crime deterrence and to signify that the location is protected.

The arming of personnel is controversial. Some medical institutions issue firearms to all officers, whereas other locations issue them only to those assigned to external areas.

Emergency Room

At least one officer must be stationed in the emergency room at all times. Depending on the crime rate, officers may have to be armed, equipped with bullet-resistant vests, and prepared to frisk people, confiscate weapons, and make arrests. Signs prohibiting weapons should be posted as well as notices of metal detectors. Disturbances occur here regularly in busy hospitals. Verbal arguments, assaults, and destruction of property may be caused by belligerent patients, visitors who are intoxicated, and rival gangs. Disturbances recurrently are the result of long waiting periods before treatment. Medical personnel can reduce a portion of disturbances if they adequately explain the reasons for delays. Emergency treatment areas should be sealed off if necessary and panic buttons available.

Newborn Nursery

Infant abduction is a particularly disturbing problem for parents, employees, and police. In 1983, the *National Center for Missing and Exploited Children* (NCMEC; http://www.ncmec.org/) created a database on infant abduction that led to the creation of guidelines for hospitals. Such offenders often impersonate medical staff and "case" the nursery prior to the crime. Countermeasures include taking footprints of infants, requiring photo ID cards of all employees and volunteers, restricting visitors, CCTV, installing an electronic surveillance system that detects infant bracelets, and not releasing birth information. If an abduction occurs, immediately notify the police, the FBI, and the NCMEC; conduct a search; check exit points; and begin a thorough investigation. Such "target hardening" at hospitals can displace kidnapping to areas outside the hospital and to the home of the infant. Parents should protect the infant by, for example, not placing pretty bows outside the home to signify a birth. Security personnel can prepare a brochure on protection at home.

"Target hardening" can displace crime. Can you think of other examples, besides the one just given, where enhanced security caused crime patterns to shift?

Pharmacy Protection and Robbery

A small percentage of the population is addicted to drugs and will do anything to obtain them. Colling notes that narcotics addiction among doctors and nurses is a much more serious problem than recognized and healthcare facilities are a major source of illegal drug traffic involving legal drugs.[20] There have been instances where medical personnel have withheld drugs from a patient for their own use or sale. One technique is to substitute flour for medication. Hospital administrators are reluctant to report these acts for fear of lawsuits. Another technique is to write a phony prescription or alter an existing one. In one case, a hospital pharmacist diverted thousands of dollars of drugs to his retail drugstore. The maintenance of specific drugs (i.e., narcotics) is strictly regulated by the *Controlled Substance Act of 1970*, enforced by the Drug Enforcement Administration (DEA). All states regulate pharmacies, and in most states the pharmacy itself and the pharmacist must be licensed.

To curb pharmacy losses, these measures are recommended: (1) maintain strict accountability and inventory control; (2) protect blank, serial-numbered prescription slips; (3) set up a camera so that a picture can be taken of prescriptions and those who receive the slip; and (4) conduct undercover investigations.

For the protection of the pharmacy, cashiering operations, and the business office, the following measures will deter burglary, robbery, and other crimes: (1) intrusion and holdup alarms integrated with CCTV, (2) bullet-resistant glass, (3) electronically operated doors, (4) patrols, and (5) key control.

Healthcare Violence and OSHA Guidelines

According to the U.S. Bureau of Labor Statistics, healthcare and social service workers have the highest incidence of assault injuries.[21] In addition to emergency rooms, several other locations in the healthcare industry are noted for potential violence. Children's hospitals, psychiatric units, and home healthcare are examples. To illustrate, in a children's hospital or pediatric unit, a child may require protection following abuse or to prevent kidnapping. If the child's parents are estranged, family strife may spill into the hospital. Protection methods include crisis intervention training for healthcare employees, gathering information on the family at the preadmission stage, checking court papers showing parental rights or restraining orders, posting photos of persons to be barred from visiting the child, and even placing a false name on the nameplate of the patient's room.[22]

Because of escalating crime at healthcare facilities and several highly publicized cases—such as the case of a man who opened fire with a semi-automatic pistol in the emergency department at USC Hospital in Los Angeles and critically injured three doctors—government intervention has occurred. California and New Jersey are among states that have developed safety standards to prevent violence in the workplace. On the federal level, the Occupational Safety and Health Administration (OSHA) has released *Guidelines for Preventing Workplace Violence for Health Care and Social Service Workers*. According to OSHA, "All employers have a general duty to provide their employees with a workplace free from recognized hazards likely to cause death or serious physical harm" and "Employers can be cited for violating the General Duty Clause if there is a recognized hazard of workplace violence in their establishments and they do nothing to prevent or abate it."[23] The OSHA guidelines are advisory in nature and focus on management commitment, work site analysis, hazard prevention and control (e.g., physical security), education and training, record keeping, and evaluation.[24]

Locker Rooms

Men and women who work in healthcare institutions are accustomed to using separate locker rooms before, during, and after shifts. Locker rooms ordinarily are located in the basement or remote locations. CCTV and patrols can be applied to areas just outside locker rooms. Panic buttons that signal trouble are useful within locker rooms. Loss prevention personnel should conduct occasional locker inspections to deter assorted problems.

Mortuary

The mortuary has been the site of morbid crimes. People, including relatives of the deceased, have stolen jewelry directly from cadavers. Gold dental work has been extracted with a pocket knife. The rare sexual perversion called *necrophilia* (sexual activity with a corpse) is a possibility in the mortuary. Also, there are cases where the wrong body was taken away for burial. A complete inventory should be conducted of the personal property of the deceased soon after death. Witnesses and appropriate paperwork should be a part of this procedure.

Patient Property

A recurring puzzle sometimes accompanies patients prior to discharge: jewelry or other personal property is missing. In addition to theft, it is possible that the property is nonexistent, is at the patient's home, or has been misplaced. To avoid negative public relations, some healthcare administrators quickly reimburse patients. But a few prevention measures are cost effective. The admitting form can contain a statement advising the patient to deposit valuables in a security envelope. These envelopes have the same serial numbers on both the envelope and the receipt. Valuables are inserted and the envelope is sealed in the presence of the patient. The patient and the clerk sign and date both the envelope and the receipt. An adequate safe is needed for these valuables.

Protection of Patient Information

Patient information requires protection. In one case, a private investigator telephoned a hospital pretending to be a physician who needed information to treat a patient. At another hospital, a medical clerk telephoned life insurance and diaper service salespeople immediately after the birth of babies. Privacy and confidentiality are subverted in such incidents. *Privacy* signifies that patients may not want certain information released for personal reasons. *Confidentiality* refers to the limitation on information revelation after a free flow of communications between the patient and medical staff members. Procedures should be implemented to obtain patient and physician approval before information is released to outsiders.

Today, electronic patient records are in need of greater protection. Sensitive information routinely is shared with noncaregivers, who use it legitimately for claim payments, research, and oversight. Transmission of patient information over the Internet or in electronic mail requires protection.[25] Many of the computer protection methods (e.g., passwords, encryption) covered in the previous chapter are applicable here.

Cooperative Efforts

In urban areas where a concentration of healthcare institutions are located, associations have formed to work toward mutual goals. Monthly meetings afford opportunities to share ideas and solutions to problems. Resources (e.g., training) are pooled, which results in lower costs.

Standards, Performance Measures, and Professionalism

The *Joint Commission on Accreditation of Healthcare Organizations* (JCAHO; http://www.jcaho.org/) is a dominant force in promoting standards in the healthcare field that affect funding from government. JCAHO standard EC 1.4 addresses how hospitals should provide a secure environment for patients, staff, and visitors. Specific written plans for security are required for the "environment of care" (EC) standards as described here:

1. Establish, support, and maintain a security management program.
2. Address security concerns regarding patients, visitors, personnel, and property.
3. Provide for identification of patients, visitors, and staff.
4. Provide access control to security sensitive areas.
5. Provide vehicular and traffic control to the emergency service area.
6. Designate personnel who are responsible for the plan's development, implementation, and monitoring.
7. Describe methods for reporting and investigating all security incidents.
8. Provide for the annual evaluation of the plan.

Other standards focus on, for example, "staff knowledge of the plans" (EC 2.1), "implementation of the plans" (EC 2.3), and "life safety management" (EC 2.6). JCAHO is particularly interested in training employees and how they react to emergencies.[26]

Because measuring the preventive role of security is not an easy task, many security departments maintain extensive record-keeping systems on a host of activities (e.g., logs of visitors, escorts, and parking notices issued). Such record-keeping systems are "keys to survival." Another avenue that helps to measure security programs is *performance standards*, which are required by JCAHO and address both broad objectives (e.g., preventing crime) and specific outcomes (e.g., establishing response time to critical incidents). This avenue, also called *benchmarking*, gives the department a mark with which to measure performance. Here are examples:

Standard: The security department will maintain 50 percent of officers certified by the IAHSS.

Performance Measurement: Security personnel training records will be reviewed in January and July and reports will be presented to the director of security.

Standard: All intrusion and panic alarm systems will be 100 percent operational and function as intended.

Performance Measurement: These systems will be field tested (activated) the first week of each month and a report will be submitted to the director of security.[27]

The ASIS Healthcare Security Committee completed a healthcare security benchmarking study in 2000. The goal of the research was to provide security practitioners with needed data to justify expenditures. Funded by Burns International through the ASIS Foundation, Inc., 1,200 hospitals were surveyed with 324 responses that yielded results that included the following: 12 percent of security staff is contracted, 76 percent is proprietary, and 10 percent is a mixture. Twenty-nine percent of hospitals plan to increase both contract and proprietary security. Twelve percent will decrease both, with plans to improve security through technology. Ninety-five percent have a security management plan in accord with JCAHO and 86 percent have a workplace violence policy in accord with OSHA. Pressing concerns were: patient protection, followed by employee and visitor protection; crime; and infant-area protection, followed by pediatric, pharmacy, and psychiatric areas. Business solutions were a priority with requirements to perform at higher levels with less funding.[28]

The professionalism of those who protect healthcare institutions is enhanced through the *International Association for Healthcare Security and Safety* (IAHSS; http://iahss.org), which was founded in 1968. It is a not-for-profit organization for hospital security and safety administrators. The IAHSS administers the Certified Healthcare Protection Administrator (CHPA) credential and publishes *The Journal of Healthcare Protection Management*. Two important purposes of this group are the development of standards for healthcare security practices and training certification. For the various certifications, students study IAHSS manuals and JCAHO security standards.

Fire and Other Disasters

"Some 10 percent of healthcare facilities have suffered a fire loss at some time in their history."[29] Compounding this problem are patients who are physically weak or mentally impaired and unable to care for themselves during an emergency.

A multitude of fire codes and standards for healthcare institutions emanate from local, state, and federal agencies. *The National Fire Protection Association 101, Life Safety Code* refers to a "total concept approach" to the fire problem, consisting of construction, detection/suppression, and staff presence.[30] Almost all states promote safety through minimum standards and healthcare licensing requirements. The federal government, for example, adopted the Life Safety Code for Medicare and Medicaid regulations in healthcare institutions.

JCAHO has worked closely with the federal government to provide adequate patient care and safety. Legislation has stated that hospitals must meet federal requirements for health and safety if they are accredited by JCAHO. All healthcare locations are subjected to OSHA, except those that are federal. At times, overlapping regulations produce confusion between JCAHO and OSHA mandates.

Fire Protection

To prevent and suppress fires, the following methods can increase safety in a healthcare environment:

1. Especially because healthcare locations use a great deal of disposables, rubbish must be collected, stored, and eliminated properly. Fire-proof receptacles are useful.
2. Flammable substances require safe storage, use, and disposal.
3. Electrical equipment and wiring should be inspected.
4. Operating and delivery rooms are subject to static electricity, which can spark a fire if close to anesthetics. These rooms should be tested for static electricity.
5. Because smoking is a recurring hazard, "no smoking" signs and sand urns will impede carelessness.
6. The person in charge of fire protection should make regular inspections.
7. A full-time fire marshal, fire engineer, or loss prevention manager should be in charge of fire protection. This individual coordinates training, evacuation plans, drills, equipment evaluation and purchasing, and liaison with local fire agencies, plus other duties.
8. Common fire protection characteristics are ionized particle detectors, sprinklers, fire-resistive construction, adequate means to egress, exit markings and illumination, and emergency power. They are stressed in the Life Safety Code.
9. The early detection and suppression of fire plus fire-resistive construction will play major roles if patients cannot be moved and must be "defended in place."

Disasters

In addition to fire, a host of other disasters are an ever-present danger. Well-designed plans, training, and liaison with outside agencies will go a long way in reducing losses if disasters strike. JCAHO has requirements for disaster preparations.

An example of a disastrous situation is a strike by healthcare workers. Associated losses are monumental: disruptions to patient care, loss of hospital income, intimidation of staff, property damage, and unfavorable publicity. Countermeasures can include formation of a strike planning committee, additional security, and enlisting the assistance of nonstriking employees and volunteers. If more than one union is at the location, management should strive for separate contract expiration dates. The preparation prior to the strike will have a definite bearing on management–union negotiations.

Career: Healthcare Security

This industry goes beyond hospitals and includes long-term care facilities, clinics, and nursing homes.

Duties: Protecting patients, visitors, employees, parking lots, pharmacies, and emergency rooms. Other duties are restraining patients and others, controlling visitation rights, investigating, conducting inspections of fire and life safety methods, and participating in continuing training. Management duties include preparing emergency plans, enforcing policies, and preparing for inspections.

Prerequisites: For management, undergraduate degree, advanced degree preferred; 5–10 years experience; CPP and or CHPA; CPR/first aid certification.

Demographics of typical practitioner: Undergraduate degree; 12–15 years in security; 6–8 years in specialty; CPP or CHPA; salary of $50,000–75,000 yr.; titles: Security Manager, Director of Safety and Security.

Source: American Society for Industrial Security, *Career Opportunities in Security* (Alexandria, VA: ASIS, 1998), p. 10.

BANKS AND FINANCIAL INSTITUTIONS

There are thousands of financial depository institutions and branches in the United States. Money, securities, checks, and other liquid assets make this industry attractive to internal and external culprits. *The range of offenses spans embezzlement and computer, credit, and loan frauds. These crimes result in greater losses while being more difficult to detect and solve than bank robbery and burglary.* Services that present particular loss problems are automated teller machines (ATMs), after-hours depositories (AHDs), and electronic fund transfer systems (EFTSs). Personnel servicing ATMs and customers have been victimized by armed robbers. AHDs also present a robbery problem, such as when a retailer makes a deposit at the end of the business day. Banks have incurred losses from fraud during the transfer of funds. Sophisticated wiretaps on a bank's funds transfer line are an ominous reality.

Regulation H

Regulation H, Code of Federal Regulations, combines the former Bank Protection Act (BPA) of 1968 and many provisions of the Bank Secrecy Act of 1986 into one document. An increase in crimes against banks and the lack of adequate countermeasures led Congress to enact the BPA, which applied to a variety of financial institutions. It established minimum standards to combat robbery, burglary, and larceny.

Even though the BPA was designed to counter losses from outsiders, a significant shortcoming of this legislation was that it did not establish standards for internal protection. For example, the savings and loan (S&L) scandal of the 1980s and 1990s, where bank executives approved risky loans to friends and so on (i.e., "the fox was guarding the hen house"), cost U.S. taxpayers billions of dollars (much more than embezzlement and bank robberies combined). Despite these drawbacks, the BPA was the first legislation reinforcing security for a large private commercial enterprise. It is impossible to ascertain the number of crimes that have been prevented because of the BPA.

Security under Regulation H

- Security procedures must be adopted to discourage robberies, burglaries, and larcenies, assist in the identification and prosecution of persons who commit such acts, and maintain records of crimes.
- The institution's board of directors must ensure that a written security program is developed and implemented.
- The board must designate a security officer to administer the security program and receive an annual report from that person.
- Program requirements include opening and closing procedures, warning signals, and safekeeping of currency and other valuables (e.g., vault controls).
- Policies, procedures, and training manuals must be developed, and initial and periodic training must be provided for employees.
- Security devices—alarm systems, tamper-resistant locks, lighting, and safes or vaults—must be selected, tested, operated, and maintained.

What are your views as to why the BPA of 1968 focused on external threats (e.g., robbery) rather than internal threats (e.g., white-collar crime, fraud)?

The *Bank Secrecy Act* was implemented to establish reporting require-ments for transactions of money to detect money laundering. In 1988, the *Anti-Drug Abuse Act* amended the Bank Secrecy Act and requires banks to report any "suspicious transactions" that may be associated with illegal drug trafficking. *The Antiterrorism and Effective Death Penalty Act of 1996* makes it a criminal offense for persons in the United States, other than those excepted by the government, to engage in financial transactions with coun-tries that condone or encourage terrorism.

A bank security officer may also be responsible for Bank Secrecy Act requirements under Regulation H. This includes ensuring that Suspicious Activity Reports (SARs) are filed with appropriate federal police agencies and the Department of the Treasury when violations of federal law are sus-pected. This includes insider abuse or money laundering. Two sample guidelines are: violations aggregating $5,000 or more where a suspect can be identified and violations aggregating $25,000 or more regardless of a poten-tial suspect.

Money laundering is a huge global problem with a conservative esti-mate of $600 billion laundered annually. Essentially, it is an attempt to make "dirty" money (i.e., obtained through illegal means, such as the drug trade) appear clean. Offenders often transfer "dirty" money, under disguised ownership, from one bank to another, globally, to increase the difficulty of tracing it.[31]

Robbery

A common feature of many financial locations is a warmer, more personal atmosphere gained through the elimination of security barriers. Although this may please customers, robbery becomes a greater threat. When a rob-bery does take place at a bank, the teller is often the only one initially knowledgeable about the crime. The situation of a lone robber passing a holdup note to the teller is typical. In any robbery situation, the danger to life must not be taken lightly. The following suggestions can improve employee reaction:

1. Institute a training program.
2. During a robbery, act cautiously and do not take any chances.
3. Activate an alarm if possible without the robber noticing.
4. Provide the robber with bait money. Tear-gas or dye packs also are important. These devices look like packs of currency and emit tear gas and red smoke (which stains clothes and the money) when carried out of a bank. A radio transmitter activates the packet.
5. Study characteristics of the bandit, especially scars, shape of eyes, height, body structure, voice, speech patterns, and other permanent features.

6. Safely note the means of transportation, license number, and vehicle description.
7. Telephone the public police.

Although robberies declined between 1996 and 1999, the bad news is that they are becoming more violent. Increasingly, hostages are being taken.[32]

In commenting on traditional and more advanced methods of bank security, one protection manager sees uniformed security officers, cash controls, and dye packs as most popular. Officers can offer comfort to customers and act as a credible witness; however, their use is subject to controversy. They may deter an amateur robber, but not a professional. Cash controls limit cash at teller stations and in the safe and vault. Initially, dye packs were a deterrent. Eventually, robbers threatened violence if they received one, and detonations have occurred inside banks. Controls on detonations and proper training are essential. Advances in protection include metal detection portals that are expensive, bullet resistive, and designed to set off an alarm and keep the inner door locked unless opened by an employee. These double doors are capable of trapping a robber, but careful planning is essential to promote safety. Another advance is the remote teller system whereby business is conducted via CCTV and pneumatic tube.[33]

Kidnapping and Extortion

A common victim of a kidnapper or extortionist is the financial executive and his or her family. However, a bank teller is another likely victim. These crimes vary; two scenarios follow. An offender kidnaps a bank employee or family member while he or she is driving the family car or is at home. The kidnapped person is traded for cash. Another approach is when an extortionist calls a bank employee at work, claims to be holding a family member, and demands cash for a safe return of the kidnapped victim. The extortionist may even confront the bank employee personally. In these situations, violence is a potential hazard, even after cash is delivered.

A precise plan and employee training are essential prior to a confrontation. The following procedures should be observed by the person in contact with the kidnappers:

1. Try to remain calm during the ordeal. Contact public police as soon as possible.
2. If a hostage is involved, ask the caller to allow the hostage to come to the telephone to speak.
3. Repeat demands to the caller to double-check any directions and procedures.
4. Try to arrange for a person-to-person payoff and transfer of the hostage.

5. If prepared, trace the call.
6. After the call, record as much information as possible (e.g., date, time, words spoken, background noises). Management should provide a standard form.
7. If the hostage is brought to the bank or if the offender confronts a bank employee personally, notify other employees with a prearranged signal.
8. Include "bait" money in any payoff.

Online Risks, Embezzlement, and Fraud

Banks have increased their exposure to crime because they are connected internally through an intranet and externally through online banking services. An employee may commit embezzlement by gaining unauthorized access to a bank's accounts payable system and creating fictitious invoices and payments to the employee's post office box. Other internal crimes are to delete all records of a friend's loan, approve fictitious loans, or tap into dormant accounts.

Online banking risks are varied and include, for example, the hacking of bank Web sites to alter information or to steal customer information. Web spoofing seeks to create a look-alike Web site to trick customers into releasing confidential account information that is exploited or sold by the hacker. A cyber-extortionist may gain access to a bank's critical systems and plant a "bomb" to destroy data unless money is paid.[34] As covered in previous chapters, sound internal controls and IT security affords protection for organizations.

Check swindles, which are a common externally perpetrated fraud, may involve the forgery of stolen checks or the manufacture of fictitious checks. Computer programs permit offenders to create corporate payroll checks that are nearly impossible to distinguish from a genuine one. A check from a real company can be scanned into a computer and printed on check stock purchased from a local office supply retailer. Another technique is to order checks from an office supply retailer using a bogus company and account number. Countermeasures for banks and other organizations include transaction reports that flag unusual activity, requiring a fingerprint for noncustomers, training, awards for employees for spotting a bogus check, and "alerts" that contain a copy of a bogus check with a photo of the suspect.[35]

Because of the growing crimes of identity theft and fraud, banks have been forced to play a greater role in preventing these problems. The Gramm-Leach-Bliley Financial Services Modernization Act, effective July 1, 2001, requires financial institutions and insurance companies to disclose to customers policies on what data they collect, with whom they share it, and how they share it. Two common scenarios are a caller to a bank who claims to have forgotten his/her customer PIN, or another scam where the pretext caller, pretending to be a bank employee, requests personal data from the bank customer. Identity theft also presents a problem when customer data is shared among banks, insurance companies, and third parties.[36]

Automatic Teller Machines

Crime has followed ATM self-service banking. Such crime is likely to increase as the number of ATMs also increases, and there is concern for safety and liability. Several state and local government bodies have passed ATM safety laws. These bills typically require surveillance cameras, adequate lighting, mirrors and low hedges to enhance visibility, and crime prevention tips to ATM card holders. As well as robbery, fraud is a problem. Although offenders watch for careless customers who do not protect their PIN numbers, a considerable amount of ATM fraud is committed by a family member or friend. "Smart cards," containing information on the customer, and biometrics will increase security.

One low-tech crime victimizing ATMs is theft of the entire machine. A truck and chains or an inexpensive lift truck are used to pull the ATM from its foundation. This technique is likely to grow because of a surge in free-standing ATMs. Countermeasures include a global positioning system that contains a sensor and transmitter attached to the ATM. When a theft occurs, location, direction, and speed are transmitted to a central station.[37]

GOVERNMENT INSTITUTIONS

The September 11, 2001 attack on the Pentagon increased concern for the protection of government buildings. But improvements in security have been occurring for several years because of attacks. In 1994, a Maryland trucker crashed a stolen plane on the White House lawn. One month later, an ex-con fired 29 rounds at the building. And then, in 1995, the bombing occurred at the Alfred P. Murrah Federal Building in Oklahoma City. The Oklahoma City bombing led former President Clinton to direct the U.S. Department of Justice to assess the vulnerability of federal office buildings in the United States. Prior to the study and publication, *Vulnerability Assessment of Federal Facilities*, there were no government-wide standards for security at federal facilities and no central database of the security in place at such facilities. Because of its expertise in court security, the U.S. Marshals Service coordinated the study that focused on the approximately 1,330 federal office buildings housing about 750,000 federal civilian employees. One major result of the study was the development of 52 standards focusing on perimeter security, entry security, interior security, and security planning. Another result of the study was the division of federal buildings into five security levels, based on staffing size, use, and the need for public access. A Level I building has ten or fewer federal employees and is a "storefront" type of operation, such as a military recruiting office. A Level V building is critical to national security, such as the Pentagon. Recommended minimum security standards apply to each security level.[38]

The process of implementing the standards is being overseen by the Interagency Security Committee, established by presidential executive order, and the General Services Administration (GSA), the government's buildings manager. The GSA has approved thousands of security recommendations from building security committees, with a price tag of hundreds of millions of dollars.[39] State and local government institutions also are involved in security efforts to protect government buildings.

Federal government security upgrades to buildings are ongoing; however, challenges remain. The GSA is developing a system to assess actual cost and an audit trail to ensure that records of work done are accurate. Federal auditors found, for example, that at one installation records showed the installation of fifteen light poles in a parking lot, but upon inspection, only two were evident. Also noted were poorly trained security officers and inadequate service from security contractors.[40] Another major problem was reported in 2000 when undercover federal agents, working for the General Accounting Office (GAO), the investigative arm of Congress, used phony IDs to enter nineteen of the most secure government buildings and two airports. The impostors were even able to drive a rental van to the interior courtyard parking lot of the Justice Department.[41]

What are your recommendations to improve security in light of the above findings? Do you think corporate buildings can be penetrated like the federal buildings?

As we know, military and nuclear weapons facilities are other examples of government locations that have been involved in security programs for years. And, security at these locations is very intense. Another aspect of government with a history of security efforts is the criminal justice system. Jails and prisons have traditionally maintained tight security for obvious reasons. Police agencies, especially following the unrest of the 1960s, have strengthened security in and around police buildings, including communications centers, evidence and weapons storage rooms, and crime labs. Following violence in the judicial system, courts have also increased security (see Figure 17-4). Because of the Sixth Amendment right of defendants to a public trial, court security is especially challenging. The U.S. Marshals Service has taken a leading role in developing court security methods. Each major component of the criminal justice system—police, courts, and

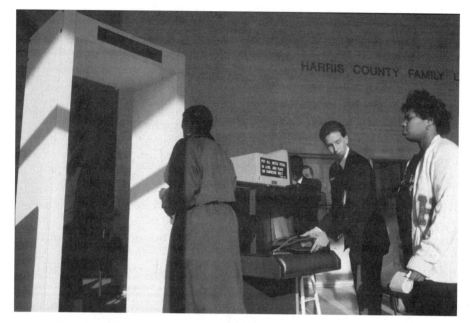

Figure 17–4 Courthouse screening. Walk-through metal detector, left; X-ray scanner, right. Courtesy: Wackenhut Corporation. Photo by Ed Burns.

corrections is connected with organizations that promote either accreditation or performance measures containing security enhancements.[42]

Search the Web

Use the search engine Google (http://www.google.com/) and type "school security" for a variety of information.

Check out the International Association of Campus Law Enforcement Administrators at http://www.iaclea.org/.

For excellent information on healthcare security, check out the International Association for Healthcare Security & Safety at http://iahss.org/.

Check out the American Bankers Association at http://www.aba.com/ for information on security, money laundering, and online banking.

CASE PROBLEMS

17A. Select two types of institutions explained in this chapter, and describe why the ones you chose are unique in terms of loss problems and prevention strategies.

17B. Choose two types of institutions from this chapter. For each, establish a priority list of the five most important measures to counter losses. Explain the reasoning behind each ranked list.

17C. Select two institutions mentioned in this chapter. (1) Refer to additional sources to gather further information, and (2) explain why you would prefer to work in one rather than the other. Maintain a bibliography.

17D. What do you think is the most demanding of the locations discussed in this chapter for a loss prevention manager? Justify your answer.

NOTES

1. Leigh Gaines, "People Power Battles Campus Crime," *Security* (August 1989), p. 44.
2. U.S. Departments of Justice and Education, *1999 Annual Report on School Safety* (Jessup, MD: U.S. Department of Education, November 1999), p. 2.
3. National Center for Education Statistics, *Indicators of School Crime and Safety, 2000* http://nces.ed.gov (May 29, 2001).
4. Scott Decker, *Increasing School Safety Through Juvenile Accountability Programs*, (Washington, D.C.: U.S. Department of Justice, December 2000), p. 3.
5. Office of Juvenile Justice and Delinquency Prevention, "Preventing Adolescent Gang Involvement" (Washington, D.C.: U.S. Department of Justice, September 2000), p. 7.
6. National Institute of Justice, *Preventing School Violence* (Washington, D.C.: U.S. Department of Justice, May 2000), p. 48.
7. Kim Rahfaldt, "Challenges School Districts Face When Securing Their Buildings and Students," *Security Technology & Design* 10 (December 2000), p. 35.
8. "School-Associated Deaths Top 50 per Year in US," *Security Concepts* (July 1996), p. 2.
9. Sandy Jaeger, "Crime Concerns on Campus," *Security Technology & Design* 12 (March 2001), p. 6.
10. Philip Purpura, *Criminal Justice: An Introduction* (Boston: Butterworth–Heinemann, 1997), pp. 32–36.
11. "Campus Sex Crimes," *Security Management* 45 (May 2001), p. 20.
12. Office of Postsecondary Education, *The Incidence of Crime on the Campuses of U.S. Postsecondary Education Institutions* (Washington, D.C.: U.S. Department of Education, January 18, 2001), pp. 1–69.
13. Bonnie S. Fisher and John J. Sloan, "University Response to the Campus Security Act of 1990: Evaluating Programs Designed to Reduce Campus Crime," *Journal of Security Administration* 16 (1993), pp. 67–77.
14. John Sloan, et al., "Policing the Contemporary University Campus: Challenging Traditional Organizational Models," *Journal of Security Administration* 23 (June 2000), pp. 1–14. And, Alan B. Jenkins, "Campus Community Oriented Policing and Problem Solving," *Campus Law Enforcement Journal* (March-April 1997), pp. 25–31.
15. Gordon P. McKinnon, editor, *Fire Protection Handbook*, 14th ed. (Boston: National Fire Protection Association, 1977), pp. 8–22.
16. Percy Bugbee, *Principles of Fire Protection* (Boston: National Fire Protection Association, 1978), p. 41.

17. Sandy Jaeger, "An Educated Risk," *Security Technology & Design* 11 (April 2001), pp. 60–67.
18. Jack Dowling, "Strategies for Student Growth," *Security Management* 44 (December 2000), pp. 91–97.
19. Russell L. Colling, *Hospital and Healthcare Security* (Boston: Butterworth–Heinemann, 2001), pp. 459–460.
20. Ibid., pp. 443–450.
21. OSHA, *Guidelines for Preventing Workplace Violence for Health Care and Social Service Workers* (Washington, D.C.: U.S. Department of Labor, 1996), p. 1.
22. P. J. Cannon, "Children's Hospitals: Hotbeds of Emotion for Broken Families," *Access Control* (September 1996), pp. 42–48.
23. OSHA, *Guidelines for Preventing Workplace Violence*, p. v.
24. Ibid., pp. 1–9.
25. Thomas Dolan, "Healthcare Security: A Very Insecure Profession," *Security Technology & Design* 9 (August 1999), p. 11. And, "Pressure Needed to Improve Security and Privacy of Electronic Health," *Business and Facility Concepts* (April 1997), pp. 21–22.
26. Bruce Morgan, "Developing a Security Management Plan," *FacilityCare* (February 1997), pp. 10–11.
27. Russell L. Colling, *Security: Keeping The Health Care Environment Safe* (Oakbrook Terrace, IL: JCAHO, 1996), pp. 34–36.
28. ASIS Healthcare Security Committee, *Healthcare Security Benchmarking Study* (Alexandria, VA: ASIS, February 2000), pp. 1–28.
29. Colling, *Hospital and Healthcare Security*, p. 490.
30. Ibid., p. 491.
31. William Schroeder, "Money Laundering," *FBI Law Enforcement Bulletin* 70 (May 2001), pp. 1–9.
32. Brian Abraham and Peter Baldassaro, "Leaving Robbers Barren," *Security Management* 45 (February 2001), pp. 42–46.
33. Terry Mann, "Policies That Pay Off," *Security Management* 44 (February 2000), pp. 42–46.
34. Jeffrey Spivey, "Banks Vault into Online Risk," *Security Management* 45 (January 2001), pp. 132–138.
35. Kevin Null, "One Bank's Fraud Fight," *Security Management* 44 (February 2000), pp. 37–41.
36. Jeanne Bonner, "When an Imposter Calls," *Access Control & Security Systems Integration* 44 (April 2001), p. 1.
37. Sandy Jaeger, "A Convenient Crime," *Security Technology & Design* 11 (April 2001), p. 6.
38. U.S. Department of Justice, *Vulnerability Assessment of Federal Facilities* (Washington, D.C.: U.S. Marshals Service, June 28, 1995).
39. "Federal Facility Update," *Security Management* (June 1996), p. 16.
40. "GSA Weighs In on Federal Facility Security," *Security Management* 44 (January 2000), p. 20.
41. Larry Anderson, "Washington: A Sitting Duck?" *Access Control & Security Systems Integration* 43 (July 2000), p. 4.
42. Purpura, *Criminal Justice*, pp. 254–257.

18

Topics of Concern

OBJECTIVES

After studying this chapter the reader will be able to:

1. List the methods by which an adversary might obtain sensitive information and list countermeasures.
2. Discuss communications security.
3. Describe the problem of terrorism and list countermeasures.
4. List strategies for executive protection.
5. Describe the problems and remedies associated with substance abuse.
6. Discuss the problem of violence in the workplace and what can be done about it.

PROTECTION OF SENSITIVE INFORMATION

Sensitive information, defined to its broadest degree, is proprietary information that, if obtained by an unauthorized person, destroyed in a disaster, or lost, can cause harm to an organization. The information often is extremely valuable (e.g., a secret formula) and may represent the lifeblood of a company. Subsequent pages emphasize espionage and countermeasures. Previous sections of this book elaborate on security and fire protection for valuables. Also, we must not forget that information pertaining to the privacy of individuals requires protection. This would include credit, medical, educational, and other records protected under various laws.

Common types of sensitive information that might be obtained by a spy are the following: product design, financial reports, engineering data, tax records, secret formulas, marketing strategies, cost reduction methods, research data, client or customer information, trade secrets, personnel records, patent information, computer programs, oil or mineral exploration maps, mergers, and contract information. ASIS reported that in 1999, *Fortune* 1000 companies sustained losses of over $45 billion from theft of proprietary information.[1]

A *trade secret*, supposedly known only to certain individuals, is a secret process that is used to produce a salable product. It may involve a series of steps or special ingredients. A famous trade secret is the formula for Coca-Cola. The holder of a trade secret must take steps to maintain secrecy from competitors. If an employee were to reveal a trade secret to a competitor, the courts could issue an injunction, prohibiting the competitor from using the secret. Money damages might be awarded.

A *patent* provides protection for an invention or design. If a competitor duplicates the device, patent laws are likely to be violated and litigation would follow. Competitors often engineer around patents.

A *trademark* includes words, symbols, logos, designs, or slogans that identify products or services as coming from a common source. McDonald's golden arches serve as an example.

Copyright provides protection for original works by giving the creator or publisher exclusive rights to the work. This type of protection covers books, magazines, musical scores, movies, and computer software programs.

Corporate Intelligence Gathering: Putting It in Perspective

Corporate intelligence involves gathering information about competitors. It ranges from the illegal activity of industrial espionage to the acceptable, universally applied practice of utilizing salespeople to monitor public business practices of other companies. Corporate intelligence gathering makes good business sense, and this is why companies such as General Electric, Digital Equipment, and Gillette have established formal intelligence programs. Because of unethical and illegal behavior by certain people and firms when gathering intelligence, the whole specialization has earned a bad reputation. But, many avenues for gathering intelligence are legal. Let us first list the reasons for corporate intelligence gathering:

- Executives should take advantage of information that is publicly available to fulfill their fiduciary duty to shareholders. Because the Cordis Corporation, a pacemaker manufacturer, for example, was unsure of why its new line did not show improved sales, it asked its salespeople to check the tactics of the competition. The salespeople found that physicians were being offered cars and boats to stay with the competition. When Cordis increased educational support for doctors, added more salespeople, and matched the giveaways, sales increased.
- Competitive intelligence is a basis for strategic planning. One intelligence seminar director found a competitor using a "dirty trick" by enrolling in his course under an assumed name.
- It is necessary, in order to be successful against global competitors. The Japanese have "deployed armies of engineers and marketing specialists" to other countries. Likewise, U.S.-based firms have set up offices abroad to gather information.

- It can be useful for the introduction of a new product. Coors did extensive chemical analysis on Gallo's wine coolers and found that it could not compete on price.[2]

The *Society of Competitive Intelligence Professionals* (http://www.scip.org/) views its vocation as an honorable profession with a code of ethics. A large part of the work focuses on research of public information and interviews with experts. The information explosion—computers, networks, data banks, and specialized publications—has enabled these professionals to find out almost anything they want about competitors.[3]

The following lists provide guidelines for information gathering. Ethical sources include:

- Published material and public documents such as court records
- Disclosures made by competitor's employees and obtained without subterfuge
- Market surveys and consultants' reports
- Financial reports and brokers' research reports
- Trade fairs, exhibits, and competitors' brochures
- Analysis of a competitor's products
- Legitimate employment interviews with people who worked for a competitor

Arguably unethical sources include:

- Camouflaged questioning and "drawing out" of a competitor's employees at a technical meeting
- Direct observation under secret conditions
- False job interviews with a competitor's employees (i.e., where there is no real intent to hire)
- Hiring a professional investigator to obtain a specific piece of information

Illegal sources include:

- Trespassing on a competitor's property
- Bribing a competitor's supplier or employee
- "Planting" your agent on the competitor's payroll
- Eavesdropping on competitors
- Theft of drawings, samples, documents, and similar property
- Blackmail and extortion.[4]

Espionage Techniques

The techniques used by adversaries to acquire sensitive information are so varied that defenders must not fall into the trap of emphasizing certain countermeasures while "leaving the back door open." For example, a company may spend hundreds of thousands of dollars defending against electronic surveillance and wiretapping while not realizing that most of the loss of sensitive information is from a few employees who are really spies for competitors.

> Defenders against espionage must not fall into the trap of emphasizing certain countermeasures while "leaving the back door open."

Three patterns of illegally acquiring sensitive information, also referred to as *espionage* or *spying*, are internal, external, and a conspiracy that combines the two. An *internal attack* can be perpetrated by an employee who sells a secret formula to a competitor, for example. An *external attack* occurs when an outsider gains unauthorized access to the premises and steals product design data. The *combined conspiracy* is seen when an employee "just happens" to leave a secret mailing list on a desk and unlocks a rear door to aid an intruder.

Various techniques are used by spies as seen in the nearby list. A spy might assemble trash from a company and an executive's home to "piece together" information. Spies may claim they are conducting a survey, as a "pretext" to acquire information. Several spies may each ask certain questions only, and then later, assemble the "big picture." A key employee might be tricked into being discovered in a compromising position (e.g., in bed with a prostitute), be photographed, and then blackmailed for information. A spy might frequent a tavern or conference populated by engineers to listen to conversations. A spy might attempt to gain employment at a target company. Sometimes, proposals for a merger, acquisition, or joint venture are used as a cover to obtain information. Salespeople, to make a sale, are known to supply excesses of information in an attempt to impress a customer. Sources of data leaks include company speeches, publications, trade meetings, disgruntled employees, and consultants. Wiretapping and planting electronic listening devices are other methods. "Reverse engineering" is a legal avenue to obtain a look at a competitor's product. The competitor simply purchases the product and dismantles it to understand the components. Patent applications, which are available to the public, can reveal valuable information. Some companies deliberately patent their failures to lead competitors astray.

The *Business Espionage Controls and Countermeasures Association* (BECCA; http//:www.espionbusiness.com/) is a professional society whose aim is "to make life as difficult and dangerous as possible for the espionage practitioner." In their *Business Espionage Report*, which highlights methods used by spies, the association noted the interception of digital telephones, pagers, teleconferencing systems, and wireless telephone headsets.[5]

Even a home computer can become a listening device. A system with a voice-data modem on the computer and a duplex speaker can be accessed by activating the modem and speakerphone. For those communicating with others on the Internet and sharing ideas, this creates a database from which a "profile" can be established. Search programs are available that quickly sift through data to produce the profile, and because the writings were posted for thousands of people to read, it would be difficult to convince a court that they were private.[6]

A good spy does not get caught, and quite often the victimized firm does not discover that it has been subjected to espionage. If the discovery is made, the company typically keeps it secret to avoid adverse publicity.

Espionage is a pervasive problem. It may take place between small, highly competitive businesses in the same city, large multinational corporations, or countries. In the *Annual Report to Congress on Foreign Economic Collection and Industrial Espionage*, a report submitted by the president to Congress, it was noted that at least 12 countries actively target U.S. proprietary information and critical technologies, and another 26 countries are involved in related suspicious incidents.[7] The obvious objectives are self-improvement and superiority—a driving force behind all businesses and governments.

Research sponsored by the American Society for Industrial Security, published as *Trends in Intellectual Property Loss*, showed an increase in reported incidents of intellectual property loss, which costs billions of dollars each year. It was noted that insiders (e.g., employees, contractors) were involved in 74 percent of the reported incidents. Foreign nationals were identified in 21 percent of the incidents, with the top five being Chinese, Canadian, French, Indian, and Japanese. The research revealed that only 76 percent of reporting companies had a formal safeguarding proprietary information (SPI) program.[8]

Countermeasures

The first step in keeping sensitive information secure is to identify and classify it according to its value. The top-level executives in a business should perform this subjective job. If a company has a DOD contract, then strict DOD criteria would apply. Each classification has rules for marking, handling, transmitting, storing, and access. The higher the classification the greater are the controls. See Table 18-1 for sample classifications, explanations, and illustrations.

Here is a list of countermeasures:

1. *Prevention* is a key strategy to protect sensitive information, which can be stolen without anything being physically missing, and this valuable corporate asset often is not covered by insurance.

Table 18-1 Classification Systems

	If Unauthorized Disclosure	*Illustrations*
*Government Classification**		
Top Secret	"Exceptionally grave damage" to national security	Vital national defense plans, new weapons, sensitive intelligence operations
Secret	"Serious damage" to national security	Significant military plans or intelligence operations
Confidential	"Identifiable damage" to national security	Strength of forces, munitions performance characteristics
Corporation Classification		
Special Controls	Survival at stake	New process or product; secret formula or recipe
Company Confidential	Serious damage	Process, customer lists; depends on value to business
Private Confidential	Identifiable damage, or could cause problems	Personnel data, price quote

*Classified by the U.S. Department of Defense in National Industrial Security Program Operating Manual (http://www.fas.org/sgp/library/nispom.htm; June 6, 2001).

2. Establish formal SPI policies and procedures. Examples include security over passwords, maintaining a "clean desk" policy so important items are not left in the open when they should be in a locked container, and restricting the release of information on a "need-to-know" basis.

3. Provide training and awareness programs for employees, especially on methods used by spies, such as "pretext" interviews.

4. Reinforce SPI programs through new employee orientation, employee handbook, and performance evaluations.

5. Carefully screen employment applicants.

6. Use employee nondisclosure agreements and employee noncompete agreements.

7. Implement physical security and access controls for people and property entering, leaving, and circulating within a facility (see Figure 18-1).

8. Secure sensitive items.

9. Review works written by employees prior to publication and their speeches, ensure protection during trade shows, and control media relations.

10. Control destruction of sensitive materials.

Figure 18–1   Sen Trac ID uses radio-frequency identification technology to provide hands-free access control and asset management to track people and products within a facility. Courtesy: Sensormatic.

11. Maintain state-of-the-art IT security. Protect all forms of electronic communication—e-mail, network, faxes, telephone, etc.
12. Use technical surveillance countermeasures (TSCM).
13. Use internal and independent security audits to strengthen protection.[9]

Destruction of Sensitive Materials

Records and documents that are simply thrown into trash bins, when appropriate, enable spies to retrieve information. The total destruction of records will impede this espionage technique. Before pollution restrictions against burning, many firms placed unwanted records in incinerators. Today, *strip-cut shredders* (producing long strips of paper 1/4-inch wide) are used by many organizations. However, security is limited. This became painfully evident in 1979, when Iranian militants stormed the U.S. Embassy in Tehran and pieced together top-secret documents that had been shredded by a strip-cut shredder. For increased security, *particle-cut shredders* (smaller pieces of paper) are the alternative (see Figure 18-2). *Cross-cut shredders* offer even higher security and are suitable for DOD classified data. The highest level of security is offered by *disintegrators*. These devices produce confetti particles through the action of a rotor and stationary knives. Disintegrators are growing in popularity because users can destroy magnetic tape,

Figure 18–2   A determined adversary may take the time to put small pieces of paper together for information.

disks, printed circuit boards, and so forth. Since the Iranian disaster, the U.S. government requires classified data to be destroyed with either a cross-cut shredder or a disintegrator.[10]

COMMUNICATIONS SECURITY

Communications security involves defenses against interception. In providing a comprehensive approach to protecting sensitive information, subfields of communications security are listed here.

- *Line security* protects communications lines of computer systems, such as a central computer and remote terminals. Line security is effective over lines an organization controls; a wiretap can occur in many locations of a line. Cryptographic security defeats wiretapping.
- *Transmission security* involves communications procedures that afford minimal advantage to an adversary bent on intercepting data communications from computer systems, telephones, radio, and other systems.
- *Emanation security* prevents undesired signal data emanations (e.g., from computer equipment) transmitted without wires (e.g., electro-magnetic or acoustic) that could be intercepted by an adversary. TEM-

PEST is the code word used by the National Security Agency for the science of eliminating undesired signal data emanations. "Shielding," discussed soon, is one strategy to reduce data emanations.

- *Technical security,* also called *technical surveillance countermeasures,* provides defenses against the interception of data communications from microphones, transmitters, or wiretaps.[11]

The above methods of attack can be used together, which is one reason why communications security is a highly complex field. What follows here primarily is technical security; however, *we must not lose sight of the importance of a comprehensive approach to protecting sensitive information.* (The discussion of computer security in Chapter 16 also provides relevant protection strategies.)

Electronic Surveillance and Wiretapping

Electronic surveillance utilizes electronic devices to covertly listen to conversations, whereas *wiretapping* pertains to the interception of telephone communications. The prevalence of these often illegal activities probably is greater than one would expect. (The legality of such acts is supported by court orders.) Because detection is so difficult, the exact extent of electronic surveillance and wiretapping and what this theft of information costs businesses is impossible to gauge.

Electronic eavesdropping technology is highly developed to the point where countermeasures (debugging) have not kept up with the art of bugging. Consequently, only the most expertly trained and experienced specialist can counter this threat.

Surveillance equipment is easy to obtain. An electronically inclined person can simply enter a local electronics store and buy all the materials necessary to make a sophisticated bug. Pre-built models are available by mail, or certain retailers will sell them if the buyer signs a statement that they will not be used for audio surveillance. Retail electronics stores sell FM transmitters or microphones that transmit sound without wires to an ordinary FM radio. Sound is broadcast over a radio several feet away after tuning to the right frequency. These FM transmitters are advertised to be used by public speakers who walk around as they talk and favor wireless microphones; the voice is transmitted and then broadcast over large speakers. They are also advertised to listen in on a baby from another room.

Miniaturization has greatly aided spying. With the advance of the microchip, transmitters are apt to be so small that these devices can be enmeshed in thick paper, as in a calendar, under a stamp, or within a nail in a wall. Bugs may be planted as a building is under construction, or a person may receive one hidden in a present or other item. Transmitters are capable of being operated by solar power (i.e., daylight) or local radio broadcast.

Bugging techniques are varied. Information from a microphone can be transmitted via a "wire run" or a radio transmitter. Bugs are concealed in a variety of objects or carried on a person. Transmitting devices can be remotely controlled with a radio signal for turning them on and off. This makes detection difficult. A device known as a carrier current transmitter is placed in wall plugs, light switches, or other electrically operated components. It obtains its power from the AC wire to which it is attached.

Many spies use a dual system. One bug is placed so that it will be found, which in many instances satisfies security and management. A second bug is more cleverly concealed.

Telephones are especially vulnerable. A "tap" occurs when a telephone conversation is intercepted. Telephone lines are available in so many places that taps are difficult to detect. A tap can be direct or wireless. With a direct tap, a pair of wires is spliced to the telephone line and then connected to a tape recorder. An FM transmitter, similar to a room bug, is employed for a wireless tap. The transmitter is connected to the line and then a receiver and tape recorder are concealed nearby. Wireless taps (and room bugs) are spotted by using special equipment. Direct taps are difficult to locate. A check of the entire line is necessary.

Because telephone traffic travels over space radio in several modes— for example, cellular, microwave, and satellite—the spy's job is made much easier and safer since no on-premises tap is required. What is required is the proper equipment for each mode. In one case a Mossad agent in Berne, Switzerland, was arrested after he tried to tap the telephone of a Hezbollah target. His technical system was a cellular telephone device that would be activated when the target telephone was put in use. The device would automatically call a second cellular telephone where the target's telephone would be monitored.[12]

Another technique transforms the telephone into a listening device whether it is in use or not. A technique known as a "hookswitch bypass" short circuits (by changing wires) the telephone hookswitch (the switch that disconnects the microphone in the mouthpiece to the outside when a person hangs up) and transforms the ordinary telephone into a bug. This is easy to detect by hanging up the telephone, placing a radio nearby (for noise), tapping into the telephone line, and listening for the radio.

When guarding against losses of sensitive information, consideration must be given to a host of methods that may be used by a spy. These include infrared transmitters that use light frequencies below the visible frequency spectrum to transmit information. This can be defeated through physical shielding (e.g., closing the drapes). Another method, a laser listening device, "bounces" laser off of a window to receive audio from the room. Inexpensive noise masking systems can defeat this technique.[13] Computer, e-mail, facsimile, and other transmissions are also subject to access by spies. A spy may conceal a tape recorder or pinhole-lens camera on the premises, or wear a camera concealed in a jacket or tie. If drawings or designs are on walls or in sight through windows, a spy, for example, stationed in another skyscraper a few blocks away might use a telescope to obtain secret data. Or, a window washer might appear at a window for surveillance. Another method is a spy disguised as a janitor to be assigned to the particular site. All of these methods by no means exhaust the skills of spies as covered earlier under "espionage techniques."

Countermeasures

The physical characteristics of a building have a bearing on opportunities for surveillance. Some of these factors are poor access control designs, inadequate soundproofing, common or shared ducts, and space above false ceilings enabling access. Comprehensive security methods will hinder spies. The in-house security team can begin countermeasures by conducting a physical search for planted devices. If a decision is made to contact a specialist, *only the most expertly trained and experienced consultant should be recruited.*

The Countermeasures Consultant

Organizations often recruit a countermeasures consultant to perform contract work. As a consumer, ask for copies of certificates of TSCM courses completed and a copy of the insurance policy for errors and omissions for TSCM services. What equipment is used? What techniques are employed for the cost? Are sweeps and meticulous physical inspections conducted for the quoted price? Watch for scare tactics. Is the consultant really a vendor trying to sell audio surveillance detection devices? Will the consultant protect confidentiality? The interviewer should request a review of past reports to clients. Were names deleted to protect confidentiality? These questions help to avoid hiring the unqualified "expert." One practitioner offered clients debugging services and used an expensive piece of equipment to conduct sweeps. After several years and hundreds of sweeps, he decided to have the equipment serviced. A service person discovered that the device was not working because it had no battery. The surprised "expert" never realized a battery was needed.

For a comprehensive countermeasures program, the competent consultant will be interested in sensitive information flow, storage, and retrieval. Extra cost will result from such an analysis, but it is often cost effective. *The employer should use an outside public telephone to contact the consultant in order not to alert a spy to impending countermeasures.*

Equipment

Detection equipment is expensive. A firm should purchase its own equipment only if it is cost effective and many sweeps will be conducted. A sample of equipment includes the nonlinear junction detector, costing $15,000, and capable of detecting radio transmitters, microphones, infrared and ultrasonic transmitters, tape recorders, and other devices hidden, even when they are not working. The telephone analyzer is another tool, costing up to $6,000 and designed for testing a variety of single and multiline telephones and fax machines. Other types of specialized equipment are on the market.[14]

Some security personnel or executives plant a bug for the sole purpose of determining if the detection specialist and his or her equipment are effective. This "test" can be construed as a criminal offense. An alternative is specially designed test transmitters, commercially available, that have no microphone pickup and therefore can be used without liability. Another technique is to place a tape recorder with a microphone in a drawer.

A tool kit and standard forms are two additional aids for the countermeasures specialist. The tool kit consists of the common tools (e.g., screwdrivers, pliers, electrical tape) used by an electrician. Standard forms facilitate good record keeping and serve as a checklist. What was checked? What tests were performed? What were the readings? Where? When? Who performed the tests? Why were the tests conducted? Over a period of time, records can be used to make comparisons while helping to answer questions.

> Who do you think has "the edge," those who seek sensitive information or those who protect it?

Another strategy to thwart listening devices is "shielding," also called *electronic soundproofing*. Basically, copper foil or screening and carbon filament are applied throughout a room to prevent acoustical or electromagnetic emanations from leaving. Although this method is very expensive (costing more than $100,000), several organizations employ it to have at least one secure room or to protect information in computers.

Equipment is available on the market that *may* frustrate telephone taps and listening devices. Scramblers, attached to telephones, alter the voice as it travels through the line. But no device or system is foolproof. Often, simple countermeasures are useful. For instance, an executive can wait until everybody is present for an important meeting, and then relocate it to a previously undisclosed location. Conversants can operate a radio at high volume during sensitive conversations, and exercise caution during telephone and other conversations.

It must be remembered that sensitive information can be collected in many different ways besides through the use of physical devices. Losses can occur through speeches and publications by employees, in company trash, and by unknowingly hiring a spy. Comprehensive, broad-based defenses are necessary.

Counterintelligence

Another avenue to protect sensitive information is *counterintelligence*, which is a broad term referring to activities that identify and counter threats by adversaries. The military and police agencies engage in counterintelligence activities. Examples include investigative and research units that collect and analyze intelligence on adversaries, internal awareness programs, and misinformation directed at adversaries. Although businesses have a different mission than the military and police, certain counterintelligence techniques, within legal guidelines, can be implemented by businesses.

Economic Espionage Act of 1996

Because intellectual property assets are often more valuable to businesses than tangible assets, Congress passed the Economic Espionage Act of 1996. This act makes it a federal crime for any person to convert a trade secret to his or her own benefit or the benefit of others with the intent or knowledge that the conversion will injure the owner of the trade secret. The penalties for any person are up to ten years of imprisonment and a fine up to $250,000. Corporations can be fined up to $5 million. If a foreign government benefits from such a crime, the penalties are even greater. The act defines *trade secret* broadly as information that the owner has taken "reasonable measures" to keep secret because of the economic value from it. Case law has further defined the act; the greater the protection and value of the information and the fewer people who know about the information, the more likely the courts will recognize its status as a protectable trade secret.[15]

The act raises two major concerns for management:

- *Protecting trade secrets.* This would include a comprehensive SPI program (see the earlier discussion).
- *Hiring employees from competitors.* Employers may violate the act if they hire employees from other firms who may bring with them trade secrets.

Prevention includes a thorough interview of applicants, ascertaining whether the applicant signed contracts or agreements with others for the protection of sensitive information, and use of a company form that signifies that the new employee understands the act's legal requirements.[16]

The act also links the economic well-being of the nation to national security interests. And, it allows the FBI to investigate foreign intelligence services bent on acquiring sensitive information of U.S. companies. At some point, a company may have to decide whether to report a violation of the act to law enforcement authorities. The disadvantages are lost time and money, unwanted publicity, and the fact that the defendant's attorney may request secrets that could then be revealed in court. Although the act offers some protection for proprietary information, this protection may depend on how a judge or attorneys in the case interpret the act. Discovery proceedings may result in information loss greater than the original loss.

Also, the case may be lost in criminal and civil courts. Therefore, management must carefully weigh decisions on legal action. Another point to consider is that the act requires businesses to protect themselves from losses, which presents liability issues relevant to due diligence.[17] *Prevention is seen here, as with many other vulnerabilities, as the key avenue for protection.*

TERRORISM

Terrorism Defined

There is general disagreement concerning how to define *terrorism*; many definitions exist.[18] This book defines *terrorism* as the use of aggressive strategies to produce fear, coercion, or violence for political, religious, or criminal ends. Terrorists often are highly trained and mobile. They are characterized by conducting surprise, violent attacks, usually to see maximum press coverage for their cause.

Terrorism has existed for centuries. Today, it includes a wide variety of methods not limited to hijacking, ambush, murder, kidnapping, bombing, chemical and biological terrorism, product tampering, and cyberterrorism. Terrorists are creative and often seek soft targets once other targets are hardened. Terrorism is a strategy to violently confront a stronger, more powerful enemy. When terrorists strike, victim emotions are heightened and revenge is a popular outcry from citizens that is often followed by government and military action. If opposing sides are unable to negotiate a solution, violence usually escalates.

History

In past decades, international terrorists targeted U.S. citizens and interests overseas. The most memorable attacks include the 1988 bombing of Pan American Flight 103 over Lockerbie, Scotland, which killed 189 Americans; the 1996 bombing of Al-Khobar Towers in Dhahran, Saudi Arabia, resulting in the deaths of 19 U.S. military personnel; and the 1998 bombing of the U.S. embassies in Kenya and Tanzania, which killed 12 Americans and many others.

The year 1993 brought with it the beginning of serious domestic terrorism. During that year change occurred with the first bombing of the World Trade Center in New York City, in which six people died and nearly 1,000 were injured. In 1995, the bombing of the Murrah Federal Building in Oklahoma City resulted in 168 deaths. A trend emerged whereby such crimes were occurring on American soil and becoming increasingly deadly.[19]

The U.S. Commission on National Security completed a study in 1999 and concluded that America will become increasingly vulnerable to attack on our homeland. The Commission also predicted that foreign states and terrorists will acquire weapons of mass destruction and mass disruption, and some will use them, resulting in American deaths.[20]

Although terrorism has been intense in the Mideast, it exists throughout the world. The tension in the Mideast and the differences between Israel and its Arab neighbors have resulted in wars, in addition to terrorism. Because the United States has a history of being pro-Israel and has led wars in Iraq and Afghanistan, the United States has been perceived as "the great Satan" and an enemy of the religion of Islam. This tension has led a minority of Middle Eastern groups to call for a "holy war." Extremists have perverted the Islamic faith in the call from God to kill Americans. This minority is violently opposed to the American way of life (e.g., equality for women, TV and films, our material possessions) because they believe it corrupts their idea of Muslim culture. Few Muslims hold these extremist and violent views. To reduce the violence, nations and groups must negotiate and reach a settlement on the issues. This is a difficult challenge, but is the avenue toward peace.

Seven Fronts Against Terrorism

Security professionals do not get involved in political disputes or correct deviant behavior. Rather, they deal with the symptoms of these problems—crime, terrorism, and so forth. Our government is charged with the duties of diplomacy and, when necessary, military action. Here is a summary or "big picture" of seven fronts to confront terrorism developed following the September 11, 2001 attack on the United States (see Figure 18-3).

- *Diplomacy.* The United States has secured a coalition of support from many nations that have deployed or pledged troops, permitted use of airspace, and shared intelligence.
- *Intelligence.* The collection of quality information that is accurate provides the foundation for action against terrorists. Many nations have provided increased intelligence support to the United States. Intelligence is gathered from many sources such as informants, spies, electronic surveillance, satellites, and drones.
- *Military.* A variety of armed services of the United States and other countries are coordinating their efforts to fight terrorists. To win support in hostile countries, U.S. psychological operations drop leaflets and radios and humanitarian aid is distributed.

Figure 18–3 Destruction of the World Trade Center in New York City following the September 11, 2001 terrorist attack.

- *Financial.* This front aims to coordinate several federal agencies and gain support from other countries in tracking and freezing terrorist assets to starve them of funding.
- *Law enforcement.* The activities of law enforcement are to investigate threats; conduct interviews, searches, and electronic surveillance; issue subpoenas; and detain and arrest. Many countries have supported criminal investigations of terrorists. The aims of law enforcement agencies are to identify, arrest, and convict offenders.
- *Homeland security.* The federal government and states have established homeland security directors to coordinate resources for protection against terrorism. The resources are broad and include coordination among public safety and emergency management agencies, medical facilities, transportation systems, utilities, infrastructure, and agencies that control access at our borders.
- *Business and organizational security.* This front covers security, fire protection, and life safety at businesses, schools, hospitals, sports arenas, utilities, and many other locations.

Business and Organizational Countermeasures Against Terrorism

When considering countermeasures against terrorism, first consider the methods used by terrorists, which go beyond bombings. The raw materials for chemical, biological, and radioactive weapons can be purchased on the open or black markets. In 1998, before his arrest by the FBI, a New Jersey physicist named Lawrence A. Maltz threatened to use biological and chemical devices. During the same year, three members of a Texas secessionist group planned to infect government officials with toxins prior to their arrest by the FBI. A disturbing trend is the increase in threats of use of weapons of mass destruction. The FBI noted that anthrax, a bacterial pathogen that can spread through contact with a powered form or by breathing an aerosol discharge, has emerged as the agent of choice among terrorists.[21] The use of anthrax as a terrorist tool became a reality in 2001 when it was mailed to politicians, the media, and others. It disrupted the postal system and caused deaths. Terrorists might obtain or build a nuclear device or simply decide to wrap radioactive material around a conventional bomb, to produce a "dirty bomb" that, when exploded, will kill and possibly shut down a city center for decades. Ventilation systems of buildings are vulnerable because these systems can be used to disperse deadly substances. Product tampering has resulted in deaths, injuries, fear, and serious economic harm to corporations.

The Internet is a source of information to build assorted weapons. Various groups publish manuals on tactics to be used to advance their cause. For example, some anti-abortion activists have written a manual on closing abortion clinics by squirting Super Glue into the locks so the clinic cannot open, drilling holes in the low points of flat roofs, and placing a garden hose in mail slots at front doors.[22]

Cyberterrorism refers to the use of computer systems and the Internet to commit terrorism. Cyberterrorism is attractive because it offers an inexpensive way to support a cause and cover tracks. A cyberterrorist can launch an attack from almost anywhere, without physical harm, while creating havoc. Cyberterrorists have the potential to disrupt international financial transactions, enter air traffic control systems to cause aircraft crashes, or remotely alter the formulas of pharmaceutical firms to cause loss of life. Countermeasures include specialists who infiltrate and operate in the world of the cyberterrorist, detection mechanisms, incident/response teams, and more research into survivability software that implements automatic defenses.[23]

Immediately following the bombings of the World Trade Center (1993, first bombing) and the Murrah Federal Building (1995) there was a flurry of security activity. However, many high-rise building security managers believed that their properties were virtually immune from terrorism. The thought was "It can't happen here." Adding weight to this view is that a building is not at risk unless it is well known, has sensitive tenants, and is very large.[24] Following the September 11, 2001 attack and anthrax threat we saw another flurry of security activity, although this one was stronger and longer lasting.

Today, following the September 11, 2001 attacks, a rethinking of security is necessary. Organizations should practice risk spreading as one method to counter terrorism. Reevaluate whether to concentrate all employees and operations in one building and in one city. Not only terrorism, but other disasters can strike.

Think critically about the following. Government buildings in Washington, D.C., and the financial district of New York City are excellent terrorist targets that this author viewed as at the top of the list prior to the September 11, 2001 attacks. These targets are still at the top of the list. Think about where terrorist strikes can harm the United States the most. We continue to concentrate so much of our nation's government and wealth in "neatly packaged targets." The plans for Washington, D.C., the financial district of New York City, and many other important and visible locations were designed many years ago in an age when planners had no idea of the threats of the twenty-first century. Although we must not be held like hostages because of the risk of terrorist attacks, we must think like terrorists to anticipate attacks and take precautions. This may mean moving operations and people to spread the risk. The destruction of the capitol dome where Congress meets and the killing of politicians would be a bold attack that would shock the world. Imagine the economic impact of a chemical, biological, or radioactive attack on Wall Street. If terrorists can level the World Trade Center towers with planes hijacked with box cutters, many scenarios are possible. An epidemic could be launched by infecting twenty or thirty suicidal terrorists who would wait until they became highly infectious before walking into government buildings, airports, schools, shopping malls, and sports arenas. Or, a bomb could contain not only an explosive, but also a chemical or biological agent, or all three. And, spreading the risk may not reduce losses from a well-coordinated, widely dispersed attack. Since there is an endless number of terrorist targets and scenarios, and financial considerations prevent protecting all locations, governments, businesses, and organizations must prioritize protection.

Let us hope that nations and groups can settle their differences. However, history tells us that this is a difficult objective to reach. If terrorism intensifies, we can hope that the combined efforts of the seven fronts cited earlier will prevent it. Also, consider the following suggestions for businesses and organizations.

- Terrorists have tremendous advantages over defenses because they search for vulnerabilities and strike almost anywhere with surprise. A British terrorism expert, Paul Wilkinson, stated, "Fighting terrorism is like a goalkeeper. You can make a hundred brilliant saves, but the only shot people remember is the one that gets past you."[25] Creative and astute security planning is essential.

- Maintain awareness of controversies that may increase exposure to terrorism.
- Reevaluate security, safety, and emergency plans. Seek cooperation with public safety agencies.
- Select a diverse committee for input for security and safety plans. Permit committee members to use their imaginations to anticipate weaknesses in protection.
- Educate people about problems and countermeasures. Include basic, simple precautions. For example, in a chemical attack, evacuate, cover your mouth with a cloth, help victims only when you are wearing protective gear, and so forth.
- Ensure that building evacuation plans provide for rapid and safe escape to areas not near the building.
- Increase employee awareness of terrorism and terrorist methods and tricks. Stifle and trick potential terrorists through creativity (e.g., avoid signs on the premises that identify departments, people, and job duties; periodically alter security methods).
- Know the business of tenants and whether they would be possible targets for violence.
- Consider the security and safety of childcare facilities used by employees.
- Intensify access controls by using a comprehensive approach covering people, vehicles, mail, deliveries, services, and any person or thing seeking access.
- Carefully plan physical security and life safety. Also, prepare contingency plans.[26]
- Carefully screen employment applicants, vendors, and others seeking to work on the premises.
- Secure and place under surveillance HVAC systems (e.g., air intake systems) and utilities.
- Maintain a pulse on employee reactions to news events of terrorism and violence. Anxiety, fear, and a change in work habits may result from shocking events. If actual victimization occurs, these symptoms will intensify, including post-traumatic stress disorder. A plan of counseling and assistance is essential to help employees.
- Once the best possible security and safety plans are implemented, remember that an offender (internal or external or both) may be studying your defenses to look for weaknesses to exploit.

Precautions for mail include:

- Prepare emergency plans, policies, and procedures for suspect mail.
- Isolate the mail area and limit access. Consider handling mail at a separate, isolated building.

Figure 18–4 The September 11, 2001 terrorist attack on the United States was followed by bioterrorism in which anthrax was spread through the mail system, necessitating precautions.

- Use gloves (see Figure 18-4) and protective masks.
- Do not touch or smell anything suspicious.
- Be suspicious of mail. See the nearby box on anthrax and the Chapter 12 figure on suspect letter and package indicators.
- Consider technology: X-ray for bombs, use letter and package tracking systems and automatic letter openers, and scan letters and send them electronically.

Official Centers for Disease Control (CDC) Health Advisory Distributed via Health Alert Network, October 12, 2001: HOW TO HANDLE ANTHRAX AND OTHER BIOLOGICAL AGENT THREATS

Many facilities in communities around the country have received anthrax threat letters. Most were empty envelopes; some have contained powdery substances. The purpose of these guidelines is to recommend procedures for handling such incidents.

Do Not Panic

1. Anthrax organisms can cause infection in the skin, gastrointestinal system, or the lungs. To do so, the organism must be rubbed into abraded skin, swallowed, or inhaled as a fine, aerosolized mist. Disease can be prevented after exposure to the anthrax spores by early treatment with the appropriate antibiotics. Anthrax is not spread from one person to another person.
2. For anthrax to be effective as a covert agent, it must be aerosolized into very small particles. This is difficult to do, and requires a great deal of technical skill and special equipment. If these small particles are inhaled, life-threatening lung infection can occur, but prompt recognition and treatment are effective.

Suspicious Unopened Letter or Package Marked with Threatening Message Such as "Anthrax":

1. Do not shake or empty the contents of any suspicious envelope or package.
2. PLACE the envelope or package in a plastic bag or some other type of container to prevent leakage of contents.
3. If you do not have any container, then COVER the envelope or package with anything (e.g., clothing, paper, trash can, etc.) and do not remove this cover.
4. Then LEAVE the room and CLOSE the door, or section off the area to prevent others from entering (i.e., keep others away).
5. WASH your hands with soap and water to prevent spreading any powder to your face.
6. What to do next . . .
   • If you are at HOME, then report the incident to local police.
   • If you are at WORK, then report the incident to local police, and notify your building security official or an available supervisor.
7. LIST all people who were in the room or area when this suspicious letter or package was recognized. Give this list to both the local public health authorities and law enforcement officials for follow-up investigations and advice.

Envelope with Powder and Powder Spills Out Onto Surface:

1. DO NOT try to CLEAN UP the powder. COVER the spilled contents immediately with anything (e.g., clothing, paper, trash can, etc.) and do not remove this cover!
2. Then LEAVE the room and CLOSE the door, or section off the area to prevent others from entering (i.e., keep others away).
3. WASH your hands with soap and water to prevent spreading any powder to your face.
4. What to do next . . .
   • If you are at HOME, then report the incident to local police.
   • If you are at WORK, then report the incident to local police, and notify your building security official or an available supervisor.

5. REMOVE heavily contaminated clothing as soon as possible and place in a plastic bag, or some other container that can be sealed. This clothing bag should be given to the emergency responders for proper handling.
6. SHOWER with soap and water as soon as possible. Do Not Use Bleach Or Other Disinfectant On Your Skin.
7. If possible, list all people who were in the room or area, especially those who had actual contact with the powder. Give this list to both the local public health authorities so that proper instructions can be given for medical follow-up, and to law enforcement officials for further investigation.

Question of Room Contamination by Aerosolization

For example: small device triggered, warning that air handling system is contaminated, or warning that a biological agent released in a public space.

1. Turn off local fans or ventilation units in the area.
2. LEAVE area immediately.
3. CLOSE the door, or section off the area to prevent others from entering (i.e., keep others away).
4. What to do next . . .
   - If you are at HOME, then dial "911" to report the incident to local police and the local FBI field office.
   - If you are at WORK, then dial "911" to report the incident to local police and the local FBI field office, and notify your building security official or an available supervisor.
5. SHUT down air handling system in the building, if possible.
6. If possible, list all people who were in the room or area. Give this list to both the local public health authorities so that proper instructions can be given for medical follow-up, and to law enforcement officials for further investigation.

International Perspective: How Is Terrorism Handled in Other Countries?

Several countries have had much more experience with terrorism than the United States. How have other countries fought terrorism?

During the 1970s, West Germany (before unification with East Germany) faced the Red Army Faction (RAF), which directed its terrorism toward "American imperialism." It carried out bombings, shooting, kidnappings, and bank robberies against U.S. and West German interests in West Germany. The West German government responded by passing laws that made it a crime to establish a terrorist organization. Police powers were also increased, such as providing police (with court approval) with the power to search entire apartment buildings for suspects. The police also could establish checkpoints on roads. They formed a crack antiterrorist unit and expanded their intelligence gathering. Initially, concessions were granted to the RAF when they took hostages; however, this prompted the RAF to take more hostages. The policy was reversed, deaths occurred, but hostage taking by the RAF declined. By the 1980s, the RAF threat was almost gone. In Italy, from the 1970s to the 1980s, the Red Brigade terrorists were known for "kneecapping," which is shooting victims in the legs to cripple them. The government responded by passing laws that made it a crime to promote violent overthrow of the government; increased police powers to stop, search, and detain suspects; and eased restrictions on wiretaps. One of the most successful tactics used by the government was to reduce the sentences of convicted terrorists if they volunteered information. Consequently, the Red Brigade began to collapse.[27]

The United Nations recommends the following to prevent and control terrorism:

1. Governments should exercise restraint, protect constitutional rights, and respect human rights.
2. Legislation should criminalize terrorism and prescribe severe penalties.
3. Government and the media should educate the public and keep it informed on ways to solve the problem.
4. Training is crucial for a professional police response.
5. Judicial groups and victims must be protected from reprisals, and the latter should receive compensation.
6. International cooperation should be promoted.[28]

EXECUTIVE PROTECTION

At home and abroad, businesses have become the target for kidnappings, extortion, assassinations, bombings, and sabotage. Terrorists use these methods to obtain money for their cause, to alter business or government policies, or to change public opinion. Organized crime groups also are participants in such criminal acts, but in contrast to terrorists, their objective almost always is money. Attacks against executives are common in Latin America, the Middle East, and Europe. But executives in the United States and other countries also have been subjected to terrorism. It appears that successful terrorist techniques employed in one country spread to other countries. This is likely to be one reason why companies are reluctant to release details of incidents or even to acknowledge terrorist occurrences. Coca-Cola, Chase Manhattan, B. F. Goodrich, and other companies have experienced terrorist assaults in the past.

Planning

A key beginning for an executive protection program is to develop a crisis management plan and team. The goals are to reduce vulnerabilities and surprises and develop contingencies. The crisis management plan can consist of threat assessments, countermeasures, policies, procedures, and lines of authority and responsibility in the event of an attack. An interdisciplinary group, if cost effective, can greatly aid the program. The group could consist of top executives, the loss prevention manager, former federal agents, counter-terrorism experts, political analysts, insurance specialists, and an attorney–negotiator.

The early stages of the plan, if not the preplanning stages, would be devoted to convincing upper management that executive protection is necessary. This objective can be supported through a quality research report that focuses on risks, seeks to anticipate (not predict) events, and answers the following questions: Which executives are possible targets? Where? When? Which individuals or groups may attack? What are their methods? What are the social and political conditions in the particular country? What role has the specific government played in past terrorist incidents? Such questions require research and intelligence gathering as well as cooperative ties to government police agencies.

The U.S. Secret Service completed a study of assassinations of public figures in the United States during the second half of the twentieth century. The findings showed that threateners do not typically make good on their threats by attacking, and attackers do not usually issue threats to the target before striking. Although threats should not be ignored, this research showed that the most serious threats are unlikely to come from those who communicate threats. So if threats are not a major signal of an attack, what are the indicators? The research found that attackers planned the attack, spoke with others about the attack, followed the target, approached the target in a controlled and secure setting, and attempted repeatedly to contact the target and visit the target's home and a location regularly visited by the target. These latter behaviors signal a probing activity to test protection and attack strategies.[29]

Education and Training

Depending on the extent of the executive protection program, many people can be brought into the education and training phase. Executives, their families, and loss prevention personnel (i.e., management, bodyguards, and uniformed officers) are top priorities. But chauffeurs, servants, gardeners, and office workers also should be knowledgeable about terrorist techniques and countermeasures that include prevention strategies, personal security, recognizing and reporting suspicious occurrences, the proper response to bomb threats or postal bombs, and skills such as defensive driving. Most in-house loss prevention personnel are not experts in dealing with executive protection. Therefore, a consultant may have to be recruited.

General Protection Strategies

Potential subjects of terrorists' interest should maintain a low profile and not broadcast their identity, affiliations, position, address, telephone number, e-mail address, net worth, or any information useful to enemies. Avoidance of publicity about future travel plans or social activities is wise. Those at risk should exercise care when communicating with others on the telephone, via e-mail or postal service, or in restaurants and should dispose of sensitive information carefully.

Avoidance of Predictable Patterns

The famous Italian politician Aldo Moro, murdered in 1978, is a classic case of a creature of habit. Moro was extremely predictable. He would leave his home in the morning to attend mass at a nearby church. Shortly after 9:00 A.M. he was en route to his office. The route was the same each morning, even though plans existed for alternatives. Although Moro was guarded by five armed men, he met an unfortunate fate. An attack characterized by military precision enabled terrorists to block Moro's vehicle and a following police car. Then, on the narrow street, four gunmen hiding behind a hedge opened fire. Eighty rounds hit the police car. Three policemen, Moro's driver, and a bodyguard were killed. Moro was dragged by his feet from the car. Almost two months later Moro was found dead in a car in Rome.

Recognition of Terrorist Tricks

A terrorist group may attempt to gain entry to an executive's residence or office under the pretext of repairing something or checking a utility meter. Repair people and government employees can be checked, before being admitted, by telephoning the employer. School authorities should be cautioned not to release an executive's child unless they telephone the executive's family to verify the caller.

Hiring bodyguards is a growth industry for the private sector. Bodyguards should be carefully screened and trained. Other employees (e.g., servants or gardeners) surrounding the executive likewise should be screened to hinder employment of those with evil motives.

Equipment appropriate for executive protection programs includes bullet-resistant vests and clothing, weapons, communications equipment, and armored vehicles. An executive personnel file should be stored in a secure location at the company's headquarters. If a kidnapping occurs, this data can be valuable. Appropriate for the file are vitae for the executive, family members, and associated employees; full names, past and present addresses and telephone numbers; and photographs, fingerprints, voice tapes, and handwriting samples.

Protection at Home

A survey of the executive's home will uncover physical security weaknesses. Deficiencies are corrected through investing in access controls, proper illumination, intrusion alarms, CCTV, protective dogs, and uniformed officers. Burglary-resistant locks, doors, and windows hinder offenders. Consideration should be given to the response time of reinforcements. For a high-risk family, a "safe room" is an asset. This is a fortified room in the house that contains a strong door and other difficult-to-penetrate characteristics. A first-aid kit, rations, and a bathroom are useful amenities. A telephone, two-way radio, and panic button connected to an external monitoring station will assist those seeking help. If weapons are stored in the room, proper training for their use is necessary.

The following list provides some protection pointers for home and family:

1. Do not put a name on the mailbox or door of the home.
2. Have an unlisted telephone number.
3. Exercise caution when receiving unexpected packages.
4. Do not provide information to strangers.
5. Beware of unknown visitors or individuals loitering outside. Call for assistance.
6. Check windows for possible observation from outside by persons with or without binoculars. Install thick curtains.
7. Make sure windows and doors are secure at all times.
8. Educate children and adults about protection.
9. Instruct children not to let strangers in the home or to supply information to outsiders.
10. When children leave the house, be sure to ascertain where they are going and who will be with them.
11. Keep a record of the names and addresses of children's playmates.
12. Tell children to refuse rides from strangers even if the stranger says that the parents know about the pickup.
13. Provide an escort for children if necessary.
14. Teach children how to seek assistance.

Protection at the Office

As with the residential setting, physical security is important at the executive's office. A survey may reveal that modifications will strengthen executive protection. The following list offers additional ideas:

1. Office windows should be curtained and contain bullet-resistant materials.
2. Equip the desk in the office with a hidden alarm button.
3. Establish policies and procedures for incoming mail and packages.
4. Beware of access by trickery.

5. Monitor access to the office by several controls.
6. Escort visitors.
7. Access during nonworking hours, by cleaning crew or maintenance people, should be monitored by uniformed officers and CCTV.
8. Educate and train employees.

Attacks While Traveling

History has shown that terrorists have a tendency to strike when executives (and politicians) are traveling. Loss prevention practitioners should consider the following countermeasures:

1. Avoid using conspicuous limousines.
2. Maintain regular maintenance for vehicles.
3. Keep the gas tank at least half full at all times.
4. Use an armored vehicle.
5. Install an alarm that foils intrusion or tampering.
6. A telephone or two-way radio will facilitate communications, especially in an emergency.
7. A remote-controlled electronic car starter will enable starting the car from a distance. This will help to activate a bomb, if one has been planted, before the driver and the executive come into range.
8. Consider installing a bomb-scan device inside the auto.
9. Headlight delay devices automatically turn headlights off one minute after ignition is stopped.
10. High-intensity lights, mounted on the rear of the vehicle, will inhibit pursuers.
11. Electronic "beepers" in vehicles will send a radio signal to those attempting to find the executive's auto in the event he or she has been hijacked in the vehicle.
12. Protect auto parking areas with physical security.
13. Avoid using assigned parking spaces.
14. Keep doors, gas cap, hood, and trunk locked.
15. Practice vehicle key control.
16. Avoid a personalized license plate or company logo on vehicle.
17. Inspect outside and inside of vehicle before entering.
18. The chauffeur should have duress signal if needed when picking up an executive.
19. Do not stop for hitchhikers, stranded motorists, accidents, or perhaps "police." It could be a trap. Use a telephone to summon aid, but keep on moving.
20. Screen and train the chauffeur and bodyguards. Include the executive and the family in training.
21. Evasive driver training is vital.
22. Have weapons in auto ready for use.
23. Maintain the secrecy of travel itineraries.

24. Be unpredictable.
25. Know routes thoroughly as well as alternative routes.
26. Use safety belts.
27. If being followed, use the telephone for assistance, continuously sound the horn or alarm, and do not stop.
28. For air travel, use commercial airlines instead of company aircraft. Unless the company institutes numerous security safeguards, the commercial means of air transportation may be safer.

Several executive protection strategies are applicable to salespeople, employees attending conferences, and others. A company should take steps to protect all employees to prevent injuries and death. Otherwise, a lawsuit or workers' compensation claim may result. Many risk managers are unaware that their workers' compensation policies do not cover employees in foreign countries.[30]

Avon Products, Inc., provides a superb illustration of an organization seeking to meet the protection needs of its employees. Initiating a global "Women and Security" program, Avon conducted extensive research on vulnerabilities of its female employees as they traveled the globe and faced greater risks than their male coworkers. The Avon security team found that South Africa, the Philippines, Russia, and Latin America were high-risk areas for women. South Africa, for example, has one of the highest levels of sexual assault in the world. Latin America is noted for abductions at ATMs. The Avon program focused on brochures, self-defense training, and one-on-one evaluations. Brochures are country-specific and include tips such as not wearing expensive-looking jewelry because street robbers do not know a genuine from a fake and avoiding public restrooms, if possible, because rapists sometimes disguise themselves as females. Self-defense training satisfied a need expressed by employees. It aims to help women avoid and deter attack. The one-on-one evaluations consist of a security staff member who observes the daily routine of the employee working overseas to offer suggestions for improved protection. The "Women and Security" program has resulted in increased safety, less anxiety, and higher productivity.[31]

Kidnap Insurance

Corporations obtain kidnap-ransom insurance policies for protection against the huge ransoms that they might be forced to pay in exchange for a kidnapped executive. Each year millions of dollars in premiums are paid to insurance companies for these policies. Of course, the insurance company requires certain protection standards to reduce the premium. Insurance companies are reluctant to admit writing these policies because terrorists may be attracted to the insured company executive. Moreover, these policies often contain a cancellation clause if the insured company discloses the existence of the policy.

Maximize Technology[32]

Here we cover a sample of technologies that assist in the protection of people. The Internet offers input for threat assessment. It contains sources (e.g., government agencies) as seen in the end-of-chapter "Search the Web," plus opportunities to check people, businesses, trip routes, and many other subjects of inquiry. The Internet also contains information of a negative nature from global activists and hate and extremist groups. "Sucks.com" sites, such as walmartsucks.com and aolsucks.com, are used to vent at companies. A variety of intelligence can be gathered from such sites.

Pinhole lens cameras, built into almost anything, serve as a witness to an attack and aid in identifying and prosecuting offenders. For advance planning, digital cameras can document travel routes, buildings, airports, etc., and images can be downloaded to a computer and transmitted to headquarters for analysis.

Portable, wireless alarm and CCTV systems offer protection for hotel rooms, vehicles, and other locations. Thermal imagers, which detect heat rather than light, can be used in total darkness to detect intruders or for search and rescue. Another portable system is the automatic external defibrillator (AED) that delivers electrical shocks to restore normal heart rate for those in cardiac arrest.

The global positioning system (GPS) found in vehicles uses a network of satellites that transmit data to ground receivers to navigate and map routes. Also, it can track the executive's vehicle and monitor speed, direction, and alarms transmitted from the vehicle. Cellular technology can be added to permit audio monitoring and remote start or kill of the engine. Remote systems are vulnerable to hacking, so defenses should include encryption.

Although air bags in vehicles offer safety, if protection specialists ram their way out of an attack, or if an attacker backs into the protected vehicle, the activation of an air bag can hinder escape. One option for careful consideration is to disconnect the air bag on the driver's side.

Insurance should be considered one of the last strategies in a long line of defenses. Insurance acts as the "backup" loss prevention strategy.

If Abduction Occurs

After an abduction takes place, the value of planning and training becomes increasingly evident. Whoever receives the kidnapper's telephone call should express a willingness to cooperate. The recipient should ask to speak to the victim; this could provide an opportunity to detect a ruse. Asking questions about the hostage (e.g., birth date, mother's maiden name) to either the hostage or the kidnapper improves the chances of discovering a trick. Prearranged codes are effective. The recipient should notify appropriate authorities after the call. If a package or letter is received, the recipient should exercise caution, limit those who touch it, and contact authorities.

People who attempt to handle the kidnapping themselves can intensify the already dangerous situation. Loss prevention personnel and public law enforcement authorities (i.e., the FBI) are skilled in investigation, intelligence gathering, and negotiating. These professionals consider the safety of the hostage first and the capture of the offenders second, although the reverse is frequently true in many foreign countries.

After an abduction, the company's policies for action should be instituted. These policies ordinarily answer such questions as who is to be notified, who is to inform the victim's family, what are the criteria for payment of the ransom, who will assemble the cash, and who will deliver it and how. Policies would further specify not disturbing the kidnapping site, whether or not to tap and record future calls, how to ensure absolute secrecy to outsiders, and use of a code word with the kidnappers to impede any person or group who might enter the picture for profit.

The crisis management team should be authorized to coordinate the company's response to the kidnapping. Because a terrorist act can take place at any time, the team members will have to be on call at all times.

Guidelines for the behavior of the hostage are as follows:

1. Do not struggle or become argumentative.
2. Try to remain calm.
3. Occupy your mind with all the incidents taking place.
4. Note direction of travel, length of time, speed, landmarks, noises, and odors.
5. Memorize the characteristics of the abductors (e.g., physical appearance, speech, or names).
6. Leave fingerprints, especially on glass.
7. Remember that an effort is being made to rescue you.
8. Do not escape unless the chances of success are in your favor.

Do you think it is possible to provide foolproof executive protection? Why or why not?

SUBSTANCE ABUSE

Substance abuse refers to human abuse of any substance that can cause personal harm or harm to others. This problem is pervasive. Millions of people abuse substances.

The following are ways in which an employee can be a substance abuser to the detriment of an organization:

1. The employee's performance can be altered by prescription or non-prescription drugs.
2. An employee obtains and uses illegal drugs at his or her work site, slows production or causes an accident.
3. The user sells illegal drugs to afford his or her habit.
4. The employee drinks alcohol or smokes marijuana before work, during breaks, or during lunch.
5. The employee sniffs glue or industrial or cleaning fluids to "get high."
6. An assembly-line worker abuses any type of substance to withstand a monotonous regimen.
7. An employee steals products or sensitive information to support a drug habit.

Substance abuse affects 12 percent of the workforce, costing organizations about $150 billion annually in lost productivity and related expenses. Compared to those who do not abuse alcohol, problem drinkers take two and one half times more absences of eight days or more and receive three times as much sick leave and accident benefits. Drug abusers are one-third less productive, have three and a half times more workplace accidents, and make five times as many workers' compensation claims as nondrug abusers.[33]

No occupation is immune to substance abuse. Those afflicted are from the ranks of blue-collar workers, white-collar workers, supervisors, managers, and professionals.

Countermeasures

Unenlightened managers ordinarily ignore substance abuse in the workplace. As with so many areas of loss prevention, when an unfortunate event occurs (e.g., drug-related crime, production decline, or accident due to substance abuse), these managers panic and react emotionally. Experienced people may be fired unnecessarily, arrests threatened, and litigation becomes a possibility. In contrast, action should begin before the first sign of abuse.

Here is a list for action against substance abuse in the workplace:

1. Form a committee of specialists to pool ideas and resources.
2. Seek legal assistance from an employment law specialist.
3. Large corporations can afford to hire a substance abuse specialist. Outsourcing is another option. Also, contact the local government-supported alcohol and substance abuse agency.
4. Prepare policies that include input from a variety of employees. Policies should focus on the company's position on abuse of substances,

including alcohol; job performance and safety as it relates to substance abuse; drug deterrence such as urinalysis; the consequences of testing positive; the responsibility of employees to seek treatment for abuse problems; available assistance; and the importance of confidentiality.

5.   Education and prevention programs can assist employees in understanding substance abuse, policies, and making informed decisions on life choices, health, and happiness.

6.   Ensure that supervisors are properly trained to recognized and report substance abuse.

7.   Drug testing must be well-planned. Questions include the following: What type of test? Who will do the testing? Cost? Who will be tested? What circumstances will necessitate a test? What controls will prevent cheating and ensure accuracy? Does the laboratory and its personnel comply with state or federal licensing and certification requirements? Are all legal issues considered?

Employee Assistance Programs (EAPs)

First introduced in the 1940s to curb the problem of alcohol abuse in the workplace, thousands of employee assistance programs (EAPs) exist today in the public and private sectors, where they incorporate a broad-based approach to such problems as substance abuse, depression, and marital and financial problems. These programs are characterized by voluntary participation by employees, referrals for serious cases, and confidentiality. The goal of EAPs is to help the employee so he or she can be retained, saving hiring and training costs.[34] Initial EAP programs were characterized by "constructive confrontation" (i.e., correct the problem or leave). Today, the philosophy is that a company has no right to interfere in private matters, but it does have a right to impose rules of behavior and performance at work.[35]

Legal Guidelines

The federal Anti-Drug Abuse Act of 1988 is an attempt to create a drug-free workplace. The law requires federal contractors (of at least $25,000) and grantees to prepare and communicate policies banning illegal substances in the workplace and to create a drug awareness program and sanctions or rehabilitation for employees abusing substances. Federal contracts and grants are subject to suspension for noncompliance or excessive workplace drug convictions.

Another form of regulation includes industries regulated by the Department of Transportation, such as airline, motor carrier, and rail, which are required to institute substance abuse programs, including drug testing. In reference to OSHA, it has issued no standards for substance abuse programs, but provides information and assistance to employers and employees. Apart from these sources, most employers are left on their own to decide on substance abuse programs, and many address the problem in some fashion.[36]

Drug Testing: The Controversy Continues

The subject of drug testing has generated considerable controversy. Chapter 6, on applicant screening, covers some of the issues and problems. The American Civil Liberties Union (ACLU) is critical of drug testing and claims that drug testing industries use exaggerated claims of its effectiveness, most workers never use illicit drugs at work, and it may hurt morale.[37] On the other hand, risk managers have seen a dramatic decrease in health insurance and workers' compensation claims following drug testing. Furthermore, those companies that don't test become a magnet for those who are abusers.[38]

Alcoholism

Alcohol is the most abused drug in America. An *alcoholic* is defined as someone who cannot function on a daily basis without consuming an alcoholic beverage.

Estimates of the number of alcoholics in the United States range between 9 and 15 million. These figures do not include the millions who are on the fringe of alcoholism. It is often a hidden disease, whereby the alcoholic hides the problem from family, friends, physicians, and himself or herself. Some major indicators are heartburn, nausea, insomnia, tremor, high blood pressure, morning cough, and liver enlargement. The alcoholic often blames factors other than alcohol for these conditions.

Today, many businesses are no longer hiding the problem. On the detection of alcoholism, a superior should notify management and obtain approval to proceed with the case. Public or private concerns that can correct the problem are contacted for information. Alcoholics Anonymous (AA), an organization for alcoholics and recovered alcoholics, run by people who have had a drinking problem, has had more success than most organizations. The employee is advised of "helping agencies," in addition to internal and external policies and procedures and what is expected of him or her by the employer regarding steps for recovery. Health insurance benefits and company disability income usually are applicable. Unless the employee takes heed of the supervisor's recommendations in seeking assistance, dismissal may occur because of poor job performance. The threat of job loss jolts many alcoholics into recognizing their serious situation and accepting treatment.

What do you think are the most successful countermeasures against substance abuse in society and in the workplace?

Types of Substances and Abuse

The explanation of four terms can assist the reader in understanding the human impact of various substance abuse categories.

- *Psychological dependence.* Users depend so much on the feeling of well-being from a substance that they feel compelled toward continued use. People can become psychologically dependent on a host of substances. Restlessness and irritability may result from deprivation of the desired substance.
- *Addiction.* Certain substances lead to physiological (or physical) addiction. This happens when the body has become so accustomed to a substance that the drugged state becomes "normal" to the body. Extreme physical discomfort results if the substance is not in the body.
- *Tolerance.* After repeated use of certain drugs, the body becomes so accustomed to the drug that increasing dosages are needed to reach the feeling of well-being afforded by earlier doses.
- *Withdrawal.* The person goes through physical and psychological upset as the body becomes used to the absence of the drug. Addicts ordinarily consume drugs to avoid pain, and possible death, from withdrawal. Symptoms vary from person to person and from substance to substance. An addict's life often revolves around obtaining the substance, by whatever means, to avoid withdrawal.

Five types of substances—narcotics, depressants, stimulants, hallucinogens, and inhalants—are discussed here.

Narcotics

Narcotics include opium, its derivatives, and their synthetic equivalents. Drugs in this category are heroin, morphine, codeine, and methadone, among others. Such drugs are used to relieve pain and induce sleep. The method of consumption is injection, oral, or inhalation. Both psychological and physiological dependence is typical, as well as a tolerance potential.

Depressants

Depressants fall into several categories: barbiturates include phenobarbital and secobarbital (Seconal); tranquilizers include Valium and Librium; non-barbiturate hypnotics include methaqualone (Quaalude); and miscellaneous depressant drugs include alcohol and chloroform. A depressant affects the central nervous system. Barbiturates ordinarily are prescribed for insomnia, whereas tranquilizers calm anxiety. Other depressants are used prior to surgery. Abuse of these drugs can lead to psychological and physiological dependence. Withdrawal is painful and can be fatal. Depressants have a tolerance potential. These drugs are taken orally or injected. They are obtained by a doctor's prescription or through illegal channels. Symptoms of depressant use are similar to that of alcohol use: drowsiness, slurred speech, disorientation, constricted pupils, irritability, and slow reflexes.

Stimulants

There are several types of stimulants; caffeine, amphetamines, and cocaine are the most common ones. These drugs affect the central nervous system and generally cause increased alertness soon after consumption, but restlessness and irritability are characteristic of long-term usage. There is a tolerance potential plus a susceptibility to dependence.

Caffeine is found in coffee, tea, cola drinks, and No-Doz. Increased alertness may be followed by insomnia, gastric irritation, and restlessness.

Amphetamines are widely used stimulants that are swallowed or injected. They are prescribed for narcolepsy (chronic sleepiness). Illegal amphetamines typically originate from legitimate sources. Abuse is characterized by anxiety, talkativeness, irritability, and dilated pupils.

Legally, cocaine is a narcotic, but physiologically it is a stimulant. It is expensive and the "high" is short-lived. The history of cocaine is interesting. It used to be an ingredient in Coca-Cola. Sigmund Freud experimented with it. The user inhales cocaine into the nose or injects it. Symptoms of abuse are similar to those of amphetamines plus damage to nasal membranes and the potential for hallucinations and hostile behavior.

Crack is a stimulant drug processed from cocaine hydrochloride by using baking soda and water and then heat to remove the hydrochloride. The pebble-sized crystal remaining, called crack, is smoked in a variety of devices. Crack is popular because it is less expensive than cocaine and when smoked it is more rapidly absorbed than snorted cocaine.

Hallucinogens

Hallucinogens can produce a trance, fright, and irrational behavior. Examples are LSD, PCP, mescaline, and psilocybin.

Marijuana is categorized by itself. It is sometimes categorized as a hallucinogen, but its actions are different from that of LSD. Both marijuana and its derivative, hashish, are widely used. Because of widespread cultivation of hemp to produce rope prior to the Civil War, marijuana grows wild in almost every state. Because of so many users today, marijuana use is controversial. Many states have decriminalized (i.e., reduced the penalty for) the offense. The effects of usage depend on the individual and the potency. There is no physiological dependence. Psychological dependence is possible. Research on tolerance is inconclusive. Millions of people smoke marijuana occasionally to feel relaxed and carefree.

LSD was popularized in the 1960s by the youth "counterculture." Use was touted as a consciousness-expanding experience. The effects vary greatly. There is no physiological dependence. Bizarre hallucinations, which can be either beautiful or terrifying, result from usage.

Inhalants

Inhaling volatile chemicals can produce intoxication. This can occur by one's own volition or by accident due to poor ventilation. Both causative factors should be understood by all employees.

Two types of volatile chemicals are volatile solvents and anesthetics. Volatile solvents include a variety of glues or liquid cements, cleaning fluid, paint thinner, and paint remover. Anesthetics are found in medical facilities for surgical purposes. Nitrous oxide (laughing gas) and ether are among the anesthetics.

Those who seek an altered state or "high" gather the substance or gas in a plastic bag and place it over the mouth and nose before breathing. Direct breathing from the container holding the substance is another method. Physiological dependence is nil, but a tolerance and psychological dependence may result. The effects are numerous and varied: intoxication, chemical odor on the person, drowsiness, stupor, and hallucinations.

WORKPLACE VIOLENCE

Two important questions on workplace violence are (1) how should it be defined, and (2) how should it be measured? The definition of workplace violence affects not only how it is measured but also its cost. As the definition expanded from "one employee attacking another" to "any violence that occurs on the job" so, too, did the cost.

The University of Iowa, in a report entitled "Workplace Violence: A Report to the Nation," found that 2 million Americans are victims of workplace violence each year. The research divided workplace violence into four categories: criminal intent (e.g., robbery), customer/client (e.g., health care environment), worker-on-worker, and personal relationship (e.g., domestic violence). About 85 percent of all workplace homicides occur under the criminal intent category and 7 percent under the worker-on-worker category. Retailers had the largest number of nonfatal violent incidents.[39] According to the Bureau of Labor Statistics, there were 645 workplace homicides in 1999, down 10 percent from 1998 and much lower than the 1,080 in 1994. Robbery was the leading motive for workplace killings.[40]

Workplace violence is costly to businesses. Losses reach into the billions of dollars each year and include medical and psychological care, lost wages, property damage, lost company goodwill, and impact on employee turnover and hiring.[41]

In putting the problem in perspective, the Bureau of Justice Statistics (BJS) noted the following rates per 1,000 adults per year (incidents not necessarily in the workplace): accident 220, personal theft 61, assault 31, death (all causes) 11, robbery 6, death from cancer 3, and homicide 0.1.[42]

Obviously, incidents of workplace violence (e.g., homicides, assaults, rapes) occurred before increased attention focused on the problem in the early 1990s. What we have witnessed is a change in the way the problem is perceived and counted. This is beneficial for gauging increases and decreases in the problem and as a foundation for planning protection with scarce resources. The United States has been known to maintain good statistics on a number of problems and freely publicize trends. From an international perspective, others may view the United States as the most violent society, when we may simply be the best at gathering data.

Do you think the United States is a violent society, or do we just maintain good data-gathering systems? Explain your viewpoint.

Legal Guidelines

There is no national law addressing violence in the workplace. OSHA has published voluntary guidelines for workers in late-night retail, healthcare, and taxicab businesses, but these guidelines are not legal requirements. Various states have enacted laws to curb violent crime at work. California and Washington passed laws aimed at reducing violence in healthcare settings. Florida, Virginia, and Washington have laws or regulations that seek to prevent robbery and homicides at late night retail establishments.

Employers who do not take measures to prevent violence in the workplace face exposure to lawsuits. Workers' compensation may cover injured employees, but the exposure of employers is much greater. Examples include premises liability and negligent hiring, training, supervision, and retention.

Contradictions in the law make protection difficult: OSHA requires a safe working environment for employees, but the Americans with Disabilities Act (ADA) can create difficulties for an employer seeking to control an employee with a mental instability. Employees have successfully sued employers for defamation because instability was mentioned. The ADA restricts "profiling" of employees through the observation of traits thought to be potentially violent.[43]

Protection Methods

What follows is a list of strategies for dealing with violence in the workplace.

1. Establish a committee to plan violence prevention and to respond to such incidents. Include specialists in security, human resources, psychology, and law.
2. Consider OSHA guidelines to curb workplace violence (see Chapter 17 under healthcare institutions).

3. Establish policies and procedures and communicate the problems of threats and violence to all employees.

4. Although human behavior cannot be accurately predicted, screen employment applicants. The ADA limits certain questions; however, these can be asked: "What was the most stressful situation you faced and how did you deal with it?" "What was the most serious incident you encountered in your work and how did you respond?"

5. Consider substance abuse testing as a strategy to prevent workplace violence. For years, BJS data has showed a relationship between violent crime and substance abuse.

6. Train managers and supervisors to recognize employees with problems and report them to the human resources department. Include training in conflict resolution and nonviolent response.

7. A history of violent behavior can help to predict its reoccurrence. The worker who becomes violent is usually male, between 25 and 45 years old, and has a history of interpersonal conflict. He tends to be a loner and may have a mental health history of paranoia or depression. He also may have a fascination with weapons.[44]

8. Managers and supervisors should be sensitive to disruptions in the workplace, such as firings. Substance abuse and domestic and financial problems also can affect the workplace; and EAP is especially helpful for such problems.

9. If a person becomes angry in the workplace, listen and show that you are interested in helping to resolve the problem. Do not get pulled into a verbal confrontation; do not argue. Acknowledge and validate the anger by showing empathy, not sympathy. Speak softly and slowly. Ensure that a witness is present. Maintain a safe distance, without being obvious, to provide an extra margin of safety. If a threat is made or if a weapon is shown, call the police.

10. Remember that outsiders (e.g., visitor, estranged spouse, robber) may be a source of violence and protection programs must be comprehensive.

11. If a violent incident occurs, a previously prepared crisis management plan becomes invaluable. Otherwise, a committee should be formed immediately after emergency first responders (i.e., police, EMS) complete their duties on the premises and affected employees and their families are assisted. At one major corporation, management was unprepared when the corporate security manager was shot. A committee was quickly formed to improve security and survey corporate plants. In addition to expenditures for physical security and training, an emphasis was placed on awareness, access controls, and alerts.[45]

Search the Web

Check out the National Counterintelligence Center on the Web at http://www.nacic.gov/ for a wealth of information on foreign intelligence threats and related links to various government agencies.

Research the Web site of the Society of Competitive Intelligence Professionals. See the employment opportunities available at http://www.scip.org/.

Use your favorite search engines and type "terrorism."

Check out the U.S. Department of State, Bureau of Consular Affairs Web page for travel warnings, resources, and services: http://travel.state.gov/.

Check out the following two sites for a wealth of anti-drug-related information: U.S. Department of Labor at http://www.dol.gov/ and the National Clearinghouse for Alcohol and Drug Information at http://www.health.org/.

Use your favorite search engines and type "violence in the workplace."

CASE PROBLEMS

18A. As the security director for a corporation engaged in research, you see the need for a communications security consultant for improved protection. What criteria would you list to select such a specialist? What questions would you ask applicants during the selection process?

18B. As the security director for a corporation with plants in the United States and Europe, prepare a list of questions to answer as you plan protection against terrorism and establish an executive protection program.

18C. As a security manager you hear through the grapevine that several employees smoke marijuana during lunch when they go to their vehicles. What do you do?

18D. You are a security manager at a plant. One day, a former employee shows up at the front gate and demands to see his estranged wife. Plus, he wants to talk with the human resources manager about benefits. How do you handle this situation?

18E. As a security manager you just received an internal telephone call from a supervisor who complains about a subordinate who became angered by a work assignment and told the supervisor that he knows where he lives and where his kids go to school. What do you do?

18F. As a corporate security director, what would you suggest to management as the top ten (prioritized) strategies for protection following the September 11, 2001 attacks and subsequent events?

18G. Of the major topics in this chapter, which one would you select as a specialization and career? Why? How would you develop such a specialization and career?

NOTES

1. Erica Thompson, "Intellectual Property," *Security Products* (January 2001), p. 18.
2. Gene Laczniak and Patrick E. Murphy, "The Ethics of Corporate Spying," *Ethics Journal* (Fall 1993), pp. 1–4.
3. "Corporate Spying: Honorable Profession," Associated Press release (April 27, 1990).
4. Worth Wade, *Industrial Espionage and Mis-use of Trade Secrets* (Ardmore, PA: Advance House, 1965).
5. *Business Espionage Report* (November 1996), pp. 3–5.
6. D. A. Nichter, "The Home Computer as a Listening Device," *Chain Link* (June 1996), p. 6.
7. "White House Reports on Espionage," *Infosecurity News* (September-October 1996), p. 14.
8. Richard Hefferman and Dan Swartwood, *Trends in Intellectual Property Loss* (Arlington, VA: ASIS, March 1996).
9. Ibid., pp. 17–32. The list of countermeasures was prepared with the assistance of this source, which emphasized survey results rather than an explanation of countermeasures.
10. Susan Thompson, "DOA: Destruction of (Almost) Anything," *Security Management* (May 1989), pp. 77–79.
11. John M. Carroll, *Computer Security*, 3rd ed. (Boston: Butterworth–Heinemann, 1996), pp. 177–277.
12. Business Espionage Controls and Countermeasures Association, "News of Hostile Activity" http://www.espionbusiness.com (June 6, 2001).
13. Tom Jones, *Surveillance Countermeasures in the Business World* (Cookeville, TN: Research Electronics International, 2000), pp. 1–17.
14. Correspondence (June 2, 2001) with Information Security Associates, Inc., Stanford, CT (isa-tscm.com/).
15. R. Mark Halligan, "Do Your Secrets Pass the Test?" *Security Management* 45 (March 2001), pp. 53–58.
16. *Legal Alert Memo* (May 20, 1997), Childs & Duff, P.A., P.O. Box 11367, Columbia, SC 29211.
17. John A. Nolan, "Economic Espionage, Proprietary Information Protection: Difficult Times Ahead," *Security Technology and Design* (January-February 1997), pp. 54–57.
18. See James M. Poland, *Understanding Terrorism* (Englewood Cliffs, NJ: Prentice-Hall, 1988), pp. 9–10.
19. Jay Albanese, *Criminal Justice* (Boston: Allyn & Bacon, 2001), pp. 95–98.
20. U.S. Commission on National Security, *New World Coming: American Security in the 21st Century* (September 15, 1999; http://www.nssg.gov/).
21. FBI, *Terrorism in the US, 1998* (Washington, D.C.: U.S. Government Printing Office, 2000), pp. 1–24.
22. "Pro-Life Terrorism: A How-To," *Harper's Magazine* (January 1995), p. 19.
23. "Tech Talk," *Security* Management 44 (June 2000), p. 38. Barry Collin, "The Future of CyberTerrorism," *Crime and Justice International* (March 1997), pp. 14–18.
24. Michael Gips, "Building in Terrorism's Shadow," *Security Management* 44 (May 2000), pp. 42–50.

25. Stefan H. Leader, "The Rise of Terrorism," *Security Management* (April 1997), pp. 34–39.
26. Ronald Decker, "How Can Companies Tackle Terrorism?" *Security Management* 44 (April 2000), p. 126–128.
27. "Terrorism: How Have Other Countries Handled It? How Should We?" *The Bill of Rights in Action* (Fall 1995), pp. 5–8.
28. United Nations, *Eighth United Nations Congress on the Prevention of Crime and the Treatment of Offenders* (July 1990), pp. 19–20.
29. Eljay Bowron, "All the World's a Staging Ground," *Security Management* 45 (April 2001), pp. 93–97.
30. William Atkinson, "Safe Travel," *Risk & Insurance* 12 (April 1, 2001), pp. 19–22.
31. Rose Shyman, "Women at Work," *Security Management* 44 (February 2000), pp. 58–62.
32. William Besse and Charles Whitehead, "New Tools of an Old Trade," *Security Management* 44 (June 2000), pp. 66–72.
33. John Ivancevich, *Human Resource Management*, 8th ed. (Boston: McGraw-Hill Irwin, 2001), p. 464.
34. John Ivancevich and William Glueck, *Foundations of Personnel*, 4th ed. (Homewood, IL: Richard D. Irwin, Inc., 1989), p. 813.
35. Ivancevich, 2001, p. 465.
36. Todd Nighswonger, "Just Say Yes to Preventing Substance Abuse," *Occupational Hazards* 62 (April 2000), pp. 39–42.
37. "Drug Testing Assailed," *Security Management* 43 (December 1999), p. 16.
38. Denise Myshko, "Just Say Yes to Drug Testing," *Risk and Insurance* 12 (April 16, 2001), pp. 44–46.
39. University of Iowa (February 2001), "Workplace Violence: A Report to the Nation," www.public-health.uiowa.edu/iprc/index.html (June 18, 2001).
40. Steven Lasky, "Workplace Violence Revisited," *Security Technology & Design* 11 (January 2001), p. 4.
41. Sandra Hughes, "Violence in the Workplace: Identifying Costs and Preventive Solutions," *Security Journal* 14 (2001), p. 69.
42. "Workplace Violence: A Growing Exaggeration?" *Security* (January 1995), p. 9.
43. Sandy Jaeger, "The Age of Rage" *Security Industry & Design* 11 (February 2001), p. 74.
44. Harvey S. Waxman, "Putting Workplace Violence in Perspective," *Security Management* (September 1995), p. 123.
45. Philip Purpura, "When the Security Manager Gets Shot: A Corporate Response," *Security Journal* (July 1993), pp. 150–157.

19

Your Future in Security and Loss Prevention

OBJECTIVES

After studying this chapter the reader will be able to:

1. Discuss security and loss prevention in the future.
2. List at least ten trends affecting security and loss prevention.
3. Discuss security and loss prevention education, research, and training.
4. Explain employment opportunities in the security and loss prevention field.

SECURITY AND LOSS PREVENTION IN THE FUTURE

Seeking to accurately predict the future is difficult and risky. However, a professional will consider many variables when making educated guesses to anticipate future events. What follows here are possibilities for the future to which the reader can apply critical thinking skills.

We begin with the anticipated market for security services and systems. Although many businesses and institutions will maintain proprietary security departments, we will see an increase in the outsourcing of partial and entire security departments to integration/management firms. These service firms will handle security functions ranging from access systems to security officers. New markets for security services will expand in developing countries as economic liberalization and expansion widen the gap between rich and poor. The privatization of correctional facilities will see enormous growth for private security service firms. Additional revenue will be generated by serving specialized prisoner populations, such as women, the elderly, and substance abusers. The future holds increasingly sophisticated devices and systems such as "intelligent" fences and robot guards. Because of the terrorist threat, contraband detection equipment, such as automated explosives detection systems and metal detectors, will become "smarter."[1] Artificial intelligence will eventually make *accurate* facial recognition of criminals on the street via CCTV a reality by going "below skin level." Instead of security command centers with numerous CCTV monitors being watched by personnel, artificial intelligence will replace the human element in evaluating and reacting to events and alert staff to observe a monitor.[2]

Future integrated security systems will perform an array of loss prevention activities beyond what is accomplished today. For example, if an intruder enters a building, not only will the system pinpoint the entry location, via a series of sensors, and activate CCTV, but simultaneously it will dispatch a robot to apprehend the intruder.

Access control systems will no longer use cards. An individual will stand in front of sophisticated sensors and positive identification will be made by the analysis of a number of characteristics: bone structure, teeth, and body odor, to name only a few. It would be especially difficult for an offender to duplicate several of these characteristics. The same sophisticated access control sensors could be placed at many locations to monitor personnel: parking lots, building entrances, elevators, high-security locations, copying machines, lunchrooms, and restrooms. Obviously, with such a system, it would be possible to know exactly where a person was at every minute of every workday. If a fire developed or if sabotage occurred, the recorded location of everybody would aid loss prevention personnel. But, will employees appreciate computer records revealing how many times and for how long they visit the restroom or other locations? Suppose a system had the capability to record every conversation, every day, within a building. This could give management the opportunity to "weed out" those persons who were counterproductive to organizational goals. Also, because this system would be capable of "recognizing" any conversations pertaining to losses, the loss prevention department could review these conversations and investigate vulnerabilities. With these possibilities in mind, one realizes the blessing and burden of technology. Are such intense measures worth sacrificing privacy? Certainly not. *Countermeasures must strike a balance between preventing losses and protecting privacy. In the future, as today, the courts will be watching and ruling as technological innovations and loss prevention strategies are applied.*

Our information age has placed a high priority on the protection of IT systems and proprietary information. It is a matter of national and business survival. There are so many ways to harm IT systems and steal information that the security planner must be very careful not to fall into the trap of emphasizing certain countermeasures while "leaving the back door open." The challenges will intensify in the future and the traditional, physical security specialist will need to make the connection to IT security through cross-training and mutual sharing of expertise.

As we progress in the era of the automatic factory (AF), loss prevention methods will change to meet the new technology. The AF operates machines that transform raw materials into finished products with limited human input. Robots with self-contained computers are an essential part of the AF. Activities such as material handling, assembly, inspection, and quality control are automated. Human input comes from a computer control center. Widespread use of "just-in-time production" also contributes to manufacturing's need for fewer workers. Production is based on the needs of retailers, which avoids costly inventory holding and producing items that do not sell well.[3]

The future use of robots is promising. They operate 24 hours a day without a coffee break or vacation. Fringe benefits such as hospitalization and pensions are unnecessary for robots. Also, robots are immune to heat, cold, noise, radiation, and other hazards.

Imagine loss prevention for a plant operated by only three managers and six technicians. If internal pilfering occurred, the number of suspects would be narrowed to nine, excluding robots. Parking lots, frequently a source of crime, would be smaller. Fires and accidents, which are often caused by human error, would be reduced.

Can you describe an example of a clash between technology and civil liberties? What were the issues and solutions?

TRENDS AFFECTING SECURITY AND LOSS PREVENTION

The twenty-first century will see no shortage of vulnerabilities or threats facing businesses and institutions. The list that follows presents trends and challenges that will have an impact on the types of specialists required for security and loss prevention and thus employment opportunities.

- The problems of crimes, fires, and accidents will remain but increase in complexity.
- Technology is both a blessing and a burden. For instance, computers make our lives easier, but they are subject to exploitation by offenders.
- The *cycle of protection* will remain: as new technology is developed, offenders will exploit it, and security specialists and offenders will remain in constant competition—one group striving to protect; the other striving to circumvent defenses. Both sides will win "battles," but neither will win the "war."
- Public police, especially on the state and local levels, will continue to lag behind the technical expertise of high-tech criminals. Consequently, private security will continue to fill the void.

- During the twenty-first century, computer viruses will be meaner and more intelligent.
- Hackers will become more sophisticated and creative. As computers affect all areas of society, the vulnerabilities are almost endless: manipulating bank records from halfway around the world, changing criminal history files and creating new identities, and remotely altering manufacturing processes.
- The protection of sensitive information (e.g., trade secrets) will become an even greater responsibility of security.
- As we become a cashless society, offenders will be ready to gain illegally from system weaknesses.
- E-business will increase along with protection needs.
- Criminal organizations will become increasingly globalized. They have taken advantage of the information and technology revolution to as great, or a greater, degree than government and business.[4]
- Top management in criminal organizations is becoming increasingly well-educated and trained. Criminals increasingly will have college degrees and experience in IT, engineering, money management, investments, and accounting.
- Criminal entrepreneurs increasingly are knowledgeable of the operations of financial institutions and related vulnerabilities. They will continue to infiltrate and manipulate financial institutions for their own purposes (e.g., money laundering), as this target becomes a top priority. Financial security professionals will continue to be challenged not only by external offenders but by internal ones as well.
- Counterfeiting will continue to be a huge business for organized criminals, especially in designer clothes, software, entertainment items, vehicle parts, and medical supplies. Counterfeiters have production facilities and distribution networks ready for new product lines.
- Twenty-first-century crime groups increasingly will own shares of multinational corporations and be involved in management decisions. This will create new challenges for security professionals.
- Satellites increasingly will assist security through instantaneous communications throughout the world. People and assets will be more easily tracked. Such technology will assist in the investigations of kidnappings and hijackings.
- Risk analysis will become more challenging for security executives because, with limited resources, priorities for protection will be established. Improved research methodologies for risk analyses must be sought for better decisions. Because not all areas of vulnerability will receive the same protection, documentation of risk analyses, research, and decisions will be extremely important.[5]
- Research shows that security managers are gaining new duties including IT security, risk management, safety, background investigations, and travel security. They are also harnessing their computers for

broader applications such as incident tracking, sharing information internally via an intranet, and conducting training.[6]

- Many security departments are facing either placement under another department (e.g., facilities management), outsourcing, or even elimination.
- Corporate and institutional changes have had an impact on employee morale. The objectives of improving quality while downsizing and other workplace issues have taken a toll on loyalty among workers. Loyalty has been an asset to protection programs. Its deterrent value today must be questioned and studied. New innovative strategies are required.
- As more and more employees are displaced from smoke-stack industries during the information and technology age, frustration-induced crime may rise.
- Women, the elderly, and the disadvantaged will make up a greater portion of the workforce. Such groups present new challenges for security. Women and the elderly require protection not only in the workplace but also at home and while traveling. Cases of domestic violence, sexual harassment, and stalking are likely to occupy more of the security professional's time. Women and the elderly will be involved in more workplace crime. If increasing numbers of disadvantaged workers are employed, they may bring with them problems of gangs and illegal drugs.[7]
- More research will focus on issues of minority group members and women in security positions. The majority of women in one study of women security managers felt they experienced relatively high levels of sex discrimination, sexual harassment, and on-the-job stress; they also felt they were not paid the same as men for the same work. Despite these issues in this male-dominated vocation, the study showed three-fourths of the women surveyed were satisfied with their careers.[8]
- Security must adapt to a multinational and multicultural workforce. As the workforce changes, security professionals must be aware of diversity and use it to the advantage of the business. Good communication can improve security and business, and even help develop new markets.
- Global markets require security to be aware of each culture and related risks.
- Twenty-first-century police will spend most of their resources and time curbing violent crimes, while their efforts against property crimes will take a lower priority. Consequently, the private sector will fill the void.
- In a speech to police leaders, Robert diGrazia, former police chief of Boston and St. Louis, said: "We are not letting the public in on our dirty little secret"; namely, "that there is little the police can do" about crime.[9]
- More and more citizens and business people are realizing that the police have limited ability and resources to curb crime. Police are

primarily "reactive"; that is, they respond to calls for service and investigate. They often are under great pressure to solve serious cases. Because of limited resources, police are not able to be more "proactive." Again, the private sector will fill the void.

- A panel of law enforcement specialists predicted that, in 2035, private security agencies will perform more than 50 percent of all law enforcement responsibilities.[10]
- Three key factors to assist protection professionals today and in the future are a broad-based education (e.g., business, security, computers), the skill to show that protection strategies have a return on investment, and the flexibility to deal with rapid change.
- Trends affecting the security and loss prevention profession point to employment opportunities in many organizations (both proprietary and contract) and government agencies and in many specialized areas.

The United States Commission on National Security/21st Century reported the following:

1. Institutions designed for another age may not be appropriate for the future.
2. Authoritarian regimes will increasingly collapse as they try to insulate their populations from free-flowing information and new economic opportunities.
3. An economically strong United States is likely to remain a primary political, military, and cultural force in the world through 2025.
4. Weapons of mass destruction (e.g., nuclear, chemical, and biological) and weapons of mass disruption (e.g., information warfare) will continue to proliferate.
5. Adversaries will resort to forms and levels of violence shocking to our sensibilities. Americans will likely die on American soil, possibly in large numbers.
6. Emerging technologies, such as advances in biotechnology, will create new moral, cultural, and economic divisions and an anti-technology backlash.
7. Energy, especially fossil fuel, will continue to have major strategic significance.
8. Minorities will be less likely to tolerate prejudicial government. Consequently, new states, international protectorates, and zones of autonomy will be born in violence.
9. Space will become a competitive military environment.
10. U.S. intelligence will face more challenging adversaries, and even excellent intelligence will not prevent all surprises.[11]

What trends do you see in the security and loss prevention field?

EDUCATION

How relevant is a college education to the loss prevention careerist? A college degree will not guarantee a job or advancement opportunities. But, with a college degree, a person has improved chances for obtaining a favored position. If two equally experienced people are vying for the same professional loss prevention position and person A has a college degree while person B does not, person A probably will get the job. Of course, other characteristics within a person's background will improve job opportunities. *Education* and *experience* are top considerations. *Training* also is important. Two other characteristics are *personality* and *common sense*. As used here, personality pertains to one's ability to get along with others. Many consider this factor to be one-half of a person's job. *Common sense* is a subjective term that is used widely. It refers to an analysis of a situation that produces the "best" solution that most people would favor.

Loss Prevention Education: Today and Tomorrow

Although business degree programs are an excellent location for security and loss prevention courses, the criminal justice (CRJ) degree programs on hundreds of campuses in the United States today are the greatest driving force behind future security and loss prevention degree programs. During the late 1960s, many police science degree programs advanced to law enforcement and then CRJ degree programs. As CRJ programs developed, so did the spectrum of course offerings: from primarily narrow police courses, CRJ programs began offering courses relating to the entire justice system (i.e., police, courts, corrections). CRJ programs became interdisciplinary because the answers to complex problems were more forthcoming from a broader spectrum of study. Likewise, security and loss prevention degree programs will evolve into broader-based, interdisciplinary loss prevention programs and will include the study of business and IT.

Academic Research

The most practical question for loss prevention researchers to address is as follows: What strategies are best to prevent and reduce losses from crimes, fires, and accidents? Ongoing evaluative research will be instrumental in strengthening successful strategies while eliminating those that are less useful.

Additional directions for research are protection against terrorism, model training programs, determining the most appropriate courses for relevant degree programs, effective job applicant screening, model statutes for licensing and regulation of the security industry, model for regulatory bodies, criteria for the selection of services and systems, evaluation of services and systems, legal issues and liabilities, strategies to improve public–private sector cooperation, privatization, private justice system (whereby decisions for or against prosecution are made by management in the private sector), centralized data bank for the compiling of loss statistics, the feasibility of tax deductions for implementing loss prevention strategies by a variety of entities and residential settings, IT security, and the use and effect of robots and other technological innovations.

As well as college and university criminal justice and loss prevention programs sharing these research questions, other curricula, such as business, insurance, safety, architecture, and engineering degree programs, are capable of providing valuable input. An interdisciplinary research effort would be most beneficial. Without adequate research, loss prevention practitioners will be hindered in their decision-making roles.

What directions for research can you suggest for the security and loss prevention field?

Training

The future direction of training largely depends on tomorrow's technological innovations, risks, and loss prevention strategies. Practitioners will need to know how to operate in an environment of new countermeasures and complex systems. But, even though loss prevention will change, many key topics taught in the training programs of today also will be taught tomorrow. Strategies against crimes, fires, and accidents will still be at the heart of training programs.

State involvement in training proprietary and service practitioners probably will increase for greater public safety. Uniformity in training will ensure that practitioners receive adequate information on basic topics such as laws of arrest, search and seizure, use of force, weapons, fire protection, and accident prevention. An interdisciplinary group would be the best choice to provide input for state-mandated training programs.

The training curriculum of tomorrow will continue to cater to the ever-increasing goal of professionalizing loss prevention personnel. The end product will be a thoroughly knowledgeable practitioner, able to provide a useful service to the community. Greater mutual respect will follow as public police and private-sector personnel share similar characteristics in education, training, salary, and professionalism.

Improved training helps to prevent costly liability suits; for example, from excessive force used by a uniformed officer. The quality of training, in terms of duration, intensity, and topics covered, is a prime consideration in such liability cases.

Programmed, *self-paced instruction* with the aid of computers will become common for loss prevention training. If the problems of turnover and constant hiring still are evident, then this method of training should be cost effective while freeing supervisory personnel for other tasks. Furthermore, new employees who learn quickly can move through the instructional program without having to wait for slower students. A varied training program may include not only programmed, self-paced instruction but also lectures, audiovisual productions, role playing, and demonstrations. *Distance learning* online will increase in popularity as students learn from remote locations.

Additional information on education and training in the security field can be obtained from the Academy of Security Educators and Trainers (ASET; http://www.personalprotection.com/).

The Concept of the Security Institute

Every state should maintain a security institute, preferably at a college or university. Three goals of a security institute are as follows:

1. Develop and conduct college and continuing education courses based upon the needs of customers.
2. Work with the state government agency that regulates the private security industry to develop training programs, conduct research, and professionalize the field.
3. Offer the institute's service area crime prevention initiatives involving security and criminal justice college students who are an unrealized and underutilized national resource to control crime.

EMPLOYMENT

Many employment opportunities can be found in the security and loss prevention field. The related field of criminal justice, which includes police, courts, corrections, probation, and parole, plus the growth of privatization, all provide opportunities and specialization for employment applicants.

Entry-level security officer positions vary widely in pay, benefits, and training. Generally, these positions do not pay as well as public police. However, there are many opportunities for employment and advancement and many part-time positions; the hours offer some flexibility; and the duties are less risky than public policing. Supervisors in security have mastered the tasks of security officers, possess broader skills, and have good human relations qualities. Managers generally have more education, training, experience, and responsibilities than supervisors. They are involved in planning, budgeting, organizing, marketing, recruiting, directing, and controlling. Other careers in this field include sales, self-employment (e.g., private investigations, consulting), and government security.

The ASIS International 2000 Employment Survey found that the average salary of top-level security professionals ranged from $42,000 to $105,000 depending on the number of locations managed.[12] The Institute of Management & Administration, which publishes *Security Director's Report*, found that the average security director earned just under $61,000 annually. This research noted that those with a master's degree earned an average of $30,000 per year more than those with a high school diploma. The CPP designation was worth an average of $7,000 more annually than what security professionals earned without a professional certification.[13]

The broad yet specialized loss prevention field extends to the alarm and insurance industries, which employ thousands of men and women. Two sources are the National Burglar and Fire Alarm Association (http://www.alarm.org/) and the Insurance Information Institute (http://www.iii.org/).

Research in 2000 on wages in security shows the average annual pay for unarmed security officers to be $16,424. Security directors average $77,550, often have a title of vice president, work in an urban area, are employed by a large corporation, possess a bachelor's degree (often a master's degree), and hold a certification (e.g., Certified Protection Professional, Certified Fraud Examiner).[14] Table 19-1 provides average annual income for security and loss prevention positions.

Sources of Employment Information

- *Online services.* The Internet is expanding into the largest database of employment listings in the world. There are several advantages: offerings are broad, time is saved by reviewing opportunities open worldwide, it is more up-to-date than most publications, and you can respond electronically. Be aware that confidentiality is limited. Look

Table 19-1   Security and Loss Prevention Annual Compensation*

Position	Average Cash Compensation
Security directors	$77,550
Security managers	54,000
Supervisors of investigations	51,662
Investigators	39,805
Supervisors of guard operations	29,500
Store detectives	25,097
Security officers	16,424

*Source: Abbott, Langer & Associates, Inc.

for services that are free. The America's Job Bank (AJB; http://www.ajb.dni.us) is a network of listings from more than 1,800 employment service offices throughout the country, and employers can list directly. Hundreds of thousands of opportunities are listed from all 50 states, plus other locations.

- *Periodicals.* Within these sources, trends in employment and employment opportunities are common topics.
- *Professional associations.* Professional organizations serve members through educational programs, publications, and a variety of strategies aimed at increasing professionalism.
- *Trade conferences.* Trade conferences, which are advertised in trade publications, are attended by people with a common interest. By attending these conferences, a loss prevention practitioner or student can learn about a variety of topics. The latest technology and professional seminars are typical features. Trade conferences provide an opportunity to meet practitioners who may be knowledgeable about employment opportunities or are actively seeking qualified people.
- *Educational institutions.* Security and loss prevention and criminal justice degree programs are another source of employment information. Usually, these programs have bulletin boards, near faculty offices, that contain career opportunities. College or university placement services or faculty members are other valuable sources.
- *Libraries.* A wealth of information for a career search is available at libraries. Examples include periodicals, newspapers, telephone books, directories, books on career strategies, and online services.
- *Government buildings.* Public buildings often contain bulletin boards that specify employment news, especially near personnel offices. Government agencies frequently search for practitioners to maintain security and safety at government buildings and installations.
- *Newspapers.* Looking under "security" in classified sections will find listings for many entry-level positions. In large urban newspapers, more specialized positions are listed. For instance, the classified and business sections of the *New York Times* often contain pertinent management positions.
- *Public employment agencies.* These agency offices operate in conjunction with the U.S. Employment Service of the Department of Labor. Personnel will provide employment information without cost and actually contact recruiters or employers.
- *Networking.* An informal network consists of people the applicant knows from past educational or employment experiences. It is a good idea for any professional to maintain contact, however slight, with peers. When employment-related problems develop and solutions are difficult to obtain, networking may be an avenue for answers. Likewise, this mutual assistance is applicable to employment searches.

- *Telephone books.* The addresses and telephone numbers of both private and public entities are abundant in telephone books. By looking up "security," "guards," "investigators," and "government offices," one can develop a list of possible employment opportunities.
- *Private employment agencies.* Almost all urban areas have private employment agencies that charge a fee. This source probably will be a last resort, and one should carefully study financial stipulations. At times, these agencies have fee-paid jobs, which means that the employer pays the fee.

Career Advice[15]

1. Read at least two good books on searching for employment and careers; both the novice and the experienced person will learn or be reminded of many excellent tips that will "polish" the career search and instill confidence.
2. Begin your search by first focusing on yourself—your abilities and background, your likes and dislikes, and your personality and people skills.
3. If you are new to the security and loss prevention field, aim to "get your foot in the door." As a college student, look for an intern position, work part-time, or do volunteer work. *Aim to graduate with experience.* As a retired government employee or if you are beginning a new career in security, market and transfer your accumulated skills and experience to this field.
4. Most people will enter new careers several times in their lives.
5. Searching for a career opportunity requires planning, patience, and perseverance. Rejections are a typical part of every search. A positive attitude will make or break your career.
6. When planning elective courses in college or when training opportunities arise, consider that employers want people with skills (e.g., writing, speaking, interviewing, computers).
7. Many students do not realize that a college education and some training programs teach the student *how to learn.* Although many bits of information studied and reproduced on examinations are forgotten months after being tested, the skills of how to study information, how to read a textbook or article, how to critically think and question, how to do research and solve problems, and how to prepare and present a report are skills for life that are repeated over and over in one's professional career. In our quickly changing information age, these skills are invaluable.
8. If you are fortunate enough to have a choice among positions, do not let salary be the only factor in your decision. Think about career potential and advancement, content of the work, free training, benefits, travel, and equipment.

9.   Exercise due diligence on potential employers. For example, speak to present employees and check the organization's financial health.
10. Five key factors influencing an individual's chances for promotion are education, training, professional development and certification, experience, and personality.
11. Avoid quitting a job before you find another. Cultivate references, even in jobs you dislike (such jobs are a learning experience).

The employment situation in the security and loss prevention field reflects a bright future. Good luck with your career!

Search the Web

Check out the following sources for employment information: Security Jobs Network at http://www.securityjobs.net/ and America's Job Bank at http://www.ajb.dni.us.

CASE PROBLEMS

19A. As a contract security supervisor with a major security service firm, you are faced with a major career decision. You have a bachelor's degree and have been with your present employer for a total of 7 years: 2 years part-time while in college, and 5 years full-time since graduating. These years have been spent at a hospital where you would like to advance to site security manager, but you face competition from one other supervisor, who also has a bachelor's degree, the same certifications and training that you possess, and about the same years of experience. The present contract site security manager is a former detective who wants to retire to Arizona within the next year or two. You have repeatedly asked managers from the security service firm (i.e., your employer) about advancement opportunities, but nothing is available. Recently, you were offered the position of in-house security and safety training officer with a nearby, urban school district. The pay is $800 less annually than what you are earning now. However, you would receive additional insurance and retirement benefits and work only day shifts, Monday through Friday. You would be the only college-educated officer on the school district security force, which is primarily composed of contract officers. The director of security is the only other in-house security officer, a retired police officer with no college degree. What career choice do you make?

19B. As a regional security manager with a major retailer, you have twelve years of retail security experience. You earned bachelor's and master's degrees and a CPP, and you worked your way through various retail security positions to your present position. The territory you work covers nearly 100 stores in six southeastern states. You are on the road each day responding to security problems and wish you could spend more time with your spouse and two children. After eight years with the same company, and no chance for advancement, you decide to consider an offer as security director with a major retailer in the New York City area. The pay is $8,000 more than what you are earning now, with similar benefits. You would have additional responsibilities, but you would travel much less. Your spouse and children do not want to move because of family and friends. What career choice do you make?

NOTES

1. Paul Bailin, "Gazing into Security's Future," *Security Management* 44 (November 2000), pp. 60–67.
2. Richard Maurer, "Where Will Security Be in 2010?" *Security Technology & Design* 10 (December 2000), pp. 12–16.
3. U.S. Department of Labor, "Futurework," *Occupational Outlook Quarterly* 44 (Summer 2000), p. 31.
4. See Richter H. Moore, "Private Security in the 21st Century: An Opinion," *Journal of Security Administration* 18, no. 1 (1995), pp. 3–13.
5. Ira S. Somerson, "The Next Generation," *Security Management* (January 1995), pp. 27–30.
6. "Security's Burden Increases," *Security Management* 45 (May 2001), p. 18.
7. "Here Comes the 21st Century: What Does It Hold for Security?" *Security Management Bulletin* (March 25, 1997), pp. 4–7.
8. "Survey Studies Women in Security," *Security Management* (February 1996), pp. 87–88.
9. Charles E. Silberman, *Criminal Violence, Criminal Justice* (New York: Vantage Books, 1978), p. 270.
10. William L. Tafoya, "The Future of Law Enforcement? A Chronology of Events," *C J International* 7 (May–June 1991), p. 4.
11. United States Commission on National Security/21st Century, *New World Coming: American Security in the 21st Century* (September 15, 1999), pp. 1–8. http://www.nssg.gov/.
12. "New Salary Survey Released," *Security Management* 44 (December 2000), p. 14.
13. "Security Directors Made Solid Salary Gains in '01," *Security Director's Report* (June 2001), p. 1.
14. *Compensation in the Security/Loss Prevention Field*, 12th ed., Abbott, Langer & Associates, Inc. (548 First St., Crete, IL 60417; Tel.: 708-672-4200). http://www.abbott-langer.com/.
15. Philip P. Purpura, *Criminal Justice: An Introduction* (Boston: Butterworth–Heinemann, 1997), Chapter 15, "Your Future in the Criminal Justice System."

Index